About This Book

The purpose of this book is to lead you through the process of developing your first significant Paradox 5 for Windows application (with multimedia features) in 14 days. This book is written around the development of a single large Paradox application. You will be building a real-world accounts receivable and payable business application with all its support features. Along the way, you will see and build smaller applications (applets), which I will use to either illustrate a point or to provide an extra feature for the main application.

Who Should Read This Book

This book assumes that you have already familiarized yourself with the Paradox 5 for Windows database product, at least at the beginner level. Following your initial introduction to the product, you can use this book to develop a first Paradox for Windows database application. The responsibility for learning what to do next, and how to do it, becomes a shared one. I will show you the way to do it, and you must step through the process with me.

Conventions

Notes: A note calls your attention to a short piece of text that you really need to see, and that is related to the normal flow of discussion.

Textbook Tips: A Textbook Tip might include a tip about Paradox technicalities, or perhaps a formal programming method.

Developer's Tips: A Developer's Tip also includes useful details, but refers to the kind of knowledge gained from experience (which is sometimes opposed to textbook knowledge).

Showstoppers: A Showstopper is a warning or cautionary note. It will tell you about things you ought *not* to do, and why.

At the end of each chapter, you will find two extra sections: *Modification Notes* and *Debugging the Process*. The *Modification Notes* section deals with the subject of borrowing existing code to create applications faster. Borrowing code, or *boilerplating*, is not a trivial topic in the real world.

Develop Your First

Paradox 5 for Windows® Application

in 14 Days

Develop Your First
Paradox 5
for Windows®
Application
in 14 Days

Lee Atkinson

SAMS
PUBLISHING

201 West 103rd Street, Indianapolis, Indiana 46290

This book is gratefully dedicated to Karen Giles, Rob Gordon, and Kevin Smith, all of Borland. When I needed your help, you were there.

International Standard Book Number: 0-672-30597-6

Library of Congress Catalog Card Number: 94-67082

97 96 95 94   4   3   2   1

Interpretation of the printing code: the rightmost double-digit number is the year of the book's printing; the rightmost single-digit, the number of the book's printing. For example, a printing code of 94-1 shows that the first printing of the book occurred in 1994.

Composed in AGaramond and MCPdigital by Sams Publishing

Printed in the United States of America

Overview

Contents

Acknowledgments

This book could not have been written, especially in the time frame that was allowed, without the support and encouragement of the folks at Sams. I would especially like to acknowledge Greg Croy, who believed in me; Dean Miller, who made sure this book came out right; Mary Inderstrodt, who made sure that this book had something to say, and said it correctly; and Wayne Blankenbeckler, who coordinated the software that went into the companion CD-ROM—and who kept me realistic. You guys are really great.

I would also like to say thanks to Jasmine Multimedia, which supplied some sample Video for Windows clips that my readers can try out with the PW Multimedia Theater, and to Microsoft Corporation for allowing us to distribute the Video for Windows runtime package with the CD-ROM. Thanks to these companies, and others like them, there is a whole new world of computing out there, like nothing we've seen before: the multimedia world.

About the Author

Lee Atkinson

Lee Atkinson first professionally entered the field of computing 25 years ago, working with punched card systems and wiring plug boards (back when core memory was made of little doughnut-shaped iron rings). He has since worked with nearly every kind of computing technology and language, on systems both large and small. He is currently an MVS/ESA systems programmer for a southeastern regional retail store where he does operating systems, storage management, and disaster recovery functions.

Introduction

The purpose of this book is to lead you through the process of developing your first significant Paradox for Windows application (with multimedia features) in 14 days. The first step in this process is yours. This book assumes that you have already familiarized yourself with the Paradox for Windows database product, at least at the beginner's level.

Following your initial introduction to the product, you can use this book to develop your first Paradox for Windows database application. Responsibility for learning what to do next, and how to do it, becomes a shared one: I will show you the way to do it, and you must step through the process with me.

In order to do all this effectively, you must understand how to use this book. Specifically, you will need to understand how the book is put together, including the printing conventions used and the organization of the chapters. You also will need to know what specific things you should do as you read each chapter—and how to effectively use the CD-ROM materials provided with the book. Finally, you'll learn about how to locate other resources that are useful for developing Paradox for Windows applications, especially applications with multimedia features.

This introduction covers all these considerations. Review this material (but don't memorize it) and then you can start developing a Paradox for Windows Multimedia Theater as the very first (but not the main) sample application. When you are done, you will have had a lot of fun, you will have some interesting and useful multimedia tools to use in future applications, and you will also have a working knowledge about developing database applications with Paradox 5 for Windows.

Printing Conventions Used in This Book

The visual design and printing conventions used in this book are calculated so that grasping the material is not only easy, but enjoyable too. Anyone who reads old books will know just how important this really is. Books from the last century, for example, often feature paragraphs that are more than one page long and sometimes consist of a single running sentence. It is very hard to follow such a book.

Hopefully, this book will do a lot better. The paragraph sizes you see here are of average length, and the sentences of moderate length. The text is frequently peppered with figures (mostly screen shots), note boxes, and ObjectPAL program listings. All these things are designed to break the material up into bite-size pieces that are easy to digest. The order in which the material is presented is important, too.

Ordinary text in this book uses the type style you are reading now. Figure captions, program listing captions, table captions, and table column heads are printed in *italic* or **bold** type. Chapter and section headings are in a larger bold type, as you have already seen.

> **Note:** Another useful formatting style is the note, like this one. This kind of box calls your attention to a short piece of text that you really need to see, and is related to the normal flow of discussion. In addition to ordinary notes like this one, you will also see Textbook Tips, Developer's Tips, and Showstoppers. A Textbook Tip might include a tip about Paradox technicalities, or perhaps a formal programming method. A Developer's Tip also includes useful details but refers to the kind of knowledge gained from experience (which is sometimes opposed to textbook knowledge). A Showstopper is a warning or cautionary note. It will tell you about things you ought *not* to do, and why.

Other type styles are also used to visually emphasize that something different is going on. ObjectPAL source code, for example, is presented in monospace type, both to make it more readable and to make it stand out on the page. For example, here is the `pushButton()` method for the Loop control button from the PW Multimedia Theater application, in monospace type:

```
method pushButton(var eventInfo Event)
  switch
    case mmfileloop = True :
      mmfileloop = False
      RunButton.killTimer()
    case mmfileloop = False :
      mmfileloop = True
      RunButton.setTimer( 1500, True )
  endSwitch
endmethod
```

Sometimes I will present a piece of code in which I want you to substitute something of your choosing. When that happens, the code will be set in monospace type, as before, but the part you should replace will be in italics, like this:

```
case mmfileloop = logicalvalue :
```

In this line of code, you are intended to substitute either the True or False logical constants in the code where the item *logicalvalue* appears.

Many of the printing conventions used in this book don't need to be explained; they just "look right" when they are used. However, you need to understand the two types of lists that can be used: the bulleted list and the numbered list.

The *bulleted list* is a list of items that can be read without regard to their order. For example, I might use a bulleted list to inform you what equipment and software your PC needs to run the sample applications in this book, as follows:

- [ ] An IBM or compatible PC, 386SX or above, running a reasonably recent version of DOS, plus Windows 3.1 (you OS/2 for Windows fans running dual boot need to stay away from Windows 3.11!). You also will need to be sure that you have installed all the multimedia drivers in DOS and Windows you need to support the CD-ROM and sound cards (mentioned later in this list).
- [ ] A hard disk with at least 10MB free space.
- [ ] An SVGA (Super VGA) video card and screen, capable of at least 640x480 pixels with 256 colors.
- [ ] Paradox 5 for Windows, of course.
- [ ] A CD-ROM drive. My own, for example, is the Creative Labs double-speed model, with a 300KB transfer rate.
- [ ] A Sound Blaster or compatible audio card. A 16-bit card is best because you can get stereo sound with it.

A *numbered list* is a list of items that must be read or performed in order. For example, to create a new Paradox for Windows application, you might begin as follows:

1. Choose **F**ile | **N**ew | **F**orm from the Desktop main menubar.
2. Click the **B**lank button in the New Form dialog box.
3. Use the Desktop toolbar to select and place various design objects (pushbuttons, text boxes, and so on) on the form.
4. Add any required ObjectPAL methods or procedures to the design objects by right-clicking each object, choosing **M**ethods from the drop-down menu, and double-clicking the method name you want to modify. When the ObjectPAL editor window appears, type in the ObjectPAL code.
5. As you complete each custom method, syntax check the code, and save the entire form by choosing **F**ile | **S**ave from the Desktop main menubar.

This sample numbered list also illustrates how I will note menu choices. The choices are listed from left to right. Beginning with the main choice first, they are separated by vertical bars (|), and the hotkey is printed in bold type.

That covers the printing conventions used here whose meanings aren't obvious at a glance. Whether I'm explaining printing conventions or meanings of terms, I have tried to structure the book so that you can just plow right ahead, using basic common sense, and still do quite well.

How the Chapters Are Organized

How the chapters are organized in this book is controlled by one simple philosophy: this is a *tutorial* book. It is very true that often the best way to learn a new subject is by doing it. That is what you will do in this book.

Now that you have gained a basic familiarity with the Paradox for Windows Desktop and its features, you will get the best kind of one-on-one instruction: a show, tell, and *do* session for each step in creating Paradox for Windows applications.

Furthermore, because the intent is to get you rolling in just 14 days, I have accordingly written exactly 14 chapters, one for each day. Each chapter title tells you what the major task for the day is, and each major section in the chapter discusses a specific action (or very small group of actions) that you must complete to continue building the application.

As the previous paragraph implies, this book is written around the development of a single, large Paradox application. You will build a real-world accounts receivable and accounts payable business application with all its support features. Along the way, you will see and build smaller applications, *applets,* which I will use to either illustrate some

point, or to provide an extra feature for the main application. In addition, you will get a lot of multimedia-related sample material from the CD-ROM. You do like lots of toys, don't you?

At the end of each chapter, you will find two extra sections. The *Modification Notes* section deals with the subject of borrowing existing code to create applications faster. Borrowing code, or *boilerplating,* is not a trivial topic in the real world. Why re-invent the wheel when you can just pop one on the car?

In fact, this book would not have been written (at least not by me), had I not been able to boilerplate the code. This entire book, including applications, was written in less than 50 days. Hopefully, the techniques I used to pull this off will come through in the book and do you some good, too. Combat buddies, and all that!

The last section of each chapter, *Debugging the Process,* covers the process of ensuring that what you just did in that chapter really works. Later in the book, I talk specifically about debugging, integration testing, and rolling out the application. It is important to verify your work as you do it, however, so I will specifically call your attention to it as you read along.

Looking at the book from a larger perspective, you will see that the chapters themselves are grouped into parts. There are four parts to the book, as follows:

- [ ] Systems Analysis and Design
- [ ] Construction
- [ ] Documentation
- [ ] Implementation

Part I, "Systems Analysis and Design," might sound like technical stuff, but it really isn't. The chapters in this part of the book are about *thinking ahead.* In this day and time, that is an activity that is all but forgotten; but it is one that makes life a whole lot easier. When you are building computer-based applications, thinking ahead is an activity that is absolutely essential.

The first chapter of both the book and this section is about building applications by *prototyping,* which means short-circuiting the method taught in the rest of the book. At least, it looks like it means that, but that really isn't true. Prototyping is a fast-path method to development, but it still depends conceptually on the methods described in the rest of the book. In this chapter, you will develop a complete preliminary application, the PW MultiMedia Theater (the MMT), in *one* day. The MMT will be used by other parts of the main application, and it's fun all by itself.

Once you have done all that dry planning work, it's time to actually build the application. This process is covered in Part II, "Construction." The pace moves a little faster here because there is more hands-on activity. This is obviously an important part of the process, too. Just as it is necessary to *plan* it all, it is necessary to *do* it all, including the details. When programming computers, go ahead, sweat the small stuff. It's the small stuff that will kill you.

Part III, "Documentation," covers how to write both printed and online documentation. In pursuit of this lofty goal, you will learn how to use both Paradox forms and the Windows Help database engine to provide hypertext, online documentation. This may be more fun than it sounds right now. You will see why when we start hooking the multimedia features into the online documentation.

Finally, Part IV, "Implementation," covers some often-neglected topics: testing, packaging, distributing, and supporting the application. Along with the planning part of the book, this is part of the driest material you must cover (maybe the editors won't notice that I'm telling you secrets), but I have to assume that you are serious about developing applications. You need to know what it really takes to do this, and this material is part of it. I'll do my best not to make it unnecessarily boring. It will work out, too, because they told me to take an informal approach, and I fully intend to take advantage of that little slip!

All in all, you and I are going to get comfortable, and I will talk you through the process of building Paradox for Windows applications, with multimedia features, and show you what I mean along the way. It'll be fun!

What To Do as You Read Each Chapter

There are a few ways you can approach using this book.

- ☐ Buy the book. Tell all your friends to buy copies, too. Work very hard at this.
- ☐ Take the book home, get a knife out, and fight with the CD-ROM inside the back cover. Try not to damage it while getting it out; but it is nearly impossible. Put the disk in the CD-ROM drive.
- ☐ Open the book and start riffling through the pages. Look at all the pictures carefully. They won't help you without reading the book, but aren't they pretty?

- [ ] Now notice that there is a multimedia theater thing with this book, and there are a lot of sound and video files to play. Run the installation procedure (that will be explained later) and start up the theater.

- [ ] Play lots of media clips, just to see what they are. Identify your favorite clips and play them over and over again.

- [ ] Get a cold glass of your favorite beverage from the refrigerator and swill about half of it in a gulp. Notice that you are feeling guilty because you just spent some hard-earned bucks and aren't doing anything but diddling around. Adjust to the fact that you aren't going to get anything out of the book this way.

This tongue-in-cheek scenario really isn't all that funny, is it? That's because both you and I have done this sort of thing before. I have bought books just out of curiosity and failed to use them through laziness. What a waste!

There is a better way to approach this book. That way involves actually reading the book and *doing* something with it as you go along. Because all the source code for the sample projects is on the CD-ROM, you don't have to retype it all. You should, however, start up Paradox for Windows and load the form, table, or whatever is being discussed when you are reading.

As you read, put your hands on the keyboard and mouse and go poke around. If I am explaining a piece of ObjectPAL code, for example, inspect the object it lives in and inspect the code right there, looking at it as a piece of a larger whole. Ask yourself questions. Why did that crazy author use that variable? How can this method (or procedure) get to that variable over there? Just why does this particular thing happen when it does? What does this thing actually *do*?

As trivial as these questions sound, they are exactly the kinds of questions that reveal what is really going on, and why things happens the way they do. In fact, you should frequently switch from design mode to run mode and watch the application carefully to see just what it does. Then go back to design mode and look at the method's code again with new eyes.

It is important to answer these questions, too, because I have deliberately left some parts of it ready for you to do the development work yourself. I have done most of the development for you: I did all the accounts receivable application and part of the accounts payable application. Therefore, whenever it is necessary for you to step in to do something, you can look at the AR forms and code and mimic them to get the AP part.

How To Use the CD-ROM Sample Materials

The CD-ROM disk contains numerous things that will be of interest to you. First, of course, are all the Paradox tables, forms, queries, reports, and everything else that appears in the book. You should use this material by being very inquisitive about it. Poke into everything, question everything. One question to always have on your mind is, "How can I use this in my own applications?"

Hopefully, the biggest thing you will carry away with you from the Paradox examples is an understanding of how the pieces of an application fit together and what Paradox features can be used to implement those ideas. After that, a lot of ObjectPAL code is included that you can use as boilerplate code. Copy and paste the code (usually with some modification, of course) into your own applications.

The second thing on the CD-ROM is important if you have never installed multimedia applications on your system. This is the Video for Windows runtime system. The VFW runtime includes all the full-motion video drivers you need to play movie clips with the Multimedia Theater you will develop in Chapter 1. Installing the VFW drivers is optional if you already have them from some other software product (such as a multimedia encyclopedia).

The third thing on the CD-ROM is just for fun. Sams has packaged some sample multimedia clips (movies) from Jasmine Multimedia on the CD-ROM, just so you can have something to prove how really neat multimedia can be.

The purpose behind the Jasmine media clips is twofold. First, they are provided just so you can have fun, as well as to give you some ideas on how you can enhance your applications with multimedia. Second, they are meant to provide you with the examples you need to better understand multimedia itself. If you, like me, are relatively new to multimedia, you will find this to be a great adventure—if sometimes an aggravating one.

The benefits gained from the CD-ROM material are both direct and indirect. You can paste some materials directly into other applications, and you will carry some in your head. Taken altogether, the experience gained from using the materials will form an invisible backdrop to your future development work, which will result in attractive, high-quality applications.

Finding Other Useful Resources

There are a number of places you can go to get more information and materials on both Paradox for Windows programming and multimedia use and programming.

For Paradox for Windows programming, I will shamelessly plug my own book, *Paradox for Windows Developer's Guide,* by Sams Publishing. There is a wealth of information in that book, if I may say so, about how Paradox works—from the inside out. If you want to get into advanced Paradox for Windows programming, that book is the place to go. I even found myself using that book as a reference while I wrote this one.

For multimedia-related material, you might do very well to begin with Ron Wodaski's "Madness" books. Yes, you read that right. Mr. Wodaski has written *Multimedia Madness, Virtual Reality Madness,* and *PC Video Madness*—also from Sams. These books contain a wealth of information on multimedia PCs. They were especially invaluable to me, because I had to write this book on such short notice (are you listening, editors?). I simply couldn't afford to spend much time researching multimedia, and I didn't have to; these books did it for me.

Now that all the preliminaries are out of the way, you can jump right in by writing a sophisticated Paradox for Windows multimedia application in just two days. That ought to lay the groundwork for a 14-day project, don't you think?

Systems Analysis
and Design

Part I requires five days to complete. In those five days, you will learn a multitude
of interesting new things, including the following:

- [ ] How to use either ObjectPAL or OLE with Paradox 5 for Windows
  multimedia programming
- [ ] How to develop applications by prototyping them
- [ ] How to begin planning a new business application, with support and
  multimedia utilities
- [ ] How to design and define the new application's database engine
- [ ] How to design and define the new application's user interfaces with
  Paradox 5 for Windows forms

Developing Applications By Prototyping

On the first two days of your 14-day stint in the Paradox for Windows salt mines, you will get a whirlwind tour of developing applications by prototyping them. In the remaining 12 days, you'll develop a classical business application in a more traditional manner (something like computer-science students do, except it's for real).

On the first day, you will find out just what prototyping is, how to do it, and what it costs and saves in effort. You will find that the cost is greater than you may have expected because it is much easier to get really involved in a project when prototyping, to the exclusion of everything around you—such as the family, the dog, and friends. This is because the fast turnaround brings visible results quickly, and therein lies the trap. Prototyping saves time, but it may destroy your mind.

What Is Prototyping, Really?

What is prototyping, really? Here it is, straight. Prototyping is cheating. It is a good kind of cheating, however, because you don't hurt anyone except yourself, and you get a lot done, quickly.

Prototyping is cheating in the sense that you do things before you really plan them. In the classical world of computer programming, that is a really stupid thing to do, because it always backfires on you. However, with tools such as the Paradox for Windows development environment and a language such as ObjectPAL that you can run as soon as you write it, the fast turnaround time from coding to running can really pay off. Try it, and if you like it, keep it.

Prototyping doesn't work in the traditional mainframe world of programming because the language tools there are all too often the old-style compilers. That means that the turnaround time from coding to running can be quite long. Furthermore, things in that environment tend to be highly interrelated, meaning that you often can't try anything until you have it all done. Fixing a problem often means reviewing the entire package, too. The interrelationships are hard-coded and have to be manually changed.

Paradox for Windows has a particular feature that lends itself very well to prototyping: its object-oriented nature. ObjectPAL is attached to objects: table frames, forms, buttons, and so on. These pieces of code attached to objects are called, as you already know, *methods* (there are procedures, too). If the code attached to one object doesn't work, very likely the effects of that failure are reasonably well-contained. You don't buy the whole farm then, you just don't get any snap beans. But the garden keeps growing.

Prototyping is the process of trying something out as soon as the concept for it becomes clear in your mind. That's how I developed the PW Multimedia Theater, which I call

the MMT. I knew I wanted some kind of multimedia player *cum* support facility for other things in the book, so I just jumped right in and built one.

With the way prototyping actually works, you end up adding functionality in layers, getting more detailed as you go along. It is neither a top-down design approach, nor a bottom-up approach. You might say it is more of a sideways-design approach. The nice thing about it is that if the whole thing turns into a topsy-turvy approach, you can just scrap the parts that don't work and do something else.

> **Developer's Tip:** I have probably written several million lines of code in my professional life, for employers, for books, and for my own commercial ventures. I figure that alone qualifies me as a developer. So here's your first Developer's hot tip. The notion that prototyping is some kind of formal discipline is nonsense. It is no more well-defined than is the concept of the "relational database" in the real world, or "object-oriented programming" for the adventurous. These things are what you want them to be, mostly, and everyone has a different opinion. But I can say this about prototyping: you need a fourth-generation tool such as Paradox for Windows so you can go fast, you need a clear notion of *what* you want to do—if not *how* to do it at first—and you need to be consistent in your approach. Being consistent means to stay organized and not miss anything.

So, whatever prototyping really is (you decide what you are going to with the word), you and I are going to develop a slick little multimedia application with Paradox for Windows by prototyping it.

We will proceed in layers, phases, or sideways, depending on how you want to look at it, but we will get the job done—and have some fun along the way. We will start with some things I knew from previous experience (which plays a major role in prototyping), and proceed to those parts that I had to invent as I went along.

As you may have already discerned, my own approach to all this is going to be one of light-hearted honesty. I fully intend to tell it like it really is, and to play the role of iconoclast to the traditional world of programming. The old way is too stuffy to be any fun, and it isn't very productive either. Besides, the editors want me to write this book in an inhumanly short period of time, so I have to do something to preserve my sanity—or perhaps to keep from discovering it again.

Author's Personal Note: The Sams editors have really goofed up this time. They told me to do something I really want to do, and that is to informally teach applications development in a practical, enjoyable way. The last time a particular friend of mine told me something like that, he was riding in a large van with me and was tired of waiting for me to get out in the traffic. So he said, "Just get out there and get you some of it!" Well, he has never since had the nerve to say that to me in a vehicle, but maybe the editors will stick to their guns. But now it's time to start developing, so let's just *get out there and get us some of it!*

Before we go ahead, there is time for a quick sneak preview of the application that will be developed in the first two chapters. Figure 1.1 shows the PW Multimedia Theater form, in all its glory.

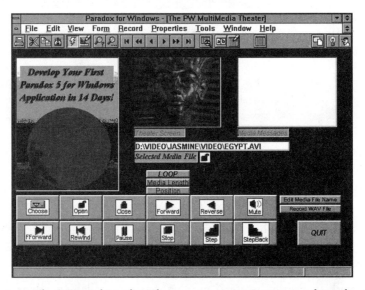

Figure 1.1. *The PW Multimedia Theater, running a Jasmine multimedia AVI movie about the Egyptian pyramids.*

Preliminary Stuff: the FORMLIST Form/Utility

The first order of business in prototyping an application is having some means of figuring out what you have already done and what you need to do next. In this regard, sometimes there is nothing as helpful as a hard copy of your code. Those of you who have used computers for text work for very long are aware that paper gives you a sense of context that a terminal simply can't. Besides, I needed some way to get my ObjectPAL code in a form I can stick in this book.

To supply this need, I have provided a *blank* form (meaning no table is attached to it) that will enumerate all the ObjectPAL sources in any form you tell it about and place the result in an ordinary text file. That form is the FORMLIST form. Figure 1.2 shows you what FORMLIST looks like (in design mode).

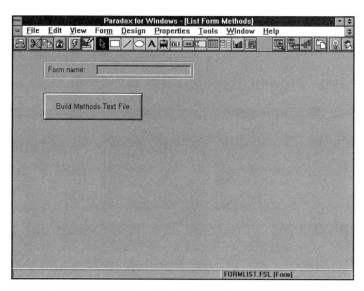

Figure 1.2. *The FORMLIST form, in design mode.*

As you can see, there are exactly two features on the FORMLIST form. There is an unnamed pushbutton, which causes the ObjectPAL source to be captured when pressed if a filename has been given.

Also there is an edit box above the pushbutton. Because I have to refer to it in the ObjectPAL code, and because I want to inform myself of the name of the form I want *inform*ation about, I have named this box inForm. (Okay, the truth: it really means "input form.")

Showstopper! If you enter the form name with its .FSL extension in the edit box, the ObjectPAL will make the form name string something like *formname*.FSL.FSL. This will hardly run, as you may expect. The code here is kind of dumb, because it is a tool for you to use while developing, not a tool for your users. That is, don't spend too much time coming up with these cute little tools; you will have no time left for the product!

Always enter the form name *without any extension* when using the FORMLIST form to get ObjectPAL source.

The FORMLIST form is a bit awkward at full-screen size, so I have also made it resize itself when it is opened. Consequently, it looks a good deal better at runtime, as shown in Figure 1.3.

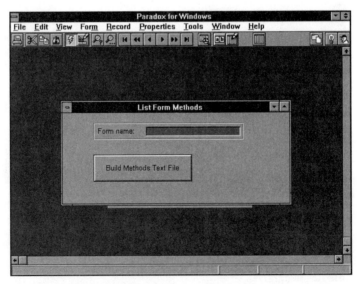

Figure 1.3. *The FORMLIST form in run mode, ready to perform.*

FORMLIST is a simple-looking, simple-acting form. Even so, it needs some ObjectPAL to do anything meaningful. The first thing to do is to control what happens when the form is opened. So choose **P**roperties | **F**orm | **M**ethods from the main menu, and then double-click open to open the edit dialog for the form's open() method. Enter the following code into the edit dialog, syntax check the method, and save the form.

```
;Attach this code to the form's open() method
method open(var eventInfo Event)
  if NOT eventInfo.isPreFilter() then
    doDefault
    setPosition(1440,1440,6500,2880)
  endif
endmethod
```

The statement if NOT eventInfo.isPreFilter() is there to keep the method from executing when every object on the form is opened. If it weren't there, you would see an awful lot of screen flashing while the form opens.

Next, the doDefault statement tells the method to go ahead and get its normal default processing out of the way. It isn't very often that you will completely override the default processing of any Paradox design object.

Finally, the setPosition(1440,1440,6500,2880) tells the form where to position and size itself on the screen in *x*, *y*, *width*, and *height* coordinates. Furthermore, these coordinates are in *twips*, which are one-twentieth of a printer's point. There are 72 printer's points per inch, so that means there are 1,440 twips per inch. Simple, right?

Seriously, if you want to get down to that level of ObjectPAL detail, the best place to go is to my other Paradox book, *Paradox for Windows Developer's Guide*, also from Sams. (Absolutely shameless. You're right.)

Note: The purpose of this book is not to teach ObjectPAL programming as such, although you will probably pick up a lot of neat stuff along the way. In that regard, I will explain what the code does, why I used it, and things like that, but I will not explain syntax, editor usage, or other things that do not directly relate to the topic of applications development.

With the form's open() method taken care of, you can deal with the pushbutton. Clearly, you want the FORMLIST application to "go get" the other form's ObjectPAL source code (all of it) and write it into a text file so you can play with it, document with it, or whatever.

Right-click the pushbutton to inspect its properties, choose **Methods...** from the object menu, and double-click the pushbutton method name to edit it. Type the following code into the edit dialog:

```
;Attach this code to the unnamed pushbutton
method pushButton(var eventInfo Event)
var
  myForm Form
endvar
  if NOT inForm.isSpace() then
    myForm.open( inForm + ".FSL" )
    myForm.enumSourceToFile( ".\\"+inForm+".TXT", True )
    myForm.close()
    setPosition(1440,1440,6500,2880)
  else
    msgInfo( "Form List", "No Form given." )
  endif
endmethod
```

As simple as the pushbutton code may be, at least it does check to see whether the user has already entered a form name in the edit box. This is taken care of in the `if` statement. The rest of the logic is simplicity itself: open the form, enumerate the source (as Borland is fond of calling this process), and close the form. The second `setPosition()` call re-establishes the FORMLIST size and position after the other form has been displayed (at its own desired size). This is necessary because Paradox sizes *all* forms on the desktop according to what you did to the most recent one.

When you have run FORMLIST, there will be a file on disk named *targetform*.TXT, where *targetform* is whatever you typed into the edit box. That's all there is to this one. It is a neat little gadget, at least to me, because this is the tool I used to extract all the ObjectPAL code for this book. In particular, I used this tool to extract all the ObjectPAL source for the PW Multimedia Theater.

The PW Multimedia Theater (MMT)

The PW Multimedia Theater, or MMT, as I will henceforth refer to it, is a really nice multimedia presentation tool that you can use just for itself, or as a presentation vehicle for other applications (as you will later see).

The list of things that I wanted MMT to do is not a modest one, especially considering that the whole project is done with ObjectPAL. There is no C language (except for the file selection dialog, but more on that later), nor is there any assembly language—just Paradox.

> **Textbook Tip:** Notice that I said "assembly language," not something
> else. That is because the Sams editors got all over my case (and rightly so,
> really) during the development of *Paradox for Windows Developer's Guide*
> for speaking of "assembler language" or just "assembler." Technically,
> they *are* right. Fact is, though, that those that *use* assembler call it just
> that among themselves—*assembler*. So, editors and readers, please forgive
> me if I mess it up from time to time. Old habits are hard to break.

Figure 1.1 showed what the MMT form looks like when you play a Jasmine AVI movie.
Even though you might not be impressed with it, I sure am. Multimedia is about the
neatest thing to come along since sliced bread, and it tickles me to no end that I can use
ObjectPAL and Paradox forms to put something like that together.

But let's get back to the immodest list of things that we want this application to do. Those
things are as follows:

- [ ] Provide an attractive, high-tech interface with which your users can play the
  three major forms of multimedia files: AVI movies, Microsoft wave (WAV)
  files, and MIDI files.

- [ ] Provide an attractive, high-tech interface with which users can select and
  display Windows bitmap (BMP) images, Postscript (EPS) images, Graphics
  Interchange Format (GIF) images, Paintbrush (PCX) images, and tagged (TIF)
  or scanner output images. (I will be referring to these kinds of images as *stills*.)

- [ ] Allow you to run the MMT stand-alone, picking and choosing what multimedia files to play, or permit you to invoke its services from another application under your full control.

- [ ] Allow the user to fully manipulate the multimedia files he or she has selected
  for playing. This includes playing forward and backward, rewinding and
  restarting a clip, stopping, pausing, and restarting a multimedia file play,
  looping AVI movies (running them in continuous play), and stepping movies
  both forward and backward a couple of frames at a time.

- [ ] Allow the user to inquire about the size and current position of a clip, even
  while it's playing. (I deliberately avoided features such as sliding horizontal
  status bars. That is just a little too much for a two-day project, but there is no
  reason you can't go back and put them in yourself.)

- [ ] Allow the user to record 10-second wave files of his own.

That list doesn't seem too long or sophisticated until you consider that what you are doing here is a full-featured multimedia programming with a database tool. Databases don't get much more flexible than that.

How the Windows multimedia drivers are controlled is covered in this chapter and the next. How I figured out what the multimedia interface and command sequences were is another matter. Frankly, you would need the tools that I have to research it properly, meaning the Windows SDK (Software Developer's Kit), which ordinary Windows users don't have. All sorts of documentation is in the SDK that the street versions of Windows don't supply. Of course, Microsoft will sell you a copy, if you come up with the bucks.

Even so, you will see enough about multimedia programming right here to do anything you might want in the future.

Designing the PWMMPLAY Form

When I begin to prototype a traditional software system, I like to doodle and draw until I get the first and most important interface reasonably straight. Fortunately, Paradox provides just the tools you need to do this without paper. You can draw forms on the screen, and if you don't like what you see, just click a form and delete it. Then do something else until it feels right.

That is exactly how I first designed MMT: by doodling it into place. So you won't have to go through the extended trial-and-error process this requires, I will show you the form as I finally left it. Figure 1.4 shows the MMT form (PWMMPLAY.FSL) in design mode, so you can see all the design objects in their places. (Some of them are invisible when the form opens in run mode.)

The design objects on this form that you must refer to in code are named something that sounds reasonable, but I will get to that in a moment.

First you should take a look at the various things that have to be set up at the form level. Then you must declare the names of any external routines you will use. There are two classes of these external routines: C language routines found in the DLL libraries GETFILE and MCIHELPR, and the multimedia interface routines found in the Windows-provided DLL named MMSYSTEM. The C language dialog, GetFile, is used to enable the user to select the media file to play. The other C language routine from the MCIHELPR DLL is named pwPositionMCIWin and is used to position the video display window (for reasons that I will talk about later). The MCI (Windows Media Control Interface) is found in the MMSYSTEM DLL, which provides the mciSendString and mciGetErrorString functions. These two functions do the bulk of the multimedia work

for MMT. There is also another form, MMSTILLS, that will be used to display the still graphic images. All of these are declared in the USES block.

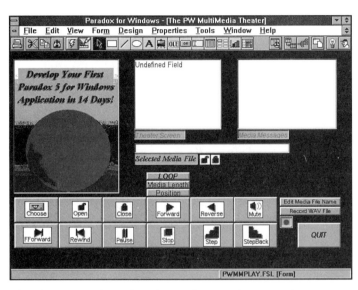

Figure 1.4. *The PW Multimedia Theater form in design mode.*

To declare the external routines, open the form in design mode and choose **P**roperties | **F**orm | **M**ethods. Then double-click Uses from the list. The ObjectPAL editor dialog opens, and you can type in (or just examine the supplied sample) code in the Uses block. Note that in the code fragments printed here, the ;BeginMethod... and ;EndMethod... comments are *not* present in the original code: they were inserted by Paradox when the FORMLIST form extracted the code. Here, then, is the PWMMPLAY USES block:

```
;¦BeginMethod¦#FormData1¦Uses¦
Uses GETFILE
  GetFileName( dllCaption CPTR ) CPTR
endUses
Uses MCIHELPR
  pwPositionMCIWin( hWnd CWORD, topx CWORD, topy CWORD,
                   width CWORD, height CWORD ) CWORD
endUses
Uses MMSYSTEM
  mciSendString( lpstrCommand CPTR, lpstrReturn CPTR,
               wReturnLng CWORD, hCallBack CWORD ) CLONG
  mciGetErrorString( dwError CLONG, lpstrReturn CPTR,
                   wLength CWORD ) CWORD
endUses
Uses ObjectPAL
```

```
   setMMStillName( sn String )
endUses
;¦EndMethod¦#FormData1¦Uses¦
```

Notice that there are actually four Uses blocks here: two for the C routines, one for the Windows MCI driver, and one for the other form. GetFile(), pwPositionMCIWin(), and the MCI interface functions are all C routines, and the names GETFILE, MCIHELPR, and MMSYSTEM correspond to the files GETFILE.DLL, MCIHELPR.DLL, and MMSYSTEM.DLL. I supplied the first two, and Microsoft supplied the other.

Developer's Tip: The GETFILE.DLL actually calls another Windows DLL, named COMMDLG.DLL. Microsoft wrote that one too, but it is redistributable by developers (at least by those that have the SDK). This DLL is necessary for GETFILE to work at all, much less properly.

The MMSYSTEM.DLL is *not* redistributable, but it will be present on any user's system that is equipped for multimedia Windows.

Notice the difference between the Uses blocks to the C-based routines and the one for the MMSTILLS form. Clearly, ObjectPAL is not the name of the other form. All you must do is declare the particular methods you will call from the other form. The form itself will be named in a String variable when it is time to open the MMSTILLS form.

There are some global variables the application needs, too. Because they are global and need to be seen by every method on the form, they should be attached directly to the form's VAR block. (Access it the same way you did the USES block.) Here is the PWMMPLAY VAR block, and again, don't add the comments stuck in there during FORMLIST processing:

```
;¦BeginMethod¦#FormData1¦Var¦
Var
  sfile String
  MBTopLeft, MBBotRight Point
  pxMBTopX, pxMBTopY, pxMBWide, pxMBHigh LongInt
  hWnd SmallInt
  muteIsOn Logical
  mmfiletype String
  mmfileloop Logical
  mmfilelength, mmfileposition LongInt
endVar
;¦EndMethod¦#FormData1¦Var¦
```

Because I assume that you already have some familiarity with the Paradox for Windows data types, I will cut straight to the chase. The following list details the use of the PWMMPLAY form variables:

`sfile String`	`sfile` is used to hold the name of the media file that the user selects via the Choose button, or by directly editing the media filename (there is another button for that).
`MBTopLeft, MBBotRight Point`	These Paradox Point variables are used to hold the top-left and bottom-right coordinates of the `MovieBox` bounding rectangle (this is the theater screen).
`pxMBTopX, pxMBTopY, pxMBWide, pxMBHigh LongInt`	These are the pixel addresses and width and height, in Windows pixels, of the MovieBox. Talk to Paradox in twips and to Windows in pixels.
`hWnd SmallInt`	`hWnd` is the Windows *handle* (identifying number) of the form itself. This will be used to tell the media player where the AVI movie window is. You have to know this so you can fit the movie inside the window (the MovieBox).
`muteIsOn Logical`	This boolean variable simply notes whether the user had clicked the Mute button or not. It is a *toggle* variable.

`mmfiletype String`	The media file type contains "AVI", "WAV", or "MID". It is used to launch differing media commands for respective file types. Sometimes this variable will contain the file extension of one of the still image formats.
`mmfileloop Logical`	Another boolean state variable. Without it, the app might loop a movie forever.
`mmfilelength, mmfileposition LongInt`	These variables record the length and current position within a media file. They are very important items: the media loop asynchronous timer logic depends upon these variables to avoid an infinite loop.

How these variables are used will become clear as I guide you through the remaining methods in PWMMPLAY. These variables are initialized in the form's open() method, as follows:

```
;¦BeginMethod¦#FormData1¦open¦
method open(var eventInfo Event)
var
  pxTop, pxBot Point
endvar
  if NOT eventInfo.isPreFilter() then
    doDefault
    maximize()
    setTitle( "The PW MultiMedia Theater" )
    MovieBox.GetBoundingBox( MBTopLeft, MBBotRight )
    pxTop = twipsToPixels( MBTopLeft )
    pxBot = twipsToPixels( MBBotRight )
    pxMBTopX = pxTop.x()
    pxMBTopY = pxTop.y()
    pxMBWide = pxBot.x() - pxTop.x() + 1
    pxMBHigh = pxBot.y() - pxTop.y() + 1
```

```
      hWnd = windowHandle()
      MediaFileName.text = ""
      sfile = ""
      muteIsOn = False
      mmfileloop = False
      mmfilelength = 0
      mmfileposition = 0
    endif
endmethod
;¦EndMethod¦#FormData1¦open¦
```

Notice that `pxTop` and `pxBot` are *local* Point type objects. They will be used in the intermediate stages of converting the bounding box locations to pixels from twips, and then discarded. The `LongInt` variable `pxMBTopX` and the other related variables are pixel positions and sizes. They are global variables defined at the form level (in the VAR block), so that they may be used by other methods later.

Once the form is open, it is up to the user to choose a media file by clicking the Choose button. Open the media file by clicking the Open button and then play the file by clicking the Forward button. The user also can manipulate and control the media file in other ways, but I will save that discussion for later.

To choose a media file, the `ChooseButton`'s `pushbutton()` method calls the form method `chooseMMFile()`, which sets the global String variable `sfile` to the selected filename. Just how `chooseMMFile()` gets the new filename is discussed in the next section. For now, just assume that it does so and take a look at what `ChooseButton` does with that filename. Here is the method's ObjectPAL code:

```
;¦BeginMethod¦#Page2.ChooseButton¦pushButton¦
method pushButton(var eventInfo Event)
var
  location SmallInt
  fv Form
endvar
  doDefault
  chooseMMFile()
  if NOT (sfile = "") then
    opengfx.visible = False
    closedgfx.visible = True
    location = sfile.search("AVI")
    if location > 0 then
      mmfiletype = sfile.substr(location,3)
    endif
    location = sfile.search("WAV")
    if location > 0 then
      mmfiletype = sfile.substr(location,3)
    endif
    location = sfile.search("MID")
    if location > 0 then
      mmfiletype = sfile.substr(location,3)
    endif
```

```
      location = sfile.search("BMP")
      if location > 0 then
        mmfiletype = sfile.substr(location,3)
      endif
      location = sfile.search("EPS")
      if location > 0 then
        mmfiletype = sfile.substr(location,3)
      endif
      location = sfile.search("GIF")
      if location > 0 then
        mmfiletype = sfile.substr(location,3)
      endif
      location = sfile.search("PCX")
      if location > 0 then
        mmfiletype = sfile.substr(location,3)
      endif
      location = sfile.search("TIF")
      if location > 0 then
        mmfiletype = sfile.substr(location,3)
      endif
      if (mmfiletype="BMP") OR (mmfiletype="EPS") OR (mmfiletype="GIF")
        OR (mmfiletype="PCX") OR (mmfiletype="TIF") then
          fv.open( "MMSTILLS.FSL" )
          fv.setMMStillName( sfile )
          fv.wait()
          mmfiletype = ""
          return
      endif
   else
      errorLog( 1, "You attempted to select a media file with a\an" +
                   "extension other than AVI, WAV, or MID." )
      errorShow( "Invalid file name", "Media File Selection" )
   endif
endmethod
;¦EndMethod¦#Page2.ChooseButton¦pushButton¦
```

After `choseMMFile()` magically supplies the selected filename in `sfile`, notice that the entire code sequence is made dependent on the actual presence of `sfile` by the `if` statement. Next, two objects named `opengfx` and `closedgfx` have their `visible` attribute set to invisible and visible, respectively. You can see these objects next to the text box reading `Selected Media File`: they are the two little padlock symbols. (See Figure 1.4.) One or the other is visible, indicating whether the user has actually opened the media file.

Following the setting of the lock (open/close) graphics, a long series of `if` statements pick out the specific file extension of the media file chosen and records it in the form variable `mmfiletype`. Also, if the media file type is one of the still image types, the MMSTILLS form is launched, and this form waits for the user to return here by closing MMSTILLS.

Now that the user has selected a media file via the Choose button, the file must be opened before it can be played. This is accomplished by clicking the Open button. The `pushbutton()` method for that object is as follows:

```
;¦BeginMethod¦#Page2.OpenButton¦pushButton¦
method pushButton(var eventInfo Event)
  mmfilelength = 0
  switch
    case mmfiletype = "AVI" : openPWMMVideo()
                              mmfilelength = LongInt(lengthPWMMVideo())
    case mmfiletype = "WAV" : openPWMMWaves()
                              mmfilelength = LongInt(lengthPWMMWaves())
    case mmfiletype = "MID" : openPWMMMidis()
                              mmfilelength = LongInt(lengthPWMMMidis())
    otherwise : msgStop( "Media File Open", "FileType not recognized" )
  endSwitch
endmethod
;¦EndMethod¦#Page2.OpenButton¦pushButton¦
```

Once again, the button's method is made very short and compact by the expedient of calling a more detailed method attached to the form. Notice that only the multimedia file types are processed here; still images are processed exclusively by the Choose button. Processing logic for still images trickles down no further into MMT methods.

When I first began to whip this form into shape, I attached the multimedia open logic directly to the button. I did the same with most of the other buttons as well. That didn't work out too well, because it made the pushbutton() methods large and unwieldy. That is why I removed all that logic and placed it in methods attached at the form level. A simple thought, you say? Yes it is, but it is just the sort of thing that prototyping is all about. If you tried shifting that much code around with traditional compiler technology, it would bog you down for days, and potentially introduce many errors. Instead, here it only simplified matters.

Back to the Open button now: In this pushbutton() method, only two things happen. A form method is called to open the media file, and once open, the length of the media file is retrieved.

By *open*, I am not referring to a traditional DOS or Windows kind of open. I mean the open accomplished by calling the MCI (Media Control Interface) and saying, "Get ready to play this file." The length is not in bytes either. For a Video for Windows movie, the length is a frame count. For a Wave file, the length might be samples or seconds. The length depends on the type of media file. See Appendix D, "Multimedia Reference Summary," for more information.

The companion piece to the multimedia open is the multimedia close, which can be invoked at any time by the user—even while the clip is still playing—by clicking the Close button. The pushbutton() method for Close is as follows:

```
;¦BeginMethod¦#Page2.CloseButton¦pushButton¦
method pushButton(var eventInfo Event)
  mmfileloop = False
  mmfilelength = 0
```

Developing Applications By Prototyping

```
  mmfileposition = 0
  switch
    case mmfiletype = "AVI" : closePWMMVideo()
    case mmfiletype = "WAV" : closePWMMWaves()
    case mmfiletype = "MID" : closePWMMMidis()
    otherwise : msgStop( "Media File Close", "FileType not recognized" )
  endSwitch
endmethod
;¦EndMethod¦#Page2.CloseButton¦pushButton¦
```

Notice that I call a form method to accomplish the MCI function. Such a separation of function (pushbutton logic from multimedia logic, in this case) is often called *encapsulation*. This technique is one you should remember for prototyping: Move code that is already working off by itself. This helps keep you from breaking finished code again when you change other code.

The next control button shown in Figure 1.4 is labeled Forward. Internally, this is the RunButton. This is an example of when prototyping can cause those little differences that can later turn out to be more than irritating. They can be downright confusing. In this case, I have left the names alone because I wanted to illustrate this trivial (and harmless) error to you. The pushbutton() ObjectPAL for RunButton is as follows:

```
;¦BeginMethod¦#Page2.RunButton¦pushButton¦
method pushButton(var eventInfo Event)
  switch
    case mmfiletype = "AVI" : fwdPWMMVideo()
    case mmfiletype = "WAV" : fwdPWMMWaves()
    case mmfiletype = "MID" : fwdPWMMMidis()
    otherwise : msgStop( "Media File Forward", "FileType not recognized" )
  endSwitch
endmethod
;¦EndMethod¦#Page2.RunButton¦pushButton¦
```

As you can see, there is nothing particularly startling about the RunButton's method. For each type of multimedia file, a corresponding form method is used to encapsulate the slightly different MCI calls.

The Forward button also has a timer() method attached to it. The first thing to understand about an object's timer() method is that it will only be used when something has called setTimer() on the object's behalf. It wouldn't be real smart for the object itself to start its own timer (this can be done, but it can easily lead to an infinite loop), but I won't keep you in suspense. The Loop button calls setTimer() for the Forward button, to make the clip loop indefinitely until the user clicks the Loop button again.

The RunButton's timer() method illustrates why it is so important to establish the clip's length at open time. Knowing the length gives something to compare to so you can know when the clip has run completely—and in turn, restart it. This method doesn't have a

20

way to shut off the loop. Remember that the loop is controlled by the Loop button. Here is the ObjectPAL for the RunButton's timer() method:

```
;¦BeginMethod¦#Page2.RunButton¦timer¦
method timer(var eventInfo TimerEvent)
  switch
    case mmfiletype = "AVI" :
      mmfileposition = LongInt(posPWMMVideo())
      if mmfileposition >= mmfilelength then
        rewindPWMMVideo()
        self.pushbutton()
      endif
    case mmfiletype = "WAV" :
      if mmfileposition >= mmfilelength then
        rewindPWMMWaves()
        self.pushbutton()
      endif
    case mmfiletype = "MID" :
      if mmfileposition >= mmfilelength then
        rewindPWMMMidis()
        self.pushbutton()
      endif
  endSwitch
endmethod
;¦EndMethod¦#Page2.RunButton¦timer¦
```

Like all the other buttons you will see on this form, logical separation is made between the types of media files in the timer() method, so that the still encapsulated MCI calls can be made for each type. Don't panic, by the way. I *will* get around to showing you how to make the MCI calls.

The other feature of interest in the timer() is the call to self.pushbutton(). What does this mean? It means that the RunButton is pushing itself, which starts the playback again. Neat, huh?

Developer's Tip: I must admit that I did not have to guess or prototype either the timer routine or the reference to self. I just borrowed and adapted the timer logic from an application called ANIMATE in my book, *Paradox for Windows Developer's Guide*. That application flies a cartoon helicopter or car across the form window using the timer logic to determine when to move the Graphic object to the next location. This is where the experience factor comes into play in prototyping. The more experience you have, the more you can boilerplate both past experience and past code. That makes for faster development. A corollary to this little story is that if you do these things constantly, they stay fresh in your mind. Don't goof off between real projects; keep working with these tools.

Because the Loop, Media Length, and Position buttons are stacked directly above the Forward button, they are discussed next. A little visual prototyping is done here because I initially could not decide where to put these buttons. I dragged them all over the form before the notion of reducing their size and stacking them hit me. They are related to playing the media file (the Forward button), right?

Something tells me that this solution is a personal preference of mine that others may not like. It is more difficult to accurately click these smaller buttons. But that is what prototyping is all about. If you prefer another look, move the buttons. Don't forget, however, to unpin their horizontal and vertical positions first. I always pin everything once I have it where I want it.

Where the Loop button goes may still be up for grabs. What this button does, however, is well-defined. Here is the ObjectPAL source for its `pushbutton()` method:

```
;¦BeginMethod¦#Page2.LoopButton¦pushButton¦
method pushButton(var eventInfo Event)
  switch
    case mmfileloop = True :
      mmfileloop = False
      RunButton.killTimer()
    case mmfileloop = False :
      mmfileloop = True
      RunButton.setTimer( 1500, True )
  endSwitch
endmethod
;¦EndMethod¦#Page2.LoopButton¦pushButton¦
```

The Loop button toggles the `mmfileloop` form variable to its other state and either sets or kills a timer for `RunButton`. I don't select file types here because the `RunButton` does that. The `setTimer()` call tells Paradox to generate a timer pop every 1,500 milliseconds (1.5 seconds) and to keep doing that (with the `True` parameter). Being able to loop a media clip indefinitely is a nice effect for just a little bit of ObjectPAL code, don't you think?

The Media Length button's function is to display the media file length in the Media Messages box (the large white box shown in Figure 1.4, with the internal name `MMMessageBox`). Here again, the media file types are separated, and the proper encapsulated MCI function is invoked. The ObjectPAL code is as follows:

```
;¦BeginMethod¦#Page2.LengthButton¦pushButton¦
method pushButton(var eventInfo Event)
  switch
    case mmfiletype = "AVI" :
      MMMessageBox.text =
      "Movie has " + lengthPWMMVideo() + " frames"
    case mmfiletype = "WAV" :
      MMMessageBox.text =
      "Wave is " + lengthPWMMWaves() + " milliseconds long"
    case mmfiletype = "MID" :
```

```
      MMMessageBox.text =
        "Midi file length is " + lengthPWMMMidis()
    otherwise : msgStop( "Media File Forward", "FileType not recognized" )
  endSwitch
endmethod
;¦EndMethod¦#Page2.LengthButton¦pushButton¦
```

The Position button performs a similar service: It displays the current media file position (even while the clip is playing) in the Media Messages box. The ObjectPAL for this task is almost identical to the Media Length button's code:

```
;¦BeginMethod¦#Page2.PositionButton¦pushButton¦
method pushButton(var eventInfo Event)
  switch
    case mmfiletype = "AVI" :
      MMMessageBox.text =
      "Movie position is " + posPWMMVideo() + " frames"
    case mmfiletype = "WAV" :
      MMMessageBox.text =
      "Wave position is " + posPWMMWaves() + " milliseconds"
    case mmfiletype = "MID" :
      MMMessageBox.text =
      "Midi file position is " + posPWMMMidis()
    otherwise : msgStop( "Media File Forward", "FileType not recognized" )
  endSwitch
endmethod
;¦EndMethod¦#Page2.PositionButton¦pushButton¦
```

That takes care of the four stacked media file run-related buttons. There are other ways, however, to run clips. You can run them backward too. That is the function of the Reverse button. Here is the pushbutton() code for Reverse:

```
;¦BeginMethod¦#Page2.ReverseButton¦pushButton¦
method pushButton(var eventInfo Event)
  switch
    case mmfiletype = "AVI" : reversePWMMVideo()
    case mmfiletype = "WAV" :
      msgStop( "Media File Player",
               "Reverse not support for WAV files" )
    case mmfiletype = "MID" :
      msgStop( "Media File Player",
               "Reverse not support for MID files" )
    otherwise : msgStop( "Media File Reverse", "FileType not recognized" )
  endSwitch
endmethod
;¦EndMethod¦#Page2.ReverseButton¦pushButton¦
```

Reverse is almost identical to its counterpart Forward, except it runs backward. You can play a movie backward, but not Wave or MIDI sound files. Note that playing a clip in reverse will look pretty jumpy unless you have a very fast computer. The media driver has to read and interpret it backward too, which takes more time.

The Mute button also has no effect on Wave or MIDI files, but that is logical. Why play sound files muted? The Mute button is only for videos; clicking the button for other files results in an error message. Here is the ObjectPAL for Mute (be quiet while you read this one, please):

```
;¦BeginMethod¦#Page2.MuteButton¦pushButton¦
method pushButton(var eventInfo Event)
  switch
    case mmfiletype = "AVI" : mutePWMMVideo()
    case mmfiletype = "WAV" :
      msgStop( "Media File Player",
               "Mute not support for WAV files" )
    case mmfiletype = "MID" :
      msgStop( "Media File Player",
               "Mute not support for MID files" )
    otherwise : msgStop( "Media File Mute", "FileType not recognized" )
  endSwitch
endmethod
;¦EndMethod¦#Page2.MuteButton¦pushButton¦
```

The repetitive structure of all these button methods might be getting boring by now. It should, because the methods are all boilerplated from the first couple of methods. Therein, however, lies a great secret of prototyping code: Be consistent *all the time*. Users and programmers alike are going to try to see uniform patters whether they exist or not. If not, errors may occur. Therefore, try to supply the uniformity (even for yourself) wherever possible. By staying consistent, you also can borrow and modify the code much more quickly.

The FForward button is for fast-forwarding the media file and is internally called RunFastButton. There is nothing surprising here, including the fact that you can't do this with sound files. FForward's pushbutton() method is as follows:

```
;¦BeginMethod¦#Page2.RunFastButton¦pushButton¦
method pushButton(var eventInfo Event)
  switch
    case mmfiletype = "AVI" : ffwdPWMMVideo()
    case mmfiletype = "WAV" :
      msgStop( "Media File Player",
               "Fast forward not support for WAV files" )
    case mmfiletype = "MID" :
      msgStop( "Media File Player",
               "Fast forward not support for MID files" )
    otherwise : msgStop( "Media File FastForward",
                         "FileType not recognized" )
  endSwitch
endmethod
;¦EndMethod¦#Page2.RunFastButton¦pushButton¦
```

The Rewind button rewinds the media file to its beginning, without having to close and re-open the media file. Here is the code, without comments:

```
;¦BeginMethod¦#Page2.RewindButton¦pushButton¦
method pushButton(var eventInfo Event)
  switch
    case mmfiletype = "AVI" : rewindPWMMVideo()
    case mmfiletype = "WAV" : rewindPWMMWaves()
    case mmfiletype = "MID" : rewindPWMMidis()
    otherwise : msgStop( "Media File Rewind", "FileType not recognized" )
  endSwitch
endmethod
;¦EndMethod¦#Page2.RewindButton¦pushButton¦
```

The Pause and Stop buttons both halt playing the media file, without closing it. Strictly speaking, you should not run a stopped file, but *resume* a paused file. Clicking the Forward button and just running it works fine. Here are the pushbutton() methods for both Pause and Stop, taken together:

```
;¦BeginMethod¦#Page2.PauseButton¦pushButton¦
method pushButton(var eventInfo Event)
  switch
    case mmfiletype = "AVI" : pausePWMMVideo()
    case mmfiletype = "WAV" : pausePWMMWaves()
    case mmfiletype = "MID" : pausePWMMidis()
    otherwise : msgStop( "Media File Pause", "FileType not recognized" )
  endSwitch
endmethod
;¦EndMethod¦#Page2.PauseButton¦pushButton¦

;¦BeginMethod¦#Page2.StopButton¦pushButton¦
method pushButton(var eventInfo Event)
  switch
    case mmfiletype = "AVI" : stopPWMMVideo()
    case mmfiletype = "WAV" : stopPWMMWaves()
    case mmfiletype = "MID" : stopPWMMidis()
    otherwise : msgStop( "Media File Stop", "FileType not recognized" )
  endSwitch
endmethod
;¦EndMethod¦#Page2.StopButton¦pushButton¦
```

The Step and StepBack buttons both move a Video for Windows movie ahead or back two frames, respectively. Note that you don't have to stop or pause first. You can click Step while the clip is playing, and MCI will halt playing while you diddle around with it. Except for their direction of movement, these two methods are nearly identical, including the fact that you can't single step with sound files again. The ObjectPAL for both methods is as follows:

```
;¦BeginMethod¦#Page2.StepButton¦pushButton¦
method pushButton(var eventInfo Event)
  switch
    case mmfiletype = "AVI" : stepPWMMVideo()
    case mmfiletype = "WAV" :
      msgStop( "Media File Player",
               "Step not support for WAV files" )
    case mmfiletype = "MID" :
```

```
        msgStop( "Media File Player",
                "Step not support for MID files" )
    otherwise : msgStop( "Media File Step", "FileType not recognized" )
  endSwitch
endmethod
;¦EndMethod¦#Page2.StepButton¦pushButton¦

;¦BeginMethod¦#Page2.StepBackButton¦pushButton¦
method pushButton(var eventInfo Event)
  switch
    case mmfiletype = "AVI" : stepbackPWMMVideo()
    case mmfiletype = "WAV" :
      msgStop( "Media File Player",
               "Stepback not support for WAV files" )
    case mmfiletype = "MID" :
      msgStop( "Media File Player",
               "Stepback not support for MID files" )
    otherwise : msgStop( "Media File StepBack", "FileType not recognized" )
  endSwitch
endmethod
;¦EndMethod¦#Page2.StepBackButton¦pushButton¦
```

Last (thank goodness), don't forget to give the user a way to get out of the application. Of course, the user can pull down the form window's control menu (using the button in the top-left corner of the window) and choose Close. But why not give your users or yourself a nice, fat, highly visible Quit button? I did, there it sits, and here is its pushbutton() method.

```
;¦BeginMethod¦#Page2.QuitButton¦pushButton¦
method pushButton(var eventInfo Event)
  close()
endmethod
;¦EndMethod¦#Page2.QuitButton¦pushButton¦
```

Whew! Enough of that! There are enough buttons on this form to decode a vault combination. They are all necessary to supply the functionality you want, and their intended functions are clear. You can look at the form and see what to do, which is one of the most highly desirable design characteristics you can have.

Adding the GetFile DLL Support to MMT

When I first began prototyping PWMMPLAY, I was quite enamored with the notion of building a multimedia application with nothing but ObjectPAL and a form. And quite obviously, that is entirely possible and easy to do.

However, there was one little glitch that I didn't like. You remember what to do now, don't you? Right, pull the offending part out and do something else. That offending part was the Paradox filebrowser, which lets you choose a filename much as you do it in PWMMPLAY. Paradox even provides a nice, attractive dialog box.

The filebrowser won't, however, return the drive name (E: in my case) as part of the returned filename string. I could have programmed around the program, using nothing but ObjectPAL, but I am a stubborn person (or I would never try to write a computer book in the first place).

I still didn't have to roll my own code, though, because I rolled it during my last book. So I went over to that directory and borrowed the code for GetFile—my handy open-filename DLL dialog applet. A couple of quick mods, bang, and I'm ready to go.

Therefore, even though GetFile is written in C (like the vitamin), I used it. I will present it here without much comment—except to say that it is so short because all it does is set up a call to the Windows COMMDLG (Common Dialogs) DLL, which does the real work. The code for GetFile is next. You can look at it and easily detect the part I changed for our multimedia application. Okay, set your teeth, here it is:

```c
#include <windows.h>
#include <dir.h>
#include <string.h>
#include "commdlg.h"

int FAR PASCAL LibMain( HANDLE hInstance, WORD wDataSeg,
                        WORD wHeapSize, LPSTR lpszCmdLine )
{
  if ( wHeapSize > 0 ) UnlockData( 0 );
  return 1;
}

LPSTR FAR PASCAL GetFileName( char *dlgTitleStr)
{
  OPENFILENAME ofn;
  char szDirName[80];            /* directory name */
  char szFile[80], szFileTitle[80];  /* file and title */
  char *szFilter[] = {
    "Video for Windows(*.AVI)",
    "*.avi",
    "Wave Sound(*.WAV)",
    "*.wav",
    "MIDI Music(*.MID)",
    "*.mid",
    "Bitmaps(*.BMP)",
    "*.bmp",
    "Bitmaps(*.DIB)",
    "*.dib",
    "Postscript(*.EPS)",
    "*.eps",
```

```
        "Gfx Ichg Fmt(*.GIF)",
        "*.gif",
        "Paintbrush(*.PCX)",
        "*.pcx",
        "Tagged(*.TIF)",
        "*.tif",
        "ALL Files(*.*)",
        "*.*",
        ""
      };

      strcpy( szDirName, "\\" );
      szFile[0] = '\0';
      ofn.lStructSize = sizeof(OPENFILENAME);
      ofn.hwndOwner = NULL;
      ofn.lpstrFilter = szFilter[0];
      ofn.lpstrCustomFilter = (LPSTR) NULL;
      ofn.nMaxCustFilter = 0L;
      ofn.nFilterIndex = 1L;
      ofn.lpstrFile= szFile;
      ofn.nMaxFile = sizeof(szFile);
      ofn.lpstrFileTitle = szFileTitle;

      ofn.nMaxFileTitle = sizeof(szFileTitle);
      ofn.lpstrInitialDir = szDirName;
      ofn.lpstrTitle = (LPSTR)dlgTitleStr;
      ofn.Flags = OFN_SHOWHELP | OFN_PATHMUSTEXIST
              | OFN_FILEMUSTEXIST;
      ofn.nFileOffset = 0;
      ofn.nFileExtension = 0;
      ofn.lpstrDefExt = (LPSTR) NULL;
      if (GetOpenFileName(&ofn))
        return ofn.lpstrFile;
      else
        return (LPSTR)"";
    }
```

As part of the C-compiler project (Borland C/C++, of course), I had to supply a Windows
DEF (definition) file. It is fairly self-explanatory, too. Here is the DEF file for GetFile:

```
LIBRARY      GETFILE
DESCRIPTION  'Get MMFile Open Name Dialog'
EXETYPE      WINDOWS
CODE         PRELOAD MOVEABLE DISCARDABLE
DATA         PRELOAD MOVEABLE SINGLE
HEAPSIZE     4096
EXPORTS      GetFileName
IMPORTS      COMMDLG.GetOpenFileName
```

Define the project, make the runtime module (the .DLL file), and so on. If all this really
bothers you, incidentally, or you cannot write C-code, you can always go back to an
ObjectPAL workaround.

It was a second glitch that made the MCIHELPR DLL necessary. In the original version
of MMT, only ObjectPAL was necessary to completely control the process of opening

and playing a Video for a Windows clip. Then, very late in the product's development process—and very late indeed in the process of producing this book—one of the final beta versions introduced what is called a "quiet change" in Paradox's internal form management functions. The result was that it was no longer possible to bind the video display window directly to the form as a child window. Paradox would no longer allow the video display window to become visible, no matter what I did. Panic!

To make this long and panicky story short, I talked to the good folks at Borland about this in some detail. It may be that by the time you see Paradox 5 for Windows, this little glitch will be resolved. They do tell me that this little problem has implications for other parts of Paradox 5 for Windows that could turn out to be important. On the other hand, the nature of the quiet change may be such that only this one application is ever affected, so the problem may not be resolved. In any case, I can't take the chance that it will be resolved, because that would mean sample code that doesn't work when you install your CD-ROM from this book.

Let's be real sure here to give the product team folks at Borland their due. Paradox 5 for Windows is a tight, dependable database package, even though I uncovered a glitch in a test version of the product. Further, in talking with the Borland team members and other beta users electronically, I was given no fewer than four usable workaround solutions to this problem. They all listened, and all pitched in to help. They saved me from a heart attack! And they'll deliver to you a really fine Windows database product— the best on the market, in fact.

Anyway, that's why MCIHELP came to exist. Its sole callable function is `pwPositionMCIWin()`, and its purpose is to allow me to position and size the video display window when it is not bound directly to the form (that is the only way I could get the display window visible again). Tomorrow, you'll see how I used this DLL, but right now you need to see what is in it.

Construction of the MCIHELPR DLL follows the same basic principles as did GETFILE, except that there is no DEF file. Instead, I simply declared the `pwPositionMCIWin()` function as exportable directly in the code. The whole thing is brutally short, because it only does one thing. Here is the MCIHELPR C language source code:

```
#include <windows.h>

#pragma argsused

int FAR PASCAL LibMain( HANDLE hInstance, WORD wDataSeg, WORD wHeapSize, LPSTR
                        lpszCmdLine )
{
  if ( wHeapSize > 0 ) UnlockData( 0 );
```

```
   return 1;
}

int FAR PASCAL _export pwPositionMCIWin( int hWnd, int topx, int topy,  int width, int
                                 height )
{
  MoveWindow( (HWND)hWnd, topx, topy, width, height, FALSE );
  return 0;
}
```

The real meat of the DLL is in the one line that calls the Windows API function, `MoveWindow()`. This is the function that puts the popup video display window where I want it, at the size and shape that I want it. I'll talk about this routine a little more tomorrow.

And now you are ready. You also know why we put some things in the Uses block for the PWMMPLAY form. It might be a good idea to just flip back momentarily and check out that form again (before moving on to Day 2).

Modification Notes

Modification notes are supposed to be notes about how to create an application by modifying it, rather than by creating it from scratch. Hmmm. Sounds kind of like prototyping to me.

Well, it *is* prototyping, and I will give away the whole store right now. The big secret to prototyping application is nothing more than this: copy and paste like crazy! Boilerplate all the code you can, and if you can't, do it anyway. Then run the code until it breaks; and then fix it. Do this until you like the way it looks and works.

You might notice my poignant sense of the ludicrous from the tongue-in-cheek approach, but my purpose is deadly serious. Do you want to develop applications fast? Do you want to develop applications with as few errors as possible? Yes? Then *borrow the code*, your own presumably, and keep your hands off the keyboard as much as possible. Every time you touch the keyboard for some original, untried purpose, you will most likely make at least one small mistake. Then you have to fix it. It is much easier to borrow, paste, and modify details.

Debugging the Process

When I first approached MMT, I could test each button as soon as I defined it. That's because I put all the logic in the button method, encapsulating nothing. That move complicated things at an exponential rate.

If I wanted to draw the form first, however, and place the design objects on it—and still encapsulate the MCI calls—how would I proceed? An easy way is to define the MCI-related methods attached to the form with nothing in them (or perhaps with just a solitary `return` statement). You can make them dummy routines; they certainly won't malfunction that way.

Defining methods as dummy routines also gives you the advantage of knowing where something broke if a test goes awry. Click a button that calls a dummy routine, and if something goes wrong, it's not in the button's method. It has to be somewhere else on the form.

That fact points to a fairly serious problem with too much encapsulation. Encapsulation means hiding some code from other parts of the code, which unfortunately sometimes means that it is *very* difficult to debug object-based or object-oriented code. You can't easily see where something went wrong.

Therefore, *test as you go*. Don't go very far past the specific task at hand before you make *sure* it works right. You will thank me for this later. And that is all the wisdom you can handle for Day 1.

2

Fleshing Out the PW Multimedia Theater

I see you made it through the first day of multimedia programming, and I'm thrilled you're back for more. That's good, because Day 1 was the warm-up; the hot stuff happens today.

The first section today is pretty lengthy, and, to be honest, has more to do with multimedia programming than with prototyping. This is where you get to see how to make all those MCI calls to the multimedia drivers.

Showstopper! The notion that prototyping applications eliminates all of the dreary detail work from applications development is a true show-stopper. There is indeed a serious temptation to "dash" the product together and let the small stuff go. Dash the proof of concept prototype together, certainly, but then sweat the small stuff. It's attention to detail that makes the detail transparent to the user, by never blowing up in his face. It's the mark of a true professional to get it *all* right.

Prototyping doesn't eliminate detail work any more than careful planning does; it's just a different way of making design decisions. Prototyping also spreads design decisions throughout the application development process, instead of concentrating them at the front end of the process.

Whether or not reading this kind of ObjectPAL code is heavy sledding for you depends on just how anxious you are to take control of those multimedia devices and files yourself. If you're anything like me, I expect you're ready to see what it takes.

I don't necessarily recommend reading the ObjectPAL in the first section word for word. Scan it, check out the comments I provide to get your bearing, and focus on the things that especially draw your interest. After all, you can go to the CD-ROM and boilerplate with this code for your own applications. The context of what *you* want to do will focus your attention in the right places at that time.

For the rest of the day, we will do some other things to flesh out the MMT, such as adding the still-image support and learning how to invoke the MMT and control it from another form. This, of course, is the real point. MMT should be a tool you can use to spice up your own applications.

Adding the Media Control Interface (MCI) String Command Support to MMT

On Day 1, I repeatedly made reference to the encapsulated, form-level methods that are used to actually call the MCI drivers. This section is where you get to meet those methods face to face.

First, look at the `chooseMMFile()` method, which is called by the Choose button's code. (Remember that the Choose button's `pushbutton()` method doesn't contain this code; it *calls* this method, which is attached to the form.) The purpose of `chooseMMFile()` is to set the `sfile` String variable to the name of the selected media file. In order to do this, the first thing that happens is a call to the `GetFile()` C-language DLL. You may remember that `GetFile()` will, in turn, call the Windows DLL COMMDLG with a request to start the open-file dialog box, with your own supplied window title and file selection types. Here is the source for the `chooseMMFile()` method:

```
;¦BeginMethod¦#FormData1¦chooseMMFile¦
method chooseMMFile()
  sfile = GetFileName( "Media File Selection" )
  if NOT (sfile = "") then
    MediaFileName.text = sfile
    opengfx.visible = False
    closedgfx.visible = True
    return
  else
    MediaFileName.text = ""
    errorLog( 1, "You attempted to select a media file with a\n" +
                "extension other than AVI, WAV, or MID." )
    errorShow( "Invalid file name", "Media File Selection" )
    return
  endif
endmethod
;¦EndMethod¦#FormData1¦chooseMMFile¦
```

There is nothing particularly startling about `chooseMMFile()`. It checks whether `GetFile()` returned a string value. If not, the user probably cancelled out of the dialog without selecting anything. This situation is handled by logging an error and showing it using the `errorLog()` and `errorShow()` Paradox library routines.

Most of the rest of the form-level methods occur in groups—a group for each of the AVI, WAV, and MID media file types. The rest of these methods also follow a particular naming convention. The method name will be of the form *function*PWMM*type*(), where *function* means something such as open or reverse. PWMM is a constant part of the method name, and *type* will be `Video`, `Waves`, or `Midis`, depending on the media type detected by the Choose button logic.

The Video media file routines come first (probably because I find PC movies more interesting that any other PC media type—bet you do, too). Scan over them, noting the comments before each method and brief explanations after each method.

The openPWMMVideo() method is the longest of the Video methods because opening an AVI file requires more customizing of the default MCI parameters to play a movie where you want it to play, in just the size box you want it to use. In this method, I also use some of the more obscure global variables, such as hWnd—the Windows handle of the form itself.

This is also the place I mentioned on Day 1, where the MCIHELPR DLL function pwPositionMCIWin() is used. As you see the method here, it is set up to tell the Media Control Interface (MCI) to use a pop-up style window for the video display window, and to use the MCIHELPR function to position and size that window the way you want it. On the other hand, you may later want to see if the approach that binds the video display window to the form will work again. I have therefore left the code for that approach in the method, as comment lines. All you have to do to switch approaches is comment out the code that uses the DLL helper function and uncomment the original code. The openPWMMVideo() source is as follows:

```
;¦BeginMethod¦#FormData1¦openPWMMVideo¦
method openPWMMVideo()
var
  mciCmdStr, ReturnString String
  ReturnCode LongInt
  twTopx, twTopy, twWide, twHigh LongInt
  twTopCorner Point
  ptTopCorner Point
endvar
  ReturnString = fill( " ", 1024 )
  if NOT (sfile = "" ) then
    mciCmdStr = "open " + sfile + " alias movie nostatic style popup"
    ReturnCode = mciSendString(mciCmdStr, ReturnString, 1024, 0)
    if NOT (0 = ReturnCode) then
      ReturnString = fill( " ", 1024 )
      mciGetErrorString( ReturnCode, ReturnString, 1024 )
      MMMessageBox.text = ReturnString
      msgStop( "Media File Open", "Open failed\nCheck media messages" )
      return
    endif
    MMMessageBox.text = ReturnString

;    ReturnString = fill( " ", 1024 )
;    mciCmdStr = "window movie handle " + strVal(hWnd)
;    ReturnCode = mciSendString(mciCmdStr, ReturnString, 1024, 0)
;    if NOT (0 = ReturnCode) then
;      ReturnString = fill( " ", 1024 )
;      mciGetErrorString( ReturnCode, ReturnString, 1024 )
;      self.MMMessageBox.text = ReturnString
;      msgStop( "Media File Open",
;              "Window definition failed\nCheck media messages" )
```

```
;      return
;    endif
;    MMMessageBox.text = ReturnString

    ReturnString = fill( " ", 1024 )
    mciCmdStr = " status movie window handle"+
    ReturnCode = mciSendString(mciCmdStr, ReturnString, 1024, 0)
    if 0 <> ReturnCode then N
      msgStop( "**Debug**", "Couldn't get AVI window handle." )
endif
    hWnd = SmallInt(numval(ReturnString))
    getposition( twTopx, twTopy, twWide, twHigh ) ; find the form's loc
    twTopCorner.setx(twTopx)
    twTopCorner.sety(twTopy)
    ptTopCorner = twipsToPixels( twTopCorner )
    ; The following code accounts for negative screen positions of the
    ; MDI client when maximized.
    if 0 > ptTopCorner.x() then
      ptTopCorner.setx(ptTopCorner.x() * -1)
    endif
    if 0 > ptTopCorner.y() then
      ptTopCorner.sety(40+ptTopCorner.y() * -1)
    else
      ptTopCorner.sety(40+ptTopCorner.y())
    endif
    pwPositionMCIWin( hWnd,
                      SmallInt(pxMBTopX-2+ptTopCorner.x()),
                      SmallInt(pxMBTopY+4+ptTopCorner.y()),
                      SmallInt(pxMBWide-2),
                      SmallInt(pxMBHigh-2) )
    ReturnString = fill( " ", 1024 )
    mciCmdStr = " realize movie normal
    ReturnCode = mciSendString(mciCmdStr, ReturnString, 1024, 0)

    ReturnString = fill( " ", 1024 )
    mciCmdStr = "window movie state show"
    ReturnCode = mciSendString(mciCmdStr, ReturnString, 1024, 0)

;    ReturnString = fill( " ", 1024 )
;    mciCmdStr = "put movie destination at " +
;                strVal(pxMBTopX+3) + " " +
;                strVal(pxMBTopY+3) + " " +
;                strVal(pxMBWide-8) + " " +
;                strVal(pxMBHigh-8)
;    MMMessageBox.text = "Place movie screen at " +
;                        strVal(pxMBTopX+3) + " " +
;                        strVal(pxMBTopY+3) + " " +
;                        strVal(pxMBWide-8) + " " +
;                        strVal(pxMBHigh-8) + " " +
;                        "(x,y,wide,high) twips"
;    ReturnCode = mciSendString(mciCmdStr, ReturnString, 1024, 0)
;    if NOT (0 = ReturnCode) then
;      ReturnString = fill( " ", 1024 )
;      mciGetErrorString( ReturnCode, ReturnString, 1024 )
;      MMMessageBox.text = ReturnString
;      msgStop( "Media File Open",
;               "Media destination failed\nCheck media messages" )
```

```
;       return
;     endif
;     MMMessageBox.text = ReturnString

     opengfx.visible = True
     closedgfx.visible = False
   else
     errorLog( 1, "You must Choose a media file first!" )
     errorShow( "Invalid choice of action", "Media File Open" )
   endif
endmethod
;¦EndMethod¦#FormData1¦openPWMMVideo¦
```

As with most of these methods, openPWMMVideo() first checks to see if sfile has anything in it. You can't open a file with no name (although you can ride through the desert on a horse with no name). Next, the MCI command string is built by simply concatenating the string parts. These parts consist of some constant values, plus the value of the sfile variable, like this:

```
mciCmdStr = "open " + sfile + " alias movie nostatic style popup"
```

You may be wondering what some of those strange constant values in the previous line of code mean. The front end of the line is fairly clear, but what does nostatic mean? The answer has to do with the color palette that the media driver will use to display video frames (which are, after all, just graphic images). The color palette available to an application is preloaded with system-defined, or static, colors. The nostatic parameter tells the driver routine to remove as many system colors from the palette as possible so that more colors will be under the video driver's control. Thus, the quality of the picture is somewhat enhanced.

In the original version of this method, it wasn't necessary to use the nostatic parameter, but when the glitch in Paradox's form handling routines appeared, the picture quality deteriorated considerably—even when using an independent pop-up window style as is done here (because the glitch involves a subtle change to palette management). If you want to see if you can use the approach that binds the video window to the form, you might try it without this parameter.

Another change you must make when binding the video window to the form, if you choose to try it, is to remove the style popup parameter from the open command string. This parameter won't work using the approach of making the form itself the video display window.

On Day 1, I introduced you to the form's Uses block. You may recall that in the Uses block, I declared the MMSYSTEM.DLL, and also declared the format of the function call I would make to that DLL. That function is your gateway to controlling the MCI

drivers. It's called the *string command interface*, and I next call it to open the AVI file, like this:

```
ReturnCode = mciSendString(mciCmdStr, ReturnString, 1024, 0)
```

For most MCI calls, `mciSendString()` returns 0 if the function was successful, and doesn't do much with the 1024-byte `ReturnString`. If there is an error, however, text describing the error is placed in `ReturnString`, where I can place it in the `MMMessageBox`. If it was successful, however, the command as I built it here not only opens the AVI file, but assigns it an *alias,* or shorthand name, of `movie`. Using this alias, I can refer to whatever movie happens to be open at the time with the same code.

If the call to `open` is successful, the next step is to identify the window that will contain the movie window. In the original code, which appears next in a block of commented lines, I wanted the movie to play in the PWMMPLAY form window, rather than creating an independent MCI window. This is accomplished with the MCI call:

```
mciCmdStr = "window movie handle " + strVal(hWnd)
```

However, Murphy was an optimist, and that approach stopped working just before this book went into production. That meant I had to do something else, meaning I had to use a pop-up style window for the video display. To accomplish this, it was also necessary to use the `hWnd` variable a little differently: Now it will refer to the video display window, not the PWMMPLAY form. I use the following MCI command string to get that window handle value:

```
mciCmdStr = "status movie window handle"
```

After obtaining the video display window's handle, I went through some rather terrible gyrations to compute where on the Windows screen the pop-up window should be placed. It's no longer defined with reference to the form window's boundaries and thus can go anywhere. Once the position and size are computed, I call the `pwPositionMCIWin()` C language routine I showed you yesterday to position and size the video display window.

Immediately following that call are two more MCI string command calls that weren't in the original code either. In the first of these, `realize movie normal`, I tell Video for Windows to realize its color palette. By this time, the video driver has defined something called a logical palette to use for playing the movie. Realizing the palette tells Windows to match up the application's logical palette with the system palette and to map any unmatched colors as intelligently as possible. The result is an enhanced color palette and a corresponding enhanced video picture. Now you know why I added the `nostatic` parameter to the `open` command: I was still trying to get that original quality back. Note that this sort of thing can be necessary when any application that has played games with the color palette launches a video clip; it isn't just because Paradox has a glitch here that I did this.

The other MCI string command is the window `movie state show` command. This wasn't in the original code, but that is only because I forgot it. This command causes the video driver to display the first frame of the clip, stop-action, before the user clicks the Forward button. I added this just because it's a nice touch that dresses up the application a little. (Well, I was fixing things anyway.)

Developer's Tip: If your tongue is hanging out a little because of the fancy stepping around I did in this method to get around a bug in a test version of Paradox, take heart. This is the kind of thing that always happens in the development of any significant piece of software. It just happened to Borland this time, and they shared it with me!

It's what happens after you find the bug that is important. You just have to find the motivation to pound the keyboard a little harder and fix the bug. Sometimes you need to do that in a tearing hurry, just as I did here, and just as Borland is doing prior to releasing the product. Nor should you be hard on Borland, or afraid of Paradox 5 for Windows. This is a really fine software package that is reliable, useful, and easy to use. It's just that sometimes when you do the really fancy things, you have to work a little harder for it. And anyway, this is a book about the real world of programming, and you just got a little taste of it. Hang in there!

Now I'll flip-flop back to the original approach of using the form window. Once the containing window has been identified, the bounding box of the movie window itself needs to be specified. This is accomplished with the MCI call:

```
mciCmdStr = "put movie destination at " +
          strVal(pxMBTopX+3) + " " +
          strVal(pxMBTopY+3) + " " +
          strVal(pxMBWide-8) + " " +
          strVal(pxMBHigh-8)
```

Now you can see why I put all those point and pixel variables in the form's `Var` block. If all these maneuvers have been successful, it remains only to make the lock graphics `opengfx` and `closedgfx` visible or invisible, as appropriate. From this point forward, I'll comment only on what is being done, not on how to make the MCI calls themselves. You need to have that explained only once, and then you can copy it, modifying only the differing details.

The `closePWMMVideo()` method is quite a bit shorter. Its code is as follows:

```
;¦BeginMethod¦#FormData1¦closePWMMVideo¦
method closePWMMVideo()
var
  mciCmdStr, ReturnString String
  ReturnCode LongInt
endVar
  ReturnString = fill( " ", 1024 )
  if NOT (sfile = "" ) then
    mciCmdStr = "close movie"
    ReturnCode = mciSendString(mciCmdStr, ReturnString, 1024, 0)
    if NOT (0 = ReturnCode) then
      ReturnString = fill( " ", 1024 )
      mciGetErrorString( ReturnCode, ReturnString, 1024 )
      MMMessageBox.text = ReturnString
      msgStop( "Media File Close", "Close failed\nCheck media messages" )
      return
    endif
    MMMessageBox.text = ReturnString
  else
    msgStop( "Media File Close", "No file specified to close" )
  endif
  MovieBox.bringToFront()
  MediaFileName.text = ""
  sfile = ""
  opengfx.visible = False
  closedgfx.visible = True
  muteIsOn = False
endmethod
;¦EndMethod¦#FormData1¦closePWMMVideo¦
```

The only remarkable things about `closePWMMVideo()` are how the global variables are reset to starting values, and how the `movie` alias eliminates the need to scrounge around for the exact filename.

Clicking the Forward button causes its `pushbutton()` to call the form method `fwdPWMMVideo` (if the user selected an AVI file, of course). Like the media close methods, playing a media file requires only one MCI call. In this case, the MCI string command is simply `play movie`, as follows:

```
;¦BeginMethod¦#FormData1¦fwdPWMMVideo¦
method fwdPWMMVideo()
var
  mciCmdStr, ReturnString String
  ReturnCode LongInt
endVar
  ReturnString = fill( " ", 1024 )
  if NOT (sfile = "" ) then
    mciCmdStr = "play movie"
    ReturnCode = mciSendString(mciCmdStr, ReturnString, 1024, 0)
    if NOT (0 = ReturnCode) then
```

```
      ReturnString = fill( " ", 1024 )
      mciGetErrorString( ReturnCode, ReturnString, 1024 )
      MMMessageBox.text = ReturnString
      msgStop( "Media File Play", "Play failed\nCheck media messages" )
      return
    endif
    MMMessageBox.text = ReturnString
  else
    msgStop( "Media File Play", "No AVI file was specified" )
  endif
endmethod
;¦EndMethod¦#FormData1¦fwdPWMMVideo¦
```

One of the things I did, both for your benefit and mine, was to place the contents of
`ReturnString` in the `MMMessageBox`, whether or not the MCI call was successful. I just
wanted to see what was going on behind the scenes, as you probably do as well. You may
want to remove some of this message-displaying activity when you build your own
applications.

Playing a movie in reverse is just like playing a movie forward, except that the MCI
command string adds the modifier reverse at the end. The presence of this token is the
only real difference between `fwdPWMMVideo()` and `reversePWMMVideo()`, whose code is as
follows:

```
;¦BeginMethod¦#FormData1¦reversePWMMVideo¦
method reversePWMMVideo()
var
  mciCmdStr, ReturnString String
  ReturnCode LongInt
endVar
  ReturnString = fill( " ", 1024 )
  if NOT (sfile = "" ) then
    mciCmdStr = "play movie reverse"
    ReturnCode = mciSendString(mciCmdStr, ReturnString, 1024, 0)
    if NOT (0 = ReturnCode) then
      ReturnString = fill( " ", 1024 )
      mciGetErrorString( ReturnCode, ReturnString, 1024 )
      MMMessageBox.text = ReturnString
      msgStop( "Media File Play-Reverse",
               "Play-reverse failed\nCheck media messages" )
      return
    endif
    MMMessageBox.text = ReturnString
  else
    msgStop( "Media File Play-Reverse",
             "No file specified to play-reverse" )
  endif
endmethod
;¦EndMethod¦#FormData1¦reversePWMMVideo¦
```

When you play a movie in reverse, its soundtrack also plays in reverse, as you would
expect. However, you cannot play a Wave or MIDI sound file in reverse, due to
differences in the media file structures, as well as their drivers.

Similarly, you can mute the sound on a movie, but it makes no sense to do so for a sound file. Muting the sound in a movie is not accomplished with a mute command (there is no such command), but with the set movie audio all off command, as follows:

```
;¦BeginMethod¦#FormData1¦mutePWMMVideo¦
method mutePWMMVideo()
var
  mciCmdStr, ReturnString String
  ReturnCode LongInt
endVar
  ReturnString = fill( " ", 1024 )
  if NOT (sfile = "" ) then
    if NOT muteIsOn then
      mciCmdStr = "set movie audio all off"
      ReturnCode = mciSendString(mciCmdStr, ReturnString, 1024, 0)
      if NOT (0 = ReturnCode) then
        ReturnString = fill( " ", 1024 )
        mciGetErrorString( ReturnCode, ReturnString, 1024 )
        MMMessageBox.text = ReturnString
        msgStop( "Media File Mute",
                 "Mute failed\nCheck media messages" )
        return
      endif
      muteIsOn = True
    else
      mciCmdStr = "set movie audio all on"
      ReturnCode = mciSendString(mciCmdStr, ReturnString, 1024, 0)
      if NOT (0 = ReturnCode) then
        ReturnString = fill( " ", 1024 )
        mciGetErrorString( ReturnCode, ReturnString, 1024 )
        MMMessageBox.text = ReturnString
        msgStop( "Media File Sound On",
                 "Sound on failed\nCheck media messages" )
        return
      endif
      muteIsOn = False
    endif
    MMMessageBox.text = ReturnString
  else
    msgStop( "Media File Mute/Sound On",
             "No file specified" )
  endif
endmethod
;¦EndMethod¦#FormData1¦mutePWMMVideo¦
```

Notice that the mutePWMMVideo() method is built to support the use of the Mute button as a *toggle switch*. If the sound is currently on, it is turned off; if off, it is turned on. This is the reason that I included the form variable muteIsOn in the form's Var block—to control the selection of the toggle action.

When the user clicks the FForward button, that pushbutton method invokes the form method ffwdPWMMVideo(). As a matter of fact, for the current release of Video for Windows (1.1a), this will have no effect. The command won't return an error, but it won't do anything either. However, I've included the method so that if a future release of Video for Windows does support this command string, you'll already have it. Here is the source code for the `ffwdPWMMVideo()` method:

```
;¦BeginMethod¦#FormData1¦ffwdPWMMVideo¦
method ffwdPWMMVideo()
var
  mciCmdStr, ReturnString String
  ReturnCode LongInt
endVar
  ReturnString = fill( " ", 1024 )
  if NOT (sfile = "" ) then
    mciCmdStr = "play movie fast"
    ReturnCode = mciSendString(mciCmdStr, ReturnString, 1024, 0)
    if NOT (0 = ReturnCode) then
      ReturnString = fill( " ", 1024 )
      mciGetErrorString( ReturnCode, ReturnString, 1024 )
      MMMessageBox.text = ReturnString
      msgStop( "Media File FastForward",
               "FastForward failed\nCheck media messages" )
      return
    endif
    MMMessageBox.text = ReturnString
  else
    msgStop( "Media File FastForward",
             "No file specified to fastforward" )
  endif
endmethod
;¦EndMethod¦#FormData1¦ffwdPWMMVideo¦
```

Notice that the `ffwdPWMMVideo()` method is exactly like the `fwdPWMMVideo()` method, except that the argument `fast` has been added to the `play movie` command string.

The next form method, `rewindPWMMVideo()`, does work. When the Rewind button is clicked and this method is invoked, the AVI file is returned to position (frame) 0, ready to play again. The ObjectPAL source for `rewindPWMMVideo()` is as follows:

```
;¦BeginMethod¦#FormData1¦rewindPWMMVideo¦
method rewindPWMMVideo()
var
  mciCmdStr, ReturnString String
  ReturnCode LongInt
endVar
  ReturnString = fill( " ", 1024 )
  if NOT (sfile = "" ) then
    mciCmdStr = "seek movie to start"
    ReturnCode = mciSendString(mciCmdStr, ReturnString, 1024, 0)
    if NOT (0 = ReturnCode) then
      ReturnString = fill( " ", 1024 )
      mciGetErrorString( ReturnCode, ReturnString, 1024 )
      MMMessageBox.text = ReturnString
```

```
        msgStop( "Media File Rewind",
                "Rewind failed\nCheck media messages" )
        return
      endif
      MMMessageBox.text = ReturnString
    else
      msgStop( "Media File Rewind",
                "No file specified to rewind" )
    endif
endmethod
; ;EndMethod;#FormData1;rewindPWMMVideo;
```

I mentioned on Day 1 that the Video for Windows MCI commands pause and stop should, strictly speaking, cause different commands to be used to start the video again. I also mentioned that just clicking the Forward button (causing a play command to be sent to the driver) works just fine. Accordingly, I'll present the pausePWMMVideo() and stopPWMMVideo() methods back to back. Indeed, these two methods' ObjectPAL source codes are identical, except that one has the MCI command pause movie, whereas the other sends a stop movie command string. Here is their source code:

```
; ;BeginMethod;#FormData1;pausePWMMVideo;
method pausePWMMVideo()
var
  mciCmdStr, ReturnString String
  ReturnCode LongInt
endVar
  ReturnString = fill( " ", 1024 )
  if NOT (sfile = "" ) then
    mciCmdStr = "pause movie"
    ReturnCode = mciSendString(mciCmdStr, ReturnString, 1024, 0)
    if NOT (0 = ReturnCode) then
      ReturnString = fill( " ", 1024 )
      mciGetErrorString( ReturnCode, ReturnString, 1024 )
      MMMessageBox.text = ReturnString
      msgStop( "Media File Pause",
                "Pause failed\nCheck media messages" )
      return
    endif
    MMMessageBox.text = ReturnString
  else
    msgStop( "Media File Pause",
              "No file specified to pause" )
  endif
endmethod
; ;EndMethod;#FormData1;pausePWMMVideo;

; ;BeginMethod;#FormData1;stopPWMMVideo;
method stopPWMMVideo()
var
  mciCmdStr, ReturnString String
  ReturnCode LongInt
endVar
  ReturnString = fill( " ", 1024 )
  if NOT (sfile = "" ) then
```

```
      mciCmdStr = "stop movie"
      ReturnCode = mciSendString(mciCmdStr, ReturnString, 1024, 0)
      if NOT (0 = ReturnCode) then
        ReturnString = fill( " ", 1024 )
        mciGetErrorString( ReturnCode, ReturnString, 1024 )
        MMMessageBox.text = ReturnString
        msgStop( "Media File Stop",
                 "Stop failed\nCheck media messages" )
        return
      endif
      MMMessageBox.text = ReturnString
   else
      msgStop( "Media File Stop",
               "No file specified to stop" )
   endif
endmethod
;¦EndMethod¦#FormData1¦stopPWMMVideo¦
```

The Step and StepBack buttons' methods call the `stepPWMMVideo()` and `stepbackPWMMVideo()` methods. These methods really are nearly identical since they use the same MCI command, differing only in the arithmetic sign on one argument. Specifically, the `step movie by` *x* MCI command string is used in both cases. The `stepPWMMVideo()` method makes this call using an *x* value of 2, and `stepbackPWMMVideo()` uses an *x* value of –2. This argument means that the AVI driver is to move the full-motion video forward or backward by two frames (no sound plays during step operations).

Some of the Microsoft Windows SDK examples use a step value of 5, which I think is too jumpy, although stepping by one frame seems to get you nowhere rather quickly. So I chose a step value of 2. As mundane as this may seem, this is a classical example of what prototyping is all about: Try it, fix it, and eventually you'll like it. The ObjectPAL source for these two methods is also presented back to back, as follows:

```
;¦BeginMethod¦#FormData1¦stepPWMMVideo¦
method stepPWMMVideo()
var
  mciCmdStr, ReturnString String
  ReturnCode LongInt
endVar
  ReturnString = fill( " ", 1024 )
  if NOT (sfile = "" ) then
    mciCmdStr = "step movie by 2"
    ReturnCode = mciSendString(mciCmdStr, ReturnString, 1024, 0)
    if NOT (0 = ReturnCode) then
      ReturnString = fill( " ", 1024 )
      mciGetErrorString( ReturnCode, ReturnString, 1024 )
      MMMessageBox.text = ReturnString
      msgStop( "Media File Step",
               "Step failed\nCheck media messages" )
      return
    endif
    MMMessageBox.text = ReturnString
  else
```

```
      msgStop( "Media File Step",
               "No file specified to step" )
  endif
endmethod
;¦EndMethod¦#FormData1¦stepPWMMVideo¦

;¦BeginMethod¦#FormData1¦stepbackPWMMVideo¦
method stepbackPWMMVideo()
var
  mciCmdStr, ReturnString String
  ReturnCode LongInt
endVar
  ReturnString = fill( " ", 1024 )
  if NOT (sfile = "" ) then
    mciCmdStr = "step movie by -2"
    ReturnCode = mciSendString(mciCmdStr, ReturnString, 1024, 0)
    if NOT (0 = ReturnCode) then
      ReturnString = fill( " ", 1024 )
      mciGetErrorString( ReturnCode, ReturnString, 1024 )
      MMMessageBox.text = ReturnString
      msgStop( "Media File StepBack",
               "StepBack failed\nCheck media messages" )
      return
    endif
    MMMessageBox.text = ReturnString
  else
    msgStop( "Media File StepBack",
             "No file specified to step back" )
  endif
endmethod
;¦EndMethod¦#FormData1¦stepbackPWMMVideo¦
```

Clicking the Position button stacked above the Forward button causes its pushbutton( )
method to call the posPWMMVideo( ) form method. This method returns the current
position of the video clip, in frames, as a string to the calling pushbutton( ) method,
which can then display it in the Media Messages box. The source for posPWMMVideo( ) is
as follows:

```
;¦BeginMethod¦#FormData1¦posPWMMVideo¦
method posPWMMVideo() String
var
  mciCmdStr, ReturnString String
  ReturnCode LongInt
endVar
  ReturnString = fill( " ", 1024 )
  if NOT (sfile = "" ) then
    mciCmdStr = "status movie position"
    ReturnCode = mciSendString(mciCmdStr, ReturnString, 1024, 0)
    if 0 = ReturnCode then
      return ReturnString
    else
      return ""
    endif
  else
    msgStop( "Media File Status", "No AVI file was specified" )
```

```
    endif
endmethod
;¦EndMethod¦#FormData1¦posPWMMVideo¦
```

In the posPWMMVideo() method, notice that the MCI driver has already converted the current media file position as a string and returned it in the ReturnString variable.

The lengthPWMMVideo() form method is likewise invoked when the stacked Media Length button is clicked. As you can see in the following source code, this method also returns a length value already encoded as a string:

```
;¦BeginMethod¦#FormData1¦lengthPWMMVideo¦
method lengthPWMMVideo() String
var
  mciCmdStr, ReturnString String
  ReturnCode LongInt
endVar
  ReturnString = fill( " ", 1024 )
  if NOT (sfile = "" ) then
    mciCmdStr = "status movie length"
    ReturnCode = mciSendString(mciCmdStr, ReturnString, 1024, 0)
    if 0 = ReturnCode then
      return ReturnString
    else
      return ""
    endif
  else
    msgStop( "Media File Status", "No AVI file was specified" )
  endif
endmethod
;¦EndMethod¦#FormData1¦lengthPWMMVideo¦
```

Next you come to the Waves group of MCI methods. As you look over these methods, you'll see that they are very much like the Video methods, but they deal with Wave files instead of AVI files.

Since you are by now becoming proficient at reading the MCI-interface method sources, I'll just present them to you in a single group, without the detailed comments previously used. Here are the Wave-related ObjectPAL sources:

```
;¦BeginMethod¦#FormData1¦openPWMMWaves¦
method openPWMMWaves()
var
  mciCmdStr, ReturnString String
  ReturnCode LongInt
endvar
  ReturnString = fill( " ", 1024 )
  if NOT (sfile = "" ) then
    mciCmdStr = "open " + sfile + " alias waves"
    ReturnCode = mciSendString(mciCmdStr, ReturnString, 1024, 0)
    if NOT (0 = ReturnCode) then
      ReturnString = fill( " ", 1024 )
      mciGetErrorString( ReturnCode, ReturnString, 1024 )
```

```
          MMMessageBox.text = ReturnString
          msgStop( "Media File Open", "Open failed\nCheck media messages" )
          return
       endif
     MMMessageBox.text = ReturnString
     opengfx.visible = True
     closedgfx.visible = False
  else
     errorLog( 1, "You must Choose a media file first!" )
     errorShow( "Invalid choice of action", "Media File Open" )
  endif
endmethod
;¦EndMethod¦#FormData1¦openPWMMWaves¦

;¦BeginMethod¦#FormData1¦closePWMMWaves¦
method closePWMMWaves()
var
  mciCmdStr, ReturnString String
  ReturnCode LongInt
endVar
  ReturnString = fill( " ", 1024 )
  if NOT (sfile = "" ) then
    mciCmdStr = "close waves"
    ReturnCode = mciSendString(mciCmdStr, ReturnString, 1024, 0)
    if NOT (0 = ReturnCode) then
      ReturnString = fill( " ", 1024 )
      mciGetErrorString( ReturnCode, ReturnString, 1024 )
      MMMessageBox.text = ReturnString
      msgStop( "Media File Close", "Close failed\nCheck media messages" )
      return
    endif
    MMMessageBox.text = ReturnString
  else
    msgStop( "Media File Close", "No file specified to close" )
  endif
  MediaFileName.text = ""
  sfile = ""
  opengfx.visible = True
  closedgfx.visible = False
endmethod
;¦EndMethod¦#FormData1¦closePWMMWaves¦

;¦BeginMethod¦#FormData1¦fwdPWMMWaves¦
method fwdPWMMWaves()
var
  mciCmdStr, ReturnString String
  ReturnCode LongInt
endVar
  ReturnString = fill( " ", 1024 )
  if NOT (sfile = "" ) then
    mciCmdStr = "play waves"
    ReturnCode = mciSendString(mciCmdStr, ReturnString, 1024, 0)
    if NOT (0 = ReturnCode) then
      ReturnString = fill( " ", 1024 )
      mciGetErrorString( ReturnCode, ReturnString, 1024 )
      MMMessageBox.text = ReturnString
```

```
      msgStop( "Media File Play", "Play failed\nCheck media messages" )
        return
      endif
      MMMessageBox.text = ReturnString
   else
      msgStop( "Media File Play", "No AVI file was specified" )
   endif
endmethod
;¦EndMethod¦#FormData1¦fwdPWMMWaves¦

;¦BeginMethod¦#FormData1¦rewindPWMMWaves¦
method rewindPWMMWaves()
var
   mciCmdStr, ReturnString String
   ReturnCode LongInt
endVar
   ReturnString = fill( " ", 1024 )
   if NOT (sfile = "" ) then
      mciCmdStr = "seek waves to start"
      ReturnCode = mciSendString(mciCmdStr, ReturnString, 1024, 0)
      if NOT (0 = ReturnCode) then
         ReturnString = fill( " ", 1024 )
         mciGetErrorString( ReturnCode, ReturnString, 1024 )
         MMMessageBox.text = ReturnString
         msgStop( "Media File Rewind",
                  "Rewind failed\nCheck media messages" )
         return
      endif
      MMMessageBox.text = ReturnString
   else
      msgStop( "Media File Rewind",
               "No file specified to rewind" )
   endif
endmethod
;¦EndMethod¦#FormData1¦rewindPWMMWaves¦

;¦BeginMethod¦#FormData1¦stopPWMMWaves¦
method stopPWMMWaves()
var
   mciCmdStr, ReturnString String
   ReturnCode LongInt
endVar
   ReturnString = fill( " ", 1024 )
   if NOT (sfile = "" ) then
      mciCmdStr = "stop waves"
      ReturnCode = mciSendString(mciCmdStr, ReturnString, 1024, 0)
      if NOT (0 = ReturnCode) then
         ReturnString = fill( " ", 1024 )
         mciGetErrorString( ReturnCode, ReturnString, 1024 )
         MMMessageBox.text = ReturnString
         msgStop( "Media File Stop",
                  "Stop failed\nCheck media messages" )
         return
      endif
      MMMessageBox.text = ReturnString
   else
```

```
        msgStop( "Media File Stop",
                "No file specified to stop" )
    endif
endmethod
;¦EndMethod¦#FormData1¦stopPWMMWaves¦

;¦BeginMethod¦#FormData1¦pausePWMMWaves¦
method pausePWMMWaves()
var
  mciCmdStr, ReturnString String
  ReturnCode LongInt
endVar
  ReturnString = fill( " ", 1024 )
  if NOT (sfile = "" ) then
    mciCmdStr = "pause waves"
    ReturnCode = mciSendString(mciCmdStr, ReturnString, 1024, 0)
    if NOT (0 = ReturnCode) then
      ReturnString = fill( " ", 1024 )
      mciGetErrorString( ReturnCode, ReturnString, 1024 )
      MMMessageBox.text = ReturnString
      msgStop( "Media File Pause",
               "Pause failed\nCheck media messages" )
      return
    endif
    MMMessageBox.text = ReturnString
  else
    msgStop( "Media File Pause",
             "No file specified to pause" )
  endif
endmethod
;¦EndMethod¦#FormData1¦pausePWMMWaves¦

;¦BeginMethod¦#FormData1¦posPWMMWaves¦
method posPWMMWaves() String
var
  mciCmdStr, ReturnString String
  ReturnCode LongInt
endVar
  ReturnString = fill( " ", 1024 )
  if NOT (sfile = "" ) then
    mciCmdStr = "status waves position"
    ReturnCode = mciSendString(mciCmdStr, ReturnString, 1024, 0)
    if 0 = ReturnCode then
      return ReturnString
    else
      return ""
    endif
  else
    msgStop( "Media File Status", "No WAV file was specified" )
  endif
endmethod
;¦EndMethod¦#FormData1¦posPWMMWaves¦

;¦BeginMethod¦#FormData1¦lengthPWMMWaves¦
method lengthPWMMWaves() String
var
  mciCmdStr, ReturnString String
```

```
    ReturnCode LongInt
  endVar
    ReturnString = fill( " ", 1024 )
    if NOT (sfile = "" ) then
      mciCmdStr = "status waves length"
      ReturnCode = mciSendString(mciCmdStr, ReturnString, 1024, 0)
      if 0 = ReturnCode then
        return ReturnString
      else
        return ""
      endif
    else
      msgStop( "Media File Status", "No WAV file was specified" )
    endif
  endmethod
;¦EndMethod¦#FormData1¦lengthPWMMWaves¦
```

Finally, there is a MIDI group of support methods. These methods will also be presented without much comment, since my purpose is neither to insult your intelligence nor put you to sleep. Here are the MIDI-related ObjectPAL sources:

```
;¦BeginMethod¦#FormData1¦openPWMMMidis¦
method openPWMMMidis()
var
  mciCmdStr, ReturnString String
  ReturnCode LongInt
endvar
  ReturnString = fill( " ", 1024 )
  if NOT (sfile = "" ) then
    mciCmdStr = "open " + sfile + " alias midis"
    ReturnCode = mciSendString(mciCmdStr, ReturnString, 1024, 0)
    if NOT (0 = ReturnCode) then
      ReturnString = fill( " ", 1024 )
      mciGetErrorString( ReturnCode, ReturnString, 1024 )
      MMMessageBox.text = ReturnString
      msgStop( "Media File Open", "Open failed\nCheck media messages" )
      return
    endif
    MMMessageBox.text = ReturnString
    opengfx.visible = True
    closedgfx.visible = False
  else
    errorLog( 1, "You must Choose a media file first!" )
    errorShow( "Invalid choice of action", "Media File Open" )
  endif
endmethod
;¦EndMethod¦#FormData1¦openPWMMMidis¦

;¦BeginMethod¦#FormData1¦closePWMMMidis¦
method closePWMMMidis()
var
  mciCmdStr, ReturnString String
  ReturnCode LongInt
endVar
  ReturnString = fill( " ", 1024 )
```

```
    if NOT (sfile = "" ) then
      mciCmdStr = "close midis"
      ReturnCode = mciSendString(mciCmdStr, ReturnString, 1024, 0)
      if NOT (0 = ReturnCode) then
        ReturnString = fill( " ", 1024 )
        mciGetErrorString( ReturnCode, ReturnString, 1024 )
        MMMessageBox.text = ReturnString
        msgStop( "Media File Close", "Close failed\nCheck media messages" )
        return
      endif
      MMMessageBox.text = ReturnString
    else
      msgStop( "Media File Close", "No file specified to close" )
    endif
    MediaFileName.text = ""
    sfile = ""
    opengfx.visible = True
    closedgfx.visible = False
endmethod
;¦EndMethod¦#FormData1¦closePWMMMidis¦

;¦BeginMethod¦#FormData1¦fwdPWMMMidis¦
method fwdPWMMMidis()
var
  mciCmdStr, ReturnString String
  ReturnCode LongInt
endVar
  ReturnString = fill( " ", 1024 )
  if NOT (sfile = "" ) then
    mciCmdStr = "play midis"
    ReturnCode = mciSendString(mciCmdStr, ReturnString, 1024, 0)
    if NOT (0 = ReturnCode) then
      ReturnString = fill( " ", 1024 )
      mciGetErrorString( ReturnCode, ReturnString, 1024 )
      MMMessageBox.text = ReturnString
      msgStop( "Media File Play", "Play failed\nCheck media messages" )
      return
    endif
    MMMessageBox.text = ReturnString
  else
    msgStop( "Media File Play", "No AVI file was specified" )
  endif
endmethod
;¦EndMethod¦#FormData1¦fwdPWMMMidis¦

;¦BeginMethod¦#FormData1¦rewindPWMMMidis¦
method rewindPWMMMidis()
var
  mciCmdStr, ReturnString String
  ReturnCode LongInt
endVar
  ReturnString = fill( " ", 1024 )
  if NOT (sfile = "" ) then
    mciCmdStr = "seek midis to start"
    ReturnCode = mciSendString(mciCmdStr, ReturnString, 1024, 0)
    if NOT (0 = ReturnCode) then
```

```
      ReturnString = fill( " ", 1024 )
      mciGetErrorString( ReturnCode, ReturnString, 1024 )
      MMMessageBox.text = ReturnString
      msgStop( "Media File Rewind",
               "Rewind failed\nCheck media messages" )
      return
    endif
    MMMessageBox.text = ReturnString
  else
    msgStop( "Media File Rewind",
             "No file specified to rewind" )
  endif
endmethod
;¦EndMethod¦#FormData1¦rewindPWMMMidis¦

;¦BeginMethod¦#FormData1¦pausePWMMMidis¦
method pausePWMMMidis()
var
  mciCmdStr, ReturnString String
  ReturnCode LongInt
endVar
  ReturnString = fill( " ", 1024 )
  if NOT (sfile = "" ) then
    mciCmdStr = "pause midis"
    ReturnCode = mciSendString(mciCmdStr, ReturnString, 1024, 0)
    if NOT (0 = ReturnCode) then
      ReturnString = fill( " ", 1024 )
      mciGetErrorString( ReturnCode, ReturnString, 1024 )
      MMMessageBox.text = ReturnString
      msgStop( "Media File Pause",
               "Pause failed\nCheck media messages" )
      return
    endif
    MMMessageBox.text = ReturnString
  else
    msgStop( "Media File Pause",
             "No file specified to pause" )
  endif
endmethod
;¦EndMethod¦#FormData1¦pausePWMMMidis¦

;¦BeginMethod¦#FormData1¦stopPWMMMidis¦
method stopPWMMMidis()
var
  mciCmdStr, ReturnString String
  ReturnCode LongInt
endVar
  ReturnString = fill( " ", 1024 )
  if NOT (sfile = "" ) then
    mciCmdStr = "stop midis"
    ReturnCode = mciSendString(mciCmdStr, ReturnString, 1024, 0)
    if NOT (0 = ReturnCode) then
      ReturnString = fill( " ", 1024 )
      mciGetErrorString( ReturnCode, ReturnString, 1024 )
      MMMessageBox.text = ReturnString
      msgStop( "Media File Stop",
               "Stop failed\nCheck media messages" )
```

```
        return
      endif
      MMMessageBox.text = ReturnString
    else
      msgStop( "Media File Stop",
               "No file specified to stop" )
    endif
  endmethod
;¦EndMethod¦#FormData1¦stopPWMMMidis¦

;¦BeginMethod¦#FormData1¦lengthPWMMMidis¦
method lengthPWMMMidis() String
var
  mciCmdStr, ReturnString String
  ReturnCode LongInt
endVar
  ReturnString = fill( " ", 1024 )
  if NOT (sfile = "" ) then
    mciCmdStr = "status midis length"
    ReturnCode = mciSendString(mciCmdStr, ReturnString, 1024, 0)
    if 0 = ReturnCode then
      return ReturnString
    else
      return ""
    endif
  else
    msgStop( "Media File Status", "No MID file was specified" )
  endif
endmethod
;¦EndMethod¦#FormData1¦lengthPWMMMidis¦

;¦BeginMethod¦#FormData1¦posPWMMMidis¦
method posPWMMMidis() String
var
  mciCmdStr, ReturnString String
  ReturnCode LongInt
endVar
  ReturnString = fill( " ", 1024 )
  if NOT (sfile = "" ) then
    mciCmdStr = "status midis position"
    ReturnCode = mciSendString(mciCmdStr, ReturnString, 1024, 0)
    if 0 = ReturnCode then
      return ReturnString
    else
      return ""
    endif
  else
    msgStop( "Media File Status", "No MID file was specified" )
  endif
endmethod
;¦EndMethod¦#FormData1¦posPWMMMidis¦
```

There is one further form method that is not called in response to any button click. This is the setMMFileName() method. This method is not, in fact, called by anything on the

PWMMPLAY form at all. Its purpose is to be called from another form or application that wants to use the MMT as a support tool. Clearly, since you would often want to set the media file to be played from another application without making the user go through the Choose button routine, some "internal" means of selecting the media file must be provided. This is it. The setMMFileName() method source is as follows, and you'll see it again later in this chapter:

```
;¦BeginMethod¦#FormData1¦setMMFileName¦
method setMMFileName( NewMMFileName String )
var
  location SmallInt
endvar
  sfile = NewMMFileName
  location = sfile.search("AVI")
  if location > 0 then
    mmfiletype = sfile.substr(location,3)
  endif
  location = sfile.search("WAV")
  if location > 0 then
    mmfiletype = sfile.substr(location,3)
  endif
  location = sfile.search("MID")
  if location > 0 then
    mmfiletype = sfile.substr(location,3)
  endif
endmethod
;¦EndMethod¦#FormData1¦setMMFileName¦
```

Adding Recording Capability to MMT

One of the neatest, yet simplest, effects provided by MMT is the capability to record 10-second Wave clips. This is kicked off by the Record button, whose pushbutton() is one of the simplest on the form. Here it is, but look and see what you might want to add, before I tell you:

```
;¦BeginMethod¦#Page2.RecordButton¦pushButton¦
method pushButton(var eventInfo Event)
  if NOT (sfile="") then
    recordPWMMWave()
  endif
endmethod
;¦EndMethod¦#Page2.RecordButton¦pushButton¦
```

What you might want to add to the record button is a little more error checking. First, as written, it will enable you to record in a file with an extension other than .WAV, if you desire. Second, it will enable you to write over a media file you may want to keep. It

could use a dialog box that prompts the user to verify that he or she indeed wants to destroy the old file in such a case. Third, it doesn't verify that the media file has been closed before trying to re-record a file; if it hasn't been closed, a sharing violation will result.

The Record button does at least verify that *some* filename was specified. However, the Selected Media File display box is a Paradox text field that does not allow input (it's not an edit field). What if the user wants to record a *new* sound file? I have just the thing: The Edit Media File Name button pops up a dialog (another form, really) and lets the user enter the filename there. Here is the method source for the Edit Media File Name button:

```
;¦BeginMethod¦#Page2.EdFileButton¦pushButton¦
method pushButton(var eventInfo Event)
var
  location SmallInt
  dlgForm Form
  dlgReturn AnyType
endvar
  dlgReturn = ""
  if dlgForm.openAsDialog( "EDMMFILE.FDL", WinStyleDefault,
                           1440,2880,6500,2880 ) then
    dlgReturn = dlgForm.wait()
  endif
  mmfiletype = ""
  sfile = String( dlgReturn )
  sfile = sfile.upper()
  if NOT (sfile = "") then
    MediaFileName.text = sfile
    opengfx.visible = False
    closedgfx.visible = True
    location = sfile.search("AVI")
    if location > 0 then
      mmfiletype = sfile.substr(location,3)
    endif
    location = sfile.search("WAV")
    if location > 0 then
      mmfiletype = sfile.substr(location,3)
    endif
    location = sfile.search("MID")
    if location > 0 then
      mmfiletype = sfile.substr(location,3)
    endif
    return
  else
    MediaFileName.text = ""
    errorLog( 1, "You attempted to select a media file with an\n" +
                "extension other than AVI, WAV, or MID." )
    errorShow( "Invalid file name", "Media File Selection" )
    return
  endif
endmethod
;¦EndMethod¦#Page2.EdFileButton¦pushButton¦
```

Notice that the Edit Media File Name method behaves much like the Choose method, except that it doesn't call the GetFile() DLL dialog routine. It separates the file types and sets key variables the same way, though.

The real difference between EdFileButton's logic and GetFile's logic lies in the manner in which input data is retrieved. For EdFileButton, the key to the matter lies in the following two ObjectPAL statements:

```
if dlgForm.openAsDialog( "EDMMFILE.FDL", WinStyleDefault,
                         1440,2880,6500,2880 ) then
  dlgReturn = dlgForm.wait()
```

If the EDMMFILE form opens properly, the method waits on a return value (dlgReturn). How a form, as opposed to a method, returns a value will be clear in the next few paragraphs, so hold that thought.

Now that you've seen the method that opens and uses the EDMMFILE dialog form, it's time to see the form itself. Figure 2.1 shows the EDMMFILE form in context, ready for the user to specify the name of the WAV file to record into.

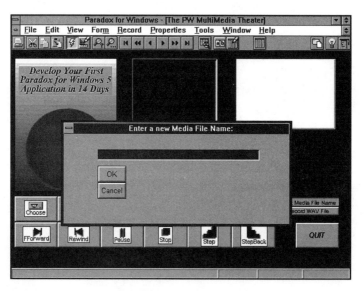

Figure 2.1. *The EDMMFILE dialog box (form).*

The EDMMFILE dialog form is simplicity itself. There is an edit field in which the user can type the name of the new WAV file, an OK button for sending the name back to the Record button, and a Cancel button for bailing out of the process.

Since the ObjectPAL attached to EDMMFILE objects is so brief, you can see it all right here. First, there is the form's open() method. Notice that EDMMFILE does not set its own position or size; the EdFileButton pushbutton() specifies these parameters when it requests that the EDMMFILE form be opened. Here is the EDMMFILE open() method:

```
;¦BeginMethod¦#FormData1¦open¦
method open(var eventInfo Event)
if NOT eventInfo.isPreFilter() then
  doDefault
  setTitle( "Enter a new Media File Name:" )
  edmmtext.text = ""
endif
endmethod
;¦EndMethod¦#FormData1¦open¦
```

Notice that there is no need for a form variable to hold the string the user types in. You can simply access the text attribute of the edmmtext edit field to get that.

The next method is for the Cancel button. Since there are so few objects on this form, I chose not to name the objects, but it's pretty clear what is going on. The Cancel button's pushbutton() method, for example, returns a null string, as follows:

```
;¦BeginMethod¦#Page2.#Button6¦pushButton¦
method pushButton(var eventInfo Event)
  close("")
endmethod
;¦EndMethod¦#Page2.#Button6¦pushButton¦
```

The pushbutton() method for the OK button is just about as complex as that for the Cancel button. It simply returns the edmmtext object. Paradox is smart enough to know that I didn't really want a box returned to the caller—I wanted its text value. I did not have to refer to the text attribute specifically to get this result:

```
;¦BeginMethod¦#Page2.#Button4¦pushButton¦
method pushButton(var eventInfo Event)
  close(edmmtext)
endmethod
;¦EndMethod¦#Page2.#Button4¦pushButton¦
```

I mentioned that you would shortly understand how a form as such could return a value to its "caller." It's the close() function that you've just seen that does it. An ordinary method would do so by using return *expression*.

That is all there is to EDMMFILE. It's a simple form that enhances the appearance and usability of a PWMMPLAY function. It's one of those nice little touches that make an application look finished.

Now the PWMMPLAY Record button can be completed. All that remains is to do the recording. That happens when the user clicks the Record button, of course. Then the `recordPWMMWave()` form method is called, and the following code executes:

```
;¦BeginMethod¦#FormData1¦recordPWMMWave¦
method recordPWMMWave()
var
  mciCmdStr, ReturnString String
  ReturnCode LongInt
endvar
  ReturnString = fill( " ", 1024 )
  if NOT (sfile = "" ) then
    mciCmdStr = "open new type waveaudio alias mywave buffer 4"
    ReturnCode = mciSendString(mciCmdStr, ReturnString, 1024, 0)
    if NOT (0 = ReturnCode) then
      ReturnString = fill( " ", 1024 )
      mciGetErrorString( ReturnCode, ReturnString, 1024 )
      MMMessageBox.text = ReturnString
      msgStop( "Media File Open", "Open failed\nCheck media messages" )
      return
    endif
    MMMessageBox.text = ReturnString
    opengfx.visible = True
    closedgfx.visible = False
    ReturnString = fill( " ", 1024 )
    mciCmdStr = "record mywave"
    ReturnCode = mciSendString(mciCmdStr, ReturnString, 1024, 0)
    if NOT (0 = ReturnCode) then
      ReturnString = fill( " ", 1024 )
      mciGetErrorString( ReturnCode, ReturnString, 1024 )
      MMMessageBox.text = ReturnString
      msgStop( "Media File Record", "Record failed\nCheck media messages" )
      return
    endif
    recording.visible = True
    sleep( 10500 )
    MMMessageBox.text = ReturnString
    ReturnString = fill( " ", 1024 )
    mciCmdStr = "stop mywave"
    recording.visible = False
    ReturnCode = mciSendString(mciCmdStr, ReturnString, 1024, 0)
    if NOT (0 = ReturnCode) then
      ReturnString = fill( " ", 1024 )
      mciGetErrorString( ReturnCode, ReturnString, 1024 )
      MMMessageBox.text = ReturnString
      msgStop( "Media File Record/Stop",
              "Record/Stop failed\nCheck media messages" )
      return
    endif
    MMMessageBox.text = ReturnString
    ReturnString = fill( " ", 1024 )
    mciCmdStr = "save mywave " + sfile
    ReturnCode = mciSendString(mciCmdStr, ReturnString, 1024, 0)
    if NOT (0 = ReturnCode) then
      ReturnString = fill( " ", 1024 )
```

```
      mciGetErrorString( ReturnCode, ReturnString, 1024 )
      MMMessageBox.text = ReturnString
      msgStop( "Media File Record/Save",
               "Record/Save failed\nCheck media messages" )
      return
    endif
    MMMessageBox.text = ReturnString
    ReturnString = fill( " ", 1024 )
    mciCmdStr = "close mywave"
    ReturnCode = mciSendString(mciCmdStr, ReturnString, 1024, 0)
    if NOT (0 = ReturnCode) then
      ReturnString = fill( " ", 1024 )
      mciGetErrorString( ReturnCode, ReturnString, 1024 )
      MMMessageBox.text = ReturnString
      msgStop( "Media File Record/Close",
               "Record/Close failed\nCheck media messages" )
      return
    endif
    MMMessageBox.text = ReturnString
    opengfx.visible = False
    closedgfx.visible = True
  else
    errorLog( 1, "You must Choose a media file first!" )
    errorShow( "Invalid choice of action", "Media File Open" )
  endif
endmethod
;¦EndMethod¦#FormData1¦recordPWMMWave¦
```

The `recordPWMMWave()` method is one of the longer methods attached to the form because it has to function more or less autonomously from everything else that goes on. The sequence of events that then goes on is as follows:

1. A new wave file is opened. The MCI string command is now `open new type waveaudio alias mywave buffer 4`, rather than `open waveaudio filename ...` as before. The important point here is that a filename is not associated with the Wave recording until *after* all recording is done.

2. The `record` command is sent to MCI (using the alias `mywave`).

3. Paradox is "turned off" for 10.5 seconds using the `sleep(10500)` ObjectPAL statement. This is much more effective than doing something like a counter loop while the method waits for the user to record. It doesn't hog the CPU this way.

4. The `stop` command is sent to MCI.

5. The `save mywave sfile` command, where *sfile* has been replaced with the string value of our old friend `sfile`. Now the Wave file is associated with a proper disk file and written to it.

6. The `close mywave` command is sent to MCI, terminating the recording session.

Although this method is a bit lengthy, it's nothing like what you'll be able to do once you finish this book, and it's trivial compared to the nice effect recording capability adds to the MMT application.

Adding the Still Images Support to MMT

Still shots are a part of multimedia also, although they may lack the glamour of full-motion video. Even so, a nice full-color photograph can be, when taken by a professional, a truly beautiful thing to behold. Still imagery is therefore a must for the PW Multimedia Theater.

If you will recall, you've already seen some of the preparatory work for MMT stills. In the ChooseButton pushbutton() method described on Day 1, you saw that the graphic image file types were detected, and the form MMSTILLS launched for them. In the next section, you will see how to hook in the MMSTILLS form and its methods as the "back end" of the MMT still images support feature.

Creating MMSTILLS Form

The first order of business is, naturally enough, to draw the MMSTILLS form itself. The appearance of the form is shown in Figure 2.2.

There are three design objects on the MMSTILLS form. A graphic object named StillBox, which has vertical and horizontal scrollbars, and two unnamed buttons, which are labeled Select Still and Close. Their uses are obvious, but the way in which MMT can directly invoke MMSTILLS requires some explanation.

First, though, some general-purpose setup is needed. Although the Select Still button doesn't need to be used when the MMT has invoked MMSTILLS and specified an image file to display, MMSTILLS can run as a stand-alone. The user in that case will want to be able to select a graphics file for display, so the GetFile() DLL is needed once again. And again, you have to declare the DLL in the form's Uses block, as follows:

```
;¦BeginMethod¦#FormData1¦Uses¦
Uses GETFILE
  GetFileName( dllCaption CPTR ) CPTR
endUses
;¦EndMethod¦#FormData1¦Uses¦
```

Whether the user has selected a file for display or MMT has specified one, a form-level variable is needed to hold the filename, so a Var block is also required. The variable is stillName, and it appears in the MMSTILLS Var block whose contents are as follows:

```
;¦BeginMethod¦#FormData1¦Var¦
Var
  stillName String
endVar
;¦EndMethod¦#FormData1¦Var¦
```

Figure 2.2. *The MMSTILLS form, while working.*

The form's open() method also needs once again to initialize any global variables and set up the form's display (by maximizing its windows in this case). The open() method does this as follows:

```
;¦BeginMethod¦#FormData1¦open¦
method open(var eventInfo Event)
if NOT eventInfo.isPreFilter() then
  doDefault
  maximize()
  stillName = ""
  StillBox.blank()
endif
endmethod
;¦EndMethod¦#FormData1¦open¦
```

Now you get to the part where MMSTILLS accepts and supports direct calls from PWMMPLAY. This is the setMMStillName() form method, which was declared back in the PWMMPLAY Uses block. setMMStillName() accepts a String as an argument, so that PWMMPLAY can call it and specify what picture to display. Here is the ObjectPAL source for setMMStillName():

```
;¦BeginMethod¦#FormData1¦setMMStillName¦
method setMMStillName( mmstillName String )
var
  mmpix Graphic
endvar
  stillName = mmstillName
  if NOT (stillName = "" ) then
    if mmpix.readFromFile( stillName ) then
      StillBox = mmpix
    endif
  endif
endmethod
;¦EndMethod¦#FormData1¦setMMStillName¦
```

Did you notice how easy this was in ObjectPAL? Just define a local Graphic variable (mmpix). If Paradox is successfully able to open and read the picture file requested by PWMMPLAY through the String argument, you can display it by simply assigning the local Graphic object to the StillBox graphic design object you painted on the form. Voila!

There are still a couple of details to take care of, however. First, you have to be able to terminate the stills viewing, to either stop the application or return to PWMMPLAY, depending on how the MMSTILLS form was opened. That is done by clicking the Close button, which erases the image and goes home, like this:

```
;¦BeginMethod¦#Page2.#Button5¦pushButton¦
method pushButton(var eventInfo Event)
  StillBox.blank()
  close(0)
endmethod
;¦EndMethod¦#Page2.#Button5¦pushButton¦
```

Last, but not least by any stretch, some means of allowing the user to pick images when running stand-alone must be provided. The Select Still button is the means, of course. The only difference between this pushbutton() method and setMMStillName() is that the Select Still button needs to use the GetFile() DLL services to select a filename. That's only one line of difference, as the following method source shows:

```
;¦BeginMethod¦#Page2.#Button3¦pushButton¦
method pushButton(var eventInfo Event)
var
  mmpix Graphic
endvar
  stillName = GetFileName( "Select a Graphic Image" )
  if NOT (stillName = "" ) then
    if mmpix.readFromFile( stillName ) then
      StillBox = mmpix
```

```
       endif
    endif
 endmethod
 ;¦EndMethod¦#Page2.#Button3¦pushButton¦
```

Once more, you get a nice effect without a lot of effort—a theme I hope you'll see throughout the book.

Calling MMT from Another Application: the TESTMMT Form

Will this guy never get through with multimedia theaters and such? If you're new to applications development of any kind, you may well be asking yourself that very question. Trust me, this is a small application, one that is well-suited to prototyping. In an application this size, it's easy to paint a form, erase it, and paint it again, until you like it—precisely because the application is small.

Developer's Tip: I confess: Yes, I've been keeping secrets from you, until now. The secret this time is that prototyping is not well-suited to all applications. It *especially* is not well-suited to really large applications. For large applications, you had better do some prior planning, for the simple reason that large applications have many interdependent parts. You can't keep track of those parts when prototyping.

There is a kicker, though. Although you should *design* a large application, you *can* prototype many, and sometimes all, of its separate parts. For example, later you and I will *design* an accounts receivable and accounts payable application. That application will require some forms for things like data entry of AP invoices. As long as the right data is collected, what does the main app care how the data entry applet does it? We will *prototype* the invoice applet, making it look however we please.

Back to business. I have mentioned several times so far that MMT is intended to be a stand-alone application for your enjoyment *and* a tool with which you can easily add multimedia shows to your other applications.

That is, other applications have to be able to both access and control MMT remotely. If I have put all the pieces in place, it should be no problem. But it's time to test-drive an MMT from another application—TESTMMT—and to put my money where my mouth is. (I wrote the check, now I'll cash it.)

I just happen to have the TESTMMT form ready to go, so I'll show it off now. After diddling around with the form in design mode for a while, I decided that simplicity is the best design approach here. Figure 2.3 shows how TESTMMT came out of that process.

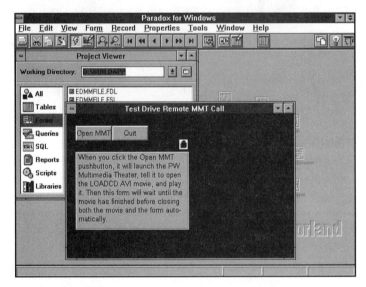

Figure 2.3. *The TESTMMT test-drive form in run mode.*

I won't show you a shot of TESTMMT actually running, because that would just be another shot of PWMMPLAY running. Silly, right? Instead, I'll just show you another shot of TESTMMT (Figure 2.4), this time in design mode so you can see all the objects on the form.

There isn't much difference, right? You should notice our old friends, the lock graphics, just above the explanatory text box. In TESTMMT, the lock graphics are used to indicate the successful opening or closing of the PWMMPLAY *form*, not a media file.

What TESTMMT does is simple. If you click the Open MMT button, TESTMMT opens the PWMMPLAY form and opens, plays, and closes a Video for Windows movie. If you click the Quit button, TESTMMT goes away.

As you should expect by now, TESTMMT has a little ObjectPAL behind it. You need to take care of the following in order to invoke PWMMPLAY:

☐ A Uses block must declare the ObjectPAL methods that will be called in that form.

☐ You need a Var block to declare a form-level Form variable.

☐ You need to do some basic setup at form (TESTMMT) open time.

☐ You need a Quit button to exit the application.

☐ The Open MMT button must contain sufficient logic to control both the PWMMPLAY form and the Video for Windows movie that will be played.

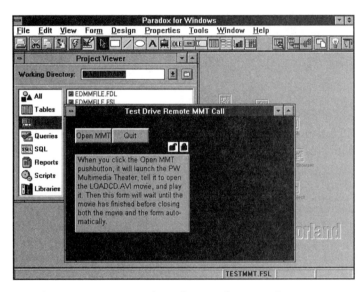

Figure 2.4. *The TESTMMT test-drive form in design mode.*

Note: So far, I've only showed you Paradox forms that have no tables attached to them: blank forms, as Borland calls them. These forms also have had a large amount of ObjectPAL associated with them, because what I've been doing is standard Windows applications, not database applications. The first thing to learn from this is that it's quite possible to use Paradox and ObjectPAL to do Windows programming both quickly and easily.

What may not be so apparent just yet is that it's equally possible to do database programming without too much ObjectPAL code. In fact, some parts of the main business application that you'll spend the next 12 days developing will have *no* ObjectPAL code.

In *Paradox for Windows Developer's Guide* (also from Sams), I found myself frequently saying, "Let the engine do the work." Although that was a more formal and internals-oriented book, there is an awful lot of truth in that statement. Wherever possible, let the engine do the work.

In this book, we will be a lot more relaxed and informal, but we will get some serious development done (we already have, if you stop to think about it). But we will observe the maxim, *Let the engine do the work.* One of the things to look for as you go along is the balance of ObjectPAL use versus simply allowing Paradox to apply default or built-in services.

In the Uses block for TESTMMT, it's not necessary to declare every method on the PWMMPLAY form, just those that will be called from TESTMMT. The ObjectPAL source for the current Uses block is as follows:

```
;¦BeginMethod¦#FormData1¦Uses¦
Uses ObjectPAL
  setMMFileName( fn String )
  openPWMMVideo()
  fwdPWMMVideo()
  closePWMMVideo()
  lengthPWMMVideo() String
  posPWMMVideo() String
endUses
;¦EndMethod¦#FormData1¦Uses¦
```

Notice that only the methods for opening and closing an AVI media file, playing it, and keeping track of the position and length of the media file are necessary, so they are the only ones declared. You may remember that previously when setMMFileName was declared in the PWMMPLAY form, its formal String argument was called newMMFileName. The fact that in the Uses block here it's called simply fn (as in *filename*) illustrates the fact that the formal argument names don't have to match, only the object types do.

The Var block for TESTMMT is short, containing only a Form variable named fv, as follows:

```
;¦BeginMethod¦#FormData1¦Var¦
Var
  fv Form
```

```
endVar
;¦EndMethod¦#FormData1¦Var¦
```

While there is no compelling reason for placing the fv Form variable at the form level as TESTMMT actually exists, I thought it a good idea to place it here anyway. The reason is that in a more complicated application using the PWMMPLAY services, more than one button or other object may be involved in controlling multimedia features. If so, then all the involved objects would need to share the Paradox variables for controlling multimedia processes.

Developer's Tip: Where to place variables, at globally or locally visible locations, is sometimes one of those decisions that depends upon both the experience level and the personal preference of the developer writing the code. There are reasons to go both ways.

On the one hand, placing variables in a globally visible location can greatly simplify development, because you can keep the total number of variables down, and you always know whether you can get to them or not.

On the other hand, global variables are sometimes prone to accidental modification by the wrong routines. Local variables are protected from other routines, and further, they go away when the current routine terminates. This can help keep the total amount of memory required for the application down to a manageable level.

All things considered, most developers, including myself, like to use local variables as long as possible, making them global only when wide viability is absolutely necessary.

TESTMMT's form open() method is also built simply . It just tells Paradox to perform default processing for the form, and sets its own size and position with the setPosition() procedure, as follows:

```
;¦BeginMethod¦#FormData1¦open¦
method open(var eventInfo Event)
   if NOT eventInfo.isPreFilter() then
     doDefault
     setPosition(1440,1440,6500,4320)
   endif
endmethod
;¦EndMethod¦#FormData1¦open¦
```

The Close button's `pushbutton()` method is even more simple. It just says, "Go home" by calling `close(0)`, like this:

```
;¦BeginMethod¦#Page2.#Button8¦pushButton¦
method pushButton(var eventInfo Event)
  close(0)
endmethod
;¦EndMethod¦#Page2.#Button8¦pushButton¦
```

Now you get to the good part. The Open MMT button's `pushbutton()` method has all the goodies for opening PWMMPLAY and the media file, and playing the media file while keeping track of matters. The secret ingredient is the `sleep()` System class procedure. Here is the method's source code:

```
;¦BeginMethod¦#Page2.#Button3¦pushButton¦
method pushButton(var eventInfo Event)
var
  vlength, vposition LongInt
endvar
  if fv.open("PWMMPLAY.FDL" ) then
    opengfx.visible = True
    closedgfx.visible = False
    fv.setMMFileName( workingDir() + "\\LOADCD.AVI" )
    fv.openPWMMVideo()
    vlength = LongInt(fv.lengthPWMMVideo())
    vposition = LongInt(fv.posPWMMVideo())
    fv.fwdPWMMVideo()
    while vposition < vlength
      sleep()                    ; yield control of the processor
      vposition = LongInt(fv.posPWMMVideo())
    endwhile
    fv.closePWMMVideo()
    fv.close()
    opengfx.visible = False
    closedgfx.visible = True
  endif
endmethod
;¦EndMethod¦#Page2.#Button3¦pushButton¦
```

Once again, the method only goes on when the PWMMPLAY form open is successful. If it is, the lock graphics are handled as before, and the media file is opened. As soon as the media file is open, the variable `vlength` is used to record the total length of the media file, and `vposition` is initialized with a first call to PWMMPLAY's `posPWMMVideo()` method.

TESTMMT "watches" the video with the `while vposition < vlength` loop. As long as the position has not caught up with the length, TESTMMT lets the movie play. The call to `sleep()` with no time argument enables Paradox to yield control of the processor often enough that the movie *can* play, and then the current position is updated again.

All that remains when you come out of the back end of the loop (indicating that the movie has finished playing) is to close the media file and to close PWMMPLAY itself.

That's too easy, you say? Well, yes, it really is. ObjectPAL programming is really not all that hard once you get the hang of it. Just figure out what you want to do and then poke around the Paradox documentation until you find a method or procedure that does what you want.

Modification Notes

You can use TESTMMT as a base from which to develop other applications. That is one of the things I had in mind while building it: to give you working boilerplate code from which you could easily begin another application without reinventing the wheel. The following list details how you might go about this process:

1. Use the Windows File Manager or equivalent tool to copy the TESTMMT.FSL form to another file. It should still be an FSL file, but you could easily copy it to another directory to separate your projects.

2. Set the Paradox working directory to the new directory, if necessary, and open the form under the new name in design mode.

3. Change the form properties, especially including the form window title to reflect the new project.

4. Edit and modify the Uses block to include the PWMMPLAY form methods that you'll be using. You might want the Wave sound functions, for example, rather than the Video for Windows functions. Or you might want them all.

5. Delete all objects from the form except the Open MMT button. Add your own design objects and do with them whatever you want. You may also want to alter the button text from "Open MMT" to something else.

6. Edit the pushbutton() method for the Open MMT button. Look for two things here. First, modify the precise MMT method calls to those you want, suitable for the media file to be played. Second, if PWMMPLAY will not reside in the same directory as the new application, make sure you include the necessary drive and path information in the call to fv.open(...).

Other methods of implementation might involve, for example, placing a Graphic object on the form, and attaching the PWMMPLAY calls to the mouseClick() method for the object. Things would otherwise work the same way, but now you would have a hotspot, similar to Windows help file hotspots.

Debugging the Process

A large part of debugging the process of building multimedia, or any other kind of Paradox application, revolves around choosing the proper method or procedure ObjectPAL calls, and getting them to function like you thought they would (or doing something else, if that doesn't work).

Nothing but experience with ObjectPAL will make that process easier, but there is something I can do for you to make the search for the right method or procedure a little quicker. I boilerplated another application from *Paradox for Windows Developer's Guide* and modified it for use here. That application is now the ObjectPAL Reference Data Summary, in the REFDATA.FSL form (or the REFDATA.FDL delivered version, which runs a little quicker).

There will be no blow-by-blow description of how this application works. I'll just show it to you and let you poke around inside it to your own satisfaction. The REFDATA form is shown in Figure 2.5.

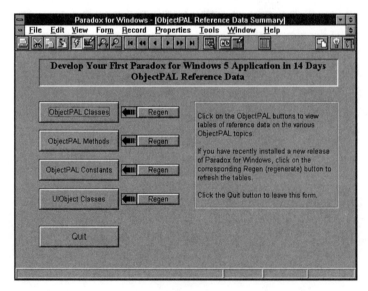

Figure 2.5. *The ObjectPAL Reference Data Summary form.*

The text box on the form makes it perfectly clear how to use the application. I'll take a few moments, however, to show you what kind of information this application places at your fingertips.

First, you can display a table of all ObjectPAL classes. It's a good idea to familiarize yourself with the class names, just so you'll have some idea where to search for more detailed information. The REFDATA class table is shown in Figure 2.6. There is only one column of information in this table, and that is just a list of the ObjectPAL class names. They do give you a high-level perspective, however, on the way Paradox packages methods and procedures (as well as how it groups objects).

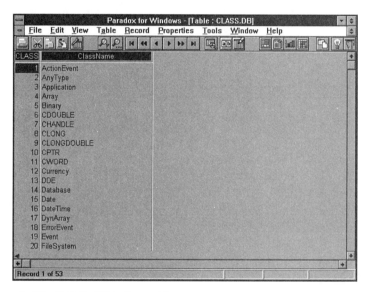

Figure 2.6. *The REFDATA class table.*

One of the most useful of the REFDATA tables is the Method table. It lists all ObjectPAL methods and procedures, grouped by class. (See? You need that high-level view already.) The Method table is shown in Figure 2.7.

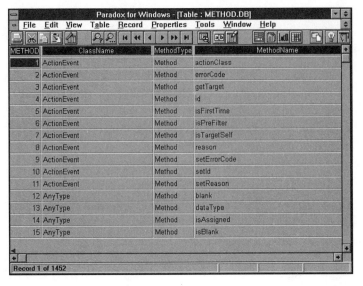

Figure 2.7. *The REFDATA method table.*

What Figure 2.7 does not show is that there are two more columns in the table. The first of these lists the appropriate arguments for the method or procedure, and the second gives the return type. Altogether, you have everything you need in this table to select a method to use, except a detailed narrative about it. But I guess we will leave Borland *something* to put in the manuals.

The REFDATA Constants table, shown in Figure 2.8, lists all the possible ObjectPAL constant names. Part of the ActionDataCommands group of constants, for example, is visible in Figure 2.8. You'll see much more of these constants later in this book when I walk you through the batch processes needed for the main business application.

Finally, Figure 2.9 shows the REFDATA UICLASS table. This table lists all the UIObject properties, arranged by UI class name. The UI classes are a further breakdown of the Paradox Class listed in the Class table. I like this table because it helps me stay straight on what UI objects can and cannot do; UI objects, for some reason, give me more trouble conceptually than any other part of Paradox for Windows. Maybe this will help you, too.

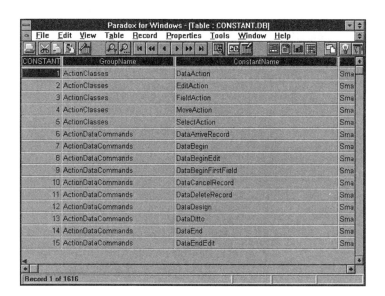

Figure 2.8. *The REFDATA constants table.*

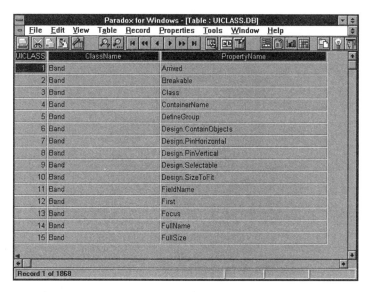

Figure 2.9. *The REFDATA UICLASS table.*

That's all for this chapter, and all for the PW Multimedia Theater and its companions as well. You'll see MMT again, but not this way, because now it's time to start in on the main application. There are only 12 days left now, and believe me, I feel your pressure. I didn't have much more time than that to write this whole book! So, whatever else you carry away from this book, I'll show you how to put this thing together *fast!*

Defining the
Application

The PW Multimedia Theater is now in place, with the tools you need to provide multimedia support for your serious applications. Today, you'll define the application to be built in the remaining 12 days of this project.

While prototyping is quite useful, and a lot of fun, serious applications require serious planning, at least if you're working on a tight schedule and require an end product that works and is stable.

In selecting an application for this book, I thought about a lot of different things that could be done. I knew I wanted a business-related application, an application that could actually be used by a real business (at least after some customizing). The application I selected is an accounts receivable and accounts payable system that can handle most of the bookkeeping needs of a small (or not so small) business.

I briefly considered wrapping the whole thing into a fully integrated general ledger system. I decided not to do that, for at least two major reasons. The first reason is time. Quite honestly, there is no way an individual programmer could build a fully integrated general ledger system in just 14 days. You could build a toy system and call it "General Ledger," yes, but you couldn't build the real thing, not even with a tool like Paradox for Windows.

The second reason is size. A real general ledger system would be quite large, and far too unwieldy to treat well in a book this size. On the other hand, I definitely wanted an application that would reflect the real world of business and could actually be used in that world—hence the AR/AP system. There is enough meat in AR/AP to provide for a very interesting and active development project, and it's perfect for a project like this one.

Introducing the Accounts Receivable and Payable System

I'll call the project you're about to undertake the DPW Accounts Receivable and Payable system because DPW is the acronym I used to name this book while communicating with the publisher (the good folks at Sams, you know). I'll also frequently refer to the application as AR/AP, and to its parts as AR or AP, as the case may be.

On each day, you'll see part of how to plan, design, and execute your plans for the AR/AP system. Each day, of course, I'll discuss both AR and AP, in parallel, to get it all in the next 12 days.

But before I begin any of that, the first order of business is to identify just exactly what it is that will be built. A first pass at the design is in order, that is. The AR/AP system will have the following characteristics:

☐ The AR system consists of the customer and receivables databases, together with all their necessary forms, utilities, documentation, reports, and batch programs.

☐ The AP system consists of the vendor and payables databases, together with all their necessary forms, utilities, documentation, reports, and batch programs.

Since we're dealing with Paradox for Windows, it may sound silly to speak of "batch programs," but the processes involved do require some off-line work. In this environment, however, it makes perfect sense to package a batch program as a form containing the necessary ObjectPAL programming. Backup and recovery utilities, query, crosstab, chart, and graph utilities will be packaged the same way—in a form presenting a nice professional appearance to the user.

When you finish the fourteenth day, you'll indeed have a complete application that you can actually use. But don't forget that this is still just a pilot project; there will be plenty of things you can do to customize the application for your own use. There will also be plenty of things you can do to further flesh it out. That's part of the fun, though.

Planning the Application Development Project

Just a moment ago, I mentioned that a serious project needs serious planning. Since that is the case, I've provided you with another toy—the DPW AR/AP Project Development Manager. From now on, I'll just refer to it as "the project manager."

The project manager is a form with two tables attached to it. The project master file is the main table, and it's arranged with one record-per-day of a development project. The project item file is a linked secondary file. This table has a compound primary key, the first part of which must be a primary key in the project master file. That is, I've defined referential integrity between the two tables. The two tables are also linked in this way in the project manager form (PROJMGR.FSL/FDL). The second part of the key in the project item file is an item number, which must be unique within its group-by-day number.

Thus, for each day of the project, you can enter and list any number of discrete tasks (items) defining the work for that day. Once an item is finished, you can open the project manager and mark the item complete by entering Yes in the Completed field of the item file. Once all the items in a day's work are complete, you can mark the whole day complete in the same way.

The project manager gives you an at-a-glance view of where you are in a project and what you need to do next. Further, with just a little boilerplating of forms and ObjectPAL code, you can adapt this project manager to other projects.

Figure 3.1 shows the project manager (PROJMGR) form opened on the desktop. As you can see in this figure, the master file fields are clustered at the top of the form and the linked items records are displayed in a table frame below that.

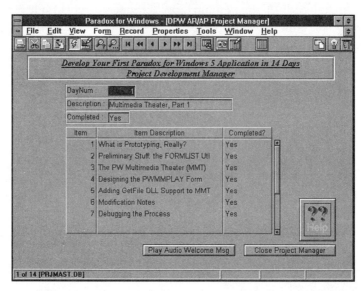

Figure 3.1. *The DPW AR/AP Project Development Manager form (PROJMGR).*

The other features of the form shown in Figure 3.1 are the Help button, the Play Audio Welcome Message button, and the Close Project Manager button. The function of the Close button is obvious: it terminates the project manager and closes the form.

The function of the Play Audio Welcome Message is also obvious and is a particular delight because it plays a Wave file recorded in my very own voice, using the Sound Blaster Wave Studio Windows app. I did my best to sound Midwestern, folks, but, shucks y'all, I'm a Southern boy and the twang *will* come through. Sorry about that.

The function of the Help button is obvious also, but produces a display that you need to see. That display is a one-page help document, which is actually just page 2 of the PROJMGR form. It's shown in Figure 3.2.

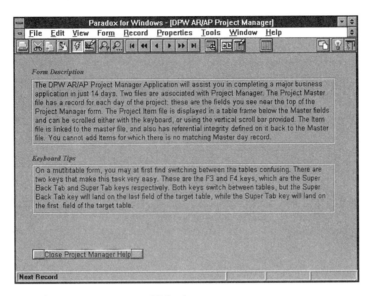

Figure 3.2. *The Project Manager Help document.*

Only a very short help document is needed for this little applet, since it mostly uses only standard Paradox for Windows features. There is a nice feature of Paradox for Windows that you may not have considered yet, however. You can move the focus to any field on the form (by clicking the field or tabbing to it) and press F6 to pop up the filter dialog.

You type in the filter criteria using syntax like you would use in the Zoom dialog (with @ and .. wildcard characters, for example). Then Paradox will only display those records in which the filtered field has contents matching your specs. For example, you could filter the Completed field of the item table so that only records having a value of Yes will display. Then you could see just how much of the project you've finished (though I noticed right away that this tends to highlight just how much you have *not* finished).

Since I suggest that you use the project manager throughout the book, I want to take a few minutes of your time now to show you how I put it together, because much of the main application is patterned after this basic structure.

Developer's Tip: The sequence of events used in constructing the project manager application is typical of a project in which you use linked tables, or other relational database features. The sequence reflects which things are dependent on what other things. In this particular case, the sequence is top-down since you need to define the *independent* (or master) table first. Then you define the *dependent* (or to-be-linked) table. Only after that do you define referential integrity on the linked table, and still later link it to the master table at form definition time.

While the design sequence is top-down from the point of view of table construction, it's definitely bottom-up from the point of view of *form* construction. A form's tables must already exist before a form can be built with the tables attached to it.

For you database analysts out there, you can think of a Paradox form as a logical view on the underlying tables. Indeed, the similarities are more than superficial since a form can completely control how users see the data and what they can do with what they see.

The project master (PRJMAST) table is both the central and simplest part of the DPW Project Development Manager. Its structure is shown in Figure 3.3.

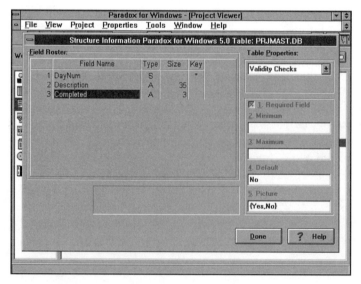

Figure 3.3. *The PRJMAST table of the project manager.*

There are just three fields in the project master table: DayNum, Description, and Completed. DayNum contains the day number of the project and corresponds exactly to the chapter number that describes that day. Description is a text description of the day's work to be done and follows the table of contents of the book pretty well, though not exactly. Completed is also a text field, but it serves the purpose of a Logical value, since its contents can be either Yes or No. I just thought this sounded better than True and False.

PRJMAST has a simple primary key composed of the DayNum field. Since it's a key field, it's automatically a required field. I could have gone further and placed minimum and maximum value validity checks against this field (limiting it, for example, to 1–14), but I thought I wouldn't do that. Without range limitations, it'll be that much easier for you to clone this application for use with other projects.

The remaining two fields in the table are explicitly required fields. Further, the Completed field additionally has a default value of No and a picture validity check of {Yes,No}. This picture field means that the data field can have one of the two listed values and nothing else. There is a side benefit to having this picture validity check: If you begin by typing either the letter Y or N, Paradox then knows what is coming and fills in the rest of the value for you.

The project item table (PRJITEM) is similar to the project master but has a little more detail. The project item table's structure is shown in Figure 3.4.

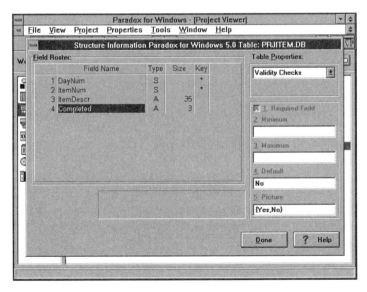

Figure 3.4. *The PRJITEM table of the project manager.*

Where the project master table had a simple key composed of DayNum, the project item table has a compound key composed of DayNum and ItemNum. The fact that the high-order part of the item table's key has the same name as the master table's primary key is significant, and will show up in just a minute.

The project item table goes beyond the project master in having item number and description fields. This allows you to associate an unlimited number of items or activities with a given day of the project. As you can see in Figure 3.4, each item can be individually checked as completed or not.

Figure 3.5 shows the item table's structure again, but makes plain that I've defined referential integrity on the item table.

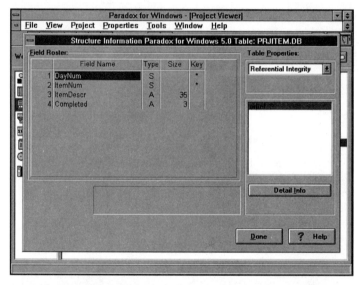

Figure 3.5. *The PRJITEM table with the referential integrity table property.*

By using referential integrity, I can guarantee that the item table never has a DayNum value that fails to match a DayNum value in the master table. This is the significance of making the high-order part of the item table's key match the primary key in the master table. Although there doesn't have to be a precise match-up of field names like this, it makes it easier to visualize and remember the nature of the referential integrity definition placed on the item table.

Figure 3.6 shows the specific nature of the referential integrity definition. Always keep in mind that referential integrity is defined on the subordinate, dependent table. Also keep in mind that table lookup is a data entry help tool, not an integrity tool, and cannot be used to guarantee linkages in the way we want here. Plenty will be said about table lookup later, but for now what we want is integrity, not data entry.

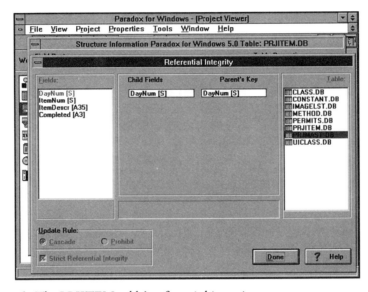

Figure 3.6. *The PRJITEM table's referential integrity structure.*

Notice in Figure 3.6 that the referential integrity structure display shows the child table fields on the left and the selected parent table and its key on the right, much as when you actually define the referential integrity relationship between the two tables.

There are two other features of the referential integrity relationship shown in Figure 3.6. First, I've accepted the default Strict Referential Integrity value: it is on. (See the checkbox at the bottom-left corner of the screen image.) Strict referential integrity means that not only *must* every item record's DayNum match a DayNum in the project master, but you cannot alter the master table in any way that would disturb the referential integrity relationship. Most specifically, strict referential integrity will prevent even previous versions of Paradox for Windows from altering the tables in any way that would disturb the relationship.

Second, I've chosen the cascade-update rule. Now, this is powerful stuff, but it's kind of like waving a gun around with the hammer back—it won't take much to pull the trigger. With cascaded updates, I can do two powerful things. If I modify a parent key field, that modification cascades to all the child records, updating every one of them. And, if I delete a parent record, the delete is cascaded, too; all the child records will be deleted with the parent record.

Showstopper! Cascaded update is a powerful tool, without a doubt. I've always been very partial to cascaded updates and deletes, but there is a less-than-good reason for that: I'm lazy. I don't want to have to manually delete all dependent records before deleting a parent record. Remember the phrase, "Let the engine do the work"?

I am sure you see that you can get yourself in a world of trouble in a heartbeat, especially if records are being deleted. A lot of data can be lost or altered beyond easy repair.

When you're choosing features like this, you may well want to choose Prohibit updates (also shown in Figure 3.6), unless you're absolutely certain that your product will be used by expert users. And even then, think about it some more.

One last thing about referential integrity. Referential integrity can be defined across two tables even if they will not be used as linked tables in a multitable form. You can open the child table directly in a table view, and the referential integrity definition will protect the table. If you'll look back for a moment to Figure 3.5 and look at the large list box in the table properties section of the dialog display, you'll see that I've named the referential integrity relationship prjref. This definition is stored with the table, in its .VAL (validity checks) file, not with a form or other instrument.

Now we can move on to the PROJMGR form design. Figure 3.1 clearly showed that this is a multitable form, with the master file defined first and the project item file linked to it. The details of the form's table linkage are shown in Figure 3.7.

When you're working with a form in design mode, you can get to the form's data model in two different ways. One of them is by choosing **F**orm|**D**ata Model from the desktop menu. This is the method illustrated in Figure 3.7. This view of the data model is a little more expansive than the other one (coming up in a moment), and I frankly like the fact that it's a little more like the previous version's view of the data model.

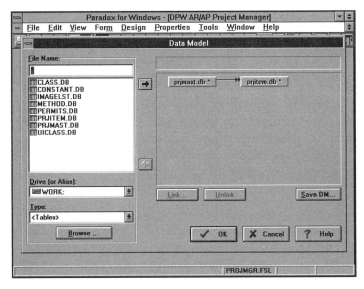

Figure 3.7. *The PROJMGR form's table linkage.*

With Paradox for Windows, defining a form's data model is relatively easy. Click the master file in the list box at the left of the display and then click the right-pointing arrow near the top of the screen to move the name into the data model display. Do the same thing with the project item file.

Now click and hold the left mouse button on the project master file in the data model window and drag the project master file onto the project item file. A line will follow the dragging mouse pointer, clearly and visually indicating that Paradox is linking the two files. The file you drag *from* is the master file, and the file you drag *to* is the linked detail file. Paradox is smart enough to know how to link these files, too. I didn't have to do a thing to tell Paradox which fields I wanted to link.

Figure 3.8 shows the other way to do the same thing, using the Data Model Designer. This, I suppose, is the chic way of doing data models. Call me old-fashioned, slow, or whatever, I just like the conventional way of going about data modeling. You can open the Data Model Designer from the form design toolbar by clicking the Data Model tool. It's the one with two documents on it, connected by an arrow.

Now, why have I walked you through the design of this simple form and its tables? I cheated, that's why. I just gave you a brief overview of the way *you* will design a really nice Accounts Receivable and Accounts Payable package. Remember this design overview.

The whole thing is not much more complicated than this with a tool like Paradox for Windows. You mostly "paint" applications. The rest is bells and whistles—Paradox itself does the really hard work for you.

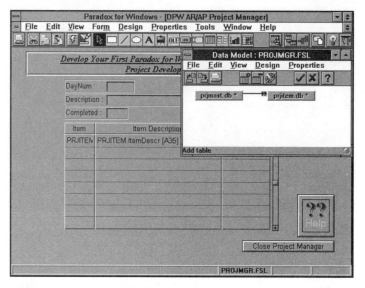

Figure 3.8. *Linking the tables with the Data Model Designer.*

Finally, Figure 3.9 shows the project manager active with Day 3 displayed and ready for you to edit. You might have noticed that all the Completed fields are marked Yes. In fact, I marked the first three days complete because you've been mostly letting me drive so far. All of that is about to change, however. You're in charge from here on out, and I'll just coach you along.

Before moving on, I am going to throw one more multimedia goody in the pot. You may recall that early in this chapter, I threatened you (oops, *informed* you) that you could hear my lovely voice by clicking the Play Audio Welcome Message button on the project manager form.

I have a confession to make right here. I didn't use the MMT to implement the playback of this Wave file. The ObjectPAL logic for playing multimedia clips is entirely contained in the PROJMGR form. I wanted an excuse to show you just one more way to access multimedia features from ObjectPAL.

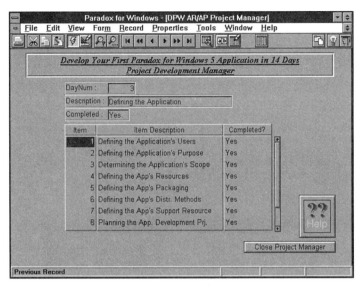

Figure 3.9. *The DPW Project Development Manager running with Day 3 displayed.*

Note: There is always more than one way to tackle a problem, and that's true here as everywhere. Later today, I will show you a couple more ways you can invoke multimedia clips using OLE objects on forms and in table frames on forms.

You'll see this in the "Modification Notes" section. At that time I'll discuss the limitations of "ObjectPAL-free" methods of playing media clips and how you might use them.

Just to get it over with quickly, here in one big lump is all the ObjectPAL source for the PROJMGR form:

```
;¦BeginMethod¦#FormData1¦Uses¦
Uses MMSYSTEM
  mciSendString( lpstrCommand CPTR, lpstrReturn CPTR,
                 wReturnLng CWORD, hCallBack CWORD ) CLONG
  mciGetErrorString( dwError CLONG, lpstrReturn CPTR,
                     wLength CWORD ) CWORD
endUses
;¦EndMethod¦#FormData1¦Uses¦
```

```
;¦BeginMethod¦#FormData1¦open¦
method open(var eventInfo Event)
  if NOT eventInfo.isPreFilter() then
  doDefault
  maximize()
  endif
endmethod
;¦EndMethod¦#FormData1¦open¦

;¦BeginMethod¦#FormData1¦playAnyMMClip¦
method playAnyMMClip( mmFName String, isLocalFile Logical )
var
  mciCmdStr, ReturnString String
  ReturnCode, mmlength, mmpos LongInt
endvar
    ReturnString = fill( " ", 1024 )
    if isLocalFile then
      mciCmdStr = "open " + workingDir() + "\\" + mmFName
                  + " alias mmclip"
    else
      mciCmdStr = "open " + mmFName + " alias mmclip"
    endif
    ReturnCode = mciSendString(mciCmdStr, ReturnString, 1024, 0)
    if NOT (0 = ReturnCode) then
      ReturnString = fill( " ", 1024 )
      mciGetErrorString( ReturnCode, ReturnString, 1024 )
      msgStop( "Media File Open", ReturnString )
      return
    endif
    ReturnString = fill( " ", 1024 )
    mciCmdStr = "play mmclip"
    ReturnCode = mciSendString(mciCmdStr, ReturnString, 1024, 0)
    if NOT (0 = ReturnCode) then
      ReturnString = fill( " ", 1024 )
      mciGetErrorString( ReturnCode, ReturnString, 1024 )
      msgStop( "Media File Play", ReturnString )
      return
    endif
    ReturnString = fill( " ", 1024 )
    mciCmdStr = "status mmclip length"
    ReturnCode = mciSendString(mciCmdStr, ReturnString, 1024, 0)
    mmlength = LongInt( ReturnString )
    ReturnString = fill( " ", 1024 )
    mciCmdStr = "status mmclip position"
    ReturnCode = mciSendString(mciCmdStr, ReturnString, 1024, 0)
    mmpos = LongInt( ReturnString )
    while mmpos < mmlength
      sleep()
      ReturnString = fill( " ", 1024 )
      mciCmdStr = "status mmclip position"
      ReturnCode = mciSendString(mciCmdStr, ReturnString, 1024, 0)
      mmpos = LongInt( ReturnString )
    endwhile
    ReturnString = fill( " ", 1024 )
    mciCmdStr = "close mmclip"
    ReturnCode = mciSendString(mciCmdStr, ReturnString, 1024, 0)
```

```
      if NOT (0 = ReturnCode) then
        ReturnString = fill( " ", 1024 )
        mciGetErrorString( ReturnCode, ReturnString, 1024 )
        msgStop( "Media File Close", ReturnString )
        return
      endif
endmethod
;¦EndMethod¦#FormData1¦playAnyMMClip¦

;¦BeginMethod¦Page2.EndHelp¦pushButton¦
method pushButton(var eventInfo Event)
  moveToPage(1)
endmethod
;¦EndMethod¦Page2.EndHelp¦pushButton¦

;¦BeginMethod¦Page1.#Button16¦pushButton¦
method pushButton(var eventInfo Event)
  playAnyMMClip( "pdmhello.wav", True )  ; clip is in local directory
endmethod
;¦EndMethod¦Page1.#Button16¦pushButton¦

;¦BeginMethod¦Page1.#Button34¦pushButton¦
method pushButton(var eventInfo Event)
 moveToPage( 2 )
 moveTo( "EndHelp" )
endmethod
;¦EndMethod¦Page1.#Button34¦pushButton¦

;¦BeginMethod¦Page1.#Button22¦pushButton¦
method pushButton(var eventInfo Event)
 close(0)
endmethod
;¦EndMethod¦Page1.#Button22¦pushButton¦
```

By now you surely recognize the Uses block for the form. It declares the multimedia mciSendString() and mciGetErrorString() functions of the Media Control Interface in MMSYSTEM.DLL. I'll also bypass describing the way the pushbuttons implement moving back and forth between the main page of the form and the help page (page 2). This is something that you can easily investigate for yourself.

There are two methods on the PROJMGR form that I really want to call your attention to. And only one of them has any real meat. These methods are as follows:

☐ The pushbutton() method for the Play Audio Welcome Message. The only thing in this method is a call to a custom method I placed on the form: playAnyMMClip("pdmhello.wav", True). That is the method that does the work—all of it, self-contained.

☐ The playAnyMMClip() form method. Notice that the first argument this method will accept is just the filename of the media clip. The second argument is a Logical type that helps us get a little fancier. This is the isLocalFile

Boolean argument. If this argument is `True`, the media file is local; that is, it has no drive or path information attached to it. You'll often want to call this method with the filename coded this way, presuming that it's in the same (working) directory.

The problem is that MCI seems to require the full drive and path information of a media file before you can open it. So when `isLocalFile` is `True`, `playAnyMMClip()` will prefix this information in the MCI `open` command string. Otherwise, it will be assumed that all drive and path information is already there (as it is when you use `GetFile()` to select the media filename).

`playAnyMMClip()` then executes some generic code to run the clip, time it to see when it's finished, and then return to the caller. You don't get to position a video window this way, but you can play any kind of media clip with this routine if your Windows setup includes drivers for the media type. This method is not limited to AVI, WAV, and MID type files.

Defining the Application's Users

Ultimately, it is the intended audience for an application that determines what the application will look like and exactly what it will do. This audience is composed of your *users,* to use the more simple and common term.

Who are the users for the PDW AR/AP system? Well, you are! That presents me with a huge problem, since it's very likely that "you" are a collection of diverse individuals. In order to get this thing off the ground, I am going to have to make a few assumptions about who you are. I certainly don't mean to pigeonhole anyone, but I am going to assume for the purposes of development that you either run a small business or are with the accounting department of a small- to medium-sized corporation.

This way we can design the application without making it too large for individual users or too small for adaptation and use by larger corporations. How would the application differ for large and small businesses? It would mainly differ in the number and kind of bells and whistles needed. Smaller businesses, for example, will need only one kind of mailing label for each of the AR and AP subsystems, whereas large corporations might want many different kinds of labels for each.

Another difference between large and small businesses can be found in the type and complexity of the batch processes required. It always turns out to be the case that larger databases need more batch support processes over interactive processes, simply because batch processes can process large amounts of data more quickly.

I have to admit, too, that the choice of application size based on presumptions about users is governed by the book itself. In this book, I can only develop and present functions that are only representative of whole classes of functions.

Another user consideration you'll need to observe later, in other development projects, is the technical background of the user base. For an application like AR/AP, for example, the user base is very likely to be more technically oriented. Most likely the users will either be accounting or computing professionals. I assume, in fact, that my readers are a mixture of just these two classes, because those are the people with the inclination, the background, and the courage to jump into a project like this one. I'm sure it's true that there are many individual readers out there who intend to use the skills they develop with this book for their own use, but those of you in this category will still fit, I feel, into the profile I've just outlined.

The kind of tools that will be developed in the course of this project, therefore, will be a little more technically oriented than would be those same tools developed for a casual user. An example of this kind of differentiation will appear when you put together the table utilities that will be used in backup, restoration, and general maintenance of the tables in the package. For the casual user, these tools would present little more to the user than simple pushbuttons that say "Do backup," for example. For you, the same table maintenance tools will offer options to copy, delete, add, and subtract tables—potentially dangerous tools in the hands of the technically disinclined.

This, then, is the profile of the intended user of the DPW AR/AP system: a user who is at least a little technically inclined in the fields of accounting or computer software development, who works in a small- to medium-sized business, and who will be responsible for developing, running, and maintaining the software.

Developer's Tip: The distinction between a technically inclined audience and a technically unsophisticated audience is one that is crucial for your future development projects. You must remember that the technically unsophisticated people who may be your later users can at the same time be quite intelligent and educated people, *and* be totally intimidated by computers. For them you must develop software that is intuitively easy to operate, does not reveal internal sophistication (no matter how tempted you are to show off), and that just doesn't fail, even when badly abused operationally. This isn't just idle flattery from me to you: if you don't realize that you're better at computers than your users, you'll set yourself up for an automatic

failure of your product—something neither of us wants. This challenge is more difficult to meet successfully than even experienced developers some-times realize.

Defining the Application's Purpose

It isn't enough just to say that the purpose of the AR/AP system is to provide accounts receivable and accounts payable services. That doesn't provide a conceptual springboard from which to launch the rest of the application design. On the other hand, it isn't yet necessary to get down to the level of record structures, either. We can aptly and usefully define the scope of the AR/AP systems as follows:

☐ The AR/AP system consists of the AR and AP subsystems. These subsystems will be nearly independent of each other for accounting purposes, but will both be launched from the same AR/AP master panel (a form that will provide for the launching of all other related forms in an organized and visually appealing way).

☐ The AR subsystem will be backed by three main tables: the customer master table, the AR master table, and the AR history table.

☐ The AR customer master table will be indexed by a simple primary key consist-ing just of the customer number. The AR master and history tables will each be indexed by a compound primary key consisting of the customer number and the date and time stamps of the AR transaction. Both the AR master and history tables will have referential integrity defined on their customer number fields, so that no AR transaction can be unrelated to a customer master record. The referential integrity definition will specify the prohibit update rule to prevent the accidental deletion of AR transactions or customer master records, and will specify strict referential integrity so that no application may modify customer or transaction records and disrupt the relational integrity.

☐ The AR subsystem will provide a single-table form solely for maintaining customer accounts. The referential integrity relationship just mentioned will prevent the accidental deletion of customer records for which there are still AR transaction records in the AR master table.

- [ ] The AR subsystem will provide a multitable form for the posting and maintenance of AR transaction records. It will also provide batch processes for the posting of mass charges based on date criteria and the transfer of completed AR transactions to the AR history tables.

- [ ] The AR subsystem will provide batch processes for backup, restoration, billing statements, mailing labels, ad hoc inquiry, and analysis of a customer's AR transactions.

- [ ] The AP subsystem will be backed by three main tables. These tables are the vendor master table, the AP master table, and the AP history table.

- [ ] The AP vendor master table will be indexed by a simple primary key consisting of just the vendor number. The AP master and history tables will each be indexed by a compound primary key consisting of the vendor number, and the date and time stamps of the AP transaction. Both the AP master and history tables will have referential integrity defined on their customer number fields, so that no AP transaction can be unrelated to a vendor master record. The referential integrity definition will specify the prohibit update rule to prevent the accidental deletion of AP transactions or customer master records, and will specify strict referential integrity so that no application may modify vendor or transaction records so as to disrupt the relational integrity.

- [ ] The AP subsystem will provide a single-table form solely for maintaining vendor accounts. The referential integrity relation just mentioned will prevent the accidental deletion of vendor records for which there are still AP transaction (invoice) records in the AP master table.

- [ ] The AP subsystem will provide a multitable form for the posting and maintenance of AP transaction records (invoices). There will also be provided batch processes for the full or partial payment of invoices based on date criteria, and the transfer of completed AP transactions to the AR history tables.

- [ ] The AP subsystem will provide batch processes for backup, restoration, invoice records, payment checks and check registers, mailing labels, ad hoc inquiry, and analysis of a vendor's AP transactions.

If all this sounds like quite a bite to chew in just 12 days, believe me, it is. It would not be possible, for me at least, if I had not already built just such a system in another context (a DOS-based system, written in C). That is, I'll be boilerplating this system, just as I've already preached that you should do whenever possible.

Determining the Application's Scope

The *scope* of an application refers simply to the degree to which you will develop the concept controlling the application. In terms of an AR/AP system, this means nothing more than determining just how many bells and whistles will be added to the system.

In one sense, the scope of the project is the degree to which you will generalize the tools made available to the user. For example, you can provide customized query forms on which the user can create just about any kind of query you might think of. Or you might make it possible to chart just about any possible trend in the numbers.

This DPW AR/AP will not have such a broad scope, just because the time you have to develop it is severely restricted. The application will thus remain a *first* application, as the book's title indicates, rather than a *commercial* application that would appeal to a broad spectrum of possible users.

This by no means implies that you cannot continue to work with the system after you finish reading this book, and to add all the bells and whistles you want. In fact, if you continue to develop the system afterward, and make it a screaming success in the marketplace, more power to you. Just tell 'em I taught you how!

Assuming that a limited scope for this version of AR/AP also does not mean that the design is going to limit the number of records that the tables can handle, for example. A Paradox for Windows table, and the Windows environment in which it all runs, is intrinsically capable of handling the large data requirements of a fair-sized corporation (assuming the server is big enough). The limitations involved will all be conceptual ones, so that you can pack your first development project in just a few days.

Defining the Application's Resources

The application's *resources* are those tools and resources that you can bring to bear on the project to create a finished product. If you were writing the application in a more traditional language, such as C, the resources available to you would mostly be just the compiler itself, your own imagination, and the time available for development. This would still be mainly true even using a language like C++, with the application frameworks (toolkits) typically available with those compiler products.

Fortunately for us 14-day types, we have all the resources of the Paradox for Windows development environment available to us. We can largely "paint" an application in an attractive GUI environment and attach support code in pieces when and where we want it, because of the object-oriented nature of this environment.

Because of the highly interactive nature of the development environment, the requirements for time as a development resource are minimized. Because of the highly visual nature of the development environment, using the imagination as a development resource is greatly enhanced. This is where the tinker-and-fix prototyping method comes into play—draw your forms the way you want them to look. Get creative, get original, and get moving!

In short, the application's resources are found in Paradox for Windows itself, together with all the built-in tools and functionality it automatically provides. With other development environments, a consideration of the resources available consumes much of the project and severely constrains what you can and cannot do. Here, resources are not that much of a consideration because you can just do whatever you want to do. That is unusual, but it's great.

Defining the Application's Packaging

Packaging for the application is also well-defined for you by the Paradox for Windows environment used to develop it. The AR/AP system will be packaged in Paradox tables, forms, and scripts.

On Day 13, I will talk about another kind of packaging to which you *will* have to pay some attention—that is, the packaging medium through which you'll deliver the application to your users.

In that kind of packaging planning, you'll have to think about compressing files for distribution, whether to deliver them on floppy disks or CD-ROM, how the user will install the product on his or her machine, and how the application must relate to the user's existing system (whether the user has to customize Windows parameters, for example).

Defining the Application's Distribution Methods

Distribution methods for the application depend on who you are, who your users are, and where you are in relation to the users. Distributing the application will come naturally to you when you give a little thought to these factors.

Several scenarios suggest themselves to me on your behalf:

☐ Corporate developers could simply hand-carry a diskette or diskettes with the application to the users who are physically located in the same offices. You might also have to install Paradox for Windows on their machines for them.

☐ Corporate developers who deal with LAN/WAN communications systems may have the option of deploying the application on the network. If you do this, you'll probably also need to ensure that you and your users are all using the Workgroups edition of Paradox for Windows.

☐ Commercial developers are well-constrained to taking orders and mailing or shipping distribution diskettes or CD-ROMs to customers of the application.

☐ Partly commercial developers and fully commercial developers both sometimes use the shareware approach to application distribution. This is probably the easiest method, since you can just upload the compressed application to the various boards and wait for folks to download it and send you money. The problem with this method is that it's the one that gives you least control over how users treat your product and whether or not they pay you for it.

The upshot is that I can't tell you how to distribute your applications. I can just give you some tips on how you might go about it, and I'll do that on Days 13 and 14.

Defining the Application's Support Resources

Support resources for your application are easy to discuss. I've seen the support resource, and it's *you!* You are your users' single greatest support resource. The only question is, Just how much are you willing to commit to supporting the users of your application? If you expect people to really use the thing, you had better be committed to supporting their use of the product. No matter how simple to use it may be, your users are going

to cover you up with questions about it, some of which will strike you as downright hard-headed; they want to do things *their* way, and that sometimes has nothing to do with what you put in the software.

There are some fairly simple means at your disposal, however, to help control being overrun by users. An important one is interactive help. Always put a help button or selection on your forms, and back it up with something decent to say about what should be going on with that form at that time. The more information, the merrier.

You also can provide both written and online documentation that the user can get to with a few simple keystrokes. This is a subject I'll help you with on Days 10 and 11. But by all means, make it easy for the user to get to some kind of information that will answer his questions, or he will bring them directly to you.

In these first three days, I've covered all the preliminary topics to actually building the AR/AP system. Tomorrow I'll get down to brass tacks and start naming the parts of the application's engine in specific detail. It's still planning, but it will start getting active from this point on.

Modification Notes

Modification notes are especially appropriate in this chapter. Now that I've told you what the main application is and what it will look like, it's only fair to tell you that I am going help you build the application by modifying the design of a similar application I've already done.

There isn't much in the way of user interface that will carry over from the previous application, since it was done in C for the DOS environment. But the structure of the tables and the basic approach to handling the data are both things that I've already done for a commercial system, and will come pretty much straight across to the Paradox for Windows environment.

I was myself quickly reminded that when you develop one application by modifying another, you don't want to get too carried away with trying to bring *everything* across. Even if you're just carrying the same application to another platform, which is exactly the case here, there is still a lot that won't make it to the new platform. In this case, that includes just about everything to do with the user interface: it's only the data model and relational implementation that will survive the transfer.

You may recall that I promised earlier in this chapter to give some brief pointers on the use of OLE 2 objects in Paradox for Windows forms to support multimedia features. You can place multimedia OLE objects on Paradox forms in two ways (each of which has two

variations, as you will see). You can select an OLE object off the toolbar and paste it right on the form, or you can define an OLE field in a table and display it in a table fram on the form.

There are two ways you can include an OLE 2 object on a Paradox form (or in any other document-oriented product). One way is by *embedding* the object so that Paradox can use it but can't get updated versions of it. The other way is by *linking* it into the document, so that the OLE server app that provides the object can keep it updated for you. Linking also costs less space in the form, since it points to the object and its server rather than just storing a copy of the object. To illustrate these concepts, I will step through embedding a Video for Windows clip in a form and linking a Wave file to a form.

First I will embed a Video for Windows clip, ELCAP.AVI, in the TESTOLE2 form. This clip, by the way, is a scene of El Capitan generated with VistaPro, image-processed by Aldus Photostyler, and animated with Photomorph. You can get freebie reduced-function versions of these products from the CD-ROM discs that come with Ron Wodaski's books *Multimedia Madness* and *Virtual Reality Madness,* both also from Sams.

In Figure 3.10, you see the first step of the OLE embedding process. Drag an OLE object from the toolbar onto the form, inspect its properties, choose **D**efine Ole, and choose **I**nsert Object.

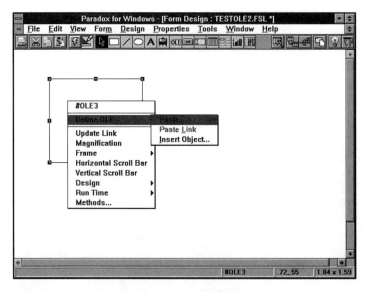

Figure 3.10. *Inserting an OLE object onto the form.*

Paradox will now show you the Insert Object Dialog box. In the Object Type list box, choose Media Clip, as shown in Figure 3.11.

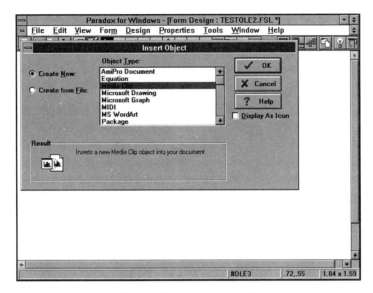

Figure 3.11. *Selecting a media clip from the Insert Object dialog box.*

Selecting a Media Clip object will then cause the Windows Media Player (which is an OLE server) to start up. Use the Media Player's File | Open command to open the ELCAP.AVI media file, as shown in Figure 3.12.

Now all you have to do is get the Media Player to send the OLE object back to Paradox. To do this, choose File | Exit & Return to TESTOLE2.FSL from the Media Player's menu. This is shown in Figure 3.13. Note that if you were updating the OLE image, rather than defining it for the first time, you could have chosen File | Update TESTOLE2.FSL.

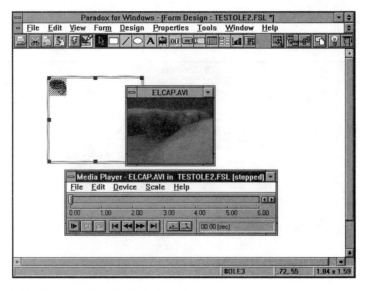

Figure 3.12. *Opening the ELCAP.AVI video.*

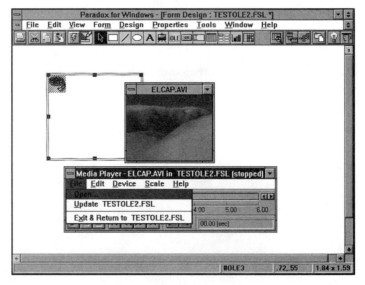

Figure 3.13. *Sending the OLE object to Paradox.*

With these actions complete, Paradox has embedded the ELCAP video in the TESTOLE2 form. The finished product is shown in Figure 3.14.

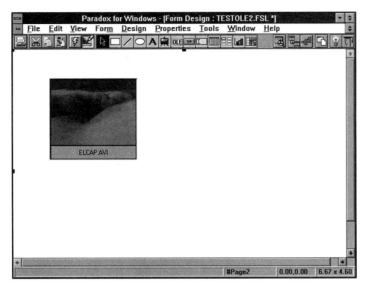

Figure 3.14. *The embedded ELCAP video, finished.*

The normal means of playing an OLE embedded clip is to double-click its icon or graphic (it can be displayed either way). However, pasting an OLE object directly on a Paradox form doesn't work quite that way at runtime (although, interestingly, it does in *design* mode). Instead, to get the media clip to run properly, you have to support it with a little ObjectPAL code. I'll get to that in just a minute. As I already mentioned, you also can do it with tables and table frames, but I will get to that in just a minute also.

As I mentioned, you also can use OLE linking to keep an updated OLE object associated (not embedded) in the form. To illustrate this process, link the MMT WELCOME.WAV audio into another Paradox OLE object, using Sound Blaster 16's Soundo'LE server. As before, open the form in design mode and place an undefined OLE object on the form. But don't do anything else yet.

Instead, open the Soundo'LE application, as shown in Figure 3.15. Note that you folks who use some equipment brand other than the Sound Blaster can work too. You have to use the drivers your manufacturer supplied instead. Another alternative is to use the Windows Media Player, which is not dependent on any particular manufacturer.

Open the media file in the Soundo'LE application. This is illustrated in Figure 3.16, and as you can see, there isn't much difference in the application's appearance yet.

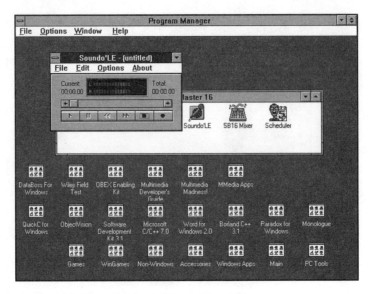

Figure 3.15. *Sound Blaster's Soundo'LE application.*

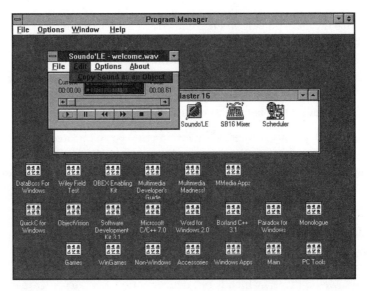

Figure 3.16. *Sound Blaster's Soundo'LE application with the WELCOME.WAV file open.*

Now switch back to the Paradox form and inspect the properties of the OLE object as you did before when embedding an object. This time, the Paste Link Soundo'LE command is active. Choose that command, as shown in Figure 3.17.

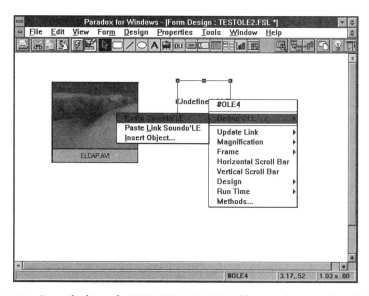

Figure 3.17. *Paste-linking the WELCOME.WAV file into the Paradox OLE object.*

The final product is shown in Figure 3.18; it's the Soundo'LE microphone icon. In most OLE-capable applications, you can run the media clip right off the form by double-clicking it with the mouse. You probably won't be surprised to learn that it works a little differently in Paradox for Windows. It takes a little ObjectPAL. Surprise, surprise!

ObjectPAL code has been attached to both the video and the sound objects' `mouseClick()` methods. The code for each object is very similar to that of the other, as follows:

```
;¦BeginMethod¦#Page2.#OLE4¦mouseClick¦
method mouseClick(var eventInfo MouseEvent)
var
  ov OLE
endvar
  ov = self
  ov.edit( "Hello Wave", 0 )
endmethod
;¦EndMethod¦#Page2.#OLE4¦mouseClick¦

;¦BeginMethod¦#Page2.#OLE3¦mouseClick¦
method mouseClick(var eventInfo MouseEvent)
var
```

```
  ov OLE
endvar
  ov = self
  ov.edit( "El Capitan", 0 )
endmethod
;¦EndMethod¦#Page2.#OLE3¦mouseClick¦
```

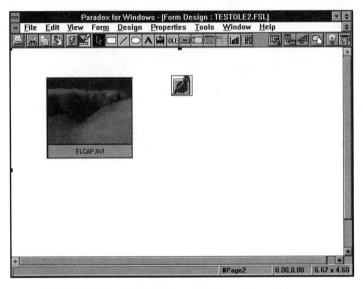

Figure 3.18. *The WELCOME.WAV sound file ready to play.*

As you can see, the method is quite simple. Define an OLE type variable and assign self to it. Then call the edit() method for the OLE variable, using as arguments a text string that (theoretically) will be the window title for the media player, and an edit command verb, which is really a SmallInt number.

How do you know what verb number number to use? You just have to know what the valid verbs for the particular OLE server are. Command verb 0 is the *primary* verb, and command verb 1 is the *secondary* verb. In the case of these two media clips, 0 means to *play* the clip, and 1 means to edit the clip. With the ObjectPAL attached to the mouseClick() methods of the OLE objects, you only need to left-click the OLE object to play the clip. This is illustrated in Figure 13.19, where the El Capitan video has been clicked and is playing.

With all that out of the way, you can look at the table, plus the table frame method, of getting OLE to handle multimedia clips. Just as when you paste an OLE object directly

on the form, you can either insert or paste-link a media object into an OLE table field. But first, of course, you have to have a table with an OLE field in it. Figure 3.20 shows the structure of the OLETAB table, in which the second field is an OLE-type field.

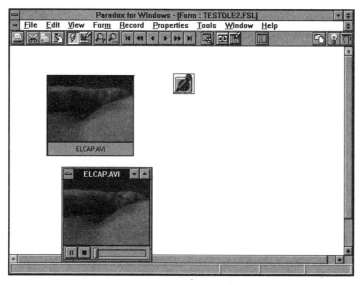

Figure 3.19. *The ELCAP video file playing after a left mouse click.*

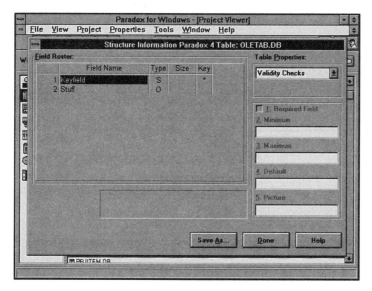

Figure 3.20. *Setting up the OLETAB table example.*

To insert or paste-link a media clip to stuff OLE field, open the table and right-click the field in the record where you want to add the OLE media clip. At this time, you will be prompted to insert the object if you have not opened the OLE server app (the Media Player, for example), or if you have opened it, you will have the option to link it as well. In this example, I have created only two records, and the OLE fields contain the LOADCD and FROG2CHK AVI clips, respectively. You'll see them shortly.

You aren't ready to play anything yet, however. First you need a form with the OLETAB bound to a table frame. The OLEFORM I created for this purpose is shown in Figure 3.21. Look at this figure and notice how deep I have made the rows. The reason for this is that it is necessary to make the rows deep enough that the clip's first frame can be displayed without "squashing" it or clipping it off short. If you don't drag out the rows like this, the clip will still be squashed when you play the clip as well.

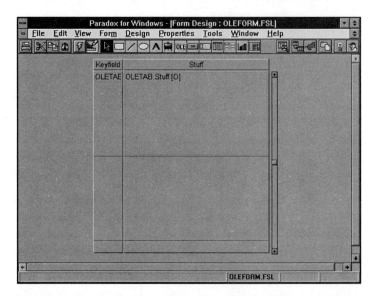

Figure 3.21. *Setting up the OLEFORM example form using a table fram.*

That's all there is to it, as far as designing the form is concerned. Now you only have to run the form and right-click the OLE field to insert the media objects. The OLEFORM sample with the media clips inserted in the OLE fields is shown in Figure 3.22.

Playing media clips managed by OLE fields is strictly according to the Microsoft standard usage. No ObjectPAL is required now, and you can just double-click the fram in its field to play the clip.

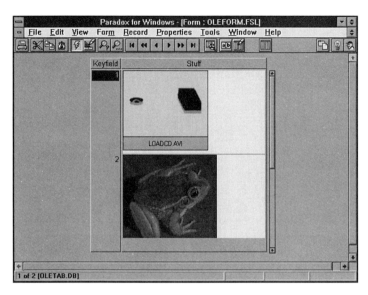

Figure 3.22. *The OLEFORM example with the OLE multimedia fields in action.*

I have saved the best method of handling OLE fields on forms for the last. This method is the most interesting and perhaps the most sophisticated because it involves a legal sort of cheating. In this method, you use a normal, unbound field to display the OLE object. Doing it this way avoids most of the difficulties associated with using true OLE fields. Thanks are due especially to Kevin Smith of Borland for the tip on this approach to multimedia. It was his suggestion to do multimedia with OLE this way: I just put the form together and dressed it up a bit.

To set up the form, you need only pick a field object from the toolbar and paste it onto a blank form. Don't define it by binding a table field or anything to it. You can, however, dress it up by playing with the frame. For the OLEMMT form, I chose an inside 3D frame. You can dress up the form by placing lots of visual cues on it that draw the user's attention to the features you want highlighted. You'll also need a couple of pushbuttons to select media clip files, to reset the unbound field to a blank state, and to close the application. The appearance of the OLEMMT form is shown in Figure 3.23.

As you can see, using a normal, unbound field, you can put together a multimedia presentation format that is almost as powerful as the original Multimedia Theater. The user can click the Open Media Clip button to pop up the file selection dialog you already saw with MMT. This button's logic also inserts the media clip into an OLE variable and then assigns that variable to the unbound field. At that point, the user is looking at the first stop-action frame of the clip (or perhaps an icon if the clip is an audio type).

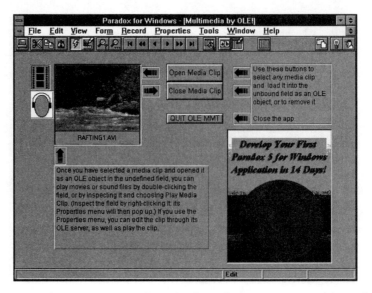

Figure 3.23. *The OLEMMT multimedia form showing a movie ready to play.*

The user can play the media clip in one of two ways. The first way is the normal procedure for an ordinary OLE field: just double-click the field to start playing. This works because the field is now (temporarily) an OLE field. When the clip begins playing, you'll see that there is a difference in the way it presents the video window from the original MMT. In OLEMMT, the video window has start and stop buttons at the bottom, plus a slider control that you can drag to position to any part of the clip (or fast-forward a sound clip).

The other method of playing the media clip involves inspecting the field (which should be showing a stop-action frame or icon) by right-clicking it. This will pop up the Properties menu, from which the user can choose Play Media Clip. Interestingly, this advanced OLE approach to multimedia permits you to edit the clip (if you have the supporting software); another of the Properties menu choices is Edit Media Clip.

And of course, when you are done playing the clip, you close it by clicking the Close Media Clip button on the form. Well, now, that sounds good and looks good. So, how do you put it together? It takes a minimal amount of ObjectPAL to select media files and control the internal OLE variables, so it's time to take a look at that source code.

First of all, you need a Uses block because the form uses the GETFILE DLL to choose files, just as with the PWMMPLAY form. This isn't strictly necessary, but it dresses up the application, and I like using it. Here is the Uses block for OLEMMT:

```
;¦BeginMethod¦#FormData1¦Uses¦
Uses GETFILE
  GetFileName( dllCaption CPTR ) CPTR
endUses
;¦EndMethod¦#FormData1¦Uses¦
```

The heart of the matter is in the Open Media Clip button's pushbutton() method. This method selects files, calls the OLE-type insertobject(), and sets up the unbound field by assigning it the value contained in the OLE variable. It also puts the form in edit mode since you can't play a media clip in view mode. Here is the ObjectPAL code for the Open Media Clip button:

```
;¦BeginMethod¦#Page2.#Button19¦pushButton¦
method pushButton(var eventInfo Event)
var
  ov OLE
  sfile String
endvar
  sfile = GetFileName( "Media File Selection" )
  if (sfile = "") then
    errorLog( 1, "You attempted to select a media file with an\n" +
                 "extension other than AVI, WAV, or MID." )
    errorShow( "Invalid file name", "Media File Selection" )
    return
  endif
  ov.insertobject(sfile,False)
  moviebox = ov
  edit()
endmethod
;¦EndMethod¦#Page2.#Button19¦pushButton¦
```

Although it is possible to select another media clip file and assign it to the unbound field without first closing it, closing the clip first and setting the field to a blank state (unbinding it again) is the normal means of terminating a media clip. Thus, you have a little ObjectPAL for the Close Media Clip button, as follows (note that edit mode is terminated here too):

```
;¦BeginMethod¦#Page2.#Button6¦pushButton¦
method pushButton(var eventInfo Event)
  endedit()
  moviebox.blank()
  self.moveto()
endmethod
;¦EndMethod¦#Page2.#Button6¦pushButton¦
```

Finally, the QUIT OLE MMT button shuts the whole thing down. Just to be on the safe side, this button's method also closes the clip. Even if the clip is already closed, this doesn't hurt, and I just like to play on the safe side of the programing street. Here is the ObjectPAL code for the QUIT button:

```
;¦BeginMethod¦#Page2.#Button8¦pushButton¦
method pushButton(var eventInfo Event)
```

```
    endedit()
    moviebox.blank()
    close()
endmethod
;¦EndMethod¦#Page2.#Button8¦pushButton¦
```

This approach to multimedia using OLE really isn't a cheater's method, since nothing was done in this form that isn't strictly legal with Paradox and ObjectPAL. But it certainly does produce the most satisfying results of all, short of the full-blown Multimedia Theater itself.

Debugging the Process

So far there hasn't been to much to debug. But in this chapter, you should notice that decisions are beginning to be made about what will go into the application, and how it will behave.

Since you're following along with me as you read this book, you won't have too much influence, for this project, on the content of those decisions. Yet it's time for you to begin questioning my decisions, about whether they are right and how you would do it differently if you were driving.

I promise I won't be offended as you do this, for two reasons. First, every person is different. If you and I worked for the same boss, who gave us each the same project just to see how we would each do it, it would come out different because *we* are different. That doesn't mean both versions of the project aren't workable; it just means that different personal styles were applied.

Second, I am developing the project with you in mind, and with some critically short time frames in mind. Your circumstances will be different, and that may require you to make some different decisions about the application and its workings.

At any rate, begin to question more and more as we go along. It will help you to more fully understand what *I* am doing, and what *you* will want to do differently later.

Defining the
Application's
Engine

This is the fourth day of the rest of your programming life. Today you'll do one of the most important things connected with the DPW AR/AP system. You'll stake out the territory—that is, you'll make the first and most fundamental decisions about what the application will look like on the inside. You'll plan the application's database engine.

In the context of older development methods, the "engine" referred to the database program, and that alone. I am using the term in a slightly new fashion here. The engine for your application consists of the Paradox for Windows software that drives everything, but you don't have to write that. From your point of view as a Paradox for Windows developer, you may as well consider the application engine to be the tables that comprise the infrastructure of the application, plus their basic relationships to one another.

That is what this chapter is about. Given the basic nature of the application's processes, which you will look at first, you can determine what tables are needed, and how they should relate to one another. And as you may have guessed, I have another neat little applet for you, which should help you maintain and manipulate those tables.

Examining the Application's Processes

The two sides of the application are the AR and AP functions. The nature of the processes involved in implementing these two parts of the system are highly parallel to one another.

At the apex of the application engine's table structure are the CUSTOMER and VENDOR tables, serving and controlling the AR and AP subsystems, respectively. These two tables maintain the data you need concerning people you want money from, and who want money from you. This is the first and most important piece of either subsystem: a controlling database to which the other tables are linked, and which in turn determines what can happen to the other tables.

For the customer table, you'll want to post charges against a customer, and post payments the customer makes, as well. This system will also be able to post a mass charge against all customers. To record all these transactions, an accounts receivable table will be attached to the customer table. It isn't desirable to enter transaction amounts directly, or only, into the customer file. One reason for this is the time lag between the posting of a charge and the posting of a payment, implying that two transactions as a pair need to be allowed for. Another good reason, of course, is that auditors like to have details about what's been going on, even if that auditor is only you.

From time to time, you'll also want to be able to move old transactions out of the way, without losing them. For this purpose an accounts receivable history table will be supplied, together with forms that will allow the user to select the records he wants to move to the history file. Many database systems would require the use of intermediary tables to hold transaction data until it's posted, but with Paradox for Windows, this will prove not to be necessary.

The accounts payable subsystem will work in a parallel fashion. To the vendor, master file will be linked an accounts payable file, which will hold the AP transactions. There will also be an accounts payable history file, serving the same purpose here that the AR history serves in its domain.

With all this in mind, there are several major processes, similar in each of the AR and AP subsystems, that have to be in place. These processes include the following:

☐ *Posting new transactions:* For AR, this will involve posting customer charges and payments to the AR master file. For AP, this will involve posting purchases (vendor invoices) and payments to the AP master file.

☐ *Payment tracking:* In this group, I include both reports that summarize the condition of accounts and identify accounts that need servicing (such as cutting a check or sending a bill), and documents for the actual payment or collection of money.

☐ *Archival and backup utilities:* These tasks are grouped together because they are so similar in nature. There are some differences, however. By *archival*, I mean moving transaction records from the AR or AP master files to their respective history files. This activity needs to be triggered by date criteria, account balance, or the manual selection of records by the user. By *backup*, I mean the regular copying of AR and AP tables to a safe location. A "safe location" doesn't have to be an underground vault; it can simply be a copy of the table by another name in the same directory. This book will not directly address the process of compressing files and storing them outside the computer.

☐ *Maintenance utilities:* Maintenance tasks include such things as table repair, new table creation, canned routines for basic statistical analysis of tables, inquiry on table and index structures, and other things in this vein. You'll get your first taste of maintenance utilities in the very next section of today's text.

☐ *Inquiry and other reporting utilities:* It's important for an application's user to be able to look at the data stored in the application in various ways. This goes beyond just giving the user a feeling of control over the application. Very often, being able to look at data in multiple ways is quite important for solving business problems. In this regard, you'll supply your users various utilities

4

supporting Paradox queries (some canned, and some under complete user control), crosstabs, charts, and graphs of the data in the system's tables.

Selecting the Application's Database Tables

As is the author's prerogative, I've cheated and have already defined and created all the major tables in the application. I didn't just do this on a whim, of course. If I want to able to lead you straight through the design and implementation of an application, I need to avoid the ever-present stopping, rethinking, and reworking of specifications that invariably accompanies any real development project. It's hard to learn that way, and not too incidentally, it's very hard to write a book that way, too.

I've also created the first table maintenance utility that will be useful as the project moves forward. This is the DPW Table Maintenance Utility. The other utilities in this category won't be designed until Day 5, and not actually created until Day 9. You get this one early, however, since it's so useful in presenting table structures and dependencies.

So, let's get busy right away by dissecting the DPW Table Utility form and its ObjectPAL methods. Figure 4.1 shows the table utility's form (TBUTIL.FSL, or .FDL for the delivered version). Take a look at that, and then I will explain how it works.

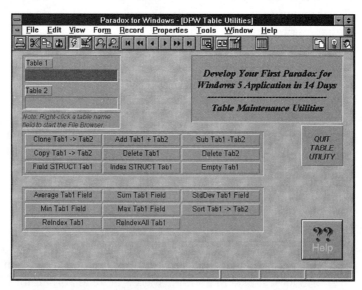

Figure 4.1. *The DPW Table Utility form.*

As Figure 4.1 shows, the table utility form has three major groups of design objects on it, plus a couple of accessories. The first group, near the top-left corner of the form, contains two edit fields, one for each of two table names that you can supply, Table 1 and Table 2. Clearly, some of the table operations involve a pair of tables.

One of the nice features of the table name fields is that you can right-click either one of them to start the Paradox file browser, from which you can pick a table name—rather than having to remember a name and type it in the field.

The second group of design objects, located just below the first group, contains controls for activating the major table manipulation functions. These objects can all be clicked to activate them, but they are packaged as text boxes with a 3D frame, rather than as pushbuttons. Why? Because it looked good to me, and nothing else. Feel free to redesign in any way that suits you.

The major table operations include cloning a table to another table (which doesn't have to exist yet), copying one table to another (which does have to be already created), adding, subtracting, emptying, and deleting tables, and displaying the structures of tables and their indexes. Note that index structure refers to the composition of secondary indexes, which you won't be using in this project.

The third group of table controls is found nearest the bottom of the form, under the others. These controls are also 3D text boxes that can be clicked. The top six controls in this group all invoke built-in Paradox table methods for performing basic statistical analysis on table fields. (The user will be prompted for the field name.)

Rebuilding secondary indexes is handled by the last two controls in the third group. The ReIndex Tab1 control prompts you first for the name of the index to rebuild, meaning that you have to know its name beforehand. You can get that information by using the Index STRUCT Tab1 control in group one. The ReIndexAll Tab1 rebuilds all secondary indexes without asking, including maintained and unmaintained indexes.

Since the form does many different things, I've provided two help screens, one for each of the two major groups of control boxes. These help screens are implemented as pages 2 and 3 of the form—a very simple and direct way to package help information with Paradox for Windows forms. (WinHelp databases will be covered, too, on Day 11.) The first help page is shown in Figure 4.2.

Defining the Application's Engine

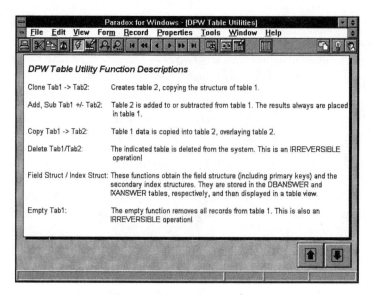

Figure 4.2. *Page 1 help for the DPW Table Utility form.*

The only remarkable thing about the help screens is the presence of the navigation pushbuttons at the bottom-right corner, plus the fact that some of the text is in color—which you can't see from the black-and-white figures.

Page 3 of the form contains the second help screen and has only the "previous-page" (up arrow) button on it. This is shown in Figure 4.3.

As I've mentioned, the interesting thing about the DPW Table Utility form isn't the help pages, it's the methods behind the table controls. As always, there is a little overhead involved in setting up a form, something you're used to by now. Here is the form's open() method, without further comment:

```
;¦BeginMethod¦#FormData1¦open¦
method open(var eventInfo Event)
  if NOT eventInfo.isPreFilter() then
    doDefault
    maximize()
  endif
endmethod
;¦EndMethod¦#FormData1¦open¦
```

The Help button and the navigation buttons on the help pages can be quickly disposed of as well. The basic procedure is to tell Paradox to go to the page you want, and make sure that some object on the target page gets the focus by using the moveTo() procedure call. The methods for the Help and help navigation buttons are as follows:

```
;¦BeginMethod¦#Page2.#Button8¦pushButton¦
method pushButton(var eventInfo Event)
  moveToPage(2)
  moveTo( p2dn )
endmethod
;¦EndMethod¦#Page2.#Button8¦pushButton¦

;¦BeginMethod¦#Page3.p2dn¦pushButton¦
method pushButton(var eventInfo Event)
  moveToPage( 3 )
  moveTo( p3up )
endmethod
;¦EndMethod¦#Page3.p2dn¦pushButton¦

;¦BeginMethod¦#Page3.p2up¦pushButton¦
method pushButton(var eventInfo Event)
  moveToPage( 1 )
  moveTo( TBName1 )
endmethod
;¦EndMethod¦#Page3.p2up¦pushButton¦

;¦BeginMethod¦#Page6.p3up¦pushButton¦
method pushButton(var eventInfo Event)
  moveToPage( 2 )
  moveTo( p2up )
endmethod
;¦EndMethod¦#Page6.p3up¦pushButton¦
```

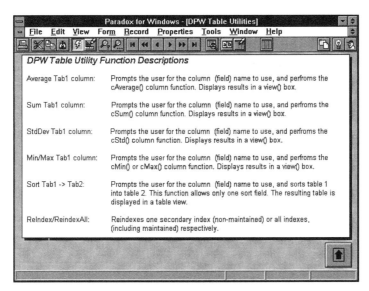

Figure 4.3. *Page 2 help for the DPW Table Utility form.*

Showstopper! With previous versions of Paradox for Windows, I got in the habit of launching things such as moveToPage() using a graphic object (a bitmap) instead of a button. This will really blow up in your face with Paradox 5 for Windows.

The table utility form originally *did* use a Help graphic, not a pushbutton. When I ran the form, I quickly noticed that Paradox will turn the page as directed, but it won't leave it there. After a few seconds, the original page will reappear, and woe betide you if you've been frantically trying to click one of the navigation buttons! What actually gets clicked is whatever was in that position on the first page.

You can work around this problem by using a pushbutton instead of a graphic object to launch something like this and by being sure to add the moveTo() call naming some object on the target page to receive the Windows focus. It works fine this way.

In many forms, you'll not want to attach method code to simple edit fields, such as the Table 1 and Table 2 fields. In this case, however, I wanted to provide some extra functionality. I wanted to be able to launch the Paradox file browser by right-clicking these fields, so that the user can look up a table name without having to remember it. The mouseRightUp() methods for these two fields are essentially the same, so here they are together:

```
;¦BeginMethod¦#Page2.#Box28.TBName1¦mouseRightUp¦
method mouseRightUp(var eventInfo MouseEvent)
var
   fbi FileBrowserInfo
   selectName String
endvar
   fbi.alias = "WORK"
   fbi.AllowableTypes = fbParadox
   fbi.FileFilters = "*.DB"
   fileBrowser( selectName, fbi )
   self = selectName
endmethod
;¦EndMethod¦#Page2.#Box28.TBName1¦mouseRightUp¦

;¦BeginMethod¦#Page2.#Box28.TBName2¦mouseRightUp¦
method mouseRightUp(var eventInfo MouseEvent)
var
   fbi FileBrowserInfo
   selectName String
endvar
   fbi.alias = "WORK"
   fbi.AllowableTypes = fbParadox
```

```
    fbi.FileFilters = "*.DB"
    fileBrowser( selectName, fbi )
    self = selectName
endmethod
;¦EndMethod¦#Page2.#Box28.TBName2¦mouseRightUp¦
```

The nifty thing about the Paradox file browser is that you don't have to know what the user's current working directory is. You can just specify that the alias name WORK be used in the FileBrowserInfo block, and tell the user to go get the filename. Earlier in the book, I supplied the GetFile() DLL to perform this function, because the MMT application had to have the drive name prefixed to the path specification. The Paradox file browser presents a very nice open-file dialog box to the user, one that is compatible in appearance to other Paradox for Windows visual features.

The first of the table operation control boxes is the CloneBox. Since this is not a pushbutton, a different method is required to activate the function, and the mouseClick() seems made to order. Here is the ObjectPAL code for CloneBox's mouseClick() method:

```
;¦BeginMethod¦#Page2.#Box42.CloneBox¦mouseClick¦
method mouseClick(var eventInfo MouseEvent)
var
  tb1, tb2 Table
endvar
  tb1.attach( TBName1 )
  tb2.attach( TBName2 )
  if tb1.isTable() AND NOT tb2.isTable() then
    message( "Cloning table..." + " " + TBName1 + "-->" + TBName2 )
    tb1.enumFieldStruct( "DBANSWER.DB" )
    tb1.enumIndexStruct( "IXANSWER.DB" )
    tb2 = create
            TBName2
            STRUCT "DBANSWER.DB"
            INDEXSTRUCT "IXANSWER.DB"
          endcreate
    msgInfo( "DPW Table Utility", TBName2+" created" )
  else
    msgStop( "DPW Table Utility", "A table is not specified correctly!" )
  endif
  tb1.unattach()
  tb2.unattach()
endmethod
;¦EndMethod¦#Page2.#Box42.CloneBox¦mouseClick¦
```

As you can see, the principal features of the cloning operation are the enumFieldStruct() method call, together with a corresponding enumIndexStruct() call. The index structure thus obtained is used to create the cloned database so that secondary indexes will not be lost in the transition. Note that cloning a table is not the same as copying a table: that is handled by the Copy Table operation (described in just a moment). Note also that many operations employ the use of two tables. In these cases, you must specify Table 2, although it doesn't have to already exist for cloning.

In fact, the clone operation uses the same enum...() calls that the field and index structure controls use. The main difference in the latter operations is that the results of the enumeration are displayed in a table view when the operation has been completed. The methods for displaying the field and index structure of a table are as follows:

```
;¦BeginMethod¦#Page2.#Box42.FieldBox¦mouseClick¦
method mouseClick(var eventInfo MouseEvent)
var
  tb1 Table
  tv TableView
endvar
  tb1.attach( TBName1 )
  if tb1.isTable()then
    message( "Getting structure of table..." + " " + TBName1 )
    tb1.enumFieldStruct( "DBANSWER.DB" )
    tv.open( "DBANSWER.DB" )
    tv.maximize()
    tv.wait()
    tv.close()
  else
    msgStop( "DPW Table Utility", "A table is not specified correctly!" )
  endif
  tb1.unattach()
endmethod
;¦EndMethod¦#Page2.#Box42.FieldBox¦mouseClick¦

;¦BeginMethod¦#Page2.#Box42.IndexBox¦mouseClick¦
method mouseClick(var eventInfo MouseEvent)
var
  tb1 Table
  tv TableView
endvar
  tb1.attach( TBName1 )
  if tb1.isTable()then
    message( "Getting index structure of table..." + " " + TBName1 )
    tb1.enumIndexStruct( "IXANSWER.DB" )
    tv.open( "IXANSWER.DB" )
    tv.maximize()
    tv.wait()
    tv.close()
  else
    msgStop( "DPW Table Utility", "A table is not specified correctly!" )
  endif
  tb1.unattach()
endmethod
;¦EndMethod¦#Page2.#Box42.IndexBox¦mouseClick¦
```

In order to display the results of the field or index enumeration, notice that a TableView variable is used to gain access to the answer tables. The sequence of operations on the table view is typical for a situation like this: open it, maximize it, wait on the user to leave the table view, and close the TableView variable.

Opening a table view is one way of associating a variable with a table object. Another way is to attach a `Table` variable to the table name. Note that you don't open a table directly. The Paradox engine always deals with your requests for interaction with a table through Paradox design objects or variables, which are not themselves the table. This raises the necessity of occasionally synchronizing the object or variable with the contents of the underlying table. You'll see how this is done as you move along through the project.

The `EmptyBox` table control uses the `attach()` method to gain access to a table to delete all the records from it. Other than that, the ObjectPAL code for emptying a table is straightforward. Here is the method code for the `EmptyBox` control:

```
;¦BeginMethod¦#Page2.#Box42.EmptyBox¦mouseClick¦
method mouseClick(var eventInfo MouseEvent)
var
  tb1 Table
endvar
  tb1.attach( TBName1 )
  if tb1.isTable()then
    message( "Emptying table... ", TBName1 )
    if tb1.empty() then
      msgInfo( "DPW Table Utility", "Table empty successful" )
    else
      msgStop( "DPW Table Utility", "Table empty FAILED!" )
    endif
  else
    msgStop( "DPW Table Utility", "A table is not specified correctly!" )
  endif
  tb1.unattach()
endmethod
;¦EndMethod¦#Page2.#Box42.EmptyBox¦mouseClick¦
```

The ObjectPAL for deleting an entire table is equally straightforward. A `Table` variable is attached using the table name string, and then you just do it, with the `delete()` method. Here is how it goes, for both the Delete Tab1 and Delete Tab2 controls:

```
;¦BeginMethod¦#Page2.#Box42.Delete1Box¦mouseClick¦
method mouseClick(var eventInfo MouseEvent)
var
  tb1 Table
endvar
  tb1.attach( TBName1 )
  if tb1.isTable()then
    message( "Deleting table... ", TBName1 )
    if tb1.delete() then
      msgInfo( "DPW Table Utility", "Table delete successful" )
    else
      msgStop( "DPW Table Utility", "Table delete FAILED!" )
    endif
  else
    msgStop( "DPW Table Utility", "A table is not specified correctly!" )
  endif
```

```
    tb1.unattach()
endmethod
;¦EndMethod¦#Page2.#Box42.Delete1Box¦mouseClick¦


;¦BeginMethod¦#Page2.#Box42.Delete2Box¦mouseClick¦
method mouseClick(var eventInfo MouseEvent)
var
  tb2 Table
endvar
  tb2.attach( TBName2 )
  if tb2.isTable()then
    message( "Deleting table... ", TBName2 )
    if tb2.delete() then
      msgInfo( "DPW Table Utility", "Table delete successful" )
    else
      msgStop( "DPW Table Utility", "Table delete FAILED!" )
    endif
  else
    msgStop( "DPW Table Utility", "A table is not specified correctly!" )
  endif
  tb2.unattach()
endmethod
;¦EndMethod¦#Page2.#Box42.Delete2Box¦mouseClick¦
```

Copying one table into another one is nearly as easy. You need two `Table` variables this time, and you tell the first table to copy itself into the other one by calling the first table's `copy()` method, as follows:

```
;¦BeginMethod¦#Page2.#Box42.CopyBox¦mouseClick¦
method mouseClick(var eventInfo MouseEvent)
var
  tb1, tb2 Table
  tv TableView
endvar
  tb1.attach( TBName1 )
  tb2.attach( TBName2 )
  if tb1.isTable() AND tb2.isTable() then
    message( "Copying table..." + " " + TBName1 + "-->" + TBName2 )
    if NOT tb1.copy( tb2 ) then
      msgStop( "DPW Table Utility", "Table copy failed" )
      tb1.unattach()
      tb2.unattach()
      return
    endif
    tv.open( TBName2 )
    tv.maximize()
    tv.wait()
    tv.close()
  else
    msgStop( "DPW Table Utility", "A table is not specified correctly!" )
  endif
  tb1.unattach()
  tb2.unattach()
endmethod
;¦EndMethod¦#Page2.#Box42.CopyBox¦mouseClick¦
```

Developer's Tip: One of the things that I've not mentioned in the discussion of the ObjectPAL code so far is the way that the table operation's logic is wrapped inside an `if tablename.isTable() ... endif` statement. This ensures that the operation is not attempted on anything other than a real Paradox table.

This sort of wrapping is always good practice. It falls not into the category of error trapping, but of error *prevention*, which is even better.

Of course, if you don't do this sort of thing, the world won't come to an end. However, you won't get much done without problems, and you could very well corrupt files that you would have rather left intact.

With the table subtraction and addition controls, the ObjectPAL logic begins to get just a little more complex. For these methods, you both perform the operation and then display the results in a table view again. Also, there is a minor, but important, peculiarity in the way the subtract() and add() methods are called. As you examine the ObjectPAL code for these methods, you may notice that the placement of arguments for subtract() and add() looks backward. Look over the code, and then I will explain why I did it that way:

```
;¦BeginMethod¦#Page2.#Box42.SubBox¦mouseClick¦
method mouseClick(var eventInfo MouseEvent)
var
  tb1, tb2 Table
  tv TableView
endvar
  tb1.attach( TBName1 )
  tb2.attach( TBName2 )
  if tb1.isTable() AND tb2.isTable() then
    message( "Subtracting table..." + " " + TBName1 + "-" + TBName2 )
    if NOT tb2.subtract( tb1 ) then
      msgStop( "DPW Table Utility", "Table subtract failed" )
      tb1.unattach()
      tb2.unattach()
      return
    endif
    tv.open( TBName1 )
    tv.maximize()
    tv.wait()
    tv.close()
  else
    msgStop( "DPW Table Utility", "A table is not specified correctly!" )
  endif
  tb1.unattach()
  tb2.unattach()
endmethod
```

```
;¦EndMethod¦#Page2.#Box42.SubBox¦mouseClick¦
;¦BeginMethod¦#Page2.#Box42.AddBox¦mouseClick¦
method mouseClick(var eventInfo MouseEvent)
var
  tb1, tb2 Table
  tv TableView
endvar
  tb1.attach( TBName1 )
  tb2.attach( TBName2 )
  if tb1.isTable() AND tb2.isTable() then
    message( "Adding table..." + " " + TBName1 + "+" + TBName2 )
    if NOT tb2.add( tb1, True, False ) then
      msgStop( "DPW Table Utility", "Table add failed" )
      tb1.unattach()
      tb2.unattach()
      return
    endif
    tv.open( TBName1 )
    tv.maximize()
    tv.wait()
    tv.close()
  else
    msgStop( "DPW Table Utility", "A table is not specified correctly!" )
  endif
  tb1.unattach()
  tb2.unattach()
endmethod
;¦EndMethod¦#Page2.#Box42.AddBox¦mouseClick¦
```

See what I mean? In both cases, I've directed table 2 to add or subtract itself from table 1. That is because, in both cases, the first table (2) examines the second table (1) to see whether its own records are present there or not. In table subtraction, if a record is in the target table, it is removed. For addition, it is added. If I had not asked table 2 to perform the operation, the results would have been left in table 2, not table 1 as I wanted.

An example can clear this matter up some more. Later, you'll develop the form that moves records from the AR (or AP) master file to its history file. Here is how you'll do that:

1. A table cursor will be used to run the master file, identify records the user wants archived, and place them in a table that you'll name ARCTEMP. At this point, the master table is unaffected by the process.

2. The ObjectPAL code will direct ARCTEMP to subtract itself from the master table by something like this: `temptab.subtract(artab)`. At this point, ARCTEMP is still there and AR has fewer records.

3. If there have been no errors so far, the ObjectPAL code will direct ARCTEMP to add itself to the ARHIST table. If this fails, an attempt will be made to re-add the records to the master table, and the process will abort.

4. If there have still been no errors anywhere in the process, the ObjectPAL code will delete the ARCTEMP table.

The value of doing things this way is obvious. It provides the maximum opportunity to back out of the process without losing any records, even in the face of errors. Another benefit isn't so obvious, and is the reason I gave you this utility early in the book: you can see how each of these operations are handled in a context that is uncomplicated by the presence of another application's needs. I cheated again, but my intentions were good!

The Sort control provides yet another little difference to be assimilated. Specifically, the Paradox sort verb is not a method at all; it's an ObjectPAL *verb* (a reserved word). Simply put, you tell Paradox what to sort, how to sort it, and where to put the results. Here is the ObjectPAL for the process; its nature is self-explanatory:

```
;¦BeginMethod¦#Page2.#Box43.SortBox¦mouseClick¦
method mouseClick(var eventInfo MouseEvent)
var
  tb1, tb2 Table
  sField String
  tv TableView
endvar
  tb1.attach( TBName1 )
  tb2.attach( TBName2 )
  if tb1.isTable() then
    sField.blank()
    try
      sField.view( "Enter the field name to sort on:" )
      sort tb1
        on sField
        to tb2
      endsort
      tv.open( TBName2 )
      tv.maximize()
      tv.wait()
      tv.close()
    onfail
      errorShow( "DPW Table Utility", "Table sort failed" )
    endtry
  else
    msgStop( "DPW Table Utility", "A table is not specified correctly!" )
    errorLog( 2, "TBUtil requires that both tables exist." )
    errorLog( 1, "Sort table specification error." )
    errorShow( "DPW Table Utility", "Table sort request was invalid" )
  endif
  tb1.unattach()
  tb2.unattach()
endmethod
;¦EndMethod¦#Page2.#Box43.SortBox¦mouseClick¦
```

The statistical operations all have in common a couple of interesting features that you'll find useful in the future. First, the `view()` method is used to both get the user's choice of field name to work on, and to display the results of the operation. Second, the `try...onfail` block is used to attempt the operation and catch any failure. Just looking at the examples is sufficient to illustrate how this is done in context, as follows:

```
;¦BeginMethod¦#Page2.#Box43.MaxBox¦mouseClick¦
method mouseClick(var eventInfo MouseEvent)
var
  tb1 Table
  sField String
  nResult Number
endvar
  tb1.attach( TBName1 )
  if tb1.isTable()then
    sField.blank()
    try
      sField.view( "Enter the field name for MaxVal:" )
      nResult = tb1.cMax( sField )
      nResult.view( sField + " column maximum value:" )
    onfail
      msgStop( "DPW Table Utility", "Couldn't compute MaxVal on that field!" )
      errorShow( "DPW Table Utility", "Column maximum value error" )
    endtry
  else
    msgStop( "DPW Table Utility", "A table is not specified correctly!" )
  endif
  tb1.unattach()
endmethod
;¦EndMethod¦#Page2.#Box43.MaxBox¦mouseClick¦

; This is the MinBox control's method. Misspelling it doesn't affect anything,
;      so I got lazy and just left it alone.
;¦BeginMethod¦#Page2.#Box43.MonBox¦mouseClick¦
method mouseClick(var eventInfo MouseEvent)
var
  tb1 Table
  sField String
  nResult Number
endvar
  tb1.attach( TBName1 )
  if tb1.isTable()then
    sField.blank()
    try
      sField.view( "Enter the field name for MinVal:" )
      nResult = tb1.cMin( sField )
      nResult.view( sField + " column minimum value:" )
    onfail
      msgStop( "DPW Table Utility", "Couldn't compute MinVal on that field!" )
      errorShow( "DPW Table Utility", "Column minimum value error" )
    endtry
  else
    msgStop( "DPW Table Utility", "A table is not specified correctly!" )
  endif
```

```
    tb1.unattach()
endmethod
;¦EndMethod¦#Page2.#Box43.MonBox¦mouseClick¦


;¦BeginMethod¦#Page2.#Box43.StdDevBox¦mouseClick¦
method mouseClick(var eventInfo MouseEvent)
var
  tb1 Table
  sField String
  nResult Number
endvar
  tb1.attach( TBName1 )
  if tb1.isTable()then
    sField.blank()
    try
      sField.view( "Enter the field name for StdDev:" )
      nResult = tb1.cStd( sField )
      nResult.view( sField + " standard deviation:" )
    onfail
      msgStop( "DPW Table Utility", "Couldn't compute StdDev on that field!" )
      errorShow( "DPW Table Utility", "Column standard deviation error" )
    endtry
  else
    msgStop( "DPW Table Utility", "A table is not specified correctly!" )
  endif
  tb1.unattach()
endmethod
;¦EndMethod¦#Page2.#Box43.StdDevBox¦mouseClick¦


;¦BeginMethod¦#Page2.#Box43.SumBox¦mouseClick¦
method mouseClick(var eventInfo MouseEvent)
var
  tb1 Table
  sField String
  nResult Number
endvar
  tb1.attach( TBName1 )
  if tb1.isTable()then
    sField.blank()
    try
      sField.view( "Enter the field name to sum:" )
      nResult = tb1.cSum( sField )
      nResult.view( sField + " column sum:" )
    onfail
      msgStop( "DPW Table Utility", "Couldn't sum that field!" )
      errorShow( "DPW Table Utility", "Column sum error" )
    endtry
  else
    msgStop( "DPW Table Utility", "A table is not specified correctly!" )
  endif
  tb1.unattach()
endmethod
;¦EndMethod¦#Page2.#Box43.SumBox¦mouseClick¦


;¦BeginMethod¦#Page2.#Box43.AverageBox¦mouseClick¦
method mouseClick(var eventInfo MouseEvent)
```

4

```
var
  tb1 Table
  sField String
  nResult Number
endvar
  tb1.attach( TBName1 )
  if tb1.isTable()then
    sField.blank()
    try
      sField.view( "Enter the field name to average:" )
      nResult = tb1.cAverage( sField )
      nResult.view( sField + " column average:" )
    onfail
      msgStop( "DPW Table Utility", "Couldn't average that field!" )
      errorShow( "DPW Table Utility", "Column average error" )
    endtry
  else
    msgStop( "DPW Table Utility", "A table is not specified correctly!" )
  endif
  tb1.unattach()
endmethod
;¦EndMethod¦#Page2.#Box43.AverageBox¦mouseClick¦
```

Rebuilding secondary indexes for a table is a more serious matter than the previous
operations and requires some careful protection of the tables involved from access by
other instances of Paradox forms. Full table-locking is required here, and any failure to
get this right can leave you with some seriously fouled-up tables. The previous examples
of the `try...onfail` method of error trapping were practice; this is the real thing. For all
table operations of this nature, be sure to use this method.

First, take a look at the `ReIndexALL` control's method. It doesn't require any user input
and is therefore the syntactically simpler of the controls. Here is its code:

```
;¦BeginMethod¦#Page2.#Box43.ReIndexAllBox¦mouseClick¦
method mouseClick(var eventInfo MouseEvent)
var
  tb1 Table
endvar
  tb1.attach( TBName1 )
  if tb1.isTable()then
    try
      tb1.setExclusive()     ; required to rebuild maintained indexes
      if tb1.lock("Full") then
        if tb1.reIndexAll() then
          msgInfo( "DPW Table Utility", "ReIndex complete" )
        else
          msgStop( "DPW Table Utility", "ReIndex FAILED!" )
          errorShow( "DPW Table Utility", "Attempted secondary re-index all" )
        endif
        tb1.unlock("Full")
      else
        msgStop( "DPW Table Utility", "Can't LOCK the table!" )
      endif
    onfail
```

```
        msgStop( "DPW Table Utility", "ReIndexAll transaction block failed!" )
        errorShow( "DPW Table Utility", "Attempted secondary re-index all" )
      endtry
    else
      msgStop( "DPW Table Utility", "A table is not specified correctly!" )
    endif
    tb1.unattach()
endmethod
;¦EndMethod¦#Page2.#Box43.ReIndexAllBox¦mouseClick¦
```

Notice that the method's code is not long, just tricky. Again, be sure to add the error handling code to this sort of table manipulation.

Re-indexing a table on a specific secondary index is more complicated because you have to get the user's selection of field name and you have to make sure that the selected name really is a field in the table. To satisfy this second requirement, the ReIndexBox's ObjectPAl first enumerates the table's structure, and uses a table cursor to attempt a locate() operation on the table, trying to find the user's selected name in the answer table's szName field.

Sound complicated? Well, it is, a little; but it's not too bad. Just take your time examining the ObjectPAl for this method, which is as follows:

4

```
;¦BeginMethod¦#Page2.#Box43.ReIndexBox¦mouseClick¦
method mouseClick(var eventInfo MouseEvent)
var
  tb1 Table
  sField String
  nResult Number
  ckTC TCursor
endvar
  tb1.attach( TBName1 )
  if tb1.isTable()then
    sField.blank()
    try
      sField.view( "Enter the secondary index name to REINDEX:" )
      tb1.enumIndexStruct( "IXANSWER.DB" )
      ckTC.open( "IXANSWER.DB" )
      if NOT ckTC.locate( "szName", sField ) then
        msgStop( "DPW Table Utility", "That field isn't an index!" )
        return
      endif
      if ckTC.bMaintained = "Y" then
        msgStop( "DPW Table Utility", "That field is auto-maintained!" )
        return
      endif
      if tb1.lock("Full") then
        if tb1.reIndex( sField ) then
          msgInfo( "DPW Table Utility", "ReIndex complete" )
        else
          msgStop( "DPW Table Utility", "ReIndex FAILED!" )
          errorShow( "DPW Table Utility", "Attempted secondary re-index on "+sField )
        endif
```

131

```
        tb1.unlock("Full")
      else
        msgStop( "DPW Table Utility", "Can't LOCK the table!" )
      endif
    onfail
      msgStop( "DPW Table Utility", "ReIndex secondary index failed!" )
      errorShow( "DPW Table Utility", "Attempted secondary re-index" )
    endtry
  else
    msgStop( "DPW Table Utility", "A table is not specified correctly!" )
  endif
  tb1.unattach()
endmethod
;¦EndMethod¦#Page2.#Box43.ReIndexBox¦mouseClick¦
```

You might have also noticed that the table cursor is used to check the table's properties for the field in the answer table's bMaintained field. If the field is automaintained by Paradox, you can't manually re-index on it.

So far I've been saving the touchy stuff for later, getting more complex as I go along. The QuitBox reverses that trend, since it has one of the simplest methods in the whole form. I'm sure you already understand everything in it. Here is the method code for getting out of the table utility form:

```
;¦BeginMethod¦#Page2.QuitBox¦mouseClick¦
method mouseClick(var eventInfo MouseEvent)
  close()
endmethod
;¦EndMethod¦#Page2.QuitBox¦mouseClick¦
```

Well, that's all for the innards of your latest toy. Now it's time to move on to a consideration of the main application's tables and their relationships.

Planning the Database Tables' Structure

One of the most important things you want to accomplish in business is getting money (sure is for me, anyway). For that reason, take a look at the table structure needed for the CUSTOMER and AR master files. Note that although I constantly refer to the AR table as a master file and it's the master storage location for AR transactions, it will be a secondary table linked to the CUSTOMER table. More on that shortly, however.

Everything in Accounts Receivable relates back to a customer account. Thus, the CUSTOMER table is the master table for Accounts Receivable. Customers will be identified primarily by their customer numbers. Their business names, the buyers

who incurred the debt by buying something from you, the billing contacts, and the company addresses are all important too. And don't forget the account balance! Figure 4.4 displays the CUSTOMER table structure.

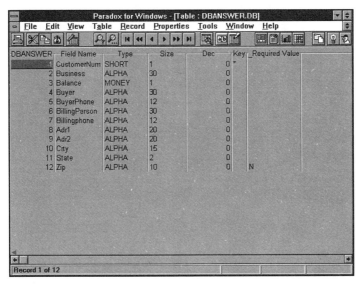

Figure 4.4. *The CUSTOMER table's structure (displayed by the Table utility).*

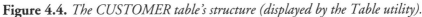

The CUSTOMER table is not surprising; it has just what you would expect in it, in simple fashion. The AR table is correspondingly simple and is keyed on the customer number. The key in this table, however, is a compound key, the second part of which is the billing number. This field is necessary to keep different receivables from the same customer separate. You might assign your own internally generated number here, or you could use something like the customer's own purchase order number. It's up to you, but the value needs to be unique to the AR table for that customer.

The AR table has fields of a more detailed nature, just as you would expect for keeping track of specific purchases made. You need to know what the customer bought, how much it cost, and whether or not the customer has paid for it yet. The AR table structure is shown in Figure 4.5.

Defining the Application's Engine

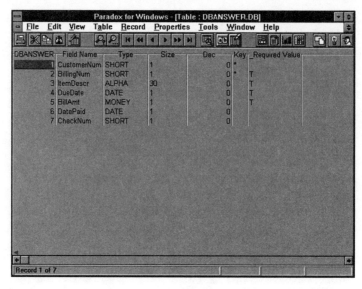

Figure 4.5. *The AR master table's structure (displayed by the Table utility).*

You'll naturally also want the AR master table to have valid contents. Specifically, allowing records in the AR table for which there is no CUSTOMER record would prevent you from collecting any money, since the debt is not associated with any person or business in that case.

You can guarantee that AR records all belong to some CUSTOMER record by defining a referential integrity relationship on the AR file with the CUSTOMER file. Now you know why I showed you how to do this in the project manager application. Here you put that knowledge to use, for the real thing. Figure 4.6 displays the referential integrity relations defined on AR with CUSTOMER.

The Accounts Payable tables are very similar to the Accounts Receivable tables, beginning with the VENDOR master table. The main difference is that the VENDOR table is keyed on the vendor number, not on a customer number. Here, *you* are the customer. The VENDOR master table's structure is displayed in Figure 4.7.

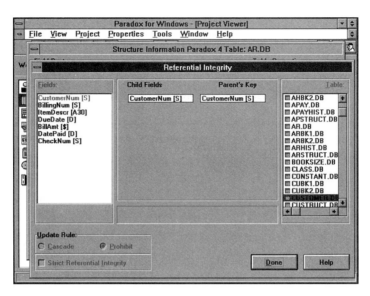

Figure 4.6. *The AR master table's referential integrity definition.*

4

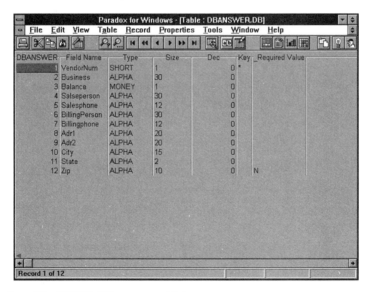

Figure 4.7. *The VENDOR master table's structure.*

Accounts Payable also has a transaction master table, which is the AP master table (APAY.DB). This table also has a compound key, composed of the vendor number and an invoice number, as shown in Figure 4.8.

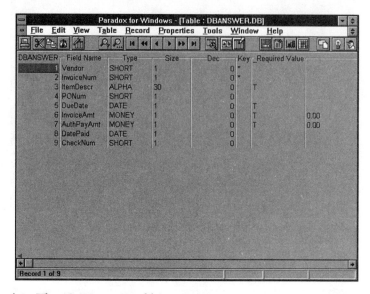

Figure 4.8. *The APAY master table's structure.*

Finally, you'll want to prevent "orphaned" AP transactions, just as you did for the AR master. Hence, another referential integrity relation, defined on the APAY table with the Vendor table, is in order. This relation is illustrated in Figure 4.9.

These, then, are the major tables needed by the DPW AR/AP system: the CUSTOMER and AR master tables, with an ARHIST archive that looks just like the AR master—and the VENDOR and APAY master tables, with an APHIST that looks just like the AP master.

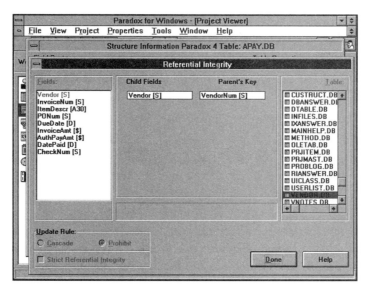

Figure 4.9. *The APAY master table's referential integrity definition.*

Planning Table Linkages

The necessary referential integrity has now been defined on all the tables that need it, but that doesn't actually link the tables. Integrity is enforced at the table level, with the Paradox database engine doing all the work for you.

Linking tables occurs within forms, not tables. In particular, the transaction posting forms for both AR and AP will be multi-table forms, having the secondary transaction file linked to the account master file. For the AR subsystem, for example, the CUSTOMER table is the master table, while the AR table is defined in the form as being the secondary table linked to the CUSTOMER table (by the customer number fields). A similar situation will exist in the AP subsystem.

Some of the application's utilities, which will implement various functions in ObjectPAL, will simulate the forms' linkages with code. This will all be done with table cursors, of the kind you've just seen demonstrated, but with a degree of detailed control of a table's records that you've not yet seen. There are three ways you can use a table cursor to control an underlying table, and there are three more ways you can use table cursors to perform the essence of the linking function inherent in multi-table forms.

The three ways you can use a table cursor on an underlying table vary in their efficiency (meaning speed of access), and are as follows:

- [ ] You can attach a table cursor to a table frame embedded in a multi-table form. Although you can delay resynchronizing the table frame display until you've processed all the records you want, this is still only moderately efficient, because the table frame UIObject (a User Interface Design Object) still sits between the table cursor and the underlying table.

- [ ] You can attach a table cursor to a table view that is open on the table. This is the least efficient method because the table view will change on the screen depending on what the table cursor is doing. This, as you may imagine, considerably slows the processing of a large number of records.

- [ ] You can open a table cursor directly on a table. This is the most efficient method for handling large numbers of records. Even though changes made in the table cursor must still be posted to the underlying table, this happens quickly, and there are no intervening display objects involved in the process. This is the method you will use to access tables with ObjectPAL methods.

With the overall method of using table cursors in hand, you must now choose a method of manually performing the table linking function in ObjectPAL code. Obviously, the method with the least coding work is the one you want. It so happens that the desired method will also be the one that is most efficient at runtime. The three methods, from least to most desirable, are as follows:

- [ ] You can hard-code a `while` or `for` loop (there is no do-loop in ObjectPAL), read every record, and manually test the field values for the ones you want. Clearly, this is the least desirable method, since you do all the work; and it will probably be slower than the other methods, though perhaps not too much so.

- [ ] You can use a `scan` *tcursor* `for` *booleanexpression*: ... `endscan` block. The *booleanexpression* is where you code your criteria for processing a record within the scan loop. This method is better, but it's still possible to do it with a little less code, letting the engine do as much of the work as possible.

- [ ] You can first code a *tcursor*.`setFilter()` method call to set the range of records the table cursor can "see," and then code a `scan` *tcursor* : ... `endscan` loop. This is the most sophisticated and most efficient method of accessing linked records, and is the one always used in this book.

Developer's Tip: You may have to combine the last two techniques in the previous list for accessing linked sets of records, if one of the criteria you need to specify involves testing a non-key or nonindex record field. `setFilter()` works only with index fields in the currently used index.

In that regard, however, you can use the `tcursor.switchIndex()` method to choose a secondary index, or call it with no arguments to switch back to the primary key. If you do this, be sure to switch indexes first, and only then call the `setFilter()` method.

Identifying the Engine's Programming Requirements

If you persist in the slightly unconventional view of viewing the application's engine as being nothing more than the tables involved (since Paradox does so much of the work of handling tables), there is no programming necessary for the engine at all.

However, it's convenient to regard a table frame open on one of these tables embedded in a form as part of the engine. The posting functions/forms for both AR and AP will embed table frames of the transaction tables in the forms, and there is some field-level programming that will need to be done there—although not very much. Most of the programming this system requires will reside in pushbutton methods attached to various user interface forms, especially for the batch processes.

The kind of programming that will be needed for the linked table frames will involve code for assisting the user in entering data, but especially for preventing the user from doing things that would foul up the integrity of the system. Even though referential integrity has been defined on the linked tables, it's still otherwise possible for a user to do something such as delete an open AR receivables transaction record, or an open AP invoice. You don't want that to happen unless the user has taken specific action to close the receivable or invoice.

Thus, most of the programming for linked table frames will revolve around trapping certain actions, examining them, and either permitting or denying them. This can be done by attaching the code to the table frame's `action()` method and calling the `eventInfo.id()` method to see what is happening. If the user is trying to delete an open transaction, for example, you can detect this by looking for the `DataDeleteRecord` event and then checking the record fields to see if their state will permit the deletion.

139

At other times, you'll want to prevent the user from changing certain fields if other fields have already been entered. Detecting this situation also means trapping action events. In this case, you would be looking for the `DataBeginEdit` action. In any case, you can stop the undesirable action by simply coding the statement `disableDefault`, which prevents Paradox from carrying out its default action (such as deleting or editing the record).

Programming an application's engine won't involve large quantities of code, but the code will be satisfyingly sophisticated.

Modification Notes

At this stage in the development process, you really can't do anything useful by simply copying an application you've done before. What you can do is look at the other application to see why you made certain design decisions.

Since I happen to have written a couple of AR/AP systems before, this is exactly what I've done here. I made several design decisions based on experience with previous systems written in other languages and other environments (both mainframe and PC-based). One of the significant design decisions was to eliminate the capability to make partial payments on an AP invoice.

It isn't actually that difficult to supply partial payment functionality, but it takes a good deal of code, and gets complicated at times. Since this is a first-application book, I chose to avoid such complications. And since the time frame here is 14 days, I also chose to eliminate lots of bulky code.

An interesting modification project for you, after you've finished this project, would be to go back and provide AP partial payment capability. Another interesting and very useful modification would be to add the capability to handle itemized invoices and item-level payment. Be warned, however, that this will get very detailed, very quickly; you'll need to start with a third AP table, the INVITEMS table, and there will be a lot of field-level programming involved.

Debugging the Process

You may have learned by now that the best way to debug the design process for an AR/AP system is to go out and buy a commercial one. After all, you can get a good Windows-based system these days for less than $100.

I'm just testing you. You and I both know that the reason you want to write the system yourself is so that it will be *your* system, and it will do what *you* want.

Just as I mentioned in the section titled "Modification Notes," there is very little program debugging that can be done at this point. That doesn't mean, however, that you should not be critical of what is going on at this time.

You should be especially critical about the specific features of the application you think you want to include at this point. Hastily assuming that you'll provide such-and-such a feature can quickly explode into vast amounts of work. It would be a very good idea for you to examine the design for AR/AP at this stage and see just how much work *you* think it will involve. It will open your eyes later and test your mettle as a Paradox for Windows programmer and developer. If you have already done a fair amount of Paradox for Windows development, you already know that it won't be too bad. On the other hand, you may well have bought this book just because you've already jumped in the deep water and tried an ambitious application on your own. Don't worry if that is the case. I certainly did a double-take or two when I first met Paradox for Windows. It's a whole different animal, isn't it?

4

5

Defining the Application's Interfaces

Today is the day that you and I become full-time partners in developing your first Paradox for Windows application. I will design and present to you the AR side of the application, plus all the extra utilities and support software, and you'll design most of the AP side.

The one exception to this plan is in the AP posting form itself. I went ahead and designed that form, and supplied the programming for the AP table frame that automatically computes vendor balance amounts and updates balances when you change or delete existing AP records.

This will be a lengthy and busy chapter. I have used 40 screen shots to display the forms, reports, and utilities designs. After all, you want a first application that really does something noticeable. Of course, this means that you'll have to get really busy, too, to keep up with your part in the AP design.

There are so many parts to the application, in fact, that you might question whether all the parts can be designed and put together in 14 days. The answer is *yes, they can.* For the parts that I did for you, I proceeded in two phases. First, I researched, designed, and built the multimedia-oriented tools (MMT and its related pieces, and the *Voice Notes!* multimedia notepad), plus the hypermedia Windows help files, in about five days. The rest of the software took about another five days. And while all this was going on, I was writing this book at a fairly steady clip. So it can be done, because that's the beauty of object-oriented tools like Paradox for Windows.

This chapter breaks up the workload into two major parts: the primary and the secondary resources required for the AR/AP system. *Primary resources* are those forms, reports, and objects used directly in the main application. *Secondary resources* are those forms, reports, and objects used in support of the application.

Defining Primary Resource for AR/AP

You first need to identify and define the primary resources required by the AR/AP application. The primary resources include the components required for multimedia support (beyond the Multimedia Theater, that is), the menus and control panels that integrate the application, the forms with which the users will interact with the application, and the reports used on a regular basis (as opposed to ad hoc reports, which come later). There are also the interface's programming requirements to think about.

Preparing for Multimedia Support

Because you already have at your disposal numerous ObjectPAL sources for driving multimedia events, you need only to identify and define those non-Paradox components that will be needed to support the application's interfaces.

It turns out that there are just two things beyond the ObjectPAL methods we'll need, and both of them are associated with plugging multimedia features into the application's Windows help files.

The first component is the CMEDIA.DLL routine, a C language routine that will enable hooking MMPLAYER calls directly into the help system for the application. Because I can't assume that all of my readers are C programmers, I have supplied both the C language sources and the runtime DLL module itself for this component. Feel free to use this DLL any way you like, in this or any other application.

The second component needed for multimedia support is also associated with the Windows help system. This is the VNOTES.INI file, which will reside in your system's \WINDOWS directory. You need this piece because the Paradox current working directory isn't the same thing as the DOS/WINDOWS current directory. We'll use the INI file to direct CMEDIA to the correct location of the WAV files used in the hypermedia help documents.

At this point, I only want to identify these components for you. You'll see the complete contents of these components on Day 7, "Building the Application's Interfaces," when you actually start building the interfaces—and on Day 11, "Writing the Application's Online Documentation," where the Windows online help system all comes together.

Integrating the Application's Interfaces with Menus and Control Panels

The first component of the AR/AP system the user will actually see is the main menu or main control panel form, from which all other functions of the system are launched. Because that's the case, it seems good to select a primary entry point to the system that's appealing to the user and fairly complete in its integration of all the remaining parts of the system.

One way to do this, of course, is with the traditional Windows blank form that has a strip menu across the top of the client area of the window. In fact, I intend to steer you away from this approach because it is one that is just not very exciting.

To illustrate this point, I put together just such a menu on a "main" form. I did not make it terribly complete, because I only intend for it to be an illustration of what you *don't* want in the system. This possible main form is MENUS.FSL (or FDL), and it is shown in Figure 5.1.

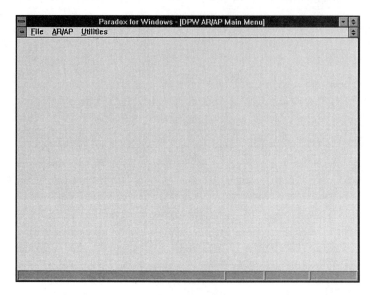

Figure 5.1. *A rather boring way to launch an application: the MENU form.*

MENUS.FSL isn't very exciting, is it? That's precisely why you are going to take another route into the application. On the other hand, don't completely discard the notion of Windows-style menus, for they have their place, and you might sometime want to use one. For that reason, I will show you how to put one together using Paradox for Windows when you start building the application on Day 6.

One of the big reasons that I often don't like traditional menuing systems is that much of the system is hidden, lurking around down in the depths of the menu's subordinate pull-down menus. Many features aren't immediately visible to the eye and therefore don't give the user a sense of power and control over the application.

That's also why I often turn to the "control panel" approach to opening and integrating the application. Modeled on the appearance of physical control panels, a control panel form puts graphical controls (pushbuttons, graphic icons, and so on) for all the system's major features right before the user's eyes. The visual appeal of the DPW AR/AP Main Selection Panel (DPWMAIN.FDL) is considerably greater than that of the traditional menu approach. Look at DPWMAIN as shown in Figure 5.2, and see whether you agree.

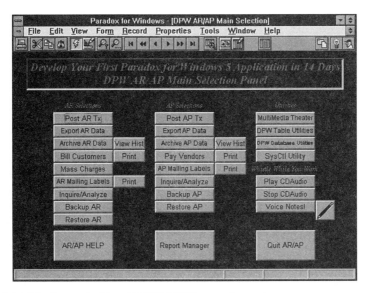

Figure 5.2. *The better-looking DPWMAIN control panel.*

DPWMAIN is the form we'll actually use as the primary entry point into the AR/AP system. Notice in Figure 5.2 that there are 33 major system controls in plain sight and in graphical form. That would be far too many to display all at once using an ordinary menu.

Identifying and Planning the Application's Forms

After DPWMAIN, which I persist in thinking of as a control panel rather than as a form, there are two forms that are the very heart of the AR/AP system. These are the AR and AP posting forms (ARPOST.FDL and APPOST.FDL). On these forms, linked views of the customer and AR tables (for AR), and of the vendor and AP tables (for AP) provide all the access the user needs to maintain the master tables, post new transactions in the system, and maintain old transactions. The ARPOST form is shown in Figure 5.3.

Notice in Figure 5.3 that all customer information is visible and available for maintenance, and all AR data is also visible and available for maintenance. You should also recall that on Day 4, "Defining the Application's Engine," I mentioned that the engine's programming would actually take place in a table frame on a form. ARPOST is the form that I referred to. When you build the form on Day 6, ObjectPAL methods will be

attached to fields in records in the AR table frame, as shown in the previous figure. These ObjectPAL methods will automate the process of updating customer balances, and also provide a little buffering against possible user mistakes in using this form.

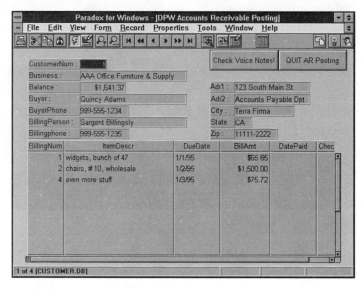

Figure 5.3. *The AR posting form, ARPOST.*

Because the posting forms are the very core of the system, I have also gone ahead and designed the AP posting form, which is shown in Figure 5.4. But don't get lazy; you go to work right after that.

Naturally, ARPOST and APPOST aren't the only forms in the system. Click most of the controls on DPWMAIN, and you'll get another form describing what you should do next. That's the case with the next AR selection control on DPWMAIN, the Export AR Data button. The AREXPORT.FDL form is shown in Figure 5.5.

The AREXPORT form provides a means for the user to export either customer or AR data to a quoted, comma-delimited ASCII text file (the so-called *DIF format*) so that it can be imported into other applications. I exported the AR data, for example, and imported the resulting file into a Quattro Pro spreadsheet while testing this part of the application.

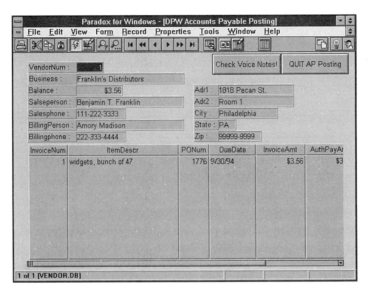

Figure 5.4. *The AP posting form, APPOST.*

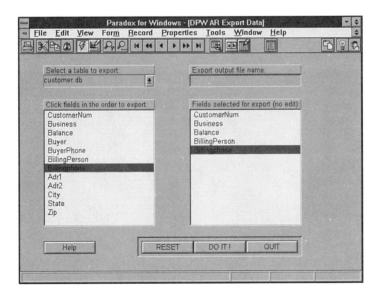

Figure 5.5. *The DPW AR Export Data form, AREXPORT.FDL.*

To enable the user to export data in the most flexible possible fashion, we'll provide a listbox on the left side of the form that displays all the fields in the currently selected table.

The user can click those fields, in any order, and they will appear in the Fields selected for export listbox on the right side of the form. At the top right of the form is an undefined edit field in which the user can name the ASCII file into which to write the exported data.

AREXPORT also provides four pushbuttons for controlling the export form's actions. The Help button will invoke the Windows help system for the application; the RESET button will deselect all fields for export, so the user can redefine them another way; the DO IT! button starts the export operation; and the QUIT button leaves the application and returns to DPWMAIN.

The next button in DPWMAIN's AR selections column is the Archive AR Data button, and ironically it's an immediate exception to my statement that most buttons call other forms. The AR archive function scans the linked customer and AR files, and "retires" AR records that have been posted as paid. That is, AR records with a nonblank DatePaid field are moved to the ARHIST table and deleted from the AR table. All the logic for this operation is contained in the `pushbutton()` method attached directly to the control button.

To the right of the Archive AR Data button, you'll see a smaller button labeled View Hist. Clicking this control button produces not another form, but a table view on the ARHIST file, so that the user can examine the AR records that were just retired. A small example of that table view is shown in Figure 5.6.

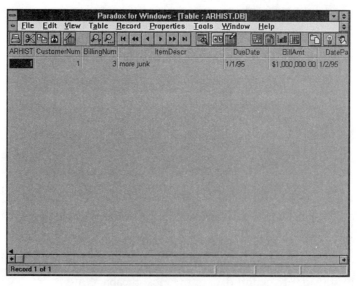

Figure 5.6. *The ARHIST table view, produced by the View Hist button.*

One of your tasks will be to clone the AR archive logic and adapt it to AP record retirement. Thus the APAYHIST table is empty, as shown in Figure 5.7, but I have already defined the AP View Hist button's ObjectPAL source for you.

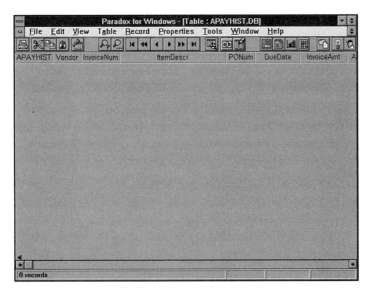

Figure 5.7. *The APHIST table view, produced by the View Hist button.*

For the moment, we'll skip over the AR Bill Customers button and its Print button, because these invoke a report. Next in the AR selections is the Mass Charges control button. Posting mass charges is a batch process, but it will require another form to control its operation. The AR Post Mass Charges form, ARMASSC.FDL, is shown in Figure 5.8.

There are three groups of controls on the left side of the ARMASSC form, and three corresponding text boxes on the right side of the form that explain what the control fields and objects do.

When the user clicks the Use Filters radio button, the mass charge run will post new charges only to customer accounts with numbers ranging from the Starting Account Number field's value to that of the Ending Account Number field. Otherwise, the mass charge will be applied to all customers in the system. In Figure 5.8, the form is set up to apply an annual renewal charge only to accounts 1 through 4.

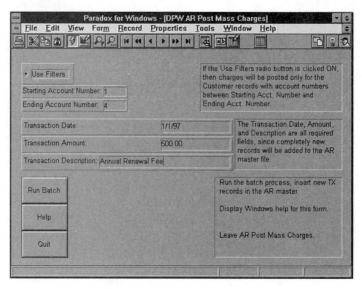

Figure 5.8. *The AR Post Mass Charges form, ARMASSC.FDL.*

The next group of fields enables input of the transaction date, amount, and description. These fields are always required because the charges posted will be meaningless without them.

The last group of controls is a set of three pushbuttons. The Run Batch button contains ObjectPAL to check the validity of the requested charges and to begin the batch run of mass charges. The Help and Quit buttons do exactly that—they go to the Windows help file, and quit the form.

Back on the DPWMAIN form, the next control is the Inquire/Analyze pushbutton. This button will start the AR Inquiry Select form (ARINQ.FDL). ARINQ is shown in Figure 5.9.

The AR/AP system will provide six canned inquiries for the user, for each of the AR and AP sides. I have designed the AR side as shown in Figure 5.9. To use one of the inquiries (which may be a true query, a report, a chart, or a crosstab), the user merely needs to click the correct radio button and then click the Launch Inquiry pushbutton. The various kinds of inquiry outputs will be discussed a little later in the section "Planning for the Application's Charts, Crosstabs, and Queries."

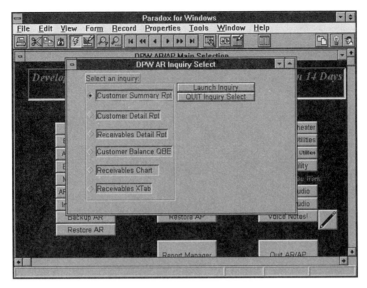

Figure 5.9. *The AR Inquiry Select form, ARINQ.FDL.*

Identifying and Planning the Application's Reports

As I just mentioned, some of the user's canned inquiries will produce report output, but there are two major reports in the AR system that need to be handled separately.

First is the DPW AR Billing Statement report, which you use to tell customers how much money they should pay. This report is launched from the DPWMAIN form using the Bill Customers button. The billing statements report is shown in Figure 5.10.

You may notice that Figure 5.10 shows the delivered version of the report. This is generally true in all the figures, but the source version (RSL files for reports) are also on the companion CD-ROM.

In order to send billing statements to customers, it would be nice to have mailing labels produced by the system. The second major report output is the AR Mailing Labels report, which is launched by the button of that same name on DPWMAIN. The mailing labels report is in the ARMAIL.RDL file, as shown in Figure 5.11.

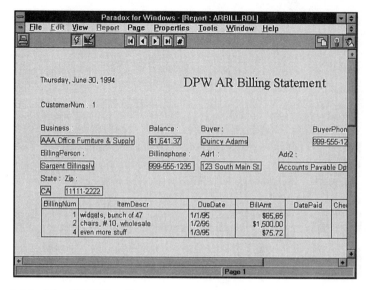

Figure 5.10. *The AR Billing Statements report, ARBILL.RDL.*

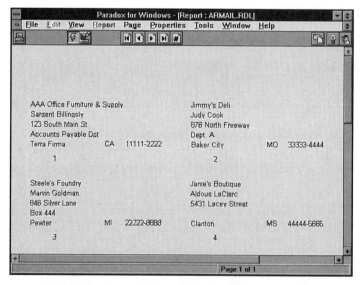

Figure 5.11. *The AR Mailing Labels report, ARMAIL.RDL.*

Having only two selections on the main control panel for reports is a little deceptive. There are actually five reports in the AR system, but three of them are used to display output from the canned user inquiries. (See Figure 5.9.)

Looking back at the main selection panel (Figure 5.2), you may notice that there are two extra pushbuttons, labeled Print, in the AR Selections column of controls. One each is attached to the right end of the report buttons. The Print buttons send the corresponding report directly to the print spooler, whereas the report buttons themselves open the reports and display them in a Paradox report window (preview mode). All reports can be previewed first and then sent to the printer from the report window; this is a built-in feature of the Paradox report window.

Identifying the Interface's Programming Requirements

One of the AR Selection's controls (Archive AR Data) doesn't open a new form. Rather, the pushbutton does all its work with ObjectPAL code attached directly to it, sending messages to the status bar at the bottom of the main selection panel's form window.

The programming required for archiving AR records should be of great interest to you. In that method you'll see how to use tables, table cursors, and dynamic arrays to do table programming without the aid of a form. The Backup AR and Restore AR buttons work this way, too, but they are covered later today (in "Planning for the Application's Backup and Recovery Functions.")

There will be some interesting programming to do for the other form-based functions as well. Both the Export AR Data and Mass Charges functions require similarly sophisticated programming. In the first of these, you'll discover how to use TextStreams, and the second will need more (and more complex) table programming.

The reports provided by the system are unique in that they require no programming at all.

Defining Secondary Resources for AR/AP

The core functionality of the AR/AP system is provided in a few relatively simple parts. But they aren't all that's required to service and maintain a system like this. There are a number of secondary resources that must be defined.

Some of the secondary resources can be considered necessary parts of the system, whereas others are just nice touches. Taken all together, however, they do seem to make for a nice,

finished system. We'll provide (you and I together) secondary resources in the form of table and database utilities, backup and recovery functions, charts, crosstabs, and queries, several batch processes, and some support utilities.

Planning the Application's Table and Database Utilities

Two utilities for working with tables and databases will be supplied with the AR/AP system. The first of these is the Table Maintenance Utility. Its form (TBUTIL.FDL) is shown in Figure 5.12.

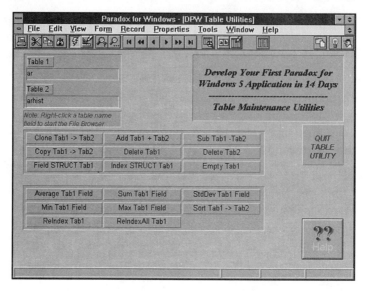

Figure 5.12. *The Table Maintenance Utility, TBUTIL.FDL.*

Using the Table Maintenance Utility, you can create, delete, and manipulate tables in a variety of ways. The form's ObjectPAL has been written especially so that table addition and subtraction works like arithmetic expressions. For example, you can add table 1 to table 2, and the result goes back into table 1. The same thing applies to table subtraction. Everything else, however, works just like the ObjectPAL commands behind them would lead you to expect.

The Database and Query Utility has a slightly different purpose. It is used to open databases, not tables, and then to verify or delete tables within that database (a database

in Paradox for Windows is simply a directory containing a collection of tables), and to work with queries in text format. The Database and Query Utility's form (DBUTIL.FDL) is shown in Figure 5.13.

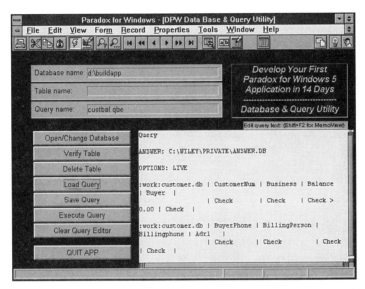

Figure 5.13. *The Database and Query Utility, DBUTIL.FDL.*

Planning for the Application's Backup and Recovery Functions

AR backup and recovery functions are launched from the DPW Main Selection panel by clicking the Backup AR and Restore AR pushbuttons. Like the archive function, these functions don't open any further forms. They simply display status messages in the status bar at the bottom of the form window.

Backup and recovery is in fact one of the trickiest parts of the entire AR/AP application. The reason is that the referential integrity relationships defined on the detail tables (discussed on Day 4) impose some very real and very tricky constraints on the manner in which you can copy tables. How I got around these constraints, as well as how you can get around them when building the AP parts of the application, is covered in detail on Day 9, "Building the Application's Support Utilities."

The main issues here are the conventions that will be used for naming backup files, how the naming process can be handled by the ObjectPAL code, and how to keep synchronized copies of the master and detail tables. Table 5.1 details the naming conventions that will be used for the AR system's backup files.

Table 5.1. AR backup filenaming conventions.

Application filename	Backup filename
CUSTOMER.DB	CUBK*nnnn*.DB
AR.DB	ARBK*nnnn*.DB
ARHIST.DB	AHBK*nnnn*.DB

The idea in selecting a backup filenaming structure is to enable the user to keep multiple versions of AR backup files. This is necessary in the real world because of auditors, year-end reporting, and similar considerations.

As you can see in Table 5.1, the naming conventions actually would permit keeping 9,999 backup versions of the AR files. That would, of course, be a silly thing to do, but the system enables it in principle.

Selecting such a naming convention presents us with the problem of keeping track of what the next backup generation or version number should be. ObjectPAL does have directory functions that will enable you to see what the last-used filename was. That won't help, however, because a user may want to overwrite a particular backup version, or may have deleted certain backup copies from the middle of the set of files.

The solution is another Windows-style INI file. This file will be named ARARC.INI, and will have an profile entry labeled `nextfilenum`. At runtime, the ObjectPAL code can simply fetch that private profile string and also give the user a chance to override the computed version number. Flexibility like this makes users happy.

Because the presence of referential integrity makes the backup and recovery process somewhat tricky, we'll also have to give some serious thought to keeping synchronized backup copies of the system tables. Part of the solution to this problem is simple: the functions will back up or restore all three of the AR tables at one time, using the same version number for each backup file copy. The other part of the solution is found in the ObjectPAL logic for backup and recovery. That will be covered on Day 9, when you actually write the code for these functions.

Planning for the Application's Charts, Crosstabs, and Queries

The ARINQ inquiry selection form contains six controls for initiating various canned inquires. (See Figure 5.9.) The first one to look at here is the AR Receivables by Date chart, shown in Figure 5.14.

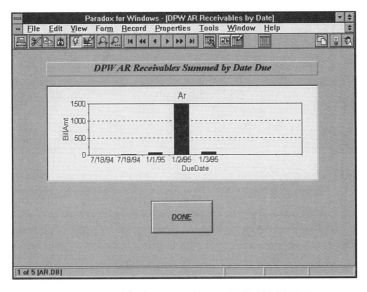

Figure 5.14. *The AR Receivables by Date chart, ARCHART.FDL.*

As you can see, the chart is embedded in the ARCHART form. It presents a simple, 1-D chart of receivables transaction amounts distributed over time.

Unlike the receivables chart, which summarizes all receivables for all customers, the AR Receivables by Date and Customer crosstab presents a tabular display of receivables transactions over time for each customer. The crosstab form, ARXTAB.FDL, is shown in Figure 5.15.

In the crosstab form, the record navigation buttons on the toolbar mean something. You can use them to navigate from one customer to another: the crosstab summarizes receivables for the currently displayed customer record.

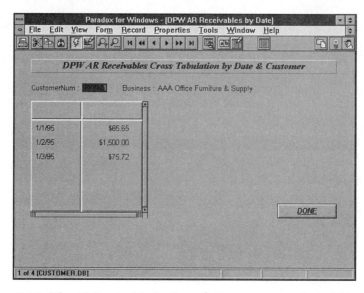

Figure 5.15. *The AR Receivables by Date & Customer crosstab, ARXTAB.FDL.*

The Customer Balance QBE selection on the ARINQ form is the true query of the six inquiries. When this query is run, the results are displayed in a table view, as shown in Figure 5.16.

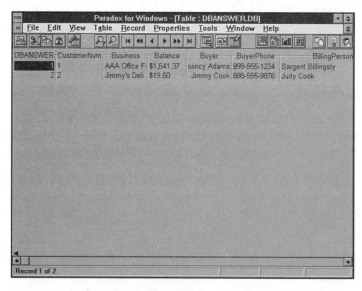

Figure 5.16. *Results from the Customer Balance QBE query displayed in a table view.*

To run this query, the ObjectPAL method for the Launch Inquiry button first reads the CUSTBAL query file (.QBE file) as a text stream, and then calls the `executeQBEString()` Paradox procedure. The resulting table view shows only those customers who still owe money.

As mentioned earlier, three of the inquiry selections are actually reports. These are the receivables detail, customer detail, and customer summary reports.

The receivables detail report/inquiry produces a report giving all receivables transaction for each customer. The resulting report, as shown in Figure 5.17, is laid out with linked tables much like that as in the AR posting form.

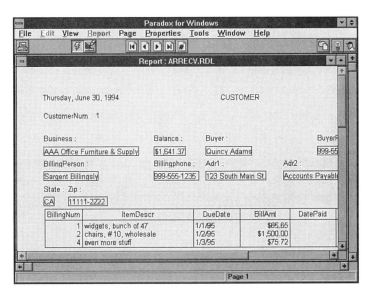

Figure 5.17. *Results from the Receivables Detail Report inquiry being displayed in a report window.*

The customer detail inquiry also produces a report, but the page layout contains just one customer record per page, with all customer table details presented in a column. This is shown in Figure 5.18.

The customer summary inquiry, by contrast, produces a report with a tabular layout, one customer record per line. This report is a summary report in that only the business name, balance, and location is included in the output. The customer summary report/inquiry is shown in Figure 5.19.

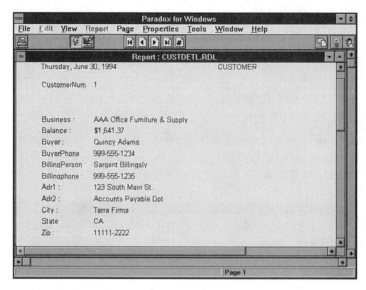

Figure 5.18. *Results from the Customer Detail Report inquiry being displayed in a report window.*

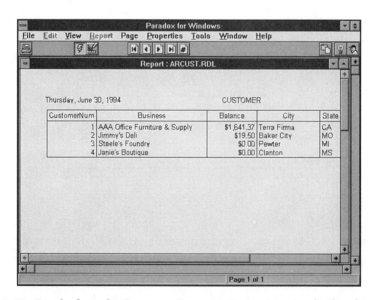

Figure 5.19. *Results from the Customer Summary Report inquiry displayed in a report window.*

Planning for the Application's Batch Processes

There are two clearly recognizable batch process controls on the DPW Main Selection Panel. These are the export and mass charge functions. One could also argue that AR record archival (retirement) and the main reports are in their own way batch processes. We'll simply accept the convention that export and mass charges are the batch processes, however.

The mass charges function has a feature that needs to be mentioned now, while planning for its implementation. You may recall that the mass charges form did not provide a way for the user to specify billing numbers for the charges. Indeed, there isn't any way to do, because many transactions will be automatically generated.

So how are you going to determine the proper billing number for each generated charge? The answer is satisfyingly sneaky. As the ObjectPAL code runs through the customer file, we'll use a table cursor with a filter placed on it to access the linked AR records for each customer record. Then with a single ObjectPAL function call, the code can simply move to the end of the visible AR records and read the last used billing number. Increment that by one, and *voila!*—you have your new billing number. This is another instance of how you can let the Paradox engine do the work for you.

Planning the Application's Support Utilities

A lot of the richness of the AR/AP application's features lies in its support utilities. For example, the application's users can run the main reports by using the DPW Main Selection Panel's control buttons, and they can run any report by using the DPW Report/ Print Manager. The Report Manager is launched by clicking the button with that label on the main selection panel.

The Report Manager is packaged in a form, RPTMGR.FDL, with several controls for streamlining report production. The RPTMGR form is shown in Figure 5.20.

The main selection panel's Windows help file has detailed instructions for using the Report Manager, so I won't go over that here. The idea is to allow printing of reports in a number of ways activated by clicking the radio buttons on the form. Many of the options require that you also enter a value in one of the fields to the left of the form. You can even do duplex printing (printing on both sides of the paper) with the Report Manager.

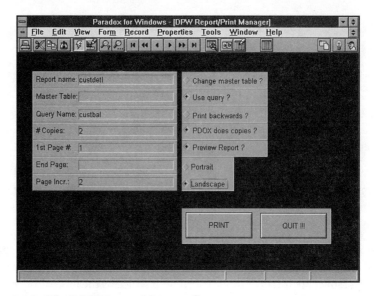

Figure 5.20. *The DPW Report Manager form.*

I want to save the System Control Panel utility for last, because there is so much to it, so now I'll jump to the Whistle While You Work stack of controls on the main selection panel. This group of utility functions provides some nifty features that, strictly speaking, aren't required to support the application. They do, however, provide a little fun and give the application a finished touch.

First, you can listen to your favorite audio CD while you work. Just click the Play CDAudio button (be sure there is a CD in the drive!) and go back to work. You can leave the main selection panel, or even Paradox, and come back to it later. The CD will continue to play. It will continue to play, in fact, until you click the Stop CDAudio button. The ObjectPAL for this feature is so simple that no supporting form is required.

I have also provided two kinds of notepad for the AR/AP application. First, you can record and play audio notes using the *Voice Notes!* application. *The Voice Notes!* form (VNOTES.FDL) is shown in Figure 5.21.

Using *Voice Notes!* is simple. Just add a record, enter the time, date, and annotation, and leave the input focus anywhere on that record. Then click the Record VNote button and start talking. Just don't forget to click the Stop Recording button when you are done, or your disk will fill up pretty quickly!

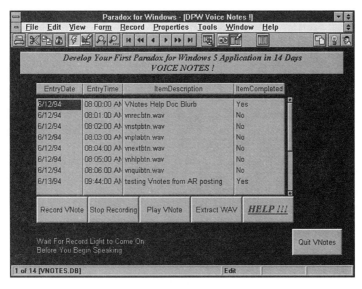

Figure 5.21. *The* Voice Notes! *(VNOTES.FDL) form.*

VNotes has its own detailed Windows help file, too. I mention this specifically because the VNotes help file isn't a normal Windows hypertext help file; it is a hypermedia help file. If you click any of the graphic images in the help file, I talk to you (I hope you like Southern-fried twang). The first page of the VNotes hypermedia help file is shown in Figure 5.22.

Because I thought you just might be curious as to how I made a Windows help file talk, I used the VNotes Windows help project as the primary example on Day 11, "Writing the Application's Online Documentation."

In Figure 5.2, you might notice that there is a little pencil graphic object tacked on to the right end of the VNotes pushbutton on the main selection panel. Click that pencil and you get the DPW NotePad, a scratchpad Windows application you can use for scratch notes. It isn't meant to be a real text editor or word processor, but it can help you clear your desk of scratch paper. The NotePad window is shown in Figure 5.23.

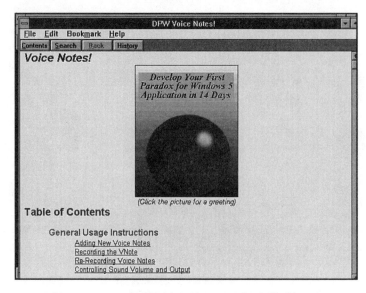

Figure 5.22. *The* Voice Notes! *Windows hypermedia help file.*

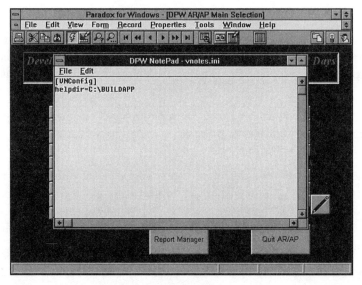

Figure 5.23. *The DPW NotePad window.*

Because NotePad is a C language Windows application, I have not included its source on the CD-ROM. For those of you who are interested, however, the application was created by modifying the EDITFILE.C program that comes with the Windows SDK.

The next several figures deal with the DPW System Control Panel. This application lets you play administrator for Paradox for Windows, and indeed, for the network, if you are on one. Of course, if you aren't an administrator, you can't play network administrator. The System Control Panel is launched by clicking the SysCtl Utility button on the main selection panel. The System Control Panel's main form is shown in Figure 5.24.

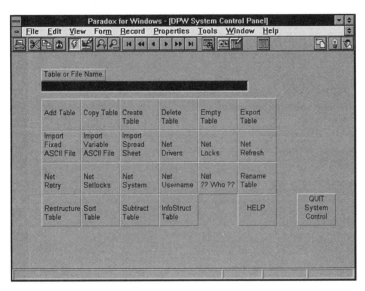

Figure 5.24. *The DPW System Control Panel (SYSCTL.FDL) form.*

As you can see, the System Control Panel provides much of the functionality of the Table Utility, but it goes much further. The System Control Panel is indeed complicated enough that I have supplied it with its own Windows help file, too. Well, maybe I cheated a little: clicking the Help button on the System Control Panel actually calls up the DPW main help and automatically navigates to the SysCtl topic, as shown in Figure 5.25.

Although the System Control Panel does a lot, it really doesn't advertise my programming prowess because it was mostly done by calling Paradox system dialog boxes. Using these dialog boxes can give your application a lot of power in a real hurry, without a lot of programming. With just a single ObjectPAL call, for example, you can launch the Add Table system dialog box, as shown in Figure 5.26.

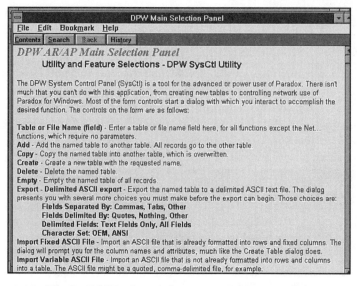

Figure 5.25. *The SysCtl Windows help topic in DPW main help.*

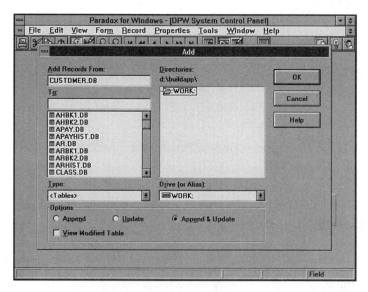

Figure 5.26. *The Paradox Add Table dialog box, launched by the System Control Panel.*

Notice in this figure that the Add Records From table name is already filled in. That's because you must specify the table name in the System Control Panel before invoking the Add dialog box. All that remains is to click the table name in the listbox to which you want to add the records.

Copying tables works almost exactly the same way, as shown in Figure 5.27.

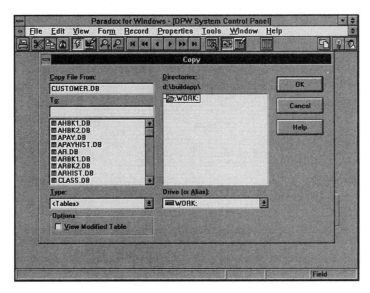

Figure 5.27. *The Paradox Copy Table dialog box, launched by the System Control Panel.*

You also can create new tables using the Create Paradox for Windows Table dialog box, as shown in Figure 5.28. This is another one of the System Control Panel selections that does require you first to enter a table name or filename.

In the other system dialog boxes you've seen so far, Paradox indicated the table name or filename passed to it by the System Control Panel by just showing the complete name. Other dialog boxes do things a little differently. The Table Export dialog box, for example, just displays an asterisk (*) in the Table Name edit field, as shown in Figure 5.29. You don't have to key in a name at this point (just click OK in the dialog box to accept the name you typed into the System Control Panel field), but it looks strange compared to the other method of displaying the name.

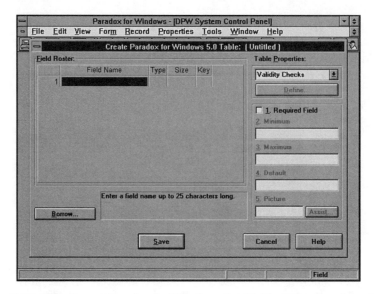

Figure 5.28. *The Create Paradox for Windows 5.0 Table dialog box, launched by the System Control Panel.*

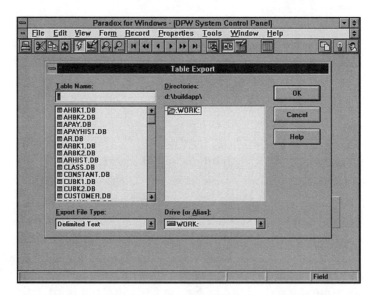

Figure 5.29. *The Paradox Table Export dialog box, launched by the System Control Panel.*

Table Export is also one of those dialog boxes that requires more than one dialog window to completely specify the requested operation. After clicking OK in the Table Export dialog window of Figure 5.29, you'll see the Delimited ASCII Export dialog box. Click its OK button, and you'll see the Text Options dialog window, shown in Figure 5.30.

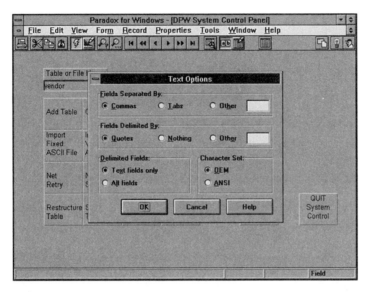

Figure 5.30. *The Paradox Table Export dialog box's Text Options window, launched by the System Control Panel.*

When you click OK in this dialog window, you are returned to the Delimited ASCII Export dialog. Click OK again, and the export function finally takes place.

The Fixed Length ASCII Import function supplies yet another dialog window format. In this dialog box, you get a combination of edit fields for naming tables and files, plus an abbreviated form of the table create dialog box, as shown in Figure 5.31.

The System Control Panel also provides several network control and display functions. The first of these to be discussed here is the Net Locks function. I actually needed this function while developing some of the code for this book, and it is the real reason why I wrote the application. Having written it, I couldn't resist passing it along to you.

Figure 5.32 illustrates the output of the Net Locks function for a table for which there are no outstanding locks.

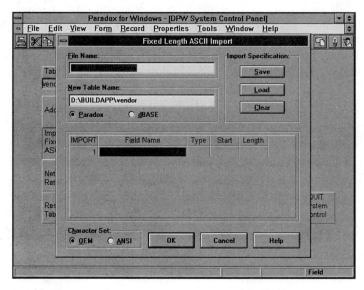

Figure 5.31. *The Paradox Fixed Length ASCII Import dialog box, launched by the System Control Panel.*

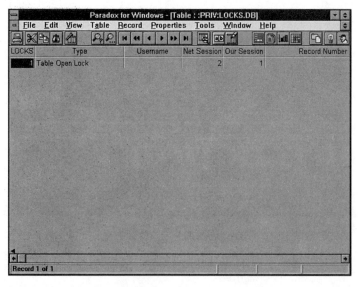

Figure 5.32. *The Paradox Net Locks table view display, launched by the System Control Panel.*

If simply investigating system-wide locks isn't enough for you, you can set them, too. Click the System Control Panel's Net Setlocks control button, and you get the Paradox Table Locks dialog box (shown in Figure 5.33) from which you can manually set or remove any lock, anywhere.

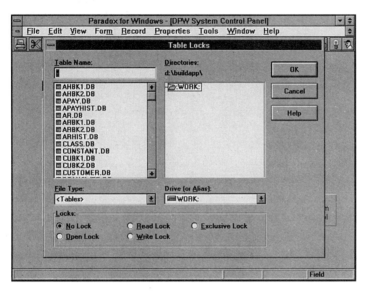

Figure 5.33. *The Paradox Table Locks dialog window, launched by the System Control Panel.*

The System Control Panel has many more features, but you can investigate those on your own. Now, it's time to move on to something that's directly related to the AR/AP system—the DPW AR/AP installation procedure.

As a matter of fact, this is the procedure you used to install the sample code from the CD-ROM to your hard drive. The point, of course, is that you can modify this form and its ObjectPAL code to suit your own needs. Because you have not only already seen, but used, this form, I will just present it for now and pass on, saving the construction details for later. The DPW Installation Procedure form (DPWINSTL.FDL) is shown in Figure 5.34.

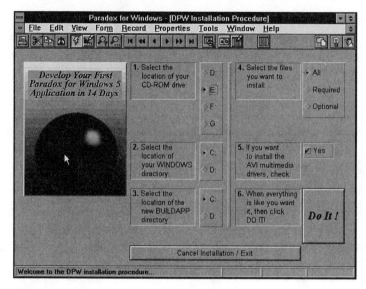

Figure 5.34. *The DPW Installation procedure form, DPWINSTL.FDL.*

Another utility that doesn't appear on the main selection panel but is quite useful is the ObjectPAL Reference Data form (REFDATA.FDL). I use this resource constantly and have borrowed it without shame from my book, *Paradox for Windows Developer's Guide.* It is just too handy for us ObjectPAL programmers not to have around. REFDATA is shown in Figure 5.35.

The REFDATA application makes it easy to find many detailed secrets of ObjectPAL, secrets that are sometime difficult or impossible to find in the manuals. Figure 5.36, for example, illustrates what I did to look up the EditEnterMemoView constant when I was writing the DBUTIL application.

Another excuse to use the REFDATA form arose while writing the System Control Panel application. You may have noticed that the controls on that form aren't true pushbuttons: they are boxes with 3D frames. To simulate pushbutton action, I wanted to change the box frames on the fly, so I looked up property name for a frame object's style using REFDATA. This is shown in Figure 5.37.

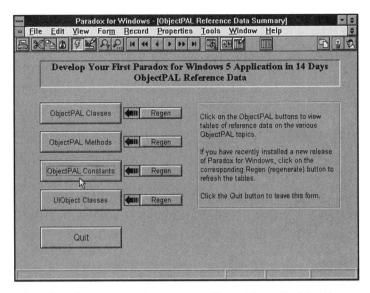

Figure 5.35. *The ObjectPAL Reference Data form, REFDATA.FDL.*

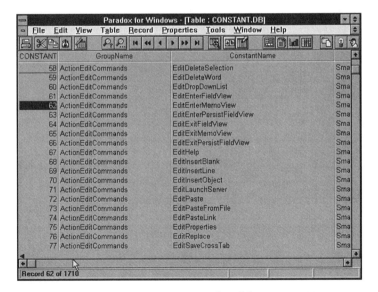

Figure 5.36. *A view of Paradox constants produced by REFDATA.*

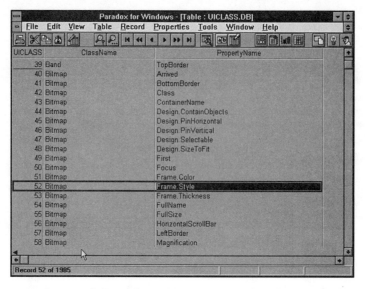

Figure 5.37. *A view of a Paradox property name produced by REFDATA.*

A final support utility form not included on the main selection panel is that old standby, FORMLIST. I use this utility constantly, too. It is the easiest way to get all the ObjectPAL code out of a form into a text file where you can see it all together (or paste it into a book). FORMLIST is shown in Figure 5.38.

The last two support functions are Paradox queries that I used to build the file list table behind the installation utility. I include these mostly as examples for you to look at when modifying DPWINSTL or creating your installation utility.

The first of the queries is APPREQ.QBE. It is used to extract from the INFILES table all those files that are required for the installation process. I then used TBUTIL to sum the FileSize column of the answer table. That sum is used in the installation utility to check the target installation drive to ensure that there is adequate free space for the installation to run to completion. The APPREQ query is shown in Figure 5.39.

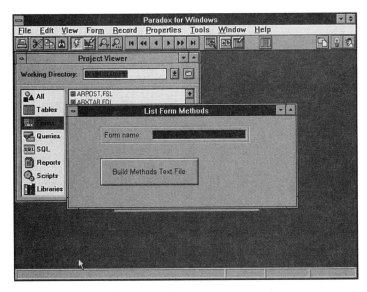

Figure 5.38. *The FORMLIST utility (FORMLIST.FDL).*

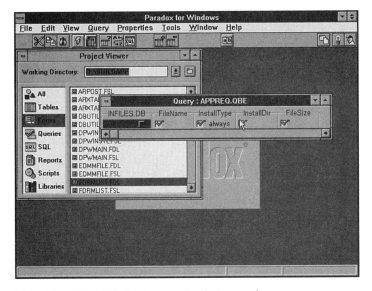

Figure 5.39. *The APPREQ.QBE query in design mode.*

Similarly, I needed a bounding size for the optional files in the installation procedure. That information can be found by running the APPOPT.QBE query, and summing the FileSize column of the answer table with the TBUTIL utility. APPOPT is shown in Figure 5.40.

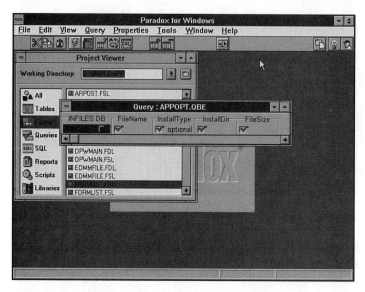

Figure 5.40. *The APPOPT.QBE query in design mode.*

All the necessary parts of the application's interfaces have been defined. I think the users will feel that they are getting their money's worth, don't you?

Planning to Share the Application's Data with Multiple Users

No specific steps will be taken in this book to share the AR/AP application's data with other users. But that doesn't mean that you cannot do so if you want.

There are three methods that you can use to share the application with multiple users:

☐ You can use OBEX (Object Exchange) to publish the application's tables, making them available to other OBEX subscribers. This method is not at all suited for sharing large tables, and it introduces the problem of integrating the

use of multiple copies of the same tables. On the other hand, if the other users need copies only for private use, this may be a good way to go about it, because you won't have many users trying to access the same tables. This method also assumes that the other users have Paradox for Windows installed on their own systems.

☐ You can simply make the application directory available on the network, so that other Paradox users can access the data live. This method also assumes that the other users have their own copies of Paradox.

☐ You can set up a server-only copy of Paradox that other users can run in order to access the data live. This method assumes that you have installed the workgroup edition of Paradox.

From your own point of view, the server-only configuration of Paradox probably makes the most sense. It means that you only have to administer one copy of everything. From the user's point of view, however, there is some performance advantage to them to using their own copy of Paradox, though that really won't amount to too much gain in performance—the data itself still has to move across the wire.

Modification Notes

Now it's your turn. At this point, you can build the forms and reports you need for the AP part of the application. Just look at how I did it for the AR part and start drawing the forms.

You also can begin to prepare for adding the ObjectPAL code later. Use the FORMLIST utility to create text files containing all the ObjectPAL code for the corresponding AR forms, and keep them ready. It will be much quicker to cut and paste ObjectPAL code from the Windows or DPW NotePad than to switch back and forth between Paradox forms, opening and closing object methods.

If you are really brave, you can just use Windows File Manager to copy the necessary forms to new names (being sure not to forget to copy all the form's files), open the new form in design mode, and start modifying. This is possible, but it can be risky business. It might be better to create the forms fresh, using the existing forms only as guides to appearance and general functionality.

You'll need to supply forms or reports for the following functions:

☐ *Export AP Data:* At the risk of contradicting myself immediately, this is one form that could easily be cloned by copying and then modifying it.

☐ *Archive AP Data:* There is no form associated with this function. Just copy the ObjectPAL code from the AR button's method and paste it into this button's method. Then be very sure to go through the code changing all references from AR to Ap tables and files. Failure to do this could be really troublesome!

☐ *Pay Vendors:* It will be easiest to simply look at the AR billing report for a general idea of layout, and then to create this report fresh. The principal differences are in the filenames, and in the fact that this report is meant to actually cut AP checks. You'll have to rearrange things some to make the data fit on the check in the right places. You'll also have to consider whether or not the checks are to have stubs. If so, detail information about individual transactions can be included.

☐ *AP Mailing Labels:* This is another one that will be easier to just create fresh. Don't forget that with Paradox for Windows, you now have the Labels Expert to help you construct the report. That makes it easiest of all.

☐ *Inquire/Analyze:* This is another form you may want to try cloning directly by copying form files to new names and modifying the resulting forms. If so, be sure to scan the Launch Inquiry pushbutton method carefully, converting all filename references to AP files.

Debugging the Process

At this point in the design, there won't be much ObjectPAL code to debug, unless you chose to clone and modify forms and reports directly. The big thing to make sure of here is that the new AP forms look like they should, and that they will open and display in Paradox. Even empty forms should be capable of being opened.

Construction

Part II requires four days to complete. In this period of time, you will perform the following tasks:

- [ ] Create the business application's database engine using permanently linked tables.
- [ ] Create the application's user interfaces using forms, menus, and control panels.
- [ ] Create the application's batch processes using ObjectPAL, including mass account updates, data export, account archival, customer billing, and customer mailing labels.
- [ ] Create the application's regular and multimedia support utilities, including the *Voice Notes!* multimedia notepad, table and database utilities, backup and recovery facilities, the report and print manager, the CDAudio player, and some system utilities for the developer.

6

Building the
Application's
Engine

Today you'll leave the design phase of the DPW AR/AP system and move into the construction phase. It is the engine itself—the principal tables—that is the focus of today's work.

As you may have already guessed, I have built the tables and provided their programming for you. But that's only so I could construct the rest of the sample material, not because you can't do it. There will be plenty for you to do shortly.

So don't slack off, just because there is no manual labor for you to do today. Indeed, pay even closer attention, because if the engine isn't right, nothing else about the application will work.

So let's get on into it: today you'll build the tables themselves, define the necessary links between them, and write the engine's required ObjectPAL code.

Building the Database Tables' Structure

The AR system is defined for the purpose of recording customers and their credit transactions. A customer may purchase goods or services from you on account, with no money up-front. It isn't advisable to do that kind of business except with established customers, naturally, but when it is done, you must keep track of the transaction and possibly bill the customer for payment.

Once an AR transaction is paid, there is no need to keep that record active: it will just be an extra record to examine when you want to produce the next billing statements. (Some call them customer invoices—I'm just a programmer, so you choose.) Therefore, it would be nice to have a place to retire, or *archive,* paid transaction records.

That in a nutshell defines and circumscribes an AR system. From this narrative definition, you can easily see that you need just three files to build an Accounts Receivable system: the CUSTOMER table, the Accounts Receivable (AR) table, and the Accounts Receivable History (ARHIST) table. You can get fancier than that, by hooking into a General Ledger system, for example, but for smaller businesses there is neither real nor legal need to do so.

The CUSTOMER table comes first because both of the other files will depend on it. The CUSTOMER table I have defined for you does have a minimal record layout, but there was a method in that choice. First, there is enough information in the CUSTOMER

record to do the basic job, and second, information beyond that minimum will likely depend on your particular business. The CUSTOMER table structure is shown in Figure 6.1.

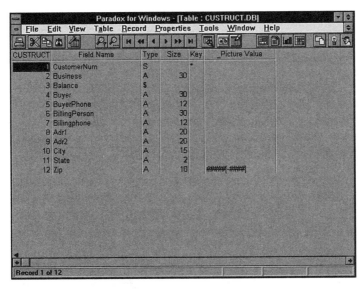

Figure 6.1. *Defining the CUSTOMER table.*

The CustomerNum field is a Paradox SmallInt type, sufficient to record up to 32,767 customer account numbers. Choosing a pure numeric type here was somewhat of a compromise: many systems use an alphanumeric field for this purpose. With a pure numeric value, however, it is easier to ensure that no invalid characters get into the account number.

The Business field is simply the name of the customer's business. It isn't a required field, so this definition doesn't exclude individual customers who aren't part of a business. The length of 30 characters will do for most business names, but you may want to lengthen this field later.

The one field without which you cannot do AR business is the Balance field. The Balance field records the customer's total outstanding debt to you, and a nonzero amount here will trigger a billing statement at billing time. This field will be automatically maintained by ObjectPAL code in the ARPOST form, so you should never have to manually enter a figure here—unless something is very wrong with the system.

In many cases, businesses that place orders with you will have a specific person who is authorized to make purchases for that business. This is the Buyer. The most important thing to know about the buyer is his or her phone number, which is recorded in the BuyerPhone field.

Another very important contact is the person at the customer's business who will receive and process the bills you send them. The name of this person is recorded in the BillingPerson field, and that person's phone number is also very important; it is recorded in the BillingPhone field.

The remaining fields in the CUSTOMER record are address fields. These fields are all fairly self-explanatory. You might take time to notice that the Zip field has a picture validation associated with it, so that AR users can enter either five- or nine-digit Zip codes with equal ease.

Each customer may have many AR transactions outstanding at any one time, so there is naturally a second detail file for the transactions: the AR, or Accounts Receivable table. You'll define its linkage to the CUSTOMER table shortly. For now, just look at the record layout for the AR table, which is shown in Figure 6.2.

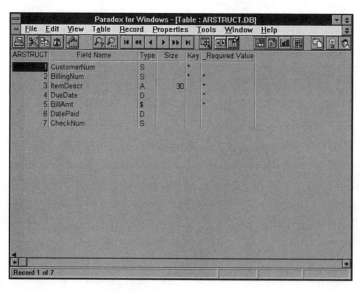

Figure 6.2. *Defining the AR table.*

CustomerNum is the first field in the AR table, and it's also the first part of the AR table's compound key. The second field of the compound key is the BillingNum, or billing number, field. These two fields taken together completely identify any possible AR transaction.

An AR transaction is further described by the ItemDescr and DueDate fields. Without these fields, you don't know what was sold to the customer, or when the bill comes due. And, of course, the BillAmt field tells you how much they owe you. Don't forget that part!

In order to determine whether or not a customer has paid an outstanding bill, the DatePaid is used to post a payment on the AR transaction. Only this field is used to post a transaction paid, because a customer may pay the debt by some means other than a check. Thus, CheckNum is provided to record check numbers, but you cannot require that it be filled in for a satisfied debt.

The accounts receivable history file, ARHIST, will be used to hold those retired AR transactions that have been posted as paid and moved over by the Archive AR Data batch process. Because the ARHIST table has exactly the same record layout as the AR table, I won't go over that again.

The VENDOR table is to Accounts Payable what the CUSTOMER table is to Accounts Receivable. The VENDOR table records the vital information on businesses from whom you make purchases. The VENDOR table structure is shown in Figure 6.3.

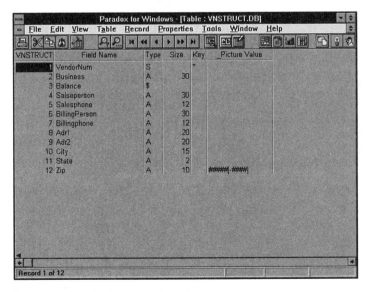

Figure 6.3. *Defining the VENDOR table.*

Rather than using a customer number, the VENDOR table uses a vendor number as its primary key. This is the VendorNum field. Also structured as a SmallInt, VendorNum is capable of recording up to 32,767 unique vendor accounts.

The VENDOR table also has a Balance field, but its significance is the amount of money you owe someone else. A nonzero value in this field should trigger check production for this vendor when you make the AP payment run. Remember that the AP checks are going to be designed and implemented by you!

The AP system also features a salesperson rather than a buyer. This field, plus the SalesPhone field, identify the culprit who helped you run up that debt. The BillingPerson also serves a mirror-image function to that of the AR system: this is the person who will be dunning you for money.

An accounts payable transaction for a vendor account is recorded in the Accounts Payable, or APAY, table. The structure of APAY is shown in Figure 6.4.

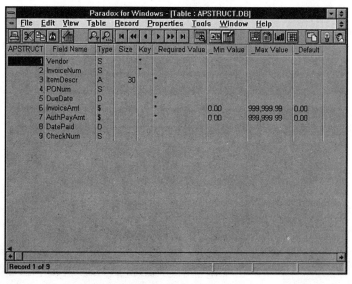

Figure 6.4. *Defining the APAY table.*

APAY has a compound key composed of the VendorNum and InvoiceNum fields. Using this compound key, any AP transaction can be uniquely identified while still remaining linked to the owning vendor record.

Much of the remainder of the APAY record looks and acts like the counterpart AR record. The main differences are the PONum, or purchase order number, field, where you record your request for goods or services, and the AuthPayAmt, or Authorized Payment Amount field. The authorized payment amount should be used to include an APAY transaction in a check amount. In other words, when you design the AP Checks function, don't include payment for a transaction until the AuthPayAmt is nonzero.

AuthPayAmt serves as an important control over the disbursing of money. You might begin by simply requiring that it match the invoice amount, InvoiceAmt, which is the amount of money the vendor says you owe. Later, you could use this field to control partial payment of invoices.

The APAYHIST table is also a mirror-image of the APAY table, so it isn't necessary to go over its structure in detail.

Building Table Linkages

In this section, you are going to link the CUSTOMER, AR, and ARHIST tables together permanently so that there can never be an AR transaction that doesn't have a valid CUSTOMER record above it. You'll also link the VENDOR, APAY, and APAYHIST tables in a similar way.

Those of you who were users of DOS Paradox systems will remember that table linkages could be defined in a DOS system only in a form: the tables could still be referenced without a form in a way that would violate the relationship between them.

That's no longer true with Paradox for Windows. Now you can define a referential integrity relationship directly on a detail table, so that nothing can modify detail records in a way that violates the relationship. The master table is also made directly aware of its dependent detail tables.

Figure 6.5 displays the details of the referential integrity relationship defined on the AR table. Note that it's the AR table, and not the CUSTOMER table, on which the relationship is defined. And, as you have no doubt figured out, I first simply defined the tables, and then came back later (using the Table Restructure dialog box) and defined the referential integrity relationship.

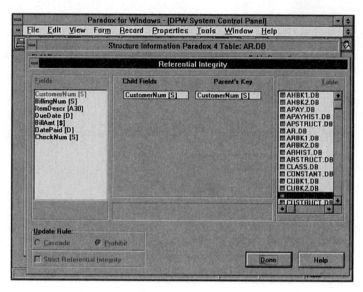

Figure 6.5. *Defining referential integrity on the CUSTOMER table.*

To define referential integrity in either the table Create or Restructure dialog boxes, first note that referential integrity is considered a table property. Normally, the Validity Checks selection is visible in the Table **P**roperties pull-down list. You have to pull down the list and select Referential Integrity in order to define the relationship. Then you can manipulate the Referential Integrity dialog box (as shown in Figure 6.5) to define the relationship on the CustomerNum field, linking it to the same field in the CUSTOMER table.

Because there is no form involved here, Paradox saves the referential integrity relationship information in the table's VAL file. Information is also stored in the master table's (CUSTOMER's) VAL file, naming the dependent tables (AR in this case). You can see this information on the master table's structure information by selecting Table **P**roperties | **D**ependent Tables in the structure dialog form. The resulting display is shown in Figure 6.6.

Before you move on, don't forget that the same relationship must be defined for the ARHIST table. As you can see in Figure 6.6, the CUSTOMER table already knows about both of those tables, plus a pair of backup tables that I created during testing.

You also need to define referential integrity on the APAY table and the APAYHIST table. The procedure is the same, but this time you'll be linking on the VendorNum field, as shown in Figure 6.7.

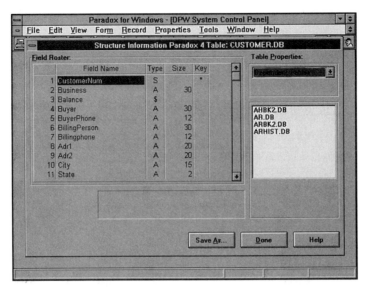

Figure 6.6. *Dependent tables of the CUSTOMER table.*

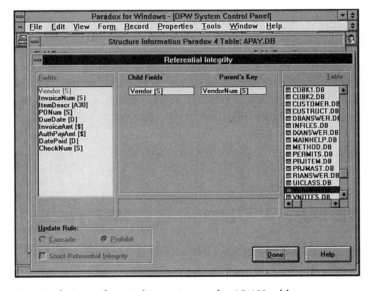

Figure 6.7. *Defining referential integrity on the APAY table.*

191

Figure 6.7 also shows a minor, but interesting, point about defining table links. The linking field names don't have to have the same name, as long as the fields have the same attributes. The Vendor field in the APAY table is linked to the VendorNum field in the VENDOR master table. Both fields are small integer types, however, so the link proceeds without problems.

Just as before, the VENDOR table also knows about its dependent tables, as shown in Figure 6.8. The only difference this time is that there are no backup tables (as yet) for the AP system.

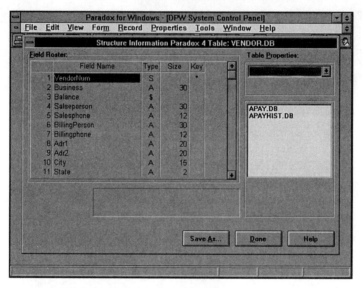

Figure 6.8. *Dependent tables of the VENDOR table.*

Writing the Engine's Support Code

As a general rule, I've done the development of the AR side of the application, and left the AP side for you do by cloning my work. One of the few exceptions was that I went ahead and wrote the APPOST form.

Here's why: The AP engine's code isn't separate from a form, but is attached to the APAY table frame in the APPOST form. I therefore have to get ahead of myself a little in order to show the engine's code before you get to Day 7, "Building the Application's Interfaces," where all the forms are actually constructed.

The same is true of the AR side of the application of course, but I did the whole thing there, anyway. In any case, you won't see all the ObjectPAL code attached to the ARPOST and APPOST forms right here: just that part of it that's being considered "engine code."

The engine's programming all has to do with the automatic maintenance of the master table's Balance field. In order for the user *not* to have to manually compute and enter new balance amounts,you are going to provide the logic to do that, at the point where detail records are added or changed—that is, in the records and fields of the AR and APAY detail table frames. Come to think of it, it might be good idea for you to start Paradox, get into the application and look at, say, the ARPOST form before you continue reading. It might give you a better sense of context as the explanation proceeds.

Now, having used my faithful friend, the FORMLIST utility, I have extracted the pertinent ObjectPAL code from the ARPOST form for your inspection. The first method that you see here is attached to the AR record in the AR table frame.

At the record level, all you need be concerned about is what to do if the user decides to delete the transaction record altogether. To handle this situation, attach the following code to the AR record in the table frame:

```
;¦BeginMethod¦#Page2.AR.#Record41¦action¦
method action(var eventInfo ActionEvent)
  if eventInfo.id() = DataDeleteRecord then
    if DatePaid.isBlank() then  ; back out only if unpaid
      balance = balance - BillAmt
    endif
  else
    doDefault
  endif
endmethod
;¦EndMethod¦#Page2.AR.#Record41¦action¦
```

This method, as you can see, first checks to determine whether the event is indeed a record deletion. If it is, the billing amount is backed out of the customer's balance field arithmetically. If it isn't a record deletion, just allow the default processing to take place.

One of the most important things the user can do, other than adding an AR transaction record, is to post that record paid. This is done, you should recall, by simply filling in the data paid field. However, some unscrupulous employee may want to unpay a bill, or to postdate it, or something of that nature. That's bad business practice, if not outright illegal, so you'll provide some logic that does enable AR transactions to be posted as paid, but not tampered with beyond that point. This is done by customizing the changeValue() method of the DatePaid field in the AR record, as follows:

```
;¦BeginMethod¦#Page2.AR.#Record41.DatePaid¦changeValue¦
method changeValue(var eventInfo ValueEvent)
  if NOT self.isBlank() then
    disableDefault
    eventInfo.setErrorCode( CanNotDepart )
    msgStop( "AR Posting", "This bill is already paid!" )
  else
    balance = balance - BillAmt  ; adjust balance for payment made
  endif
endmethod
;¦EndMethod¦#Page2.AR.#Record41.DatePaid¦changeValue¦
```

As you can see, if the DatePaid field has already been entered, the default value posting action is disabled, the user isn't allowed to leave the field, and an error message box is displayed. Otherwise the user is allowed to enter the date paid value or post the transaction paid.

The next thing that can happen is that the user changes his or her mind and decides that the billing amount wasn't right. The record doesn't need to be deleted, but the billing amount does needs to be changed. That's fine, as long as the customer hasn't already paid the bill. If the customer has, a change at this time could be construed as an effort to get more (illegal) money out of the customer. You can customize the changeValue() method in the DatePaid field to handle this situation, as follows:

```
;¦BeginMethod¦#Page2.AR.#Record41.BillAmt¦changeValue¦
method changeValue(var eventInfo ValueEvent)
var
  oldval, newval Number
endvar
  if NOT DatePaid.isBlank() then
    disableDefault
    eventInfo.setErrorCode( CanNotDepart )
    msgStop( "AR Posting", "This bill is already paid!" )
  else
    oldval = self.value      ; value not posted to table yet
    newval = eventInfo.newValue()
    if NOT oldval.isBlank() then
      balance = balance - oldval  ; back it out
      balance = balance + newval  ; strike new balace
    endif
  endif
endmethod
;¦EndMethod¦#Page2.AR.#Record41.BillAmt¦changeValue¦
```

Before arithmetically adjusting the balance, the DatePaid field is once again checked to see if the record has been posted as paid. If it has been, the action isn't permitted and an error message box is displayed.

On the other hand, if this is a legal adjustment, the action is permitted. There is an interesting bit of ObjectPAL legerdemain at work here that permits you to inspect both the old and new values of a field in the changeValue() method, at the same time. This trick is found in the following two lines of code:

```
oldval = self.value      ; value not posted to table yet
newval = eventInfo.newValue()
```

With the old and new values of the field in hand, the customer balance can be adjusted if the old value was not blank (which would mean that the balance had never yet been affected by this transaction, as when the transaction is first added to the table). I don't know about you, but it sometimes seems to me that it's not the huge, hulking programs that are especially impressive, it is the small, but slick, touch like this one that does the trick.

Moving on now, there is one more critical field that a user might try to improperly change. If a transaction has already been posted as paid, it doesn't make sense to permit a change to the due date of the record. The only reasons I can think of for doing this are once again not completely on the up-and-up. So you add the code to prevent that little slip, as follows:

```
;¦BeginMethod¦#Page2.AR.#Record41.DueDate¦changeValue¦
method changeValue(var eventInfo ValueEvent)
  if NOT DatePaid.isBlank() then
    disableDefault
    eventInfo.setErrorCode( CanNotDepart )
    msgStop( "AR Posting", "This bill is already paid!" )
  endif
endmethod
;¦EndMethod¦#Page2.AR.#Record41.DueDate¦changeValue¦
```

The same sorts of things have to happen on the AP side of the ledger as well. Because you don't need as much explanation now, I will just introduce the methods as they appear, concentrating only on differences from the AR system. First, you'll adjust the vendor balance when the record is deleted—if the transaction isn't already posted as paid (which would have done the necessary adjusting at that time), as follows:

6

```
;¦BeginMethod¦#Page2.APAY.#Record41¦action¦
method action(var eventInfo ActionEvent)
  if eventInfo.id() = DataDeleteRecord then
    if DatePaid.isBlank() then  ; back out only if unpaid
      balance = balance - InvoiceAmt
    endif
  else
    doDefault
  endif
endmethod
;¦EndMethod¦#Page2.APAY.#Record41¦action¦
```

Next, you can enable a record to be posted as paid if it hasn't already been so posted, and if the authorized amount matches the invoice amount correctly. Here's how that's done:

```
;|BeginMethod|#Page2.APAY.#Record41.DatePaid|changeValue|
method changeValue(var eventInfo ValueEvent)
  if NOT self.isBlank() then
    disableDefault
    eventInfo.setErrorCode( CanNotDepart )
    msgStop( "AP Posting", "This invoice is already paid!" )
  else
    if ( AuthPayAmt.isBlank() ) OR ( AuthPayAmt <> InvoiceAmt ) then
      disableDefault
      eventInfo.setErrorCode( CanNotDepart )
      msgStop( "AP Posting", "Authorized pay amount must equal invoice." )
    else
      balance = balance - AuthPayAmt   ; adjust balance for payment made
    endif
  endif
endmethod
;|EndMethod|#Page2.APAY.#Record41.DatePaid|changeValue|
```

Along those same lines, you don't want the authorized amount to be tampered with if it won't match the invoice amount. You can stop just such an improper update like this (notice that the new value is checked before it can be posted to the underlying record):

```
;|BeginMethod|#Page2.APAY.#Record41.AuthPayAmt|changeValue|
method changeValue(var eventInfo ValueEvent)
var
  newval Currency
endvar
  newval = eventInfo.newValue()
  if ( newval = InvoiceAmt ) then
    doDefault
  else
    disableDefault
    eventInfo.setErrorCode( CanNotDepart )
    msgStop( "AP Posting", "Partial or overpayments not allowed." )
  endif
endmethod
;|EndMethod|#Page2.APAY.#Record41.AuthPayAmt|changeValue|
```

Similarly, you don't want to allow any change to the invoice amount if the invoice has already been paid, and you don't want to adjust the balance if there is an invalid old value for the transaction, as follows:

```
;|BeginMethod|#Page2.APAY.#Record41.InvoiceAmt|changeValue|
method changeValue(var eventInfo ValueEvent)
var
  oldval, newval Number
endvar
  if NOT DatePaid.isBlank() then
    disableDefault
    eventInfo.setErrorCode( CanNotDepart )
    msgStop( "AP Posting", "This invoice is already paid!" )
```

```
    else
      oldval = self.value      ; value not posted to table yet
      newval = eventInfo.newValue()
      if NOT oldval.isBlank() then
        balance = balance - oldval  ; back it out
        balance = balance + newval  ; strike new balace
      endif
    endif
endmethod
;¦EndMethod¦#Page2.APAY.#Record41.InvoiceAmt¦changeValue¦
```

Last but not least, you still want to guard against changing the due date if the record has already been posted as paid. Once again, here's how:

```
;¦BeginMethod¦#Page2.APAY.#Record41.DueDate¦changeValue¦
method changeValue(var eventInfo ValueEvent)
  if NOT DatePaid.isBlank() then
    disableDefault
    eventInfo.setErrorCode( CanNotDepart )
    msgStop( "AP Posting", "This invoice is already paid!" )
  endif
endmethod
;¦EndMethod¦#Page2.APAY.#Record41.DueDate¦changeValue¦
```

Now, there really isn't that much code in the "engine," but the code that's there provides for some really nice automation in maintaining the balance field, and for preventing several possible glaring user errors.

Modification Notes

You may want to modify the minimal record layouts of the AR and AP files to include more information that specifically applies to your business. It's okay to do that, as long as you're adding new fields.

If you want to restructure the tables so that existing fields are modified, however, you'll need to observe the following considerations:

- ☐ Much of the ObjectPAL in the systems depends on particular field names, and in some cases, particular field sizes present in the records. If you change field names and sizes, you'll need to examine all the ObjectPAL code to ensure that the modifications won't cause failures of the ObjectPAL methods.

- ☐ If you should want to increase the capacity of the CustomerNum or VendorNum key fields, you may have a tricky job ahead of you. The reason isn't that the fields are keys, per se, but that they are the anchoring fields in the referential integrity relationships you have defined on the master and detail tables. If you want to make the CustomerNum field an alphanumeric field, for example, you'll need to remove the referential integrity relationships with the AR and ARHIST tables, and then restructure all the tables in the same way.

6

After restructuring, be sure to check the KeyViol and Problems tables in your private directory: you may have to manually re-enter some records into the new tables with the correct new format. Following that, be sure to re-establish the referential integrity relationship between the master and detail tables. If you ever let foreign records get into the detail tables, you may find that some of the processes don't work as they should any more.

Debugging the Process

Debugging the engine's code is easy, because all you have to do is enter transactions, and try to do everything you can think of to them. It may be easy, but it is also very important not to go past this point until you're sure that the logic is working correctly.

If you do go past this point, and the logic isn't working right, you're going to have some very corrupted tables on your hands. And that may mean a long process of manually correcting the data—after you have corrected the errors.

To test the engine's code, you could perform the following steps:

1. Add a new transaction record. Make sure the master table's balance field is updated correctly.

2. Add another transaction record. Check the balance field, modify the transaction amount, and check the balance field again.

3. Add a couple more transactions just to have some data to play with. Check the balance field each time. Then modify some of the numbers and see what happens to the balance.

4. Delete one of the transactions that has not been posted as paid. The balance field should be decreased accordingly.

5. Now post one or more of the transactions as paid (fill in the date paid field). The balance field should be decreased by the amount of the transaction.

6. Try to modify one of the posted-as-paid records in an improper way. You should get only error messages, but no changes to the tables should occur.

7. Delete one or more of the posted-as-paid records. Nothing should happen to the master table's balance field.

Building the Application's Interface

There is so much to do in setting up the application's interfaces that you designed in one day, you'll now require three days to build. Any faster than that, and you'd need to be superhuman to get it all in place, and this chapter would have to be much too long.

Today, you'll just concentrate on the main ingredients of the primary system interfaces: setting up multimedia support, building the menus and control panels you'll need, and building the posting forms, export data forms, mass charges form for AR, and the inquiry selection panel forms.

It only takes one paragraph to describe it, but—hold on to your hats—it will take considerable effort to do it. And don't forget: I'll explicitly develop the AR side, and a little of the AP side, but you have a lot of work to do, too. So get ready.

Setting Up for Multimedia Support

On Day 5, you identified two pieces that would be needed to support multimedia operations. These pieces are the CMEDIA.DLL and the VNOTES.INI file that will reside in the Windows directory. Both of these pieces are needed for supporting the *Voice Notes!* hypermedia help file.

VNOTES.INI is the simplest of the resources used anywhere in the entire application. It is an initialization file in the standard Windows format, as follows:

```
[VNConfig]
helpdir=d:\buildapp
```

The DPW Installation Procedure (DPWINSTL.FDL) will customize this file and place it in the Windows directory. You'll see how that's done later, but now the question is, *Why do you need this file at all?*

Remember that the purpose of VNOTES.INI is to guide the CMEDIA.DLL routines to the right spot to find the sound files that will be played in the VNOTES hypermedia Windows help file. This guidance is needed because the Paradox current working directory is not the same thing as a DOS or Windows current directory.

Unless you have set it to be something else, the DOS current directory is *drive:*\PARADOX\PRIVATE while Paradox is running. Even if you have set your private directory's name to something else, it still very likely won't be your own \BUILDAPP directory. Therefore, CMEDIA is almost certain to go to the wrong directory for the .WAV files—unless you tell it where to look, using the VNOTES.INI file.

CMEDIA.DLL contains the multimedia player routine that you need to be able to invoke from a Windows help document, and this is the culprit that needs guidance to

find its sound files. This routine is the C-language playAnyMMClip() function. You should recognize the name from the PW Multimedia Theater. This function is just a C language conversion of the routine by that same name that you already saw written in ObjectPAL.

Because this isn't a C programming book, I will present the code for CMEDIA.C without much comment, except to say that C is English-like enough that you can probably recognize the meaning of most of the code lines. Here is the source for CMEDIA.C:

```c
#include <windows.h>
#include <mmsystem.h>
#include <string.h>
#include <stdlib.h>

#pragma argsused

int FAR PASCAL LibMain( HANDLE hInstance, WORD wDataSeg,
                        WORD wHeapSize, LPSTR lpszCmdLine )
{
  if ( wHeapSize > 0 ) UnlockData( 0 );
  return 1;
}

void FAR PASCAL playAnyMMClip( char *mmfilename,
                               char *inifile,
                               char *inisection,
                               char *inientry )
{
  char mciCmdStr[255];
  char fullMMName[255];
  char ReturnString[1025];
  DWORD ReturnCode, mmlength, mmpos;

/*
  The calling application must supply an INI file, with a section
  and an entry that specifies the PATH to use to access the MMfile.
  for Voice Notes! for example, the vnotes.ini file looks like this:
    [VNConfig]
    helpdir=d:\buildapp
  or wherever the user installed the DPW apps.
*/
  GetPrivateProfileString( inisection, inientry,
    "", fullMMName, sizeof(fullMMName), inifile );
  strcat( fullMMName, "\\" );
  strcat( fullMMName, mmfilename );
  memset( ReturnString, ' ', 1024 );
  strcpy( mciCmdStr, "open " );
  strcat( mciCmdStr, fullMMName );
  strcat( mciCmdStr, " alias mmclip" );
  ReturnCode = mciSendString(mciCmdStr, ReturnString, 1024, 0);
  if ( ReturnCode ) {
    memset( ReturnString, ' ', 1024 );
```

7

```
   mciGetErrorString( ReturnCode, ReturnString, 1024 );
   strcat( ReturnString, "\n" );
   strcat( ReturnString, fullMMName );
   MessageBox( NULL, ReturnString, "CMedia Player", MB_OK );
   return;
 }
 memset( ReturnString, ' ', 1024 );
 strcpy( mciCmdStr, "play mmclip" );
 ReturnCode = mciSendString(mciCmdStr, ReturnString, 1024, 0);
 if ( ReturnCode ) {
   memset( ReturnString, ' ', 1024 );
   mciGetErrorString( ReturnCode, ReturnString, 1024 );
   MessageBox( NULL, ReturnString, "CMedia Player", MB_OK );
   return;
 }
 memset( ReturnString, ' ', 1024 );
 strcpy( mciCmdStr, "status mmclip length" );
 ReturnCode = mciSendString(mciCmdStr, ReturnString, 1024, 0);
 mmlength = atol( ReturnString );
 memset( ReturnString, ' ', 1024 );
 strcpy( mciCmdStr, "status mmclip position" );
 ReturnCode = mciSendString(mciCmdStr, ReturnString, 1024, 0);
 mmpos = atol( ReturnString );
 while ( mmpos < mmlength ) {
   Yield();
   memset( ReturnString, ' ', 1024 );
   strcpy( mciCmdStr, "status mmclip position" );
   ReturnCode = mciSendString(mciCmdStr, ReturnString, 1024, 0);
   mmpos = atol( ReturnString );
 }
 memset( ReturnString, ' ', 1024 );
 strcpy( mciCmdStr, "close mmclip" );
 ReturnCode = mciSendString(mciCmdStr, ReturnString, 1024, 0);
 if ( ReturnCode ) {
   memset( ReturnString, ' ', 1024 );
   mciGetErrorString( ReturnCode, ReturnString, 1024 );
   MessageBox( NULL, ReturnString, "CMedia Player", MB_OK );
   return;
 }
 return;
}
```

As is my habit (probably from writing C books), I always present all the pieces needed for a C program to compile correctly. Thus, because CMEDIA.C is a Windows DLL package, it needs its .DEF (definition) file so that the compiler will know what to do with the module. Here is the CMEDIA.DEF file for CMEDIA.DLL:

```
LIBRARY      CMEDIA
DESCRIPTION 'C MMedia Player'
EXETYPE      WINDOWS
CODE         PRELOAD MOVEABLE DISCARDABLE
DATA         PRELOAD MOVEABLE SINGLE
HEAPSIZE     4096
EXPORTS      playAnyMMClip
IMPORTS      MMSYSTEM.mciSendString
             MMSYSTEM.mciGetErrorString
```

Well, enough of that C stuff. You'll see how I used CMEDIA.DLL on Day 11, "Writing the Application's Online Documentation," when I put the VNOTES.HLP Windows help file together. Until then, let's just get on with the more interesting Paradox programming.

Creating Menus and Control Panels

This section and the next will be quite brief: you have already seen the menus and forms that are presented here. The only difference is that these screen shots of the forms were taken while the documents were in design mode. I am including them here to give you a sense of context for what follows later today in "Writing the Interface's Support Code."

First, let's revisit the MENUS form. Recall that the MENUS form implements the standard Windows menu method of integrating the application. The appearance of that form is quite boring (as you may recall), as shown in Figure 7.1.

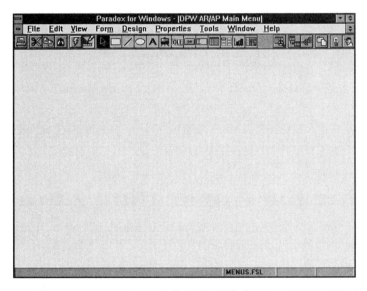

Figure 7.1. *The way you won't do it: the MENUS form, MENUS.FSL, in design mode.*

In the MENUS form, all the code you need to write will be attached to the page object (with the exception of the form's open() and close() methods). Specifically, you'll customize the built-in methods arrive() and menuAction() for the page.

The DPWMAIN form is a bit more interesting—quite a bit, I hope. It is chock-full of buttons and controls, in an I-mean-business format. Everything the application's users need to run AR/AP is visible on the form's window, as shown in Figure 7.2.

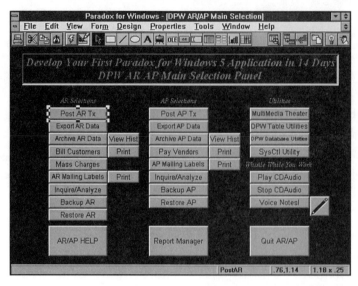

Figure 7.2. *The way you'll do it: the DPWMAIN control panel, DPWMAIN.FSL.*

There are so many objects to which you'll be attaching code that I will just wait until you get there to even try to enumerate them all.

Creating the Application's Forms

After the DPWMAIN form, there are just three more main forms that you'll build and write code for today. These are the ARPOST, APPOST, and ARINQ forms. (These aren't all the forms, of course, just the ones you'll do today.)

As I mentioned on Day 6, ARPOST and APPOST are the repositories of both the form programming and their respective engine's programming. The ARPOST form is shown in Figure 7.3, once again in design mode.

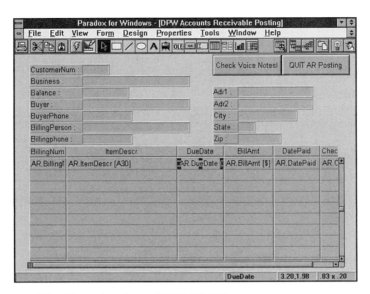

Figure 7.3. *The AR posting form, ARPOST.FSL.*

The APPOST form is almost exactly parallel to the ARPOST form in design, construction, and purpose. APPOST is shown in Figure 7.4.

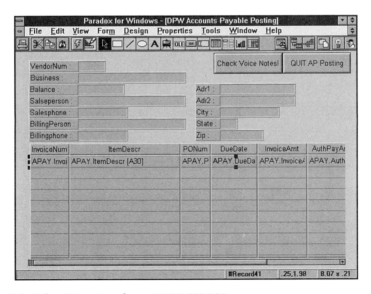

Figure 7.4. *The AP posting form, APPOST.FSL.*

Finally, you have the AR Inquiry Selection form ARINQ. I have not developed the AP-side form for this one: that's part of the exercise for you to complete. But the AP-side form will surely be almost exactly the same, just as the posting form was. Figure 7.5 shows the ARINQ form, with the object tree opened on the design window, so that you can see how I put it together.

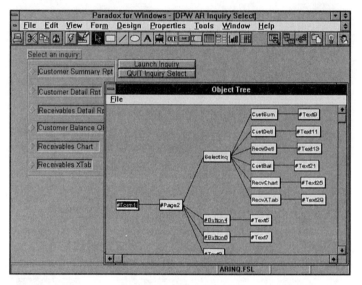

Figure 7.5. *The AR Inquiry Select form, ARINQ.FSL.*

I included the object tree in Figure 7.5 because it's not easily discernible where to attach the code the first time you try to program with radio buttons. It really isn't hard, but it might fool you the first time around.

Writing the Interface's Support Code

Now that you have come to the real programming part of the chapter, I will go over the MENUS form first because I want to explain why I didn't use this approach to integrating the application. Besides, menus aren't all bad, and you might want to use these techniques in another place. The MENUS form's methods begin with the form open() and close() methods. Take a look at them now, and see if you can discover what is different about them, compared to the forms you have already seen early in this book:

```
;¦BeginMethod¦#FormData1¦open¦
method open(var eventInfo Event)
  if NOT eventInfo.isPreFilter() then
    doDefault
    hideSpeedBar()
    maximize()
  endif
endmethod
;¦EndMethod¦#FormData1¦open¦

;¦BeginMethod¦#FormData1¦close¦
method close(var eventInfo Event)
  if NOT eventInfo.isPreFilter() then
    showSpeedBar()
  endif
endmethod
;¦EndMethod¦#FormData1¦close¦
```

You're right: that was too easy. The difference in these methods is that I have added a single line of code that hides and shows the toolbar in the open() and close() methods, respectively.

Hiding the toolbar is the default action for MENUS, but the visibility of the toolbar is also under the user's control. There will be menu options (**File** | **S**how Speedbar and **File** | **H**ide Speedbar) for this very purpose.

You should be aware, however, that the speedbar methods are carryovers from Paradox for Windows 4.5. These objects are now known as toolbars, but the speedbar methods remain in Paradox as undocumented methods, for upward compatibility purposes. In the next release, however, you may have to change this nomenclature.

To control Paradox menus, you first customize the page object's arrive() methods, where you define the menus and their contents. You'll use Menu variables and define their attributes with the addText() and addPopUp() methods. Here is the MENUS page's arrive() method, with customized menu definitions:

```
;¦BeginMethod¦MainPage¦arrive¦
method arrive(var eventInfo MoveEvent)
var
  mainMenu Menu
  filemenu, appsmenu, utilsmenu PopUpMenu
  refmenu, demomenu PopUpMenu
endvar
  filemenu.addText( "&Show Speedbar" )
  filemenu.addText( "&Hide Speedbar" )
  filemenu.addText("E&xit")
  mainMenu.addPopUp( "&File", filemenu )

  appsmenu.addText("&DPW Main")
  mainMenu.addPopUp( "&AR/AP", appsmenu )

  utilsmenu.addText("&Table Utility")
```

```
    utilsmenu.addText("&Database Utility")
    utilsmenu.addText("&SysCtl")
    utilsmenu.addText("&Report Mgr")
    mainMenu.addPopUp( "&Utilities", utilsmenu )

    mainMenu.show()
  endmethod
;¦EndMethod¦MainPage¦arrive¦
```

In defining the menu items' text, you should notice that the & character is placed just before the hotkey character selection for the item.

Defining the menu contents doesn't yet tell Paradox what to do when one of the new menu items is selected by the user. This is done in the page's `menuAction()` method, where you reproduce every item's text in a gigantic `switch` statement, and supply the code that's to be executed when the item is selected. Here is how the `menuAction()` method must be customized:

```
;¦BeginMethod¦MainPage¦menuAction¦
method menuAction(var eventInfo MenuEvent)
var
  mChoice String
  fv Form
endvar
  mChoice = eventInfo.menuChoice()
  switch
    case mChoice = "&Hide Speedbar" : hideSpeedBar()
    case mChoice = "&Show Speedbar" : showSpeedBar()
    case mChoice = "E&xit" : close()
    case mChoice = "&DPW Main" :       fv.open( "DPWMAIN.FDL" )
                                       fv.wait()
    case mChoice = "&Database Utility" : fv.open( "DBUTIL.FDL" )
                                       fv.wait()
    case mChoice = "&Table Utility" : fv.open( "TBUTIL.FDL" )
                                       fv.wait()
    case mChoice = "&SysCtl" :          fv.open( "SYSCTL.FDL" )
                                       fv.wait()
    case mChoice = "&Report Mgr" : fv.open( "RPTMGR.FDL" )
                                       fv.wait()
  endswitch
endmethod
;¦EndMethod¦MainPage¦menuAction¦
```

Well, that's enough about defining Windows style menus. You won't be using this approach to integrating the application for two reasons. First, it takes a lot of typing, and believe it or not, I am not a touch typist, so typing is dreary work for me, indeed. If you like typing, you may certainly use this approach—it won't hurt my feelings at all. Second, however, there is the consideration that the resulting forms looks so bland. It has no visual appeal.

Even if you don't like my design for the DPW Main Selection Panel, you must admit there is certainly more going on in the form window than there was in the menu version.

I kind of like the black background; it gives me a three-dimensional feeling, as if the control objects are just hanging out there in space.

Before you get down to the nuts and bolts of the DPWMAIN form's insides, I will just comment that some of the ObjectPAL methods will be covered again later, in much more detail. I have still included all the form's methods here for the sake of completeness.

DPWMAIN first of all has a Uses block because it will communicate with the MMPLAYER multimedia interface. Because I am certain that you remember this setup, I won't say anything further about it. The DPWMAIN Uses block is as follows:

```
;¦BeginMethod¦#FormData1¦Uses¦
Uses MMSYSTEM
  mciSendString( lpstrCommand CPTR, lpstrReturn CPTR,
                 wReturnLng CWORD, hCallBack CWORD ) CLONG
  mciGetErrorString( dwError CLONG, lpstrReturn CPTR,
                     wLength CWORD ) CWORD
endUses
;¦EndMethod¦#FormData1¦Uses¦
```

The DPWMAIN open() is similarly familiar. It just sets up the window, triggers default processing, and goes away, like this:

```
;¦BeginMethod¦#FormData1¦open¦
method open(var eventInfo Event)
  if NOT eventInfo.isPreFilter() then
    doDefault
    maximize()
  endif
endmethod
;¦EndMethod¦#FormData1¦open¦
```

There is a Help button on the DPWMAIN form, so some code is required to call the Windows help engine. Here is the pushbutton() method for that purpose:

```
;¦BeginMethod¦#Page2.HelpBtn¦pushButton¦
method pushButton(var eventInfo Event)
  helpShowContext( "DPWMAIN.HLP", 1 )
endmethod
;¦EndMethod¦#Page2.HelpBtn¦pushButton¦
```

When I put the pencil graphic object on the form for invoking the DPW NotePad, I didn't even name the object. Paradox therefore used a default *noise name* to identify the graphic, #Page2.#Bitmap72. The method's code just invokes the Windows application editfile.exe, as follows:

```
;¦BeginMethod¦#Page2.#Bitmap72¦mouseClick¦
method mouseClick(var eventInfo MouseEvent)
  self.frame.style = Inside3DFrame
  execute( workingDir() + "\\editfile.exe", No, WinStyleDefault )
  self.frame.style = Outside3DFrame
endmethod
;¦EndMethod¦#Page2.#Bitmap72¦mouseClick¦
```

7

Note that you can invoke any Windows or DOS application using the execute() call.

Invoking the DPW System Control Panel is nearly as easy. Because SYSCTL is a form, you need a form variable, and an open() and wait() call. After waiting for the called form to return, I called the maximize() function again, just in case the other application did something to window sizing. The code for all this is as follows:

```
;¦BeginMethod¦#Page2.GoSysCtl¦pushButton¦
method pushButton(var eventInfo Event)
var
  fv Form
endvar
  fv.open( "SYSCTL.FDL" )
  fv.wait()
  maximize()
endmethod
;¦EndMethod¦#Page2.GoSysCtl¦pushButton¦
```

Evidently, I didn't think to name the four Print tab buttons when I added them to the form. The first of these, button 68, is for the AP Mailing Labels direct print function. As you can see, this is one of the functions I have left for you to complete:

```
;¦BeginMethod¦#Page2.#Button68¦pushButton¦
method pushButton(var eventInfo Event)
  msgInfo( "DPW AP Function", "You need to implement this function!" )
endmethod
;¦EndMethod¦#Page2.#Button68¦pushButton¦
```

Button 66 is also a Print button: it is the Pay Vendors direct print button. You also need to implement this function, as the ObjectPAL source shows:

```
;¦BeginMethod¦#Page2.#Button66¦pushButton¦
method pushButton(var eventInfo Event)
  msgInfo( "DPW AP Function", "You need to implement this function!" )
endmethod
;¦EndMethod¦#Page2.#Button66¦pushButton¦
```

How you'll implement those two unfinished buttons can be seen by examining the code for button 64. This is the code that invokes the direct print function for AR Mailing Labels, as follows:

```
;¦BeginMethod¦#Page2.#Button64¦pushButton¦
method pushButton(var eventInfo Event)
var
  ri  ReportPrintInfo
  rep Report
endvar
  ri.name = ":work:armail.rdl"
  rep.print( ri )
  maximize()
endmethod
;¦EndMethod¦#Page2.#Button64¦pushButton¦
```

As you can see, it's quite easy to launch a report. Just print() the report using the appropriate ReportPrintInfo structure, and away you go. Exactly the same approach is used for button 62, which is the direct print button for AR Billing, as follows:

```
;¦BeginMethod¦#Page2.#Button62¦pushButton¦
method pushButton(var eventInfo Event)
var
  ri  ReportPrintInfo
  rep Report
endvar
  ri.name = ":work:arbill.rdl"
  rep.print( ri )
  maximize()
endmethod
;¦EndMethod¦#Page2.#Button62¦pushButton¦
```

The ViewAPHist tab button invokes a table view of the APATHIST table. You just open, maximize, wait, and close the TableView variable, like this:

```
;¦BeginMethod¦#Page2.ViewAPHist¦pushButton¦
method pushButton(var eventInfo Event)
var
  tv TableView
endvar
  tv.open( ":work:apayhist.db" )
  tv.maximize()
  tv.wait()
  tv.close()
endmethod
;¦EndMethod¦#Page2.ViewAPHist¦pushButton¦
```

The ViewARHist tab button works just the same way, and here is the ObjectPAL for it:

```
;¦BeginMethod¦#Page2.ViewARHist¦pushButton¦
method pushButton(var eventInfo Event)
var
  tv TableView
endvar
  tv.open( ":work:arhist.db" )
  tv.maximize()
  tv.wait()
  tv.close()
endmethod
;¦EndMethod¦#Page2.ViewARHist¦pushButton¦
```

AR Mass Charges is a batch function that you'll implement in detail on Day 8, "Building the Application's Batch Processes." Launching it, however, is a task for DPWMAIN, and that involves only another form's launch, as before. Here is the code for launching mass charges:

```
;¦BeginMethod¦#Page2.ARMassCharge¦pushButton¦
method pushButton(var eventInfo Event)
var
  fv Form
```

```
endvar
  fv.open( "ARMASSC.FDL" )
  fv.wait()
endmethod
;¦EndMethod¦#Page2.ARMassCharge¦pushButton¦
```

Launching the Report Manager is likewise just an exercise in opening and waiting on a form variable. The only difference is in the form name specified:

```
;¦BeginMethod¦#Page2.RptMgrBtn¦pushButton¦
method pushButton(var eventInfo Event)
var
  fv Form
endvar
  fv.open( "RPTMGR.FSL" )
  fv.wait()
endmethod
;¦EndMethod¦#Page2.RptMgrBtn¦pushButton¦
```

The APBackup button is another one that I have left for you to complete on your own, as is the APRestore button. Here are their rather empty pushbutton() methods:

```
;¦BeginMethod¦#Page2.APBackup¦pushButton¦
method pushButton(var eventInfo Event)
  msgInfo( "DPW AP Function", "You need to implement this function!" )
endmethod
;¦EndMethod¦#Page2.APBackup¦pushButton¦

;¦BeginMethod¦#Page2.APRestore¦pushButton¦
method pushButton(var eventInfo Event)
  msgInfo( "DPW AP Function", "You need to implement this function!" )
endmethod
;¦EndMethod¦#Page2.APRestore¦pushButton¦
```

ARRestore is another matter altogether. Although this ObjectPAL code will be dissected in detail on Day 9, I wanted to present all the DPWMAIN code in one place, so here is the AR restore routine, with comments deferred:

```
;¦BeginMethod¦#Page2.ARRestore¦pushButton¦
method pushButton(var eventInfo Event)
var
  lpstr, cwdir, dlgreturn, bkupname String
  newarcnum SmallInt
  tb, tb2 Table
endvar
  cwdir = workingDir() + "\\ararc.ini"
  lpstr = readProfileString( cwdir, "ARARC", "nextfilenum" )
  newarcnum = SmallInt( lpstr )
  dlgreturn = msgYesNoCancel( "DPW AR Restore",
                              "The current backup file number is " +
                              StrVal(newarcnum) + "\n" +
                              "Do you want to choose another version?" )
  switch
    case dlgreturn = "Yes" :
      newarcnum.view( "Change file number:")
```

```
    case dlgreturn = "No" :
      message( "DPW AR Restore: Default backup file number accepted." )
    case dlgreturn = "Cancel" :
      message( "DPW AR Restore run aborted..." )
      sleep( 1000 )
      return
  endswitch

  message( "DPW AR Restore: Beginning Customer restore..." )
  bkupname = workingDir() + "\\cubk" + StrVal(newarcnum) + ".db"
  tb.attach( ":work:customer.db" )
  tb2.attach( bkupname )
  tb2.setReadOnly(Yes)
  if tb2.copy( tb ) then
    message( "DPW AR Restore: Customer table restore OK" )
    sleep( 1000 )
  else
    errorShow( "DPW AR Restore", "Customer table restore failed" )
  endif

  message( "DPW AR Restore: Beginning AR restore..." )
  bkupname = workingDir() + "\\arbk" + StrVal(newarcnum) + ".db"
  tb.attach( ":work:ar.db" )
  tb2.attach( bkupname )
  tb2.setReadOnly(Yes)
  if tb2.copy( tb ) then
    message( "DPW AR Restore: AR table restore OK" )
    sleep( 1000 )
  else
    errorShow( "DPW AR Restore", "AR table restore failed" )
  endif

  message( "DPW AR Restore: Beginning ARHIST restore..." )
  bkupname = workingDir() + "\\ahbk" + StrVal(newarcnum) + ".db"
  tb.attach( ":work:arhist.db" )
  tb2.attach( bkupname )
  tb2.setReadOnly(Yes)
  if tb2.copy( tb ) then
    message( "DPW AR Restore: ARHIST table restore OK" )
    sleep( 1000 )
  else
    errorShow( "DPW AR Restore", "ARHIST table restore failed" )
  endif

  message( "DPW AR Restore: Complete!" )
endmethod

;¦EndMethod¦#Page2.ARRestore¦pushButton¦
```

AR backup falls into the same category as the restore function. It is shown here for the sole purpose of presenting all the DWMAIN code complete and together at least once:

```
;¦BeginMethod¦#Page2.ARBackup¦pushButton¦
method pushButton(var eventInfo Event)
var
  lpstr, cwdir, dlgreturn, bkupname String
```

```
     newarcnum SmallInt
     tb, tb2 Table
  endvar
     cwdir = workingDir() + "\\ararc.ini"
     lpstr = readProfileString( cwdir, "ARARC", "nextfilenum" )
     newarcnum = SmallInt( lpstr ) + 1
     dlgreturn = msgYesNoCancel( "DPW AR Backup",
                                 "The next backup file number is " +
                                 StrVal(newarcnum) + "\n" +
                                 "Do you want to reset it?" )
     switch
       case dlgreturn = "Yes" :
         newarcnum.view( "Change file number:")
       case dlgreturn = "No" :
         message( "DPW AR Backup: Default backup file number accepted." )
       case dlgreturn = "Cancel" :
         message( "DPW AR Backup run aborted..." )
         sleep( 1000 )
         return
     endswitch
     message( "DPW AR Backup: New backup file number = " + StrVal(newarcnum) )
     writeProfileString( cwdir, "ARARC", "nextfilenum",
                         StrVal(newarcnum) )

     message( "DPW AR Backup: Beginning Customer back up..." )
     bkupname = workingDir() + "\\cubk" + StrVal(newarcnum) + ".db"
     tb.attach( ":work:customer.db" )
     tb2.attach( bkupname )
     if tb.copy( tb2 ) then
       message( "DPW AR Backup: Customer table back up OK" )
       sleep( 1000 )
     else
       errorShow( "DPW AR Backup", "Customer table back up failed" )
     endif

     message( "DPW AR Backup: Beginning AR back up..." )
     bkupname = workingDir() + "\\arbk" + StrVal(newarcnum) + ".db"
     tb.attach( ":work:ar.db" )
     tb.setReadOnly(Yes)
     tb2.attach( bkupname )
     if tb.copy( tb2 ) then
       message( "DPW AR Backup: AR table back up OK" )
       sleep( 1000 )
     else
       errorShow( "DPW AR Backup", "AR table back up failed" )
     endif

     message( "DPW AR Backup: Beginning ARHIST back up..." )
     bkupname = workingDir() + "\\ahbk" + StrVal(newarcnum) + ".db"
     tb.attach( ":work:arhist.db" )
     tb.setReadOnly(Yes)
     tb2.attach( bkupname )
     if tb.copy( tb2 ) then
       message( "DPW AR Backup: ARHIST table back up OK" )
       sleep( 1000 )
     else
```

```
        errorShow( "DPW AR Backup", "ARHIST table back up failed" )
      endif

    message( "DPW AR Backup: Complete!" )
endmethod

;¦EndMethod¦#Page2.ARBackup¦pushButton¦
```

The *Voice Notes!* application will also be covered in detail on Day 9, but invoking it in the first place certainly belongs here. The means is just your old familiar friend, the forms launch, as follows:

```
;¦BeginMethod¦#Page2.GoVoiceNotes¦pushButton¦
method pushButton(var eventInfo Event)
var
  fv Form
endvar
  fv.open( "VNOTES.FDL" )
  fv.wait()
  maximize()
endmethod
;¦EndMethod¦#Page2.GoVoiceNotes¦pushButton¦
```

At last, a really easy one! The Quit button does nothing but make the whole thing go away. It calls the `close()` method, like this:

```
;¦BeginMethod¦#Page2.QuitBtn¦pushButton¦
method pushButton(var eventInfo Event)
  close(0)
endmethod
;¦EndMethod¦#Page2.QuitBtn¦pushButton¦
```

Audio CD support is one of the fun things I decided to add to this application. I'll also go over this function on Day 9, but if you look closely, you'll probably recognize everything in the Stop CDAudio button's method right now:

```
;¦BeginMethod¦#Page2.GoStopCD¦pushButton¦
method pushButton(var eventInfo Event)
var
  mciCmdStr, ReturnString String
  ReturnCode LongInt
endvar
    ReturnString = fill( " ", 1024 )
    mciCmdStr = "stop cdaudio"
    ReturnCode = mciSendString(mciCmdStr, ReturnString, 1024, 0)
    if NOT (0 = ReturnCode) then
      ReturnString = fill( " ", 1024 )
      mciGetErrorString( ReturnCode, ReturnString, 1024 )
      msgStop( "CDAudio Stop", ReturnString )
      return
    endif
    ReturnString = fill( " ", 1024 )
    mciCmdStr = "close cdaudio"
    ReturnCode = mciSendString(mciCmdStr, ReturnString, 1024, 0)
    if NOT (0 = ReturnCode) then
```

```
            ReturnString = fill( " ", 1024 )
            mciGetErrorString( ReturnCode, ReturnString, 1024 )
            msgStop( "CDAudio Close", ReturnString )
            return
        endif
endmethod
;¦EndMethod¦#Page2.GoStopCD¦pushButton¦
```

Likewise for Play CDAudio, I'm sure. By now, multimedia programming is getting to be pretty ho-hum stuff, right? Not for me—I never get tired of it! Here is the Play CDAudio button's code:

```
;¦BeginMethod¦#Page2.GoPlayCD¦pushButton¦
method pushButton(var eventInfo Event)
var
  mciCmdStr, ReturnString String
  ReturnCode LongInt
endvar
    ReturnString = fill( " ", 1024 )
    mciCmdStr = "open cdaudio"
    ReturnCode = mciSendString(mciCmdStr, ReturnString, 1024, 0)
    if NOT (0 = ReturnCode) then
      ReturnString = fill( " ", 1024 )
      mciGetErrorString( ReturnCode, ReturnString, 1024 )
      msgStop( "CDAudio Open", ReturnString )
      return
    endif
    ReturnString = fill( " ", 1024 )
    mciCmdStr = "play cdaudio"
    ReturnCode = mciSendString(mciCmdStr, ReturnString, 1024, 0)
    if NOT (0 = ReturnCode) then
      ReturnString = fill( " ", 1024 )
      mciGetErrorString( ReturnCode, ReturnString, 1024 )
      msgStop( "CDAudio Play", ReturnString )
      return
    endif
endmethod
;¦EndMethod¦#Page2.GoPlayCD¦pushButton¦
```

Launching the database and tables utilities is also only a matter of launching the correct forms, just as before. Here is the code for both of these pushbutton() methods, without further ado:

```
;¦BeginMethod¦#Page2.GoDBUtil¦pushButton¦
method pushButton(var eventInfo Event)
var
  fv Form
endvar
  fv.open( "DBUTIL.FDL" )
  fv.wait()
  maximize()
endmethod
;¦EndMethod¦#Page2.GoDBUtil¦pushButton¦

;¦BeginMethod¦#Page2.GoTBUtil¦pushButton¦
```

```
method pushButton(var eventInfo Event)
var
  fv Form
endvar
  fv.open( "TBUTIL.FDL" )
  fv.wait()
  maximize()
endmethod
;¦EndMethod¦#Page2.GoTBUtil¦pushButton¦
```

Remember the Multimedia Theater? Here it is again, integrated into the DPW Main Selection Panel. And again, it's just a forms launch, as follows:

```
;¦BeginMethod¦#Page2.GoMMT¦pushButton¦
method pushButton(var eventInfo Event)
var
  fv Form
endvar
  fv.open( "PWMMPLAY.FDL" )
  fv.wait()
  maximize()
endmethod
;¦EndMethod¦#Page2.GoMMT¦pushButton¦
```

By now it's becoming pretty clear even to me that the AR/AP application is fairly well modularized, with a lot of the code being interface or invocation code. That's the case once more with the APPOST forms launch, which is attached to the PostAP button, like this:

```
;¦BeginMethod¦#Page2.PostAP¦pushButton¦
method pushButton(var eventInfo Event)
var
  fv Form
endvar
  fv.open( "APPOST.FDL" )
  fv.wait()
endmethod
;¦EndMethod¦#Page2.PostAP¦pushButton¦
```

Next, there is a whole string of functions that I have left for you to implement, including AP export, AP archive, AP checks, AP mailing labels, and AP Inquire/Analyze. Even though I have done the majority of development for the system, I have left plenty for you to do. Just remember to use what I have provided, cloning it wherever possible, rather than keying it up by brute force. Here is the string of "blank" methods I have left as placeholders for you:

```
;¦BeginMethod¦#Page2.ExportAP¦pushButton¦
method pushButton(var eventInfo Event)
  msgInfo( "DPW AP Function", "You need to implement this function!" )
endmethod
;¦EndMethod¦#Page2.ExportAP¦pushButton¦

;¦BeginMethod¦#Page2.ArchiveAP¦pushButton¦
```

```
method pushButton(var eventInfo Event)
  msgInfo( "DPW AP Function", "You need to implement this function!" )
endmethod
;¦EndMethod¦#Page2.ArchiveAP¦pushButton¦

;¦BeginMethod¦#Page2.APPay¦pushButton¦
method pushButton(var eventInfo Event)
  msgInfo( "DPW AP Function", "You need to implement this function!" )
endmethod
;¦EndMethod¦#Page2.APPay¦pushButton¦

;¦BeginMethod¦#Page2.APMail¦pushButton¦
method pushButton(var eventInfo Event)
  msgInfo( "DPW AP Function", "You need to implement this function!" )
endmethod
;¦EndMethod¦#Page2.APMail¦pushButton¦

;¦BeginMethod¦#Page2.APQuery¦pushButton¦
method pushButton(var eventInfo Event)
  msgInfo( "DPW AP Function", "You need to implement this function!" )
endmethod
;¦EndMethod¦#Page2.APQuery¦pushButton¦
```

Now it's back to the same old grind: more forms' launches. Here is the ObjectPAL method for the AR Inquire/Analyze pushbutton:

```
;¦BeginMethod¦#Page2.ARQuery¦pushButton¦
method pushButton(var eventInfo Event)
var
  fv Form
endvar
  fv.open( "ARINQ.FDL" )
  fv.wait()
  maximize()
endmethod
;¦EndMethod¦#Page2.ARQuery¦pushButton¦
```

Here is something a little different. The ARMail pushbutton launches the AR Mailing Labels report, but not with the report print() method. This time, you won't launch a form; you'll open a report in preview mode (that is, display the report in a report window). To preview a report, you don't use the print() method, you simply open() it, as follows:

```
;¦BeginMethod¦#Page2.ARMail¦pushButton¦
method pushButton(var eventInfo Event)
var
  ri  ReportPrintInfo
  rep Report
endvar
  ri.name = ":work:armail.rdl"
  rep.open( ri )  ; open on desktop for user to verify / launch
  maximize()
endmethod
;¦EndMethod¦#Page2.ARMail¦pushButton¦
```

The AR billing report works the same way. Because this isn't a direct print launch, just open() the report, using the ReportPrintInfo structure, as follows:

```
;¦BeginMethod¦#Page2.ARBill¦pushButton¦
method pushButton(var eventInfo Event)
var
  ri  ReportPrintInfo
  rep Report
endvar
  ri.name = ":work:arbill.rdl"
  rep.open( ri )  ; open on desktop for user to verify / launch
  maximize()
endmethod
;¦EndMethod¦#Page2.ARBill¦pushButton¦
```

The AR Archive function is another one of those batch functions for which I will save a detailed discussion at a later time (on Day 8). In the interests of presenting all the code in one place, however, here is the AR Archive function's logic, with no comment for now:

```
;¦BeginMethod¦#Page2.ArchiveAR¦pushButton¦
method pushButton(var eventInfo Event)
var
  tb1, tb2 Table
  tcar, tchist TCursor
  arRec DynArray[] AnyType
endvar
  message( "DPW AR starting record retirement to history file." )
  sleep(500)
  message( "DPW AR creating temporary transaction table." )
  tb1.attach( ":work:ar.db" )
  tb2.attach( ":work:artemp.db" )
  if tb1.isTable() AND NOT tb2.isTable() then
    tb1.enumFieldStruct( ":work:DBANSWER.DB" )
    tb1.enumIndexStruct( ":work:IXANSWER.DB" )
    tb2 = create
          ":work:artemp.db"
          STRUCT ":work:DBANSWER.DB"
          INDEXSTRUCT ":work:IXANSWER.DB"
        endcreate
  else
    msgStop( "DPW AR Archive", "Could not create temp table!" )
    tb1.unattach()
    tb2.unattach()
    return
  endif
  tb1.unattach()
  tb2.unattach()
  message( "DPW AR locating receivables for retirement." )
  if NOT tcar.open( ":work:ar.db" ) then
    msgStop( "DPW AR Archive", "Could not open AR.DB!" )
    return
  endif
  if NOT tchist.open( ":work:artemp.db" ) then
    msgStop( "DPW AR Archive", "Could not open AR.DB!" )
```

7

```
    tcar.close()
    return
  endif
  tcar.edit()
  tchist.edit()
  tchist.end()
  scan tcar for (tcar.DatePaid.isBlank() = False) :
    tcar.copyToArray( arRec )
    tchist.insertAfterRecord()
    tchist.copyFromArray( arRec )
    tcar.deleteRecord()
    loop     ; don't let scan move the record pointer, delete did it
  endscan
  tcar.endEdit()
  tchist.endEdit()
  tcar.close()
  tchist.close()
  message( "DPW AR adding temporary transaction table to history." )
  tb1.attach( ":work:arhist.db" )
  tb2.attach( ":work:artemp.db" )
  if tb1.isTable() AND tb2.isTable() then
    if NOT tb2.add( tb1, True, False ) then
      msgStop( "DPW AR Archive", "Table add failed" )
      tb1.unattach()
      tb2.unattach()
      return
    endif
  else
    msgStop( "DPW AR Archive", "A table is not specified correctly!" )
  endif
  tb1.unattach()
  tb2.unattach()
  tb1.attach( ":work:artemp.db" )
  if tb1.isTable()then
    message( "DPW AR deleting table... ", ":work:artemp.db" )
    if NOT tb1.delete() then
      msgStop( "DPW AR Archive", "Temp Table delete FAILED!" )
      return
    endif
  else
    msgStop( "DPW AR Archive", "A table is not specified correctly!" )
    return
  endif
  tb1.unattach()
  message( "DPW AR record retirement to history file complete." )
endmethod
;¦EndMethod¦#Page2.ArchiveAR¦pushButton¦
```

That was quite a load of code! The AR Export function is a relief by comparison. It's back to the same old form's launch for this one:

```
;¦BeginMethod¦#Page2.ExportAR¦pushButton¦
method pushButton(var eventInfo Event)
var
  fv Form
endvar
```

```
  fv.open( "AREXPORT.FDL" )
  fv.wait()
endmethod
;¦EndMethod¦#Page2.ExportAR¦pushButton¦
```

If you were wondering what happened to the ARPOST launch, I saved it for last. And
here it is, now:

```
;¦BeginMethod¦#Page2.PostAR¦pushButton¦
method pushButton(var eventInfo Event)
var
  fv Form
endvar
  fv.open( "ARPOST.FDL" )
  fv.wait()
endmethod
;¦EndMethod¦#Page2.PostAR¦pushButton¦
```

Saving the ARPOST launch for last in the presentation of the DPWMAIN form's
method makes a good transition into the ARPOST form itself.

The ARPOST form's methods are presented here all together just as before; even the
engine's code has already been presented. I am still working the theory that, at least once,
you need to see it all together and in context. At least I can skip over detailed comment
on the engine's code this time.

The ARPOST open() and close() form methods are old hat. Like the shoe commercial
says, "Just do it." Note, however, that you are attaching code to the open() method, but
simply calling the close() method. And here are the methods:

```
;¦BeginMethod¦#FormData1¦open¦
method open(var eventInfo Event)
  if NOT eventInfo.isPreFilter() then
    doDefault
    maximize()
  endif
endmethod
;¦EndMethod¦#FormData1¦open¦

;¦BeginMethod¦#Page2.#Button56¦pushButton¦
method pushButton(var eventInfo Event)
  close(0)
endmethod
;¦EndMethod¦#Page2.#Button56¦pushButton¦
```

I hope you're not discouraged by the fact that programming real systems involves a good
deal of repetitive work, such as forms launches and the like. That's the way it is in the real
world, and it's always the price of building anything useful. Just ignore the repetition,
and think of the result that it produces.

Such is the case with the Check VNOTES pushbutton on the ARPOST form. It's the same old forms launch, but it launches the user right into the world of multimedia applications that you can use. Here is the pushbutton() method for the Check VNOTES button:

```
;¦BeginMethod¦#Page2.#Button54¦pushButton¦
method pushButton(var eventInfo Event)
var
  fv Form
endvar
  fv.open( "VNOTES.FDL" )
  fv.wait()
endmethod
;¦EndMethod¦#Page2.#Button54¦pushButton¦
```

You should recognize the next method. It's the record delete logic for the AR engine. This code is attached to the record within the table frame. I present it intact and without further comment, for the sake of completeness:

```
;¦BeginMethod¦#Page2.AR.#Record41¦action¦
method action(var eventInfo ActionEvent)
  if eventInfo.id() = DataDeleteRecord then
    if DatePaid.isBlank() then  ; back out only if unpaid
      balance = balance - BillAmt
    endif
  else
    doDefault
  endif
endmethod
;¦EndMethod¦#Page2.AR.#Record41¦action¦
```

In like manner, you have already seen the changeValue() methods for the DatePaid, BillAmt, and DueDate AR fields. And in like manner, I present them without further comment:

```
;¦BeginMethod¦#Page2.AR.#Record41.DatePaid¦changeValue¦
method changeValue(var eventInfo ValueEvent)
  if NOT self.isBlank() then
    disableDefault
    eventInfo.setErrorCode( CanNotDepart )
    msgStop( "AR Posting", "This bill is already paid!" )
  else
    balance = balance - BillAmt  ; adjust balance for payment made
  endif
endmethod
;¦EndMethod¦#Page2.AR.#Record41.DatePaid¦changeValue¦

;¦BeginMethod¦#Page2.AR.#Record41.BillAmt¦changeValue¦
method changeValue(var eventInfo ValueEvent)
var
  oldval, newval Number
endvar
  if NOT DatePaid.isBlank() then
    disableDefault
    eventInfo.setErrorCode( CanNotDepart )
```

```
      msgStop( "AR Posting", "This bill is already paid!" )
    else
      oldval = self.value      ; value not posted to table yet
      newval = eventInfo.newValue()
      if NOT oldval.isBlank() then
        balance = balance - oldval  ; back it out
        balance = balance + newval  ; strike new balace
      endif
    endif
endmethod
;¦EndMethod¦#Page2.AR.#Record41.BillAmt¦changeValue¦

;¦BeginMethod¦#Page2.AR.#Record41.DueDate¦changeValue¦
method changeValue(var eventInfo ValueEvent)
  if NOT DatePaid.isBlank() then
    disableDefault
    eventInfo.setErrorCode( CanNotDepart )
    msgStop( "AR Posting", "This bill is already paid!" )
  endif
endmethod
;¦EndMethod¦#Page2.AR.#Record41.DueDate¦changeValue¦
```

I realize that it is perhaps confusing to treat some of a form's methods as if they were part of another entity, the engine. That's both the curse and the beauty of an object-oriented system like Paradox for Windows. There is no code apart from an object, and in this case, there's nowhere to put the engine's code but in the table frame that displayed part of the engine's tables.

The exact situation also applies in the APPOST form. There is a little code for the form, and there is a lot of code for the AP engine. Because the sequence of statements is by now so familiar, here is all the code for the form's open, close, and VNOTES launch, in one bite:

```
;¦BeginMethod¦#FormData1¦open¦
method open(var eventInfo Event)
  if NOT eventInfo.isPreFilter() then
    doDefault
    maximize()
  endif
endmethod
;¦EndMethod¦#FormData1¦open¦

;¦BeginMethod¦#Page2.#Button59¦pushButton¦
method pushButton(var eventInfo Event)
  close(0)
endmethod
;¦EndMethod¦#Page2.#Button59¦pushButton¦

;¦BeginMethod¦#Page2.#Button61¦pushButton¦
method pushButton(var eventInfo Event)
var
  fv Form
endvar
```

7

```
    fv.open( "VNOTES.FDL" )
    fv.wait()
endmethod
;¦EndMethod¦#Page2.#Button61¦pushButton¦
```

And you have already seen the engine's code, too. It is likewise presented in one bite, because you're already familiar with it. Take heart, though. New things come immediately afterward. Here are the AP engine's methods:

```
;¦BeginMethod¦#Page2.APAY.#Record41¦action¦
method action(var eventInfo ActionEvent)
  if eventInfo.id() = DataDeleteRecord then
    if DatePaid.isBlank() then  ; back out only if unpaid
      balance = balance - InvoiceAmt
    endif
  else
    doDefault
  endif
endmethod
;¦EndMethod¦#Page2.APAY.#Record41¦action¦

;¦BeginMethod¦#Page2.APAY.#Record41.DatePaid¦changeValue¦
method changeValue(var eventInfo ValueEvent)
  if NOT self.isBlank() then
    disableDefault
    eventInfo.setErrorCode( CanNotDepart )
    msgStop( "AP Posting", "This invoice is already paid!" )
  else
    if ( AuthPayAmt.isBlank() ) OR ( AuthPayAmt <> InvoiceAmt ) then
      disableDefault
      eventInfo.setErrorCode( CanNotDepart )
      msgStop( "AP Posting", "Authorized pay amount must equal invoice." )
    else
      balance = balance - AuthPayAmt  ; adjust balance for payment made
    endif
  endif
endmethod
;¦EndMethod¦#Page2.APAY.#Record41.DatePaid¦changeValue¦

;¦BeginMethod¦#Page2.APAY.#Record41.AuthPayAmt¦changeValue¦
method changeValue(var eventInfo ValueEvent)
var
  newval Currency
endvar
  newval = eventInfo.newValue()
  if ( newval = InvoiceAmt ) then
    doDefault
  else
    disableDefault
    eventInfo.setErrorCode( CanNotDepart )
    msgStop( "AP Posting", "Partial or overpayments not allowed." )
  endif
endmethod
;¦EndMethod¦#Page2.APAY.#Record41.AuthPayAmt¦changeValue¦

;¦BeginMethod¦#Page2.APAY.#Record41.InvoiceAmt¦changeValue¦
method changeValue(var eventInfo ValueEvent)
```

```
var
  oldval, newval Number
endvar
  if NOT DatePaid.isBlank() then
    disableDefault
    eventInfo.setErrorCode( CanNotDepart )
    msgStop( "AP Posting", "This invoice is already paid!" )
  else
    oldval = self.value      ; value not posted to table yet
    newval = eventInfo.newValue()
    if NOT oldval.isBlank() then
      balance = balance - oldval  ; back it out
      balance = balance + newval  ; strike new balace
    endif
  endif
endmethod
;¦EndMethod¦#Page2.APAY.#Record41.InvoiceAmt¦changeValue¦

;¦BeginMethod¦#Page2.APAY.#Record41.DueDate¦changeValue¦
method changeValue(var eventInfo ValueEvent)
  if NOT DatePaid.isBlank() then
    disableDefault
    eventInfo.setErrorCode( CanNotDepart )
    msgStop( "AP Posting", "This invoice is already paid!" )
  endif
endmethod
;¦EndMethod¦#Page2.APAY.#Record41.DueDate¦changeValue¦
```

Even though you have seen some of the preceding code listings before, I hope I was right in thinking that it is important to see all the code for a form together in one place. I know it is for me because it gives me a sense of the connections between the parts.

But now, onward to new horizons. You haven't yet seen the ARINQ form's methods, so you should wake up now! They are mercifully few, and are packaged in a somewhat different manner. You'll need to observe them carefully, because you have to duplicate them soon for the AP system.

Before I begin talking about the methods on the ARINQ form, look back for a moment at Figure 7.5, where the form is shown. Notice that I opened the object tree on the form for this figure. Now you're about to discover why I did.

Look at Figure 7.5 closely, and you'll soon realize that the stack of six radio buttons is actually just one field, named SelectInq. This field can have six, and only six, discrete possible values: the values of the individual radio buttons. Notice also that each individual radio button is given an explicit name. I did not leave them with their default Paradox noise names. This point will be important for writing the ObjectPAL code that initializes the radio button field to its starting value.

It might be profitable to stop a moment and review how a radio button field can be placed on a form and defined so that the ObjectPAL methods can work with it. First, just click

225

the field tool on the toolbar and drag a new, undefined field onto the form. The result is demonstrated in Figure 7.6.

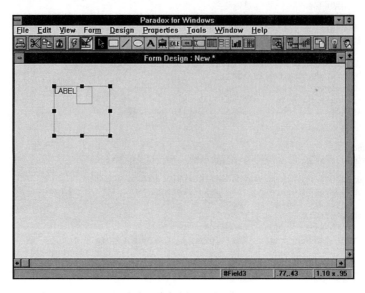

Figure 7.6. *Placing a new undefined field on the form.*

So far, there isn't much to the new field. Next, however, right-click the new field object to display its properties list. In the properties list, click the Display type selection, which will produce yet another pop-up menu. From that menu, click the Radio Buttons selection.

Now you should see the Define List dialog box, as shown in Figure 7.7. In that dialog box, in the Item field, I have typed three text values, Item1, Item2, and Item3. The three text values each moved, as they were entered, to the right into the listbox labeled Item List.

Each text item will now become the label for one of the radio buttons. After clicking OK in the Define list dialog box, you'll see the form again, but now the undefined field looks like a radio button field, as shown in Figure 7.8. Notice that the text items I entered in the dialog box are now the labels for the radio buttons. The text value for the radio button that's clicked at runtime will be the value of the whole field. This is important: remember it when you initialize the form in the open() method.

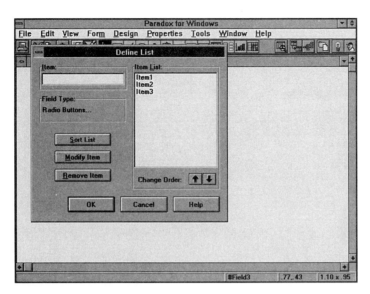

Figure 7.7. *Defining list items for the radio button labels.*

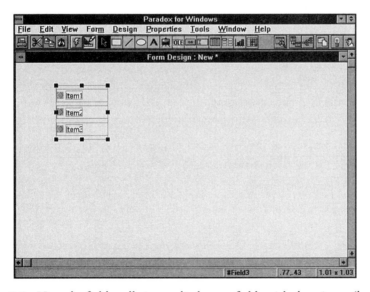

Figure 7.8. *Now the field really is a radio button field, with three items (buttons).*

227

In Figure 7.9, you can see how I have begun to give the field a little life. I have made the page a gray color, and the radio button field is gray as well. Furthermore, I have assigned the field frame a 3D style to pick it up off the form's surface.

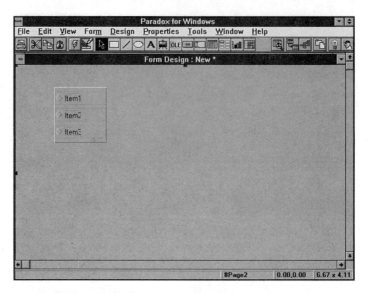

Figure 7.9. *Working with the field's attributes to spruce it up.*

As a final touch, I selected each text field within the buttons (remember that contained objects have to be clicked more than once to select them), and gave them each an inside 3D frame. This really puts the finishing touch on the appearance of the radio button field.

Go back now and look at the ARINQ form's open() method. This is where I initialized the radio button field. Here is the source for that method:

```
;¦BeginMethod¦#FormData1¦open¦
method open(var eventInfo Event)
  if NOT eventInfo.isPreFilter() then
    doDefault
    setPosition( 1440, 220, 6500, 4320 )
    SelectInq.value = "Customer Summary Rpt."
    SelectInq.CustSum.pushButton()
  endif
endmethod
;¦EndMethod¦#FormData1¦open¦
```

Notice that the radio button field was initialized in two steps. First I assigned the field as a whole the value of "Customer Summary Rpt." Notice too that this is exactly the same as the text for the first radio button: it is really important not to misspell this one!

Second, I caused the desired radio button to click itself by coding the pushbutton() call to that very button. This is why each individual button must be named. They cannot be accessed for this purpose otherwise. The call reads like this:

```
SelectInq.CustSum.pushButton()
```

Now the radio button field has the correct initial value, and the display object has the correct appearance: the button is clicked—and all without the user having to do anything to set it up!

The ARINQ close() method is most uninspiring by comparison, but it does its job. It makes the ARINQ form go away, as usual. Here is the close() method in all its beauty:

```
;¦BeginMethod¦#Page2.#Button6¦pushButton¦
method pushButton(var eventInfo Event)
  close(0)
endmethod
;¦EndMethod¦#Page2.#Button6¦pushButton¦
```

Good, now we're past the boring stuff. The Launch Inquiry button comes next, and it must decode the state and value of the SelectInq radio button field in order to proceed. It does this with a rather large switch statement, as follows:

```
;¦BeginMethod¦#Page2.#Button4¦pushButton¦
method pushButton(var eventInfo Event)
var
  ri  ReportPrintInfo
  rep Report
  qbf TextStream
  qtl,qtext String
  tv  TableView
  fv  Form
endvar
  switch
    case SelectInq.value = "Customer Summary Rpt." :
      ri.name = ":work:arcust.rdl"
      rep.open( ri )
    case SelectInq.value = "Customer Detail Rpt." :
      ri.name = ":work:custdetl.rdl"
      rep.open( ri )
```

```
      case SelectInq.value = "Receivables Detail Rpt." :
        ri.name = ":work:arrecv.rdl"
        rep.open( ri )
      case SelectInq.value = "Customer Balance QBE" :
        qtext.blank()
        qbf.open( ":work:custbal.qbe","r" )
        while NOT qbf.eof()
          qbf.readLine( qtl )
          qtext = String( qtext, qtl, "\n" )
        endwhile
        qbf.close()
        if executeQBEString( qtext, ":work:dbanswer.db" ) then
          tv.open( ":work:dbanswer.db" )
          tv.maximize()
          tv.wait()
        else
          msgStop( "DPW AR Inquiry", "Query execution FAILED!" )
        endif
      case SelectInq.value = "Receivables Chart" :
        fv.open( ":work:archart.fdl" )
        fv.wait()
      case SelectInq.value = "Receivables XTab" :
        fv.open( ":work:arxtab.fdl" )
        fv.wait()
    endswitch
    setPosition( 1440, 220, 6500, 4320 )
  endmethod
;¦EndMethod¦#Page2.#Button4¦pushButton¦
```

The switch statement contains a case statement for each of the six possible values of the SelectInq radio button field. Remember that each possible value is also the value of the text field for each individual radio button. It is therefore of the utmost importance that you spell the text labels in the case statements precisely as you did when you defined them in the Define list dialog box. If you don't do that, nothing gets hit, and nothing will happen when you choose Launch Inquiry!

Creating the Application's Charts, Crosstabs, and Queries

This is the home stretch for building the AR/AP application's interfaces. All that remains today is to create the charts, crosstabs, and inquiries (which include both a query and some reports) for the application. It will be a walk in the park, relatively speaking, so just go through the process at just about light speed. Got your seat belt on?

There is just one chart for the system, though of course you can add as many as you like to the system. The chart is embedded in the form ARCHART, which is shown, in design mode, in Figure 7.10.

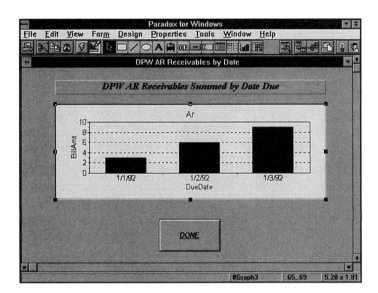

Figure 7.10. *Creating ARCHART.FSL.*

To create the chart, open a new form, using the AR table. But select a blank *layout* (noting that this is different from a blank *form*), because you're going to provide the form's contents.

There are three objects on the form: the title text, the chart itself, and the DONE button—I got tired of quitting, so I just got "done." Of these objects, only the chart needs any comment. You can inspect the form yourself and see that everything else is just what you have seen before.

First drag a chart object onto the form and position and size it the way you want it. Then right-click it to see the properties list, from which you can define the chart. You should select the AR.DB to back the chart, of course.

After that, it is a simple matter of right-clicking the components of the chart, meaning mainly the *x*- and *y*-axes, to define the fields on which they are to be based. Yes, it really is that simple. Ain't Paradox nice?

The crosstab is very nearly as simple. You create a new form on the CUSTOMER table and link it to the AR table, master to slave. But you still choose the blank layout style.

You drag a crosstab object onto the screen and define that much as you did the chart. For a crosstab, however, you define the columns, rows, and summaries (which are the essence of the crosstab). Now add the required text title and DONE button and you're, well, done. It really is still that easy, and the result is shown in Figure 7.11.

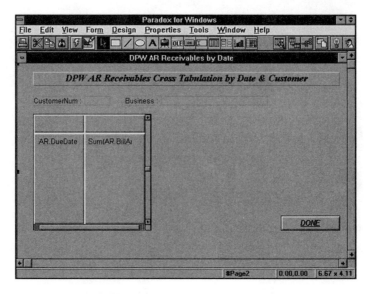

Figure 7.11. *Creating ARXTAB.FSL.*

Creating a query is even easier. The CUSTBAL query is shown in Figure 7.12. It is obvious that I created a new query and then just checked everything in the record. As a last touch, I required that only records with a balance field greater than zero be selected, by specifying that criteria in the Balance field.

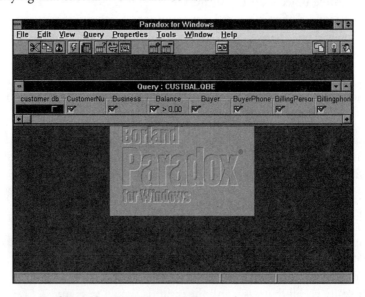

Figure 7.12. *Defining the CUSTBAL.QBE query.*

Getting the reports used in the inquiries was not much more complicated because I allowed Paradox to use defaults wherever possible. Paradox is great for getting things rolling quickly—the default manner of doing things is usually at least somewhat acceptable—and then you have the Experts, too. You can define your own Experts if you want.

The first report you'll see here is the customer summary report, ARCUST.RSL. This report really is a default report, with just a few of the fields removed from the tabular layout. It is shown in Figure 7.13.

For the receivables detail report, I did something a little different. I created a default report, but then I added a band and grouped the report on the CustomerNum field. The result is shown in Figure 7.14.

The reason that I wanted to group on the customer number, however, is because I wanted a page break after each customer. Thus, there could possibly be several pages per customer, but never more than one customer per page. In Figure 7.15, the receivables detail report is shown scrolled down so that you can see where I put the page break. (To add a page break, just click in the open area to the left of the vertical rule, where you see the break symbol in the figure).

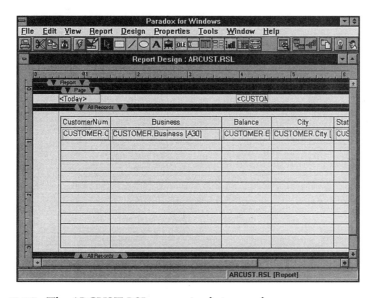

Figure 7.13. *The ARCUST.RSL report, in design mode.*

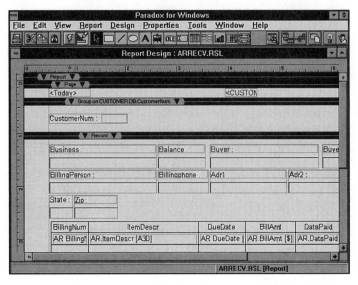

Figure 7.14. *Creating the receivables detail report, ARRECV.RSL, grouping on CustomerNum.*

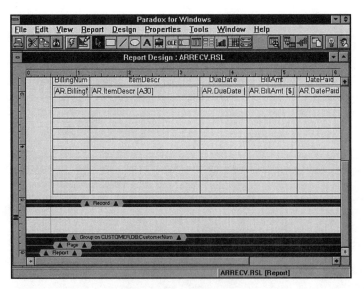

Figure 7.15. *Adding a page break to the ARRECV.RSL report, in the bottom group band, to break after every customer.*

And, last of all, you have the customer detail report, in which everything known about each customer is printed. There is a group band in this report too, so that each customer's information is printed on a separate page. The page break is placed in the bottom group band exactly as before. The customer detail report is shown in Figure 7.16.

Modification Notes

In the DPWMAIN form, there were several places where dummy ObjectPAL code was inserted, to identify the work you have ahead of you.

You can go right now and find those methods and plan what will happen when the user clicks the buttons. Get as specific as deciding on what the form or report names will be. You also can go ahead and write a lot of the code, particularly the kind that just launches other forms, or perhaps a report. Finally, you can go ahead and design an AP Inquire/Analyze form, using the one I did as a model. You can even design and create the various inquiries, whether they be charts, crosstabs, queries, or reports hiding under the covers.

What you shouldn't do yet is write the ObjectPAL code for the batch processes and other code that's embedded directly in the DPWMAIN form, as pushbutton() methods. It would be best if you waited until I've discussed those features in detail before you go ahead with that part.

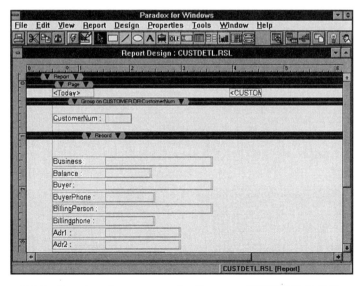

Figure 7.16. *Creating the customer detail report, CUSTDETL.RSL.*

Debugging the Process

The way Paradox works, you can put as much of your part of the AP side into place as you want. Then go ahead and click the buttons to see what will happen. That's exactly how I wrote the AR side, and part of the AP side, too.

If you failed to put something into place, you'll find that out very quickly, and it is the best way to find those little lost details. Click 'em all to see what happens. Then fix things by adding the parts you left out, or typed wrong, or whatever, until clicking the buttons yields the results you want.

I am fully aware that this doesn't sound like high-tech programmer talk. That's one of the nicest things about programming Paradox for Windows. You can do some real programming, getting amazing results, without being a high-tech programmer. Experiment and enjoy: it's hard to break things in this environment so badly that you can't get out of it somehow!

8

Building the Application's Batch Process

In the first seven days of this project, you designed and built the primary system interfaces for the DPW AR/AP accounting system, plus lots of other neat toys besides. Things are moving along at a rapid clip now, indeed.

Today is the day to begin filling in all the nice little details without which the application really isn't an application yet. However, these "nice little details" aren't by any means trivial. Some serious programming is going to take place today, including the following programming activities:

- ☐ Adding the ObjectPAL methods necessary to implement the AR data export function. This will be a detailed exercise in programming drop-down and plain listboxes, strings and TextStreams, and advanced table cursor programming.

- ☐ Supplying the ObjectPAL code necessary for the DPWMAIN form to carry out AR transaction archival, or record retirement. This will involve more table and table cursor handling.

- ☐ Coding the ObjectPAL methods for posting mass charges to AR customers. This is again a fairly advanced project, using tables and table cursors.

- ☐ Creating the AR billing report, which you'll use to bill your customers. This is a free ride, by comparison to the previous activities.

- ☐ Creating the AR mailing labels report, also a walk in the park after all that table cursor manipulation.

As you can see, rest period is over! This will be another busy day.

Exporting Data from the Application

No serious software package today is caught without the means to export its data for use by other applications. It is something that users have demanded by refusing to use packages that don't offer the feature. You can hardly fail to follow suit in the DPW AR/AP accounting system, so the first batch process you'll implement today will be the AR data export feature.

The export function will scan either the CUSTOMER or AR table, display the table's fields for the user to select from, and, when requested to do so, create a text file in quoted, comma-delimited format (sometimes called DIF, or Data Interchange Format.)

That doesn't sound too bad, but you'll have to master some more-advanced ObjectPAL programming techniques to pull it off. But before you get down into that, review the

AREXPORT form in somewhat more detail than before, as a prelude to programming the form itself. Figure 8.1 shows the AREXPORT form, and there is nothing new visible so far.

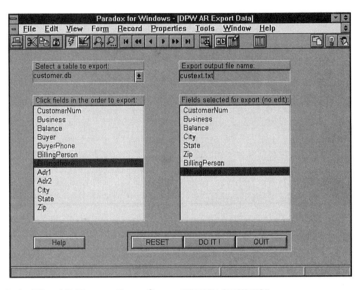

Figure 8.1. *The AR Export Data form, AREXPORT.FSL.*

Just for the sake of completeness, and to give you a feeling for the objective here, I exported a few fields from the CUSTOMER table, and edited the resulting text file in the DPW NotePad. The results of that operation are shown in Figure 8.2.

As you can see in Figure 8.2, it isn't necessary to select all the record's fields, nor is it necessary to select them in any particular order. The output text file, after all, isn't a table and has no keys or indexes: it's just data.

How you get from here to there is another matter, though. There is first the issue of allowing the user to select which of the two tables will be exported. This is taken care of by the drop-down listbox (the field SelectDB, really), from which the user can choose either the CUSTOMER or AR tables.

Drop-down listboxes are defined in much the same manner as plain listboxes. This point is illustrated in Figure 8.3, where I am defining the SelectDB field's list entries.

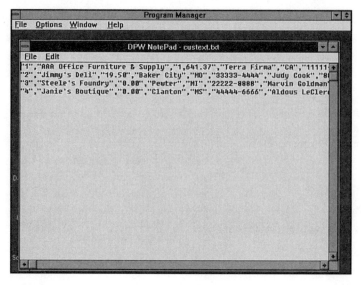

Figure 8.2. *The results of exporting the CUSTOMER table, in file CUSTEXT.TXT.*

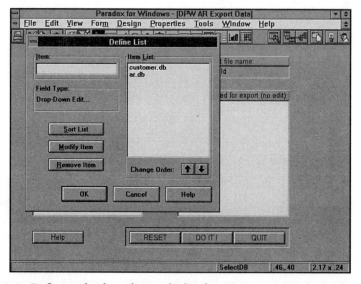

Figure 8.3. *Defining the drop-down edit list for AR Export (to select either CUS-TOMER or AR tables).*

One important thing to remember about list objects, drop-down or otherwise, is that they are fields, and contain another object which is the list itself. Both of these objects should be named, and not allowed to remain with the default noise name.

This important point is illustrated in Figure 8.4, where I have opened the object tree to explode the listbox's detailed structure. In this figure, you can see that I have used the object tree to select the entire field.

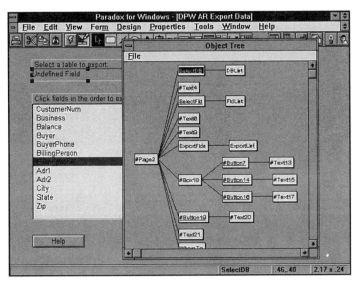

Figure 8.4. *Using the object tree to display the drop-down list field structure* (SelectDB).

Keep in mind, too, that you can click the object tree to select an object on the form. That's quite important, for sometimes you either can't tell what you have selected (no selection handles will appear), or you just can't select an object without using the object tree.

This point is illustrated in Figure 8.5, where I have used the object tree to select the list interior to the drop-down list field. As you can see, there are no visible selection handles when the list itself (DBList) is selected. Although you couldn't see what you had done, you could have clicked on the drop-down button to select the list, but you could not have inspected its properties. And you need to do that to name the list.

241

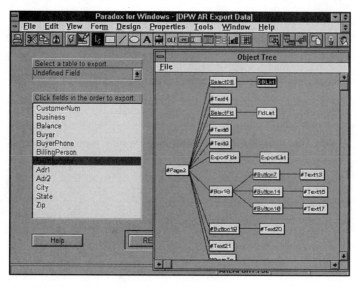

Figure 8.5. *Using the object tree to display the drop-down list structure (DBList).*

Figure 8.6, is a little deceptive. It is a depiction of the definition of the plain listbox SelectFld, which contains the list FldList. Take a look at the figure and see if you can guess what isn't quite right about it.

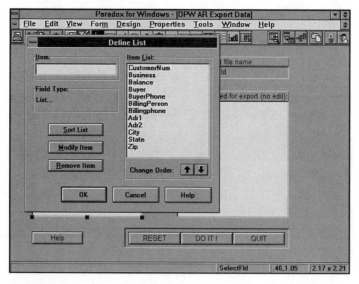

Figure 8.6. *Defining the field selection listbox items for AR Export.*

The thing about the Define List dialog box shown in Figure 8.6 is that there are entry items apparently defined. The problem is, I didn't define them! Not directly, that is.

When I created the `SelectFld` listbox, I left it entirely undefined, because the ObjectPAL behind the form will fill in the list when the user selects one of the tables for export. So how did the entries get in the listbox definition?

Fortunately, the answer is both simple and unthreatening. While I worked on the form, I switched back and forth several times between design and run modes. After switching back to design mode, after running the form, the list entries were left over, you might say. Then I saved the form that way. No worries, though, because the ObjectPAL code also clears out the listbox when the form is opened, so it starts fresh every time.

Figure 8.7 shows the object tree being used to examine the detailed structure of the `SelectFld` field; it contains the list named `FldList`. Again, name both the field and the contained list, so they can be accessed by ObjectPAL code.

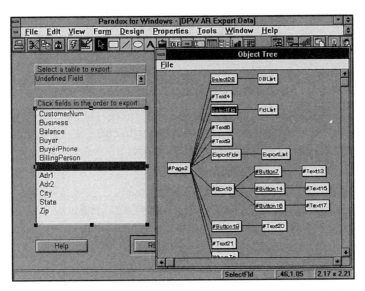

Figure 8.7. *Using the object tree to examine the* `SelectFld` *listbox field structure.*

In Figure 8.8, you see a slight variation on the previous figure. It is the `FldList` list object that's selected this time, and because this isn't a drop-down list, you can see that the selection handles are visible, and they even manage to convey that it is the interior object that's currently selected.

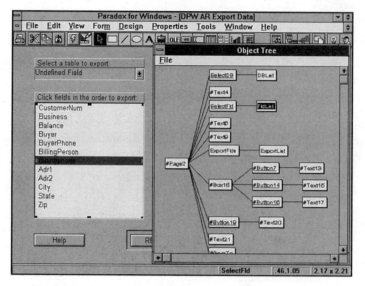

Figure 8.8. *Using the object tree to examine the* `FldList` *listbox list structure.*

At this point, you should be thoroughly familiar with the structure and construction of the form and its listboxes. The `ExportFlds` listbox field and `ExportList` list are done the same way as the others, but don't allow the user to select anything.

Now you can begin programming for the export function. The programming is in two parts: programming for the drop-down and plain listboxes, and the programming that will actually drive the export function.

To begin with, take a look at the form's `open()` method, paying special attention to the lines of codes that initialize the listboxes. You should immediately see why it is important to name every part of a listbox:

```
;¦BeginMethod¦#FormData1¦open¦
method open(var eventInfo Event)
  if NOT eventInfo.isPreFilter() then
    doDefault
    maximize()
    SelectDB.DBList.list.Selection = 1   ; default to customer.db
    SelectDB.value = SelectDB.DBList.list.value ; show it
    SelectFld.FldList.list.count = 0     ; do nothing until user does
    ExportFlds.ExportList.list.count = 0 ; initial reset for selected list
  endif
endmethod
;¦EndMethod¦#FormData1¦open¦
```

Table 8.1 summarizes the list attributes that you can use to work with listboxes. With these attributes, you can access and control a list's value, item count, and current selection.

Table 8.1. ObjectPAl list attributes for working with list objects.

Attribute Name	Attribute Use
`fieldname.listname.list.count`	Set to 0 to empty, access for information
`fieldname.listname.list.value`	Access or set the value of the current selection
`fieldname.listname.list.selection`	Set the current selection

In the `open()` method, every one of these attributes is used. For the `SelectDB` field, the selection is set to 1, the first entry in the list, and the value of that selection is extracted to initialize the field value itself (both entities have values.) You won't need to set the field's value again. The user will do that by clicking on a selection.

The help button and quit button ObjectPAl are by now old hat. I will just show those methods together and go on. Here they are:

```
;¦BeginMethod¦#Page2.#Button19¦pushButton¦
method pushButton(var eventInfo Event)
  helpShowContext( "AREXPORT.HLP", 1 )
endmethod
;¦EndMethod¦#Page2.#Button19¦pushButton¦

;¦BeginMethod¦#Page2.#Box18.#Button16¦pushButton¦
method pushButton(var eventInfo Event)
  close(0)
endmethod
;¦EndMethod¦#Page2.#Box18.#Button16¦pushButton¦
```

I have left the Do It! pushbutton with its default noise name, but it is next. The ObjectPAL for the Do It! runs in several discrete steps, as follows:

☐ Check the value of the WhereTo edit field to see if the user specified an output text filename. If not, show an error and return to the form.

☐ Check the ExportFlds listbox to see if any fields have been selected for export. If not, show an error and return to the form.

☐ Open a table cursor on the table currently selected in the SelectDB drop-down listbox. If unable, show an error and return to the form.

☐ Create the text file (open a TextStream) with the name found in the WhereTo field. If unable, show an error and return to the form.

☐ Get the number of fields selected for export from the ExportFlds listbox by using the count attribute.

☐ Set the `visible` attribute for `ExportFlds.ExportList` to `False`. Leaving the fields in the listbox visible drastically slows down the next step.

☐ Examine every record in the selected table using a `scan` loop. Within the `scan` loop, use a `for` loop to check and extract each of the selected fields from `ExportFlds.ExportList`. Use the table cursor to get each field's type and make sure that it is a type that can be exported. If it is, get the string value of the field and package it with quotation marks and commas, as necessary, and add that string fragment to the string output line. When the string output line is complete, put it in the text file using the `writeLine()` TextStream method.

☐ Set the `visible` attribute for `ExportFlds.ExportList` to `True`. This enables the user to see the fields again, and is a visual cue that the export is completed.

☐ Close both the TCursor and TextStream variables. You're done!

Now that you know how the whole thing goes, here is the ObjectPAL code that does these things:

```
;|BeginMethod|#Page2.#Box18.#Button14|pushButton|
method pushButton(var eventInfo Event)
var
  ts     TextStream
  lpstr  String
  tc     TCursor
  i, k   SmallInt
  hold   AnyType
endvar
  if WhereTo.isBlank() then
    msgStop( "DPW AR Export", "No output file name was given" )
    return
  endif
  if 0 = ExportFlds.ExportList.list.count then
    msgStop( "DPW AR Export", "No fields were selected for export" )
    return
  endif
  if NOT tc.open( SelectDB.DBList.list.value ) then
    msgStop( "DPW AR Export", "Could not open the selected table" )
    return
  endif
  if NOT ts.create( WhereTo.value ) then
    msgStop( "DPW AR Export", "Could not create/open the export file" )
    return
  endif
  k = ExportFlds.ExportList.list.count
  ExportFlds.ExportList.visible = False
  scan tc :
    lpstr = ""
    for i from 1 to k
      lpstr = lpstr + "\""
      ExportFlds.ExportList.list.selection = i
      if (tc.fieldType( ExportFlds.ExportList.list.value ) <> "MEMO") AND
         (tc.fieldType( ExportFlds.ExportList.list.value ) <> "FMTMEMO") AND
```

```
      (tc.fieldType( ExportFlds.ExportList.list.value ) <> "BINARYBLOB") AND
      (tc.fieldType( ExportFlds.ExportList.list.value ) <> "OLEOBJ") AND
      (tc.fieldType( ExportFlds.ExportList.list.value ) <> "GRAPHIC") then
      tc.fieldValue( ExportFlds.ExportList.list.value, hold )
      lpstr = lpstr + StrVal(hold)
    endif
    if i = k then
      lpstr = lpstr + "\""
    else
      lpstr = lpstr + "\","
    endif
  endfor
  ts.writeLine( lpstr )
 endscan
 ExportFlds.ExportList.visible = True
 tc.close()
 ts.close()
endmethod
;¦EndMethod¦#Page2.#Box18.#Button14¦pushButton¦
```

The Reset button on the AREXPORT form is also stuck with its default noise name, but I happen to know that it is #Button7. Its function is to clear the ExportFlds listbox, so that the user can start over again clean selecting fields for export. Using the count list attribute it is very easy to do this. Just set it to zero, as follows:

```
;¦BeginMethod¦#Page2.#Box18.#Button7¦pushButton¦
method pushButton(var eventInfo Event)
  ExportFlds.ExportList.list.count = 0
endmethod
;¦EndMethod¦#Page2.#Box18.#Button7¦pushButton¦
```

The idea behind the AREXPORT form is to enable the user to click fields in the left-hand listbox to select them for export. When a field is clicked on, it should naturally show up in the right-hand listbox. As you might expect, however, this doesn't happen by magic; you have to make it happen. To add a clicked field to the other listbox, you have to first identify the selection that was clicked, get its value, and add that entry to the other list.

That task is somewhat simplified by the fact that I mentioned earlier: A listbox field has a value, which is just the value of the list entry that's currently selected. Thus, you can customize the newValue() method for the SelectFld list as follows:

```
;¦BeginMethod¦#Page2.SelectFld¦newValue¦
method newValue(var eventInfo Event)
  if eventInfo.reason() = EditValue then
    ExportFlds.ExportList.list.selection =
        ExportFlds.ExportList.list.count + 1    ; next exported item
    ExportFlds.ExportList.list.value =
        self.FldList.list.value
  endif
endmethod
;¦EndMethod¦#Page2.SelectFld¦newValue¦
```

Checking to see whether eventInfo.reason() = EditValue is the cause for the newValue() calls just verifies that the event is being handled only because the user clicked an entry. This will be important in the next method to be discussed, but hold on to it for now, and see how the entry is transferred to ExportFlds.

Adding the entry to the ExportFlds.ExportList listbox proceeds in two steps. First set the selection for the list to count plus one. This moves the selection off the end of the present list, something like you do to add a record to a table in a table view.

Second, set the value of the new entry to the value of self. Remember that this method is the newValue() method for SelectFld which knows its own value. It takes a few words to say it, but if you look back at the method's code, you'll see that only two statements do the actual work.

The next method, the newValue() method for the SelectDB field, checks not only for the EditValue event, but for the StartUpValue event as well. Remember that this is the drop-down list for selecting either the CUSTOMER or AR tables. Thus, you are trapping new value events when the user selected a different table, or opening the form assigned an initial value here.

The SelectDB newValue() method must go a little further, however, because it must go get the field list for the selected table, and place the list in the SelectFld listbox. This is done with a table cursor, as follows:

```
;¦BeginMethod¦#Page2.SelectDB¦newValue¦
method newValue(var eventInfo Event)
var
  tc       TCursor
  i, k LongInt
endvar
  if eventInfo.reason() = EditValue or
     eventInfo.reason() = StartUpValue then
    SelectFld.FldList.list.count = 0
    ExportFlds.ExportList.list.count = 0
    tc.open( self.DBList.list.value )
    SelectFld.FldList.visible = False
    k = tc.nFields()
    for i from 1 to k
      SelectFld.FldList.list.selection = i
      SelectFld.FldList.list.value = tc.fieldName( SmallInt(i) )
    endfor
    SelectFld.FldList.visible = True
    tc.close()
  endif
endmethod
;¦EndMethod¦#Page2.SelectDB¦newValue¦
```

Here is what just happened in this method, in more detail:

☐ Both the `SelectDB` and `ExportFlds` listboxes are emptied, by setting their `count` attributes to zero.

☐ The table cursor is opened on the selected table, and the list in `SelectFld` is made invisible (so the code will run much faster). The table cursor is used to determine how many fields are in the selected table's records.

☐ A `for` loop retrieves each field's name, using the table cursor, and places the name in the current list selection as its value.

Bingo! List programming is really easy to do, once you get the drift of what is going on.

Archiving Account Data for the Auditors

In this section I will go back and look at just one method, the `pushbutton()` method for the AR Archive Data button from the DPWMAIN form. You may recall that retiring AR transaction data doesn't open a new form: it just puts messages in the window's status bar as work progresses.

Because there is just the one method, it will be listed, but interrupted by my comments from time to time, contrary to my previous habits of presenting ObjectPAL code.

The first order of business is to declare a few variables for use within the method. This is done at the beginning of the method, as always, and as follows:

```
;|BeginMethod|#Page2.ArchiveAR|pushButton|
method pushButton(var eventInfo Event)
var
  tb1, tb2 Table
  tcar, tchist TCursor
  arRec DynArray[] AnyType
endvar
```

One of the design goals of this method is to segment the work, so that if it fails, the minimum possible damage is done to the original tables. One way to go about ensuring this level of security is to do everything in a temporary table first. Then if all is well, use the temporary table to move transaction records to the history file. On the other hand, if things don't go well, the temporary table is still sitting there, with your data intact. Recovery might be a little awkward, but at least recovery would be possible.

Accordingly, the second order of business is to clone the AR table, creating the temporary work table. If this doesn't happen properly, everything stops, an error message is displayed in the status bar, and the method returns to the form with no further processing. The code to clone the AR to the temporary table, incidentally, was stolen without remorse from the DPW Table Utility, and it looks like this:

```
message( "DPW AR starting record retirement to history file." )
sleep(500)
message( "DPW AR creating temporary transaction table." )
tb1.attach( ":work:ar.db" )
tb2.attach( ":work:artemp.db" )
if tb1.isTable() AND NOT tb2.isTable() then
  tb1.enumFieldStruct( ":work:DBANSWER.DB" )
  tb1.enumIndexStruct( ":work:IXANSWER.DB" )
  tb2 = create
        ":work:artemp.db"
        STRUCT ":work:DBANSWER.DB"
        INDEXSTRUCT ":work:IXANSWER.DB"
      endcreate
else
  msgStop( "DPW AR Archive", "Could not create temp table!" )
  tb1.unattach()
  tb2.unattach()
  return
endif
tb1.unattach()
tb2.unattach()
```

Presuming that you now have a temporary table to work with, it is time to open the AR and ARHIST files. The open() calls are couched in terms of if statements so that the method won't accidentally proceed if the open operations fail, as follows:

```
message( "DPW AR locating receivables for retirement." )
if NOT tcar.open( ":work:ar.db" ) then
  msgStop( "DPW AR Archive", "Could not open AR.DB!" )
  return
endif
if NOT tchist.open( ":work:artemp.db" ) then
  msgStop( "DPW AR Archive", "Could not open AR.DB!" )
  tcar.close()
  return
endif
```

As you can see, this method only looks lengthy. It is really composed of a few sections of relatively brief code. The section of code that does all the real work, locating transactions that have been posted as paid, is built as a single scan loop passing over the entire AR table. If such a record is found, it is first copied to the temporary table, and then deleted from the AR table. Look at the code for this process, and then I'll tell you one more little secret about scan loops that I first discovered with DOS Paradox. Here it is:

```
tcar.edit()
tchist.edit()
tchist.end()
scan tcar for (tcar.DatePaid.isBlank() = False) :
  tcar.copyToArray( arRec )
  tchist.insertAfterRecord()
```

```
      tchist.copyFromArray( arRec )
      tcar.deleteRecord()
      loop       ; don't let scan move the record pointer, delete did it
    endscan
    tcar.endEdit()
    tchist.endEdit()
    tcar.close()
    tchist.close()
```

The little secret that I mentioned has to do with the `loop` statement inside the `scan` loop, right after the `deleteRecord()` call. The fact is, deleting the record automatically advances the current record position down to the next record, the one that wasn't deleted. If you now enable scan to reach the bottom of the loop, the record pointer will advance again, and you'll thus miss the one right after the deleted record. The `loop` statement goes back to the top of the loop early, avoiding that mistake.

In this scan loop, by the way, the `scan for` syntax is used, so that every pass through the loop will be for a record that should, in fact, be deleted. Thus, the `loop` statement is used in every pass through the loop.

Following the `scan` loop, there are a bunch of posted-as-paid records sitting in the temporary table, and only there. If something should happen, such as a power failure at this point, you can always come back and add the temporary table manually to the history file.

If all goes well, however, adding the posted records to the history file is the job of the next section of the code. The logic for this little bit of code was also stolen without embarrassment of any kind (I freely plagiarize my own work, and you should form the same habit—with your work, that is). The table `add()` call is arranged so that the records are added to the history file, leaving the temporary table alone for the moment, as follows:

```
message( "DPW AR adding temporary transaction table to history." )
tb1.attach( ":work:arhist.db" )
tb2.attach( ":work:artemp.db" )
if tb1.isTable() AND tb2.isTable() then
  if NOT tb2.add( tb1, True, False ) then
    msgStop( "DPW AR Archive", "Table add failed" )
    tb1.unattach()
    tb2.unattach()
    return
  endif
else
  msgStop( "DPW AR Archive", "A table is not specified correctly!" )
endif
tb1.unattach()
tb2.unattach()
```

Now the posted records live in two places: in the history file, and also still in the temporary table. Cleaning up by deleting the temporary table is the only task that remains. That's accomplished by a simple call to the table `delete()` method, like this:

```
tb1.attach( ":work:artemp.db" )
if tb1.isTable()then
  message( "DPW AR deleting table... ", ":work:artemp.db" )
  if NOT tb1.delete() then
    msgStop( "DPW AR Archive", "Temp Table delete FAILED!" )
    return
  endif
else
  msgStop( "DPW AR Archive", "A table is not specified correctly!" )
  return
endif
tb1.unattach()
message( "DPW AR record retirement to history file complete." )
endmethod
;¦EndMethod¦#Page2.ArchiveAR¦pushButton¦
```

There you are! Archiving paid transaction records wasn't as bad as you thought it was going to be, was it? The thought for the day here is to break up intimidating tasks into more digestible chunks.

Posting Mass Charges to Customers

Another one of those jobs that seems to be intimidating on the surface is found in the AR mass charge batch procedure. If you haven't done something like this before, I'm sure you're wondering how you're going to get all those new records in the AR table in some organized way.

The answer is the same one you just used. A table cursor and a scan loop will do the job very nicely once more. Before you get into the insides of mass posting AR records, however, take a refresher look at the form that drives this process. The ARMASSC form is shown in Figure 8.9.

The mass charges process requires that you do three things correctly:

☐ Account for the possibility that the user will want to perform the task on only a part of the customer base. You'll provide the filter button and fields for this purpose.

☐ Provide the means to construct AR transaction records with the right transaction date, amount, and description. If one of these items is missing, then the mass charge posting will put a lot of junk records in the AR file in a big hurry.

☐ Get all the new records in the AR file in the right places, and only for the selected customers, if filtering is in force.

That may sound intimidating, but it's not. Go through the ObjectPAL one piece at a time, just as before, and knock it down to size. It's always nice to come up to speed smoothly, so you start with as many other listings with the form's open() method. It's nothing you haven't seen before, and here it is:

```
;¦BeginMethod¦#FormData1¦open¦
method open(var eventInfo Event)
  if NOT eventInfo.isPreFilter() then
    doDefault
    maximize()
  endif
endmethod
;¦EndMethod¦#FormData1¦open¦
```

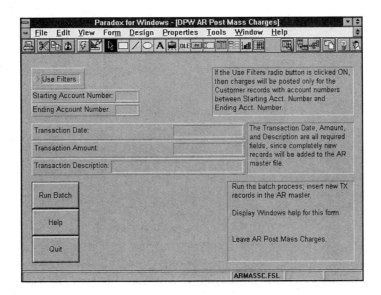

Figure 8.9. *Reviewing the AR Mass Charges form, ARMASSC.FSL.*

Two more easy ones are the methods for the Help and Quit buttons. They also are nothing you haven't seen before by now, and here they are, too:

```
;¦BeginMethod¦#Page2.QuitButton¦pushButton¦
method pushButton(var eventInfo Event)
  close(0)
endmethod
;¦EndMethod¦#Page2.QuitButton¦pushButton¦
```

```
;¦BeginMethod¦#Page2.HelpButton¦pushButton¦
method pushButton(var eventInfo Event)
  helpShowContext( "ARMASSC.HLP", 1 )
endmethod
;¦EndMethod¦#Page2.HelpButton¦pushButton¦
```

Warmed up, now? Good, because here comes the good stuff. When the Run Batch button is clicked, this is what happens (I have inserted my comments in the middle of this code, too):

```
;¦BeginMethod¦#Page2.RunButton¦pushButton¦
method pushButton(var eventInfo Event)
var
  custtc, artc TCursor
  newbillnum SmallInt
endvar
```

After declaring a small handful of local variables, the method immediately checks the vital transaction input fields. If these fields are blank (not entered), nothing can happen, for these are required fields (and are marked required in the table structure).

```
if TXDate.isBlank() then
  msgStop( "DPW AR Mass Post", "You must supply a valid date." )
  return
endif
if TXAmount.isBlank() then
  msgStop( "DPW AR Mass Post", "You must supply a transaction amount." )
  return
endif
if TXDescription.isBlank() then
  msgStop( "DPW AR Mass Post", "You must supply a description." )
  return
endif
```

Of course, the next most important thing is that one be able to open the necessary tables, meaning the CUSTOMER and AR tables. Failure to open the tables also is disastrous, and causes a return back to the form, as follows:

```
if NOT custtc.open( "customer" ) then
  msgStop( "DPW AR Mass Post", "Could not open customer table." )
  return
endif
if NOT artc.open( "ar" ) then
  msgStop( "DPW AR Mass Post", "Could not open AR table." )
  custtc.close()
  return
endif
```

Next, the filter conditions must be checked, because they are going to be used to call the ObjectPAL setFilter() method for the CUSTOMER table cursor. Using setFilter()

greatly simplifies the later scan loop logic, which would otherwise have to check the field values manually for every record. Notice in the following fragment that I have actually validated only the `StartAcct` field; you may want to add code to validate the `EndAcct` field as well:

```
if UseFiltBtn then
  if (StartAcct.isBlank()) OR (StartAcct < 1) then
    msgStop( "DPW AR Mass Post", "Starting account must be >= 1." )
    custtc.close()
    artc.close()
    return
  endif
  custtc.setFilter( StartAcct, EndAcct )
endif
```

All the preliminaries are now out of the way. The following scan loop will access either all CUSTOMER records, or just the selected group, depending on whether the previous `setFilter()` call actually executed. As you look at this next fragment of the method's code, notice that I used the `setFilter()` call again as a shortcut method of getting to the linked AR records for each customer record. It's quite a handy little trick, and here is how it is done:

```
  message( "DPW AR Mass Post... All input fields verified." )
  custtc.edit()
  scan custtc :
    artc.setFilter( custtc.CustomerNum, 1, 32767 )
    artc.end()
    if artc.isEmpty() then
      newbillnum = 1
    else
      newbillnum = artc.BillingNum + 1
    endif
    message( "Adding AR record for customer: " +
             Strval(custtc.CustomerNum) )
    artc.edit()
    artc.insertAfterRecord()
    artc.CustomerNum = custtc.CustomerNum
    artc.BillingNum = newbillnum
    artc.ItemDescr = TXDescription
    artc.DueDate = TXDate
    artc.BillAmt = TXAmount
    artc.endEdit()
    custtc.Balance = custtc.Balance + TXAmount
  endscan
  custtc.endEdit()
  message( "DPW AR Mass Post... Posting COMPLETE." )
endmethod
;|EndMethod|#Page2.RunButton|pushButton|
```

A couple of closing comments are in order about the scan loop in this last code fragment. Right after the inner `setFilter()` call was made to get to the linked AR records, you

should notice that the `artc.end()` call is made to position the table cursor at the end of the group of linked records.

Then, after entering edit mode, a new record is inserted in the AR table using the `insertAfterRecord()` call. It is imperative that you use this form of record insertion here, or you'll be trying to place a new AR record out of order.

In some instances you would get away with that, as powerful as Paradox is. But there is one circumstance in which you would not get away with, and that's when there were no linked records to begin with. In that case, if you have chosen the simpler-looking `insertRecord()` type of call, Paradox could stop the whole show.

The reason, of course, is that this type of record insertion attempts to add the new record before the current record. If there is no current record, everything comes tumbling down.

Well, that's that. You have just finished the most difficult parts of the system, and the most critical, too. You'll just coast for the rest of the day, creating only a couple of reports—the main system reports.

Invoicing Customers for Payment

I have included the main system reports in the chapter on building batch processes, because report production is a batch process. You start the report running, and then you go away until it is complete.

The first, and most important, report is the AR Billing Statement report. Without this report, you can't notify your customers to pay their bills. You go broke that way.

One of the really nice things about Paradox for Windows that I have mentioned before is how often the default service provided by Paradox is adequate for one's needs. That's very nearly the case for the billing report. I created a default report, moved the fields around a little, changed the heading text, and added a group band so that I could force a page break where I want one.

Figure 8.10 shows the results of these preliminary manipulations. As you can see there, it is pretty much a standard report, and that's why you should have no problem building the parallel reports on the AP side.

After adding a group band, grouping on `CustomerNum`, just scroll the report design screen down and click in the bottom group band where you want the page break to occur. Even customer detail transactions may take several pages; you want a break before the next customer's data. This is shown in Figure 8.11.

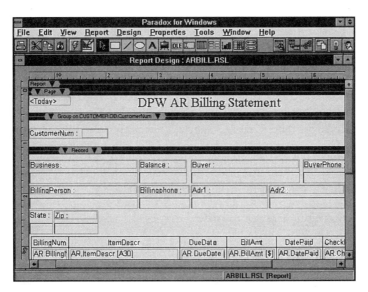

Figure 8.10. *Grouping the AR Billing Statement report (ARBILL.RSL) by CustomerNum.*

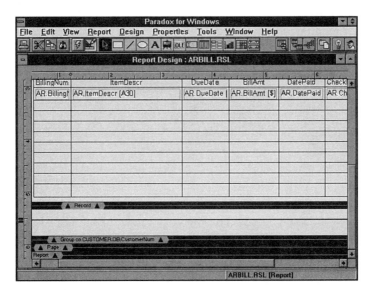

Figure 8.11. *Page breaking in the ARBILL.RSL report after each customer's statement.*

And that's all there is to the AR Billing Statement report. What could be easier than that?

Creating Customer Mailing Labels

Creating the AR Mailing Labels report was even easier because I used the Labels Expert to create it. To use the Labels expert, select **File** | **New** | **Report** from the desktop menu. You'll now see the New Report dialog box. The dialog box contains four buttons from which you can select a report design approach: Blank, Report Expert, Label Expert, and the Data Model buttons. Click the Label Expert button and just answer a few questions.

What the Label Expert does is to create a report with a multi-record object on it, as shown in Figure 8.12. The field layout doesn't initially look like the one in Figure 8.12, so I moved the fields around a bit to suit my own taste.

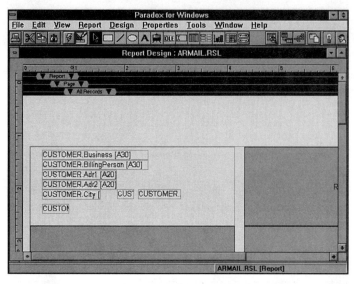

Figure 8.12. *Setting up the Ar Mailing Labels (ARMAIL.RSL) report as a multi-record object.*

Furthermore, the Label Expert didn't have precisely the kind of label layout I wanted, so I just took the first available one. That happened to be for three-up (three across) labels. My laser printer labels are two-up, and a slightly different size. So I right-clicked the multi-record object and opened the Record Layout dialog box, as shown in Figure 8.13. In that dialog box, I defined the number of labels across and down the page, the separation distances between individual labels, and the sequence Paradox will place data in the individual record areas (left to right, and then down).

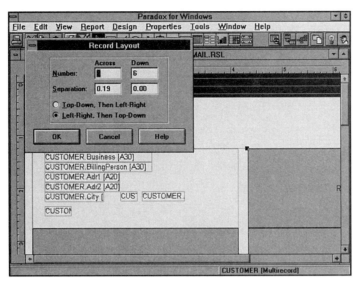

Figure 8.13. *Using the Record Layout dialog box to arrange the multi-record object for the mailing labels.*

Now my basic format is like I want it, but the label records are still a slightly different physical size from my labels. To remedy this situation, I clicked on the "token" record, and when its sizing handles appeared, I just dragged the size into submission. Notice in Figure 8.14 that while you're sizing a record, Paradox displays (in the status bar at the bottom left of the window) the object's current sizing information. Because I could see that, and I knew the actual size of my labels, it was quite easy to accurately size the label record.

One last shot about creating mailing labels. If you don't get the label record size exactly right, the first few labels will look like they fit on the page correctly. But then the label areas will begin to creep up or down the page, moving farther and farther out of line. I suggest that you experiment with your label layouts by printing them on black stock paper. You can place the plain paper printout over a real label page, hold it up to the light, and see what is going on.

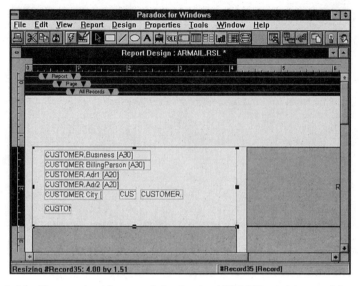

Figure 8.14. *Fine-tuning the record size in the ARMAIL multi-record layout, to avoid "creeping print."*

Modification Notes

Having read this chapter with the utmost attention (right?), you now need to bring the AP side of the application up to par. Specifically, you need to

- ☐ Modify the AP Export Data button's method in DPWMAIN to provide the ObjectPAL code for exporting VENDOR and APAY data. You can follow the AR version almost exactly, except for table and field names, to do this.

- ☐ Modify the AP Archive Data button's method in DPWMAIN to provide the ObjectPAL code for retiring posted-as-paid APAY records. You also can clone my code here, with very few changes, to accomplish this.

- ☐ Supply other batch functions. You'll naturally not want to build a batch mass payment to vendors function, but if there is some other batch function similar to this one, you can clone this code to build it. Always remember, boilerplating the code is both the fastest and the safest way to go. The only danger lies in not changing everything that should differ, and in not accounting for slightly different function requirements.

8

☐ Use the Paradox Label Expert to create your AP Mailing Labels. This should literally be only a few minutes' work.

☐ Create the Pay Vendors report, a convenient euphemism for writing AP checks and paying your honest debts. The watchword here is to use the Paradox defaults wherever you can, and then to just make the report match your blank check forms.

Debugging the Process

Today's workload wasn't as heavy as yesterday's, but some of the things you accomplished today were sophisticated. You should accordingly wring out everything to see if it works right. Even if it seemed right to me, it may not be exactly what you need. And I did once make a mistake, back in '53. Thought I had goofed, but I was wrong. Check me anyway; if you expected me to be perfect, you consulted the wrong genie.

Second, clone my work and create this chapter's parts of the AP system. Then really wring it out. Click every button, try every feature, and try to enter data that should mess things up. When it does mess up (and it will), go back and try to prevent that from happening by adding and/or correcting your ObjectPAL code.

Building the
Application's
Support Utilities

Today you're going to see a ton of code. As is true of most applications I've seen, the core of the application is actually quite compact. The surrounding support and utility code are what's voluminous. That fact is no less true here than elsewhere. Today you'll put all the rest of the utilities and support code together, and there is quite a lot of it.

But that's fine, because today you finish the whole thing. There will be a little documenting to do. (OK, a *lot* of documenting—I wrote this book about it, didn't I?) There will be a little testing to do. And there will be a little packaging for distribution to do. But all of that is nothing compared to what you're about to accomplish: a complete, functioning application that you can be proud of!

Creating the *Voice Notes!* Multimedia Audio Notepad Application

It's hard to say whether I like the Multimedia Theater or the *Voice Notes!* audio notepad better, because they are both multimedia-based. Multimedia is the thing, and I suppose I like them equally well, just in somewhat different ways.

At any rate, it's the *Voice Notes!* application that you now turn to. To refresh your memory about the VNOTES form, it is shown again in Figure 9.1.

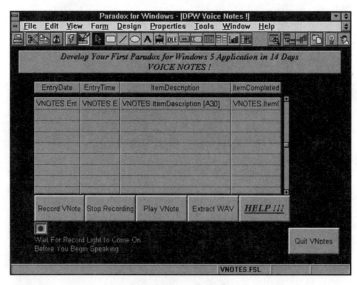

Figure 9.1. *The* Voice Notes! *form, VNOTES.FSL.*

As you might recall, you can insert a new record (making sure it is posted to the underlying table), and then, leaving the focus anywhere on the record, click the Record VNote button to make yourself a note. One important trick to remember is to click the Stop Recording button when you're done, so that your multigigabyte drive won't fill up. As a rough guess, it seems as if one second of recording time takes about 75KB of disk space.

The note, of course, is a WAV file, and is stored in the VNOTES table as a BLOB (Binary Large OBject) field. That's not too hard to arrange, and you have already seen a great deal of multimedia programming, so there won't be much to surprise you in this application. It is just that the pieces are put together in a new, pleasing (to me, anyway), and useful fashion.

As all multimedia forms do, this one requires the use of both a Uses and a Var block attached to the form for the multimedia overhead stuff. Because you're already familiar with all of that, plus the normal things you do at form open time, here are those three pieces without much comment:

```
;¦BeginMethod¦#FormData1¦Uses¦
Uses MMSYSTEM
  mciSendString( lpstrCommand CPTR, lpstrReturn CPTR,
                 wReturnLng CWORD, hCallBack CWORD ) CLONG
  mciGetErrorString( dwError CLONG, lpstrReturn CPTR,
                     wLength CWORD ) CWORD
endUses
;¦EndMethod¦#FormData1¦Uses¦

;¦BeginMethod¦#FormData1¦Var¦
Var
  isRecording Logical
endVar
;¦EndMethod¦#FormData1¦Var¦

;¦BeginMethod¦#FormData1¦open¦
method open(var eventInfo Event)
  if NOT eventInfo.isPreFilter() then
    doDefault
    maximize()
    isRecording = False
  endif
endmethod
;¦EndMethod¦#FormData1¦open¦
```

The only thing at all out of the ordinary in the open() method just presented is the line that initializes the isRecording variable to a value of False. You can surely guess what that variable is for.

The HELP!!! button has a simple method, one that you're accustomed to. It just calls the Windows help application for VNOTES. But there is nothing simple or ordinary about the VNOTES.HLP help file, as you'll discover on Day 11. Here is the help engine call:

```
;¦BeginMethod¦#Page2.#Button19¦pushButton¦
method pushButton(var eventInfo Event)
  helpShowTopic( workingDir() + "\\VNOTES.HLP", "contents" )
endmethod
;¦EndMethod¦#Page2.#Button19¦pushButton¦
```

One of the nice features about VNotes is that you can use it as a general-purpose recording tool, and extract the resulting messages to stand-alone WAV files at your leisure. The Extract WAV button still has the noise name #Button17, but it does exactly what it sounds like it should. Here is its code:

```
;¦BeginMethod¦#Page2.#Button17¦pushButton¦
method pushButton(var eventInfo Event)
var
  sfile String
  vtc TCursor
  theMessage Binary
endvar
  if NOT isRecording then
    vtc.attach(VNOTES)
    if isBlank( vtc.VNote ) then
      msgStop( "VNOTES!", "There is no message to extract!" )
      return
    endif
    sfile = workingDir() + "\\VNOTES.WAV"
    sfile.view( "Enter WAV file name for extract:" )
    theMessage = vtc.VNote
    if NOT theMessage.writeToFile( sfile ) then
      msgStop( "VNOTES!", "Couldn't extract the message to a file." )
      return
    endif
  endif
endmethod
;¦EndMethod¦#Page2.#Button17¦pushButton¦
```

Notice that the first thing the extract WAV logic checks for is whether you're already recording at this time. It would, of course, be senseless to try to extract a WAV file while you're recording one at the same time.

The method also double-checks to see whether there is any message at all stored for the current record. It would also be senseless to extract a nonexistent audio file. But if all other things are equal, a table cursor is used to get to the BLOB field, placing it in a Binary type variable. Then the Binary method, writeToFile() is used to get the audio into the external WAV file. Piece of cake.

The Stop Recording button also still has a noise name: #Button15. In order to stop recording, just the opposite logic from the previous case is employed: you must be recording in order to stop. If that's the case, the MCI strings to stop recording, save the WAV file, and are sent to MMPLAYER to close it. After that, the WAV file is loaded into the BLOB field, unless there is an error. It's a bit verbose, but really quite straightforward, as follows:

```
;¦BeginMethod¦#Page2.#Button15¦pushButton¦
method pushButton(var eventInfo Event)
var
  mciCmdStr, ReturnString, sfile String
  ReturnCode LongInt
  vtc TCursor
  theMessage Binary
endvar
  if isRecording then
    if NOT VNOTES.editing then
      msgStop( "VNOTES!", "Table is not in edit mode!" )
      return
    endif
    vtc.attach(VNOTES)
    sfile = workingDir() + "\\VNOTES.WAV"
    ReturnString = fill( " ", 1024 )
    mciCmdStr = "stop mywave"
    RecordLight.visible = False
    ReturnCode = mciSendString(mciCmdStr, ReturnString, 1024, 0)
    if NOT (0 = ReturnCode) then
      ReturnString = fill( " ", 1024 )
      mciGetErrorString( ReturnCode, ReturnString, 1024 )
      msgStop( "Media File Record/Stop", ReturnString )
      return
    endif
    ReturnString = fill( " ", 1024 )
    mciCmdStr = "save mywave " + sfile
    ReturnCode = mciSendString(mciCmdStr, ReturnString, 1024, 0)
    if NOT (0 = ReturnCode) then
      ReturnString = fill( " ", 1024 )
      mciGetErrorString( ReturnCode, ReturnString, 1024 )
      msgStop( "Media File Record/Save", ReturnString )
      return
    endif
    ReturnString = fill( " ", 1024 )
    mciCmdStr = "close mywave"
    ReturnCode = mciSendString(mciCmdStr, ReturnString, 1024, 0)
    if NOT (0 = ReturnCode) then
      ReturnString = fill( " ", 1024 )
      mciGetErrorString( ReturnCode, ReturnString, 1024 )
      msgStop( "Media File Record/Close", ReturnString )
      return
    endif
    if theMessage.readFromFile( sfile ) then
      vtc.VNote = theMessage
    else
      msgStop( "VNOTES!", "Couldn't read the sound file!" )
    endif
    isRecording = False
  endif
endmethod
;¦EndMethod¦#Page2.#Button15¦pushButton¦
```

Taking a quick break, I'll just present and pass over the Quit VNotes button's pushbutton() method. Here it is:

```
;¦BeginMethod¦#Page2.#Button10¦pushButton¦
method pushButton(var eventInfo Event)
  close(0)
endmethod
;¦EndMethod¦#Page2.#Button10¦pushButton¦
```

An audio notepad that can record but not play back would be kind of useless, so naturally there is a `Play VNote` button (whose noise name is `#Button8`). Actually, a WAV file must be extracted first in order to play it: it cannot be accessed by MMPLAYER buried within a table's .MB file.

Therefore, the play button extracts the BLOB field to a temporary external WAV file to play it, using a table cursor to access the field as before. The remainder of the method is exactly the same kind of multimedia playback logic you have already seen. Here is how the `Play VNote` button works:

```
;¦BeginMethod¦#Page2.#Button8¦pushButton¦
method pushButton(var eventInfo Event)
var
  mciCmdStr, ReturnString, sfile String
  ReturnCode, mmpos, mmlength LongInt
  vtc TCursor
  theMessage Binary
endvar
  if NOT isRecording then
    vtc.attach(VNOTES)
    if isBlank( vtc.VNote ) then
      msgStop( "VNOTES!", "There is no message to play!" )
      return
    endif
    sfile = workingDir() + "\\VNOTES.WAV"
    theMessage = vtc.VNote
    if NOT theMessage.writeToFile( sfile ) then
      msgStop( "VNOTES!", "Couldn't extract the message to a file." )
      return
    endif
    ReturnString = fill( " ", 1024 )
    mciCmdStr = "open " + sfile + " alias mmclip"
    ReturnCode = mciSendString(mciCmdStr, ReturnString, 1024, 0)
    if NOT (0 = ReturnCode) then
      ReturnString = fill( " ", 1024 )
      mciGetErrorString( ReturnCode, ReturnString, 1024 )
      msgStop( "Media File Open", ReturnString )
      return
    endif
    ReturnString = fill( " ", 1024 )
    mciCmdStr = "play mmclip"
    ReturnCode = mciSendString(mciCmdStr, ReturnString, 1024, 0)
    if NOT (0 = ReturnCode) then
      ReturnString = fill( " ", 1024 )
      mciGetErrorString( ReturnCode, ReturnString, 1024 )
      msgStop( "Media File Play", ReturnString )
      return
    endif
```

```
      ReturnString = fill( " ", 1024 )
      mciCmdStr = "status mmclip length"
      ReturnCode = mciSendString(mciCmdStr, ReturnString, 1024, 0)
      mmlength = LongInt( ReturnString )
      ReturnString = fill( " ", 1024 )
      mciCmdStr = "status mmclip position"
      ReturnCode = mciSendString(mciCmdStr, ReturnString, 1024, 0)
      mmpos = LongInt( ReturnString )
      while mmpos < mmlength
        sleep()
        ReturnString = fill( " ", 1024 )
        mciCmdStr = "status mmclip position"
        ReturnCode = mciSendString(mciCmdStr, ReturnString, 1024, 0)
        mmpos = LongInt( ReturnString )
      endwhile
      ReturnString = fill( " ", 1024 )
      mciCmdStr = "close mmclip"
      ReturnCode = mciSendString(mciCmdStr, ReturnString, 1024, 0)
      if NOT (0 = ReturnCode) then
        ReturnString = fill( " ", 1024 )
        mciGetErrorString( ReturnCode, ReturnString, 1024 )
        msgStop( "Media File Close", ReturnString )
        return
      endif
    endif
  endif
endmethod
;¦EndMethod¦#Page2.#Button8¦pushButton¦
```

To record a VNote, when the Record VNote button is clicked, a couple of extra things
have to happen. First the table must be in edit mode, or the audio message cannot be
stored. Also, because it would contradict the scheme of the application to have an audio
message with no text annotation at all, that's checked, too—no annotation (description
field), no message. If these two things are okay, recording can proceed.

The only other unusual thing that the Record VNote button method must do is to turn
on the recording light, the bright red dot, when it is time to talk (it is turned off by the
Stop Recording button). With all that in mind, look at the ObjectPAL for the Record
VNote button:

```
;¦BeginMethod¦#Page2.#Button6¦pushButton¦
method pushButton(var eventInfo Event)
var
  mciCmdStr, ReturnString String
  ReturnCode LongInt
  vtc TCursor
  theMessage Binary
endvar
  if NOT VNOTES.editing then
    msgStop( "VNOTES!", "Table is not in edit mode!" )
    return
  endif
  vtc.attach(VNOTES)
  if isBlank( vtc.EntryDate ) OR isBlank( EntryTime )
```

```
      OR isBlank( vtc.ItemDescription ) then
      msgStop( "VNOTES!", "Annotate the record before recording." )
      return
    endif
    ReturnString = fill( " ", 1024 )
    mciCmdStr = "open new type waveaudio alias mywave buffer 4"
    ReturnCode = mciSendString(mciCmdStr, ReturnString, 1024, 0)
    if NOT (0 = ReturnCode) then
      ReturnString = fill( " ", 1024 )
      mciGetErrorString( ReturnCode, ReturnString, 1024 )
      msgStop( "Media File Open", ReturnString )
      return
    endif
    ReturnString = fill( " ", 1024 )
    mciCmdStr = "record mywave"
    ReturnCode = mciSendString(mciCmdStr, ReturnString, 1024, 0)
    if NOT (0 = ReturnCode) then
      ReturnString = fill( " ", 1024 )
      mciGetErrorString( ReturnCode, ReturnString, 1024 )
      msgStop( "Media File Record", ReturnString )
      return
    endif
    RecordLight.visible = True
    isRecording = True
  endmethod
;¦EndMethod¦#Page2.#Button6¦pushButton¦
```

Just to be sure that the VNOTES table is, in fact, in edit mode, you do it for the user when the VNOTES table frame is opened. The method is simplicity itself. Just attach the following code to the table frame's open() method:

```
;¦BeginMethod¦#Page2.VNOTES¦open¦
method open(var eventInfo Event)
  edit()    ; Must be in edit mode to do anything !
endmethod
;¦EndMethod¦#Page2.VNOTES¦open¦
```

Likewise, it's a good idea to end edit mode when the table frame is closed (such as when the user has exited the application). This, too, is simplicity incarnate. Just attach the following code to the table frame's close() method:

```
;¦BeginMethod¦#Page2.VNOTES¦close¦
method close(var eventInfo Event)
  endEdit()
endmethod
;¦EndMethod¦#Page2.VNOTES¦close¦
```

And that's all there is to the *Voice Notes!* application. As you can see, it really doesn't take all that much code to produce a thoroughly impressive application with Paradox for Windows.

Creating the Application's Table and Database Utilities

You've already seen the Table Maintenance Utility on Day 4. I won't bore you by presenting all that code again, but I will go so far as to show you the form again, just by way of reminder that the utility properly belongs here, with its fellows. The Table Maintenance Utility form is shown (again) in Figure 9.2.

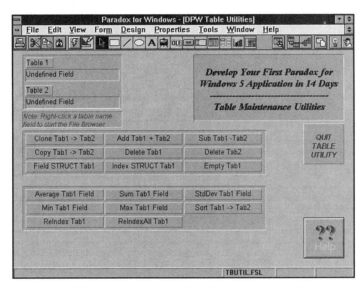

Figure 9.2. *The Table Maintenance Utility form, TBUTIL.FSL.*

You have also seen the Database and Query Utility (see Figure 9.3 to see it again), but you haven't yet seen how it works. So this time you get the whole load.

A *database* in Paradox is just a directory, but Borland has thoughtfully provided a Database class, and some methods to go along with it. You take advantage of these methods in the DBUTIL form. Although the utility can access a table sufficiently to either verify its validity, or to delete it, the main purpose of the utility is to load, save, edit, and run queries, in their native text format (QBE files are text files). If you want the ultimate flexibility in building and running Paradox queries, this utility is for you.

Because several of the forms' button controls access the same database and/or query, the utility has some important variables defined at the form level, in the Var block. Here are the contents of the Var block:

```
;¦BeginMethod¦#FormData1¦Var¦
Var
  aDB  Database
  aTB  Table
  aQBE Query
endVar
;¦EndMethod¦#FormData1¦Var¦
```

The form's open() method has just the usual baggage in it, as follows:

```
;¦BeginMethod¦#FormData1¦open¦
method open(var eventInfo Event)
  if NOT eventInfo.isPreFilter() then
    doDefault
    maximize()
  endif
endmethod
;¦EndMethod¦#FormData1¦open¦
```

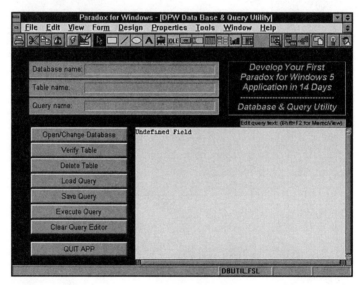

Figure 9.3. *The Database and Query Manager form, DBUTIL.FSL.*

Something you may find a bit more interesting is the use of the mouseEnter() and mouseExit() methods, which are attached to most of the design objects on the form. These methods do nothing more surprising than simply placing a message in the status bar when the user moves the mouse over the button or box, or whatever, and erasing it when the mouse leaves the object. It just lets you know what would happen, if you click that object. It's one of the niceties that only the finest software offers. Here are the mouseEnter() and mouseExit() methods for the LodQBBTN (Load Query Button):

```
;¦BeginMethod¦#Page2.LodQBBtn¦mouseEnter¦
method mouseEnter(var eventInfo MouseEvent)
  message( "Load a query file named in QBName to editor..." )
endmethod
;¦EndMethod¦#Page2.LodQBBtn¦mouseEnter¦

;¦BeginMethod¦#Page2.LodQBBtn¦mouseExit¦
method mouseExit(var eventInfo MouseEvent)
  message ( "" )
endmethod
;¦EndMethod¦#Page2.LodQBBtn¦mouseExit¦
```

9

Because QBE files are text files, and because you'll execute the query (if requested to) from a string, the Load Query button's method opens the QBE file as a TextStream. Then it reads the file and builds one, long string composed of the files text lines separated by the \n (newline) character. It is short and to the point, as follows:

```
;¦BeginMethod¦#Page2.LodQBBtn¦pushButton¦
method pushButton(var eventInfo Event)
var
  qbf TextStream
  qtl String
  i SmallInt
endvar
  QBEText.blank()
  QBEText.font.typeface = "Courier New"
  qbf.open( ":dbCurrent:"+StrVal(QBName),"r" )
  while NOT qbf.eof()
    qbf.readLine( qtl )
    QBEText = String( QBEText, qtl, "\n" )
  endwhile
  qbf.close()
endmethod
;¦EndMethod¦#Page2.LodQBBtn¦pushButton¦
```

Because it's impossible to edit the query text in its field box unless the field is in memo view, just make sure that this happens when the user lands in the query text box. Also make sure that memo view is terminated when the user leaves the field. This is handled by the field's arrive() and depart() methods, as follows:

```
;¦BeginMethod¦#Page2.QBEText¦arrive¦
method arrive(var eventInfo MoveEvent)
  action( EditEnterMemoView )
endmethod
;¦EndMethod¦#Page2.QBEText¦arrive¦

;¦BeginMethod¦#Page2.QBEText¦depart¦
method depart(var eventInfo MoveEvent)
  action( EditExitMemoView )
endmethod
;¦EndMethod¦#Page2.QBEText¦depart¦
```

And, as before, you also provide nice status messages when the mouse moves over the query text box, using the `mouseEnter()` and `mouseExit()` methods, like this:

```
;¦BeginMethod¦#Page2.QBEText¦mouseEnter¦
method mouseEnter(var eventInfo MouseEvent)
  message( "Query Editor: enter/edit query text..." )
endmethod
;¦EndMethod¦#Page2.QBEText¦mouseEnter¦

;¦BeginMethod¦#Page2.QBEText¦mouseExit¦
method mouseExit(var eventInfo MouseEvent)
  message( "" )
endmethod
;¦EndMethod¦#Page2.QBEText¦mouseExit¦
```

`mouseEnter()` and `mouseExit()` methods are also provided for the `Clear Query` button, as follows:

```
;¦BeginMethod¦#Page2.ClrQBBtn¦mouseEnter¦
method mouseEnter(var eventInfo MouseEvent)
  message( "Clear query editor box (leaves file alone)..." )
endmethod
;¦EndMethod¦#Page2.ClrQBBtn¦mouseEnter¦

;¦BeginMethod¦#Page2.ClrQBBtn¦mouseExit¦
method mouseExit(var eventInfo MouseEvent)
  message ( "" )
endmethod
;¦EndMethod¦#Page2.ClrQBBtn¦mouseExit¦
```

Clearing the query text itself is really easy. You just use the `blank()` method on the query text field, like this:

```
;¦BeginMethod¦#Page2.ClrQBBtn¦pushButton¦
method pushButton(var eventInfo Event)
  QBEText.blank()
endmethod
;¦EndMethod¦#Page2.ClrQBBtn¦pushButton¦
```

The `Quit` button is by now such a fixture in your mind, I trust, that I can present all three of that button's methods in one lump. Here they are, if you want to look at them (you might want to check me out to see if I am slacking anywhere):

```
;¦BeginMethod¦#Page2.QuitBtn¦mouseEnter¦
method mouseEnter(var eventInfo MouseEvent)
  message( "Leave the Data Base & Query Utility..." )
endmethod
;¦EndMethod¦#Page2.QuitBtn¦mouseEnter¦

;¦BeginMethod¦#Page2.QuitBtn¦mouseExit¦
method mouseExit(var eventInfo MouseEvent)
  message ( "" )
endmethod
;¦EndMethod¦#Page2.QuitBtn¦mouseExit¦
```

```
;¦BeginMethod¦#Page2.QuitBtn¦pushButton¦
method pushButton(var eventInfo Event)
  close()
endmethod
;¦EndMethod¦#Page2.QuitBtn¦pushButton¦
```

The same thing would be true of the Execute Query button, except that I want you to look at the `pushbutton()` method in particular. So here are the `mouseEnter()` and `mouseExit()` methods, in a hurry:

```
;¦BeginMethod¦#Page2.XeqQBBtn¦mouseEnter¦
method mouseEnter(var eventInfo MouseEvent)
  message( "Execute the query in the query editor box..." )
endmethod
;¦EndMethod¦#Page2.XeqQBBtn¦mouseEnter¦

;¦BeginMethod¦#Page2.XeqQBBtn¦mouseExit¦
method mouseExit(var eventInfo MouseEvent)
  message ( "" )
endmethod
;¦EndMethod¦#Page2.XeqQBBtn¦mouseExit¦
```

Now you come to the Execute Query `pushbutton()` method. It has a couple of features that bear at least quick scrutiny. While the method checks the `DBName` (and `QBName`) fields to see if they are blank or not, this may not be all the protection you need here. Notice in the following method's code that the notation `:dbCurrent:` is used to refer to the currently open database. This is a *reserved word* notation, like `:work:`. The problem is that if the user has entered the directory *cum* database name, but has not clicked the `Open/Change Database` button, this method may well fail. Look and see for yourself:

```
;¦BeginMethod¦#Page2.XeqQBBtn¦pushButton¦
method pushButton(var eventInfo Event)
var
  ansTab, tabname, qbfile String
  tv TableView
endvar
  if NOT ( DBName.isBlank()
        OR QBName.isBlank() ) then
    ansTab = ":dbCurrent:DBANSWER.DB"
    tabname = ":dbCurrent:" + StrVal(TBName)
    qbfile = ":dbCurrent:" + StrVal( QBName )
    if executeQBEFile( qbfile, ansTab ) then
      tv.open( ansTab )
      tv.maximize()
    else
      msgStop( "DPW DBUtil",
               "Query execution FAILED!" )
    endif
  else
    msgStop( "DPW DBUtil",
             "You must enter the DATABASE and QUERY names first!" )
  endif
endmethod
;¦EndMethod¦#Page2.XeqQBBtn¦pushButton¦
```

The Save Query button avoids this problem. But before you get to that, take a quick look at the mouse...() methods for this button. They are the very things you should expect for these methods by now:

```
;¦BeginMethod¦#Page2.SavQBBtn¦mouseEnter¦
method mouseEnter(var eventInfo MouseEvent)
  message( "Save edited query to file named in QBName..." )
endmethod
;¦EndMethod¦#Page2.SavQBBtn¦mouseEnter¦

;¦BeginMethod¦#Page2.SavQBBtn¦mouseExit¦
method mouseExit(var eventInfo MouseEvent)
  message ( "" )
endmethod
;¦EndMethod¦#Page2.SavQBBtn¦mouseExit¦
```

The Save Query button gets around the problem of the opened or not opened database by using the aDB global Database variable that was defined in the Var block. You haven't seen it yet, but the Open/Change Database button's code will set this variable if the database is successfully opened. So you can avoid stubbing your toe on an unopened database by calling aDB.isAssigned(), as follows:

```
;¦BeginMethod¦#Page2.SavQBBtn¦pushButton¦
method pushButton(var eventInfo Event)
var
  qString String
endvar
  qString = QBEText
  if not qString.isBlank() then
    if not QBName.isBlank() then
      if aDB.isAssigned() then
        if writeQBE( qString, ":dbCurrent:"+QBName ) then
          msgInfo( "DPW DBUtil",
                   "Query successfully saved!" )
        else
          msgStop( "DPW DBUtil",
                   "Query save FAILED!" )
        endif
      else
        msgStop( "DPW DBUtil",
                 "Open a database to save query!" )
      endif
    else
      msgStop( "DPW DBUtil", "Query file name not yet entered!" )
    endif
  else
    msgStop( "DPW DBUtil", "Can't save blank query text!" )
  endif
endmethod
;¦EndMethod¦#Page2.SavQBBtn¦pushButton¦
```

In the meantime, the Delete Table button is sitting there just waiting to do something. It can do something if the table name has been entered, the entered name corresponds

to a valid table, and the database has been successfully opened. And this time, I'll just lump all three of the Delete Table methods together. Here is how they work:

```
;¦BeginMethod¦#Page2.DelTBBtn¦mouseEnter¦
method mouseEnter(var eventInfo MouseEvent)
  message( "Delete table named in TBName..." )
endmethod
;¦EndMethod¦#Page2.DelTBBtn¦mouseEnter¦

;¦BeginMethod¦#Page2.DelTBBtn¦mouseExit¦
method mouseExit(var eventInfo MouseEvent)
  message ( "" )
endmethod
;¦EndMethod¦#Page2.DelTBBtn¦mouseExit¦

;¦BeginMethod¦#Page2.DelTBBtn¦pushButton¦
method pushButton(var eventInfo Event)
var
  stuff String
endvar
  if (aDB.isAssigned()) and (NOT TBName.isSpace()) then
    if aDB.isTable( TBName ) then
      if "Yes" = msgQuestion( "DPW DBUtil",
            "Do you really want to delete the selected table?" ) then
        if aDB.delete( TBName ) then
          msgInfo( "DPW DBUtil", StrVal( TBName ) + " was deleted." )
        else
          msgStop( "DPW DBUtil", StrVal( TBName ) + " delete FAILED." )
        endif
      else
        msgInfo( "DPW DBUtil", "Aborted table delete." )
      endif
    else
      msgInfo( "DPW DBUtil", StrVal( TBName ) + " was not found." )
    endif
  else
    errorLog( 1, "Either the database has not been opened, or\n" +
                 "you have not provided a table name." )
    errorShow( "DPW DBUtil", "Deleting table" )
    stuff = DBName
    stuff.view( "Current database name:" )
    stuff = TBName
    stuff.view( "Current table name:" )
  endif
endmethod
;¦EndMethod¦#Page2.DelTBBtn¦pushButton¦
```

Verifying a table when the Verify Table button is clicked works along precisely the same lines. The methods are so similar, I will present them forthwith:

```
;¦BeginMethod¦#Page2.VerTBBtn¦mouseEnter¦
method mouseEnter(var eventInfo MouseEvent)
  message( "Verify table named in TBName..." )
endmethod
;¦EndMethod¦#Page2.VerTBBtn¦mouseEnter¦
```

```
;¦BeginMethod¦#Page2.VerTBBtn¦mouseExit¦
method mouseExit(var eventInfo MouseEvent)
  message ( "" )
endmethod
;¦EndMethod¦#Page2.VerTBBtn¦mouseExit¦

;¦BeginMethod¦#Page2.VerTBBtn¦pushButton¦
method pushButton(var eventInfo Event)
var
  stuff String
endvar
  if (aDB.isAssigned()) and (NOT TBName.isSpace()) then
    if aDB.isTable( TBName ) then
      msgInfo( "DPW DBUtil",
               StrVal( TBName ) + " is a valid table." )
    else
      msgStop( "DPW DBUtil",
               StrVal( TBName ) + " was not found." )
    endif
  else
    errorLog( 1, "Either the database has not been opened, or\n" +
                 "you have not provided a table name." )
    errorShow( "DPW DBUtil", "Verifying table" )
    stuff = DBName
    stuff.view( "Current database name:" )
    stuff = TBName
    stuff.view( "Current table name:" )
  endif
endmethod
;¦EndMethod¦#Page2.VerTBBtn¦pushButton¦
```

The Open/Change Database button is the biggie in this form. Once more I'll lump all three of this button's method's together and show them to you. Take a look, and then I'll describe what happens when a database is opened:

```
;¦BeginMethod¦#Page2.ChgDBBtn¦mouseEnter¦
method mouseEnter(var eventInfo MouseEvent)
  message( "Change or open data base for first time..." )
endmethod
;¦EndMethod¦#Page2.ChgDBBtn¦mouseEnter¦

;¦BeginMethod¦#Page2.ChgDBBtn¦mouseExit¦
method mouseExit(var eventInfo MouseEvent)
  message ( "" )
endmethod
;¦EndMethod¦#Page2.ChgDBBtn¦mouseExit¦

;¦BeginMethod¦#Page2.ChgDBBtn¦pushButton¦
method pushButton(var eventInfo Event)
var
  dbAlias String
endvar
  if aDB.isAssigned() then
    aDB.close()
  endif
  if NOT DBName.isBlank() then
```

```
      dbAlias = DBName
      addAlias( "dbCurrent", "Standard", dbAlias )
      if not aDB.open( "dbCurrent" ) then
        msgStop( "DPW DBUtil", "Database open FAILED!" )
      else
        msgInfo( "DPW DBUtil", StrVal(dbAlias) + " Database opened." )
      endif
    else
      errorLog( 1, "You have not named a database yet." )
      errorShow( "DPW DBUtil", "Opening a new database" )
    endif
  endmethod
  ;|EndMethod|#Page2.ChgDBBtn|pushButton|
```

First of all, the ChgDBBtn pushbutton() method assumes that if the database is already open, you mean to change it. Thus, any open database is closed, right up front.

After that, all that's required is that you have entered a valid database name. That means a valid directory name without a trailing slash. If this is in order, the new database name is associated with the dbCurrent alias, and the database is opened using the dbCurrent alias. Another piece of cake, you say? You bet.

The remaining methods on the DBUTIL form are all housekeeping functions: they are the mouseEnter() and mouseExit() methods for the query and table name input fields, as follows:

```
;|BeginMethod|#Page2.QBName|mouseEnter|
method mouseEnter(var eventInfo MouseEvent)
  message( "QBName: Enter queryname.QBE ..." )
endmethod
;|EndMethod|#Page2.QBName|mouseEnter|

;|BeginMethod|#Page2.QBName|mouseExit|
method mouseExit(var eventInfo MouseEvent)
  message ( "" )
endmethod
;|EndMethod|#Page2.QBName|mouseExit|

;|BeginMethod|#Page2.TBName|mouseEnter|
method mouseEnter(var eventInfo MouseEvent)
  message( "TBName: Enter a table name..." )
endmethod
;|EndMethod|#Page2.TBName|mouseEnter|

;|BeginMethod|#Page2.TBName|mouseExit|
method mouseExit(var eventInfo MouseEvent)
  message ( "" )
endmethod
;|EndMethod|#Page2.TBName|mouseExit|

;|BeginMethod|#Page2.DBName|mouseEnter|
method mouseEnter(var eventInfo MouseEvent)
  message( "DBName: Enter a drive:\\directory path..." )
endmethod
```

```
;¦EndMethod¦#Page2.DBName¦mouseEnter¦

;¦BeginMethod¦#Page2.DBName¦mouseExit¦
method mouseExit(var eventInfo MouseEvent)
  message ( "" )
endmethod
;¦EndMethod¦#Page2.DBName¦mouseExit¦
```

Creating the Application's Backup and Recovery Functions

The AR archival and export functions were two of the most important, and most difficult, functions you have yet seen implemented. The ones you're about to see—the backup and restore functions—are equally tricky and at least as important.

The backup and restore functions, you may recall, don't have their own form. They execute immediately when their respective buttons are clicked on the DPWMAIN form. Just to illustrate that point graphically, I took another shot of the main selection panel screen and "fuzzed" (defocused) everything but these two buttons (I used Aldus Photostyler to do this). Here is the result, in Figure 9.4.

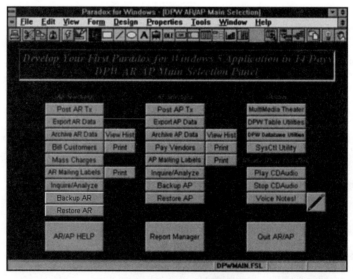

Figure 9.4. *The Backup AR and Restore AR buttons on the DPWMAIN form.*

Turning now to the ObjectPAL implementation of the backup process, remember that this method is extracted from the DPWMAIN form by itself. Therefore, I will spread my comments on the code all through the code again.

The method begins by declaring a handful of variables that will be used internally, as follows:

```
;¦BeginMethod¦#Page2.ARBackup¦pushButton¦
method pushButton(var eventInfo Event)
var
  lpstr, cwdir, dlgreturn, bkupname String
  newarcnum SmallInt
  tb, tb2 Table
endvar
```

Next, the current working directory (the *Paradox* directory, remember) is determined just in case you didn't leave all this good sample code stashed in the \BUILDAPP directory. The ARARC.INI file is accessed, using the readProfileString() System class procedure, to read the nextfilenum string value. Once that's converted to a numeric value and incremented, the user is prompted, and offered the opportunity to override the generated next file number (the new backup version number). Whether the user does or doesn't override the version number, it is written back into the profile entry for use next time. Here is the code for the process so far:

```
cwdir = workingDir() + "\\ararc.ini"
lpstr = readProfileString( cwdir, "ARARC", "nextfilenum" )
newarcnum = SmallInt( lpstr ) + 1
dlgreturn = msgYesNoCancel( "DPW AR Backup",
                            "The next backup file number is " +
                            StrVal(newarcnum) + "\n" +
                            "Do you want to reset it?" )
switch
  case dlgreturn = "Yes" :
    newarcnum.view( "Change file number:")
  case dlgreturn = "No" :
    message( "DPW AR Backup: Default backup file number accepted." )
  case dlgreturn = "Cancel" :
    message( "DPW AR Backup run aborted..." )
    sleep( 1000 )
    return
endswitch
message( "DPW AR Backup: New backup file number = " + StrVal(newarcnum) )
writeProfileString( cwdir, "ARARC", "nextfilenum",
                    StrVal(newarcnum) )
```

After notifying the user with a status bar message, the customer table backup begins. The first step is to construct the backup filename from the selected version number, and then table cursors are attached to both the customer and backup files. At that point, backing up the customer file is as simple as calling the Table class copy() method, as follows:

```
message( "DPW AR Backup: Beginning Customer back up..." )
```

```
bkupname = workingDir() + "\\cubk" + StrVal(newarcnum) + ".db"
tb.attach( ":work:customer.db" )
tb2.attach( bkupname )
if tb.copy( tb2 ) then
  message( "DPW AR Backup: Customer table back up OK" )
  sleep( 1000 )
else
  errorShow( "DPW AR Backup", "Customer table back up failed" )
endif
```

Before moving on to the rest of the backup procedure, here is a point well worth reiterating. The back up version of the customer table will not retain any record (in its VAL file) of the referential integrity relationship that was defined between it and its detail tables. That fact will figure into procedures you need to know a little later.

The procedure for backing up the AR file is almost identical to that for the customer table. There is one notable difference: There is an extra statement in the code that sets the ReadOnly attribute for the AR table during the copy operation. If you don't do this, the referential integrity relationship will prevent the copy altogether. Also remember that the referential integrity relationship will still be noted in this and the ARHIST back up versions. Here is the procedure for backing up the AR table:

```
message( "DPW AR Backup: Beginning AR back up..." )
bkupname = workingDir() + "\\arbk" + StrVal(newarcnum) + ".db"
tb.attach( ":work:ar.db" )
tb.setReadOnly(Yes)
tb2.attach( bkupname )
if tb.copy( tb2 ) then
  message( "DPW AR Backup: AR table back up OK" )
  sleep( 1000 )
else
  errorShow( "DPW AR Backup", "AR table back up failed" )
endif
```

Last comes the backup code for the ARHIST table. This process observes the same requirements as the AR table's backup process:

```
message( "DPW AR Backup: Beginning ARHIST back up..." )
bkupname = workingDir() + "\\ahbk" + StrVal(newarcnum) + ".db"
tb.attach( ":work:arhist.db" )
tb.setReadOnly(Yes)
tb2.attach( bkupname )
if tb.copy( tb2 ) then
  message( "DPW AR Backup: ARHIST table back up OK" )
  sleep( 1000 )
else
  errorShow( "DPW AR Backup", "ARHIST table back up failed" )
endif
```

The only thing remaining now is to notify the user, who has been sitting patiently all this time, that the backup process is now complete. A simple message() call does this:

```
   message( "DPW AR Backup: Complete!" )
endmethod
;¦EndMethod¦#Page2.ARBackup¦pushButton¦
```

The AR restore function is closely parallel to the backup function. The way it behaves when you run it, however, may be a little startling if you don't know what to expect. A first clue about this is that any peculiarities arise, as before, because of the referential integrity relationships defined among the tables.

First, there are the requisite variables, just as before:

```
;¦BeginMethod¦#Page2.ARRestore¦pushButton¦
method pushButton(var eventInfo Event)
var
  lpstr, cwdir, dlgreturn, bkupname String
  newarcnum SmallInt
  tb, tb2 Table
endvar
```

Fetching the version number to use from the INI file is also much like before, except that it's not incremented this time: the restore is creating a new backup version. The user is, however, given a chance to override the expected version number, just in case it is desired to restore a backup version other than the most current one. The code is as follows:

```
cwdir = workingDir() + "\\ararc.ini"
lpstr = readProfileString( cwdir, "ARARC", "nextfilenum" )
newarcnum = SmallInt( lpstr )
dlgreturn = msgYesNoCancel( "DPW AR Restore",
                           "The current backup file number is " +
                           StrVal(newarcnum) + "\n" +
                           "Do you want to choose another version?" )
switch
  case dlgreturn = "Yes" :
    newarcnum.view( "Change file number:")
  case dlgreturn = "No" :
    message( "DPW AR Restore: Default backup file number accepted." )
  case dlgreturn = "Cancel" :
    message( "DPW AR Restore run aborted..." )
    sleep( 1000 )
    return
endswitch
```

The customer table restore is very familiar, too, with only the direction of table movement being reversed, and the ReadOnly attribute being set for the customer table this time, too. What happens when you run this code is another matter, but check it out before I tell you what that means.

```
message( "DPW AR Restore: Beginning Customer restore..." )
bkupname = workingDir() + "\\cubk" + StrVal(newarcnum) + ".db"
tb.attach( ":work:customer.db" )
tb2.attach( bkupname )
tb2.setReadOnly(Yes)
if tb2.copy( tb ) then
```

```
    message( "DPW AR Restore: Customer table restore OK" )
    sleep( 1000 )
else
    errorShow( "DPW AR Restore", "Customer table restore failed" )
endif
```

Although the customer table can be backed up no matter what (as long as there is room for the back up copies), it's not true that the customer table can be restored under any circumstances.

In fact, as long as the original customer table still exists, it cannot be restored, due to the presence of the referential integrity relationship. Now, this won't stop the restore run altogether: you'll get an error message box stating that the customer tables still has detail tables. Click OK in this box, and the copy fails, but the ObjectPAL code keeps on running (the AR and ARHIST tables will be restored even after this error).

There is a way around this situation. You won't like it, though. You can simply use Windows File Manager or DOS to completely delete the CUSTOMER table and all its family of files. Then the restore will work perfectly.

I told you that you wouldn't like it, and neither do I, really. But it is the price that must be paid to keep the referential integrity relationships on the tables. I consider that to be far more important than a mere inconvenience while restoring files. Likely enough, if you have to restore, they will have been lost anyway, and this won't crop up. Not only that, but if you remove the referential integrity relationship from the tables, you'll very soon end up with tables so hopelessly out of kilter that you'll wish you had left well enough alone. That's experience speaking, people!

With all the gritty stuff out of the way, you can go right along with the rest of the restore procedure. It is so predictable by now that I can just show it to you and move on. Here it is:

```
message( "DPW AR Restore: Beginning AR restore..." )
bkupname = workingDir() + "\\arbk" + StrVal(newarcnum) + ".db"
tb.attach( ":work:ar.db" )
tb2.attach( bkupname )
tb2.setReadOnly(Yes)
if tb2.copy( tb ) then
  message( "DPW AR Restore: AR table restore OK" )
  sleep( 1000 )
else
  errorShow( "DPW AR Restore", "AR table restore failed" )
endif

message( "DPW AR Restore: Beginning ARHIST restore..." )
bkupname = workingDir() + "\\ahbk" + StrVal(newarcnum) + ".db"
tb.attach( ":work:arhist.db" )
tb2.attach( bkupname )
tb2.setReadOnly(Yes)
```

```
    if tb2.copy( tb ) then
      message( "DPW AR Restore: ARHIST table restore OK" )
      sleep( 1000 )
    else
      errorShow( "DPW AR Restore", "ARHIST table restore failed" )
    endif

    message( "DPW AR Restore: Complete!" )
  endmethod

;¦EndMethod¦#Page2.ARRestore¦pushButton¦
```

A final note about backing up and restoring files is in order here. In spite of the possible inconvenience in restoring linked tables, think about one question for a moment. What will happen, someday, if you don't make regular backup runs? I'll bet you come up with the same answer that I do.

Creating Utilities for You and the User

The following sections cover a number of utilities that are either too much fun or too useful to leave out. Just as a worker who grudgingly exerts only the absolute minimum of effort is considered substandard, software that presents only a Spartan array of features also is considered undesirable.

Well, you aren't going to let that happen! Going even beyond the Multimedia Theater, the *Voice Notes!* audio notepad, and all the built-in and extra utility features, there is more! You'll give them music, lights, action!

Actually, I'm not kidding—at least not too much. The very first of the support utilities is the CDAudio Player. That's the music part, anyway. This is followed by the System Control Panel and Report Manager, two very powerful tools. Lastly, and mostly for you rather than your users, the FormList utility and the ObjectPAL Reference Data utility are covered.

The CDAudio Player

The CDAudio Player was one of the first features I put into place while developing all the parts of the AR/AP main selection panel. I'm sure there is no doubt why I did it that way! It was fun to do, and it has provided hours of enjoyment while I finished this book (which, I assure you, was much harder to complete than the software).

Because the CDAudio controls are on the main selection panel that you have seen so often, and because I still wanted to highlight their existence, I used the fuzzy picture trick

again to show you the CDAudio controls. Once more, they are the only objects in the picture in focus in Figure 9.5, just so you'll be sure to look at them.

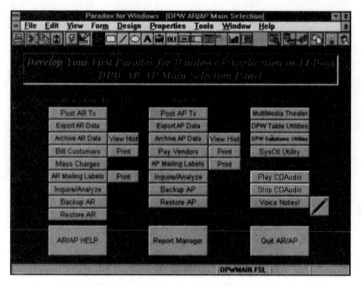

Figure 9.5. *The Play CDAudio and Stop CDAudio buttons on the DPWMAIN form.*

The CDAudio Player has just two buttons, and just two ObjectPAL methods to go with them. Those methods cannot stand alone, however, because they are multimedia-oriented. You might recall that the DPWMAIN form, from which these methods are taken, also has the Uses and Var blocks with the right things in them to support the MCI string command interface calls. That was one of several reasons I had for insisting (on Day 7) on showing you all of a form's methods together.

The one secret to playing audio CDs on your computer's CD-ROM drive is opening and playing the right kind of device type: the cdaudio device type. And that's the only secret. Other than that, you already know how to send string commands to the MCI string command interface. Once more, I am impressed with just how easy it is to play multimedia material with your computer. That's a credit both to Microsoft for the MCI interfaces, and to Borland for the ObjectPAL language.

Without further ado, then, here is the ObjectPAL source code for the Play CDAudio control button:

```
;¦BeginMethod¦#Page2.GoPlayCD¦pushButton¦
method pushButton(var eventInfo Event)
```

```
var
  mciCmdStr, ReturnString String
  ReturnCode LongInt
endvar
    ReturnString = fill( " ", 1024 )
    mciCmdStr = "open cdaudio"
    ReturnCode = mciSendString(mciCmdStr, ReturnString, 1024, 0)
    if NOT (0 = ReturnCode) then
      ReturnString = fill( " ", 1024 )
      mciGetErrorString( ReturnCode, ReturnString, 1024 )
      msgStop( "CDAudio Open", ReturnString )
      return
    endif
    ReturnString = fill( " ", 1024 )
    mciCmdStr = "play cdaudio"
    ReturnCode = mciSendString(mciCmdStr, ReturnString, 1024, 0)
    if NOT (0 = ReturnCode) then
      ReturnString = fill( " ", 1024 )
      mciGetErrorString( ReturnCode, ReturnString, 1024 )
      msgStop( "CDAudio Play", ReturnString )
      return
    endif
endmethod
;¦EndMethod¦#Page2.GoPlayCD¦pushButton¦
```

You see? It really was that easy! The ObjectPAL code for the Stop CDaudio button is similarly simple, as follows:

```
;¦BeginMethod¦#Page2.GoStopCD¦pushButton¦
method pushButton(var eventInfo Event)
var
  mciCmdStr, ReturnString String
  ReturnCode LongInt
endvar
    ReturnString = fill( " ", 1024 )
    mciCmdStr = "stop cdaudio"
    ReturnCode = mciSendString(mciCmdStr, ReturnString, 1024, 0)
    if NOT (0 = ReturnCode) then
      ReturnString = fill( " ", 1024 )
      mciGetErrorString( ReturnCode, ReturnString, 1024 )
      msgStop( "CDAudio Stop", ReturnString )
      return
    endif
    ReturnString = fill( " ", 1024 )
    mciCmdStr = "close cdaudio"
    ReturnCode = mciSendString(mciCmdStr, ReturnString, 1024, 0)
    if NOT (0 = ReturnCode) then
      ReturnString = fill( " ", 1024 )
      mciGetErrorString( ReturnCode, ReturnString, 1024 )
      msgStop( "CDAudio Close", ReturnString )
      return
    endif
endmethod
;¦EndMethod¦#Page2.GoStopCD¦pushButton¦
```

That's all there is to playing CDAudio on your Windows machine. Enjoy.

The DPW System Control Panel

The System Control Panel is a power tool for the system administrator or power user. You can do an abundance of things with this utility, as is made plain in Figure 9.6, where the SYSCTL.FSL form is shown.

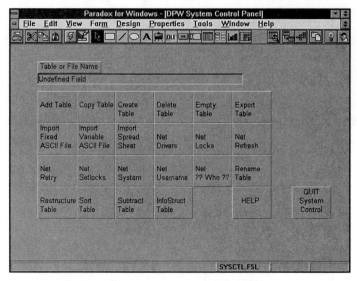

Figure 9.6. *The System Control Panel form, SYSCTL.FSL.*

In order to discuss the ObjectPAL methods attached to objects in SYSCTL, there are a couple of things that need to be mentioned. One of those things is that I left all the design objects with their default noise names. Bad news, because now I have to correlate all the methods to their control objects, so that you can tell what they are.

The other thing involves the reason I keep saying "control objects" rather than buttons. That's because there aren't any buttons: every button-like object on the form is actually a text box with an outside 3D frame style.

I chose to use text boxes for the control "button" objects because I liked the appearance it gives. It's something like a real control panel with flush-mounted pushbuttons in a rectangular array. Of course, that does introduce a slight programming problem, because I still wanted the control "buttons" to respond when clicked by appearing to be depressed momentarily.

That programming requirement turns out to be no problem at all. All you have to do is set another frame style (an inside 3D frame), do whatever it is you want the "button" to do, and restore the frame style. It is done just like this:

```
self.frame.style = Inside3DFrame
; ............. do other things here ..............
self.frame.style = Outside3DFrame
```

The SYSCTL form open() is the same one you have been using, it seems. Its contents are the usual, as follows:

```
;¦BeginMethod¦#FormData1¦open¦
method open(var eventInfo Event)
  if NOT eventInfo.isPreFilter() then
    doDefault
    maximize()
  endif
endmethod
;¦EndMethod¦#FormData1¦open¦
```

The Help button is a perfect example of the frame style manipulation just described. The "button" appears to depress when clicked, the help file is displayed, and when the help engine returns, the "button" appears to pop back out. Here is the code for it:

```
;¦BeginMethod¦#Page2.#Text11¦mouseClick¦
method mouseClick(var eventInfo MouseEvent)
  self.frame.style = Inside3DFrame
  helpShowContext( "dpwmain.hlp", LongInt(28) )
  self.frame.style = Outside3DFrame
endmethod
;¦EndMethod¦#Page2.#Text11¦mouseClick¦
```

The Quit button behaves a little differently. The frame style is changed to the inside 3D style, but never restored. Why do that, when the next action is to go away? The code is as follows:

```
;¦BeginMethod¦#Page2.#Text33¦mouseClick¦
method mouseClick(var eventInfo MouseEvent)
  self.frame.style = Inside3DFrame
  close(0)
endmethod
;¦EndMethod¦#Page2.#Text33¦mouseClick¦
```

All the remaining SYSCTL methods manipulate the frame exactly as described. They all also use one of the built-in Paradox System class dialog boxes to perform the work. For that reason, and to conserve space, I will just introduce the button control's method by simply stating its name.

Here is the mouseClick() method for the Restructure Table control:

```
;¦BeginMethod¦#Page2.#Text29¦mouseClick¦
method mouseClick(var eventInfo MouseEvent)
```

```
      self.frame.style = Inside3DFrame
      if NOT isTable(TFName) then
        msgStop( "DPW SysCtl Panel", "Enter a table name first" )
      else
        dlgRestructure( TFName )
      endif
      self.frame.style = Outside3DFrame
    endmethod
    ;¦EndMethod¦#Page2.#Text29¦mouseClick¦
```

Here is the mouseClick() method for the Sort Table control:

```
    ;¦BeginMethod¦#Page2.#Text28¦mouseClick¦
    method mouseClick(var eventInfo MouseEvent)
      self.frame.style = Inside3DFrame
      if NOT isTable(TFName) then
        msgStop( "DPW SysCtl Panel", "Enter a table name first" )
      else
        dlgSort( TFName )
      endif
      self.frame.style = Outside3DFrame
    endmethod
    ;¦EndMethod¦#Page2.#Text28¦mouseClick¦
```

Here is the mouseClick() method for the Subtract Table control:

```
    ;¦BeginMethod¦#Page2.#Text27¦mouseClick¦
    method mouseClick(var eventInfo MouseEvent)
      self.frame.style = Inside3DFrame
      if NOT isTable(TFName) then
        msgStop( "DPW SysCtl Panel", "Enter a table name first" )
      else
        dlgSubtract( TFName )
      endif
      self.frame.style = Outside3DFrame
    endmethod
    ;¦EndMethod¦#Page2.#Text27¦mouseClick¦
```

Here is the mouseClick() method for the InfoStruct Table control:

```
    ;¦BeginMethod¦#Page2.#Text26¦mouseClick¦
    method mouseClick(var eventInfo MouseEvent)
      self.frame.style = Inside3DFrame
      if NOT isTable(TFName) then
        msgStop( "DPW SysCtl Panel", "Enter a table name first" )
      else
        dlgTableInfo( TFName )
      endif
      self.frame.style = Outside3DFrame
    endmethod
    ;¦EndMethod¦#Page2.#Text26¦mouseClick¦
```

Here is the mouseClick() method for the Net Retry control:

```
    ;¦BeginMethod¦#Page2.#Text23¦mouseClick¦
    method mouseClick(var eventInfo MouseEvent)
      self.frame.style = Inside3DFrame
```

```
  dlgNetRetry()
  self.frame.style = Outside3DFrame
endmethod
;¦EndMethod¦#Page2.#Text23¦mouseClick¦
```

Here is the `mouseClick()` method for the Net Setlocks control:

```
;¦BeginMethod¦#Page2.#Text22¦mouseClick¦
method mouseClick(var eventInfo MouseEvent)
  self.frame.style = Inside3DFrame
  dlgNetSetLocks()
  self.frame.style = Outside3DFrame
endmethod
;¦EndMethod¦#Page2.#Text22¦mouseClick¦
```

Here is the `mouseClick()` method for the Net System control:

```
;¦BeginMethod¦#Page2.#Text21¦mouseClick¦
method mouseClick(var eventInfo MouseEvent)
  self.frame.style = Inside3DFrame
  dlgNetSystem()
  self.frame.style = Outside3DFrame
endmethod
;¦EndMethod¦#Page2.#Text21¦mouseClick¦
```

Here is the `mouseClick()` method for the Net UserName control:

```
;¦BeginMethod¦#Page2.#Text20¦mouseClick¦
method mouseClick(var eventInfo MouseEvent)
  self.frame.style = Inside3DFrame
  dlgNetUsername()
  self.frame.style = Outside3DFrame
endmethod
;¦EndMethod¦#Page2.#Text20¦mouseClick¦
```

Here is the `mouseClick()` method for the Net ??Who?? control:

```
;¦BeginMethod¦#Page2.#Text19¦mouseClick¦
method mouseClick(var eventInfo MouseEvent)
  self.frame.style = Inside3DFrame
  dlgNetWho()
  self.frame.style = Outside3DFrame
endmethod
;¦EndMethod¦#Page2.#Text19¦mouseClick¦
```

Here is the `mouseClick()` method for the Rename Table control:

```
;¦BeginMethod¦#Page2.#Text18¦mouseClick¦
method mouseClick(var eventInfo MouseEvent)
  self.frame.style = Inside3DFrame
  if NOT isTable(TFName) then
    msgStop( "DPW SysCtl Panel", "Enter a table name first" )
  else
    dlgRename( TFName )
  endif
  self.frame.style = Outside3DFrame
endmethod
```

```
;¦EndMethod¦#Page2.#Text18¦mouseClick¦
```

Here is the `mouseClick()` method for the Import Fixed ASCII File control:

```
;¦BeginMethod¦#Page2.#Text17¦mouseClick¦
method mouseClick(var eventInfo MouseEvent)
  self.frame.style = Inside3DFrame
  if TFName.isBlank() then
    msgStop( "DPW SysCtl Panel", "Enter a file name first" )
  else
    dlgImportASCIIFix( TFName )
  endif
  self.frame.style = Outside3DFrame
endmethod
;¦EndMethod¦#Page2.#Text17¦mouseClick¦
```

Here is the `mouseClick()` method for the Import Variable ASCII File control:

```
;¦BeginMethod¦#Page2.#Text16¦mouseClick¦
method mouseClick(var eventInfo MouseEvent)
  self.frame.style = Inside3DFrame
  if TFName.isBlank() then
    msgStop( "DPW SysCtl Panel", "Enter a file name first" )
  else
    dlgImportASCIIVar( TFName )
  endif
  self.frame.style = Outside3DFrame
endmethod
;¦EndMethod¦#Page2.#Text16¦mouseClick¦
```

Here is the `mouseClick()` method for the Import Spreadsheet control:

```
;¦BeginMethod¦#Page2.#Text15¦mouseClick¦
method mouseClick(var eventInfo MouseEvent)
  self.frame.style = Inside3DFrame
  if TFName.isBlank() then
    msgStop( "DPW SysCtl Panel", "Enter a file name first" )
  else
    dlgImportSpreadSheet( TFName )
  endif
  self.frame.style = Outside3DFrame
endmethod
;¦EndMethod¦#Page2.#Text15¦mouseClick¦
```

Here is the `mouseClick()` method for the Net Drivers control:

```
;¦BeginMethod¦#Page2.#Text14¦mouseClick¦
method mouseClick(var eventInfo MouseEvent)
  self.frame.style = Inside3DFrame
  dlgNetDrivers()
  self.frame.style = Outside3DFrame
endmethod
;¦EndMethod¦#Page2.#Text14¦mouseClick¦
```

Here is the `mouseClick()` method for the Net Locks control:

```
;¦BeginMethod¦#Page2.#Text13¦mouseClick¦
```

```
method mouseClick(var eventInfo MouseEvent)
  self.frame.style = Inside3DFrame
  dlgNetLocks()
  self.frame.style = Outside3DFrame
endmethod
;¦EndMethod¦#Page2.#Text13¦mouseClick¦
```

Here is the mouseClick() method for the Net Refresh control:

```
;¦BeginMethod¦#Page2.#Text12¦mouseClick¦
method mouseClick(var eventInfo MouseEvent)
  self.frame.style = Inside3DFrame
  dlgNetRefresh()
  self.frame.style = Outside3DFrame
endmethod
;¦EndMethod¦#Page2.#Text12¦mouseClick¦
```

Here is the mouseClick() method for the Export Table control:

```
;¦BeginMethod¦#Page2.#Text10¦mouseClick¦
method mouseClick(var eventInfo MouseEvent)
  self.frame.style = Inside3DFrame
  if NOT isTable(TFName) then
    msgStop( "DPW SysCtl Panel", "Enter a table name first" )
  else
    dlgExport( TFName )
  endif
  self.frame.style = Outside3DFrame
endmethod
;¦EndMethod¦#Page2.#Text10¦mouseClick¦
```

Here is the mouseClick() method for the Empty Table control:

```
;¦BeginMethod¦#Page2.#Text9¦mouseClick¦
method mouseClick(var eventInfo MouseEvent)
  self.frame.style = Inside3DFrame
  if NOT isTable(TFName) then
    msgStop( "DPW SysCtl Panel", "Enter a table name first" )
  else
    dlgEmpty( TFName )
  endif
  self.frame.style = Outside3DFrame
endmethod
;¦EndMethod¦#Page2.#Text9¦mouseClick¦
```

Here is the mouseClick() method for the Delete Table control:

```
;¦BeginMethod¦#Page2.#Text8¦mouseClick¦
method mouseClick(var eventInfo MouseEvent)
  self.frame.style = Inside3DFrame
  if NOT isTable(TFName) then
    msgStop( "DPW SysCtl Panel", "Enter a table name first" )
  else
    dlgDelete( TFName )
  endif
  self.frame.style = Outside3DFrame
endmethod
```

```
;¦EndMethod¦#Page2.#Text8¦mouseClick¦
```

Here is the `mouseClick()` method for the Create Table control:

```
;¦BeginMethod¦#Page2.#Text7¦mouseClick¦
method mouseClick(var eventInfo MouseEvent)
  self.frame.style = Inside3DFrame
  if TFName.isBlank() then
    msgStop( "DPW SysCtl Panel", "Enter a table name first" )
  else
    dlgCreate( TFName )
  endif
  self.frame.style = Outside3DFrame
endmethod
;¦EndMethod¦#Page2.#Text7¦mouseClick¦
```

Here is the `mouseClick()` method for the Copy Table control:

```
;¦BeginMethod¦#Page2.#Text6¦mouseClick¦
method mouseClick(var eventInfo MouseEvent)
  self.frame.style = Inside3DFrame
  if NOT isTable(TFName) then
    msgStop( "DPW SysCtl Panel", "Enter a table name first" )
  else
    dlgCopy( TFName )
  endif
  self.frame.style = Outside3DFrame
endmethod
;¦EndMethod¦#Page2.#Text6¦mouseClick¦
```

Here is the `mouseClick()` method for the Add Table control:

```
;¦BeginMethod¦#Page2.#Text5¦mouseClick¦
method mouseClick(var eventInfo MouseEvent)
  self.frame.style = Inside3DFrame
  if NOT isTable(TFName) then
    msgStop( "DPW SysCtl Panel", "Enter a table name first" )
  else
    dlgAdd( TFName )
  endif
  self.frame.style = Outside3DFrame
endmethod
;¦EndMethod¦#Page2.#Text5¦mouseClick¦
```

As you can see, the methods in SYSCTL are highly repetitive in form (pardon the pun), but the effects they can achieve are very satisfying.

The Report Manager

On Day 5 you saw how to use the Report Manager for various printing tasks, including duplex printing with either a dot-matrix or laser printer. Now you'll see how to write ObjectPAL for controlling reports in such a detailed manner.

The secret to the flexible control of reports is the ReportPrintInfo structure. Fill that structure in correctly, call Paradox, and let the engine do the work. Thus, most of the ObjectPAL code in the Report Manager's methods involve collecting and checking user inputs from fields and radio buttons. The layout of the fields and radio buttons is shown in Figure 9.7.

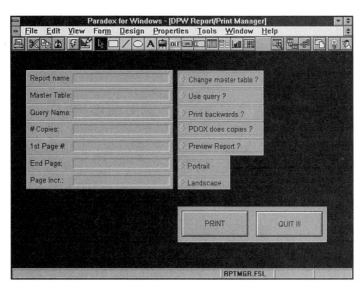

Figure 9.7. *The Report/Print Manager form, RPTMGR.FSL.*

RPTMGR has a Var block that's used to hold the queryString variable. This variable will be used when the user wants to run the report against query output, rather than against the master table directly. The Var block looks like this:

```
;¦BeginMethod¦#FormData1¦Var¦
Var
  queryString String
endVar
;¦EndMethod¦#FormData1¦Var¦
```

The open() method for RPTMGR is also a little more involved than usual. All the buttons and fields are initialized to beginning values after performing default actions, as follows:

```
;¦BeginMethod¦#FormData1¦open¦
method open(var eventInfo Event)
  if Not eventInfo.isPreFilter() then
    doDefault
    maximize()
```

```
      queryString.blank()
      RptReport = ""
      RptTable = ""
      RptQuery = ""
      RptCopies = 1
      RptFirstP = 1
      RptPageInc = 1
      RtpChgTab = False
      RptUseQuery = False
      RptBkwds = False
      RptPXCopies = False
      RptOrient = "Portrait"
      PButton.pushbutton()
   endif
endmethod
;¦EndMethod¦#FormData1¦open¦
```

The RPTMGR form's `close()` method is still the normal thing, however. Its code is as follows:

```
;¦BeginMethod¦#Page2.#Box41.RptQuit¦pushButton¦
method pushButton(var eventInfo Event)
   close()
endmethod
;¦EndMethod¦#Page2.#Box41.RptQuit¦pushButton¦
```

I gave the Print button the internal name of `RptDOIT` in honor of my DOS Paradox experiences. It is in this button's method that all the action takes place. That action is surprisingly simple, too. It is a little lengthy, but quite straightforward. Take a look at it, and then I will make some final comments on it.

```
;¦BeginMethod¦#Page2.#Box41.RptDOIT¦pushButton¦
method pushButton(var eventInfo Event)
var
   qbf TextStream
   qtl String
   ri ReportPrintInfo
   rep Report
endvar
   if RptReport.isBlank() then
     errorLog( 2, "You must specify a report name!" )
     errorLog( 1, "Report specification error" )
     errorShow( "DPW Laser Duplex Reports", "DPW error log..." )
     fail()
   endif
   ri.name = RptReport
   if RptChgTab = True then
     if NOT RptTable.isBlank() then
       ri.masterTable = RptTable
     endif
   endif
   if RptUseQuery = True then
     if NOT RptQuery.isBlank() then
       queryString.blank()
       qbf.open( RptQuery,"r" )
```

```
        while NOT qbf.eof()
          qbf.readLine( qtl )
          queryString = String( queryString, qtl, "\n" )
        endwhile
        qbf.close()
        ri.queryString = queryString
      endif
  endif
  if PrtBkwds = True then
    ri.printBackwards = True
  else
    ri.printBackwards = False
  endif
  if RptPXCopies = True then
    ri.makeCopies = True
  else
    ri.makeCopies = False
  endif
  if NOT RptCopies.isBlank() then
    ri.nCopies = RptCopies
  endif
  if NOT RptFirstP.isBlank() then
    ri.startPage = RptFirstP
  endif
  if NOT RptLastP.isBlank() then
    ri.endPage = RptLastP
  endif
  if NOT RptPageInc.isBlank() then
    ri.pageIncrement = RptPageInc
  endif
  switch
    case RptOrient = "Portrait" : ri.orient = PrintPortrait
    case RptOrient = "Landscape" : ri.orient = PrintLandscape
  endswitch
  if RptPreview then
    rep.open( ri )
  else
    rep.print( ri )
  endif
endmethod
;¦EndMethod¦#Page2.#Box41.RptDOIT¦pushButton¦
```

The first thing that had to happen in the method, of course, is to check for a report name input from the user. No report, no print. Next, a check is made to see if the user wants to change the master table for the report. You might want to use this option, for example, with a report on the AR table that you want to run against the ARHIST table for a change.

Following those checks, any requested query is loaded. The technique used for this purpose is the same one you saw earlier today. The entire query file is loaded into a single String object, with the text lines separated by a \n (newline) character. Notice that, if used, the entire query string is placed into the ReportPrintInfo structure.

The remaining actions taken by the method all read radio button settings, and set the
`ReportPrintInfo` structure accordingly. If the request was for preview mode, the report
is opened, otherwise it is `printed`.

The Form List Form

To use the FormList utility, you just name the source version of the form you want the
ObjectPAL from, and click the Build Methods Text button. This somewhat unassuming
form is shown in Figure 9.8. It is a utility that really is just for you, and not the end users
of your software. They should be getting only the delivered forms anyway, right?

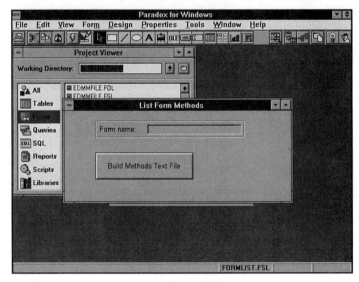

Figure 9.8. *The Form List Utility form, FORMLIST.FSL.*

For Paradox developers (that includes you, now), however, this little utility is a blessing.
This utility is how I got all the source listings for the forms into this book, for example.
Without it, I would still be typing, I guess.

The FORMLIST `open()` method is standard fare, so here it is without comment:

```
;¦BeginMethod¦#FormData1¦open¦
method open(var eventInfo Event)
  if NOT eventInfo.isPreFilter() then
    doDefault
    setPosition(1440,1440,6500,2880)
  endif
```

```
endmethod
;¦EndMethod¦#FormData1¦open¦
```

When you punch the go-button, FORMLIST checks for a filled-in form name, and calls the `enumSourceToFile()` method, as follows:

```
;¦BeginMethod¦#Page2.#Button6¦pushButton¦
method pushButton(var eventInfo Event)
var
  myForm Form
endvar
  if NOT inForm.isSpace() then
    myForm.open( inForm + ".FSL" )
    myForm.enumSourceToFile( ".\\"+inForm+".TXT", True )
    myForm.close()
    setPosition(1440,1440,6500,2880)
  else
    msgInfo( "Form List", "No Form given." )
  endif
endmethod
;¦EndMethod¦#Page2.#Button6¦pushButton¦
```

There you are! You get a whole lot of candy for just a dime with this utility.

The ObjectPAL Reference Summary Application

The ObjectPAL Reference Summary utility is another one that only you and I can use. But it is one that I use constantly while writing ObjectPAL. I use it to find methods, constants, and properties that I know must be there, but whose names I cannot for the moment recall. You can look up a method's or procedure's call syntax, too, something I often need. Figure 9.9 will refresh your memory about the form's appearance.

All the reference data is stored in a series of tables (which you get with the book's CD-ROM). To refer to the material, click the button for the subject. If the tables don't yet exist, or you have installed a new release of Paradox, you can refresh the tables by clicking the corresponding Regen buttons. Once again, Paradox makes it easy.

The REFDATA form's `open()` and `close()` methods are still old hat for you, so here they are with no comment:

```
;¦BeginMethod¦#FormData1¦open¦
method open(var eventInfo Event)
  if NOT eventInfo.isPreFilter() then
    setTitle( "ObjectPAL Reference Data Summary" )
    doDefault
    maximize()
  endif
endmethod
```

```
;¦EndMethod¦#FormData1¦open¦

;¦BeginMethod¦#Page2.#Button10¦pushButton¦
method pushButton(var eventInfo Event)
  close()
endmethod
;¦EndMethod¦#Page2.#Button10¦pushButton¦
```

Next there appears a few methods calling enumRTL...() methods (short for *enumerate RunTime Library*), and directing Paradox to place the results in tables, as follows:

```
;¦BeginMethod¦#Page2.#Button52¦pushButton¦
method pushButton(var eventInfo Event)
  enumRTLClassNames( "class.db" )
endmethod
;¦EndMethod¦#Page2.#Button52¦pushButton¦

;¦BeginMethod¦#Page2.#Button49¦pushButton¦
method pushButton(var eventInfo Event)
  enumRTLMethods( "method.db" )
endmethod
;¦EndMethod¦#Page2.#Button49¦pushButton¦

;¦BeginMethod¦#Page2.#Button46¦pushButton¦
method pushButton(var eventInfo Event)
  enumRTLConstants( "constant.db" )
endmethod
;¦EndMethod¦#Page2.#Button46¦pushButton¦

;¦BeginMethod¦#Page2.#Button43¦pushButton¦
method pushButton(var eventInfo Event)
  enumUIClasses( "uiclass.db" )
endmethod
;¦EndMethod¦#Page2.#Button43¦pushButton¦
```

The remaining methods all open table views on the reference data. There is nothing startling here, either, so just take a look at the code, and then go on to the next section:

```
;¦BeginMethod¦#Page2.#Button38¦pushButton¦
method pushButton(var eventInfo Event)
var
QS TableView
endvar
QS.open("uiclass")
QS.maximize()
endmethod
;¦EndMethod¦#Page2.#Button38¦pushButton¦

;¦BeginMethod¦#Page2.#Button59¦pushButton¦
method pushButton(var eventInfo Event)
var
QS TableView
endvar
QS.open("constant")
QS.maximize()
endmethod
```

```
;¦EndMethod¦#Page2.#Button59¦pushButton¦

;¦BeginMethod¦#Page2.#Button60¦pushButton¦
method pushButton(var eventInfo Event)
var
QS TableView
endvar
QS.open("method")
QS.maximize()
endmethod
;¦EndMethod¦#Page2.#Button60¦pushButton¦

;¦BeginMethod¦#Page2.#Button61¦pushButton¦
method pushButton(var eventInfo Event)
var
QS TableView
endvar
QS.open("class")
QS.maximize()
endmethod
;¦EndMethod¦#Page2.#Button61¦pushButton¦
```

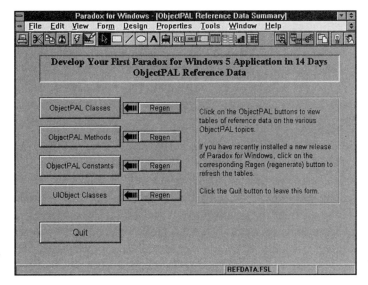

Figure 9.9. *The ObjectPAL Reference Data form, REFDATA.FSL.*

I hope that you find the REFDATA application to be as handy as I have. It's one of those things you can get hooked on. In fact, during early release testing of new Paradox versions, I sometimes found it to be more reliable than the preliminary documentation (when there is preliminary documentation).

Sharing the Application's Data with Multiple Users

In the planning stages, it was sufficient to merely mention the kinds of network data sharing that might interest you. At this point, however, it is time to discuss the programming implications of deploying your application on a network.

The first thing you should always do if your application is on a network is *password protect* the tables. You can do this through the desktop, or through ObjectPAL using the protect() method. Through the desktop you can define both owner and auxiliary passwords. ObjectPAL will permit only the definition of an owner password with the protect() method.

When the tables are password protected, you should provide some kind of an initial sign-on panel, where a user can supply a password, and your ObjectPAL code can log the user in by calling the addPassword() Session class method. That is, declare a Session class variable and use it to call the method, like this:

```
var
  password Session
endvar
  password.addPassword( userinputstring )
...
```

When the user logs off (for which you should provide an interface, as well), your code should call the removePassword() Session class method.

You must also understand Paradox locks in order to deploy your application on a network. Paradox supports both automatic and explicit locks, and table and record locks.

Paradox will automatically place a record lock on a table record while you're editing it in a table view or table frame, and release it when you move off the record. Paradox will also place a table lock on a table for some intensive batch operations, such as sorting or copying tables.

However, when you open a table cursor on a table, as is often done throughout this book, there is no UI object on top of the table, and Paradox isn't automatically controlling the table's or record's locks. You must do that in ObjectPAL code in these instances.

First of all, you can lock an individual record while the ObjectPAL edits the record. For example, if an ObjectPAL method is updating the AR table, using a table cursor named artc, you could code something like this:

```
artc.edit()              ; go into edit mode
if artc,lockRecord() then ; be  sure we have the lock
  ...                    ; do editing stuff here
```

```
endif
artc.unlockRecord()        ; don't forget this!
artc.endEdit()             ; or this!
```

If your code is going to do something on a larger scale, to the whole table for example, you can place a table lock on the table. You may recall that you did this in the TBUTIL form for the `ReIndexAll` function. The code there looked like this:

```
var
  tb1 Table
endvar
  tb1.attach( TBName1 )
  if tb1.isTable()then
    try
      tb1.setExclusive()    ; required to rebuild maintained indexes
      if tb1.lock("Full") then
        if tb1.reIndexAll() then
          msgInfo( "DPW Table Utility", "ReIndex complete" )
        else
          msgStop( "DPW Table Utility", "ReIndex FAILED!" )
          errorShow( "DPW Table Utility", "Attempted secondary re-index all" )
        endif
        tb1.unlock("Full")
      else
        msgStop( "DPW Table Utility", "Can't LOCK the table!" )
      endif
    onfail
      msgStop( "DPW Table Utility", "ReIndexAll transaction block failed!" )
      errorShow( "DPW Table Utility", "Attempted secondary re-index all" )
    endtry
  else
    msgStop( "DPW Table Utility", "A table is not specified correctly!" )
  endif
  tb1.unattach()
```

Notice in this code fragment how locks are set, and how the lock is tested, too. You don't always get the lock you ask for, so be sure to check it. It is important to package sensitive code, such as locking and unlocking code, in `if...then` and `try...fail` blocks so that you don't let any unexpected conditions get by you. Table 9.1 summarizes the table locks that you can set, and what access rights these locks give you and other users on the network.

Table 9.1. Locks you can place on tables, with summaries of users' rights.

Lock level	Your rights	Other users' rights	Locks other users can place
None	None	All	All
Open	Read, Write	Read, Write	All except exclusive

continues

Table 9.1. continued

Lock level	Your rights	Other users' rights	Locks other users can place
Read	Read, Write	Read	Open, Read
Write	Read, Write	Read	Open
Exclusive (full)	All	None	None

There is one final type of lock method that you need to know about: the Sessions class `lock()` method. This type of lock is important because it will permit you to lock more than one table simultaneously. This could be critical, for example, if you were updating both the CUSTOMER and AR tables together. Therefor you need to be sure that neither is disturbed while the update is in flight. There is a corresponding multitable Sessions class `unlock()` also.

Modification Notes

Wow! We're done! Well, I'm done anyway. You still have to clone my code for the AP backup and restore features, but that shouldn't be difficult at all. Just copy it, and be doubly sure you change all the table names: CUSTOMER becomes VENDOR, AR becomes AP, and ARHIST becomes APHIST. Modify the backup template names, too. CUBK*nnnn* should become VNBK*nnnn*, and so on. Oh, and don't forget that you'll need an APARC.INI file to record the back up version numbers

And come to think of it, you aren't *done* done, either. You still have a lot of work to do in documenting the now-running application, and finally in deploying it to your users.

Debugging the Process

Debugging the AP backup and restore procedures should take your entire attention for a little while. Don't just clone my code and assume that it will work. Try it several times, making sure that the version numbering scheme works, that the tables actually get copied correctly, and most importantly, that you can get them back.

Enough said. Now go to Part III of the book and learn how to write documentation. This is the part that all programmers love to hate, but they shouldn't. I have seen many applications that could have been great, but were useless due to inadequate documentation. And besides, you'll learn how to create not just hypertext documentation, but hypermedia documentation as well.

Documentation

Part III requires just two days to complete. But in those two days, you may learn something you didn't quite expect. You will see how to do the following:

☐ Create the application's written documentation. You'll get tips on writing, from yours truly—but you will just have to live with that.

☐ Create the application's online documentation using Paradox forms or the Windows help compiler. With the Windows help compiler, you'll also learn how to create hypermedia online documentation, not just hypertext.

Writing the
Application's
Printed
Documentation

There is something solid about a book that makes it an extension of one's self, a projection of one's own mind. There is a sense of context that clings to the printed page, which is impossible to duplicate with a computer, even though hypermedia (covered on Day 11) is beginning to make some limited strides in that direction.

A printed message gives its owner and reader a sense of power and control over the subject matter, which cannot be duplicated by other means. Online hypertext documentation can, therefore, have a large, possibly decisive, effect on the potential buyer of a piece of software; but the application isn't complete until there is a *book* that goes with it. I, along with many other buyers of commercial software, may indeed migrate toward the application that has nice online features; but for me, the printed documentation is a given that's not negotiable.

If you think about it for a moment (and I certainly have), this very human psychology is what makes the market for books like this one possible; and it's books like this one that make commercial software more viable in the marketplace. If that weren't true, why did you buy this book about Paradox for Windows? You and I both would like to think that this book serves a useful purpose, each for our own reasons.

Printed documentation in whatever form it may take, bundled manual or commercial book like this one, is what the philosophers would call the *sine qua non* (Latin for "without which not") of a truly finished application. That being the case, today I will take you on a brief—but hopefully helpful—tour of the art and craft of documenting your applications. Yep. You're going to have to turn writer to do the documentation. I'm still learning, too, but perhaps I can help a little.

How Much Documentation is Enough?

This chapter will stand out in the book for its lack of figures, source code, and other paraphernalia of software documentation and explanation. It will be just you and I discussing the merits of various aspects of the writing craft and learning how to tie that craft to the world of software. In particular, I'll talk about large writing projects, and what it takes to bring one off.

That thought leads to the question posed by this section's title: Just how much documentation is enough documentation for your application? The answer is, *a lot.* I say that because in 25 years of documenting software (and a few spent in writing these books, too), I have learned that the very first rule of any kind of writing is that you cannot assume

that the reader automatically knows what you're talking about. If you don't say it, how can the reader know what you're talking about? The most common mistake that beginning writers make is to assume that the reader knows something. My editors can tell you that I still sometimes do this, in spite of having had published somewhere in the vicinity of a half-million or so words in several books. Oh, well.

The point is clear, however. You have to say it all, in print. Otherwise, the reader, who is your software user, won't know what is going on. The reader might not verbalize what is wrong, but he will certainly be aware that the documentation is gappy, disorganized, or confusing.

So, again, how much is a lot? It is enough to cover the what, where, why, and how of every feature of the application. Name every form, field, button, and table. Tell what each does and how that will affect other parts of a software's function. A list of things is just a list: documentation is a discussion of things and their relationships. Therefore, even a moderately sized application is likely to require a large document—20, 50, or even more pages.

Of course, there is a lot, and then there is a *lot* of documentation. I admit that this is a slightly gray area, because you may produce a completely adequate Paradox for Windows document that's shorter than this one. That's a confession: I seem to have trouble bringing in a book project in anything less than a thousand pages. I can do it (this book being a case in point), but it hurts!

This last point raises the twin issues of controlling the document's development and of so-called writer's block. Speaking of the second phenomenon first: there is no such thing as writer's block when writing documentation. If you wrote an application, you obviously have something to say about how it was put together and how it should work. Just get out there and say it. In fact, if you do have writer's block about the documentation, it most likely means that you're stumbling over an inadequacy of the application itself. If the program behaves poorly, is poorly targeted, or is sloppily constructed, your comments about it are going to be confusing. Get the application squeaky clean, and then the words will come on their own.

Returning to the issue of controlling the document, think about this: if you're consistently running over the planned document size (my face is red, here), it may be that you have lost sight of what you set out to do with the words. Are you heading toward a clearly defined goal? Is what you're saying in the text really related to *what the user needs to know* about the software? The old rule, "plan the work and work the plan," applies here. The language style you select will have something to do with this; but as a rule, don't be chatty, because it will only confuse the reader further.

10

About the *second* first rule of writing: if it isn't working you hard, then you aren't writing; you're just diddling around, and the result will be worthless. These are strong words, but the point isn't an idle one. I have found that writing isn't a trivial endeavor. It requires lots of intelligently applied thought and hard work.

The concept of intelligently applied hard work leads to the *third* first rule of successful writing. (You're right; they are all first rules because they are equally important.) That rule is that if you plan and organize the contents of the document correctly, the document will nearly write itself. With practice, you'll learn to recognize that correctly organized state. The whole document will seem to gel in your mind, permitting you to write the parts in any order. Furthermore, when the document is properly organized, the size will take care of itself. Organizing your documentation is the subject of the next section.

Organizing the Documentation's Contents

There are many similarities to writing text and writing computer programs. One of those similarities isn't bottom-up design! Attempting to design a document beginning with details and formulating the larger perspective from them will lead directly to a phased-out state of mind.

Being *phased out* means being deflected away from the goal at hand to something (anything) else. Now, if you have not yet established the major goals for the document by using a top-down design approach, how are you going to stick to the pursuit of those goals? A very good question, is it not? There do exist those mad, genius types who can write a book or other document backward like that, but they tend to be flaky and unable to produce consistently on demand and on schedule. That's not very conducive to getting a product to market on time.

A top-down approach to designing the document, then, is the way to go for serious documentation. Constructing an ordinary outline of the document, with just the major bullets in it at first, is the ideal way to begin. In this age of the word processor, going back to add further detail is no problem: just insert the lines under the major heads, one level at a time.

What the major heads contain, and what sequence they should appear in, is a little problematic. Both decisions depend on the audience. Are you writing internal documentation for specialists? You might then safely assume that the readers are familiar with certain basic procedures, or rules of the game. Documentation for insiders typically leaves

a lot unsaid (or perhaps said elsewhere). Are you writing documentation for end users? Then you'll need to be very careful to mentally approach the subject in the same fashion and sequence in which your readers will approach it. What do such readers want to know first when they initially approach a software package that's new to them? Where should they go from there? Have you used a packaging style that they aren't familiar with, that will give them few clues as to how to proceed? Then you had better spell out what they need to know about the environment, and how they may navigate around in it.

Sometimes it's difficult to answer these questions. I experienced just this dilemma in designing this book. My readers (you, that is) are a combination of the insider and the newcomer. You already have some experience with Paradox for Windows, but you initially had no clear notion where I might head with this book (how could you, until you had seen what was going to be built?).

Thus, the design of this book was quite problematic for me, even after I began writing it. It got reorganized a few times as various points popped up, and when various means of helping you along occurred to me. This was especially a problem in that some of the ObjectPAL in the applications used some fairly sophisticated techniques; yet I had to assume (because of the target audience I was assigned) that you were still somewhat new to Paradox for Windows programming.

It was because of these and similar considerations that you and I rambled around a bit, playing with multimedia tools in the first four chapters. I wanted to introduce them immediately because multimedia is such neat stuff; and maybe that's all you were aware of at the time. There was, however, another hidden purpose: repeated exposure to some fairly complex ObjectPAL, for the simple reason that it is exposure to a new topic that begins to put you at ease with the new terrain.

This perceived need to take you immediately into the realm of ObjectPAL programming dictated both the placement and the content of those first four chapters. The particular depth to which I carried you there, of course, depended on something else—the multimedia programming itself. I like multimedia, as do many of you, and I have also long hated computer books that only hint at what might be done and then move on without telling the reader how to do it. So let's be honest here: I wanted to play with the multimedia tools because it's fun, and I made the assumption that you did too. Hope I was right!

What does all this have to do with content and organization of a document? It is simply that there are *two* viewpoints, not merely one, to consider in selecting the document's content. It is true that the overt needs of the audience are the highest governing rule in document design decisions. Yet it is also true that there is an implicit assumption on the part of the author that he and the reader have shared interests, so that what *you* want to put into the document has something to do with the decisions as well.

It would be good for your documentation if you were conscious of the implicit assumptions that you must make in order to write at all. If you're not, the writing may run away from you. When you're conscious of those assumptions, however, you can use them to enhance the readability of your prose. Because example is a good way of teaching, here are the specific assumptions I made about you while I wrote this book:

☐ You and I share an interest in Paradox for Windows programming because that's the tool you need to produce significant applications. We also share an interest in multimedia programming, just because it is fascinating.

☐ Still being a little new to serious Paradox programming, you first wanted to know what I did to bring the application together in a working package. In this regard, I also assumed that you were aware of the fact that I simplified the application a little (to avoid overloading you with repetitive details). I assumed that there is a balance you wanted to see in the application. That is, the application shouldn't be too simple—because you want it to actually do something useful—and not too detailed either. And I assumed that you approve of this deliberate approach.

☐ Because there is always more than one way to get something done, I also assumed that you next wanted to know why I did things the way I did. I made this assumption because why a tool is used in a certain way reveals how the tool works the way it does.

It may well be that these assumptions did not appear on the surface of the text very often. They were certainly there, however, and they greatly influenced what I chose to say, when I chose to say it, and how I chose to say it.

If you and I do our jobs well, the readers will be edified, their questions will get answered, and they will never suspect all the thought that went into making the document what it is (unless you write a chapter like this one, and spill your guts!). The moral is clear: a document will have the right content and organization when writing becomes a thinking game to you, not merely a matter of pounding the keyboard.

I still haven't touched on the matter of fleshing out the document's design. Whether I am writing a book like this one, or pulling technical documentation together, I use three principles of thought. In the document design phase of writing, I try always to consider *coverage, flow,* and *completeness.*

So far, this chapter has discussed coverage and flow. That is, finding all the major heads that need to go into the document and sequencing them so that they make sense from the reader's point of view.

At this point, you must make the trickiest transition in writing—moving from an overview of the subject to its details. The flow, or sequencing of topics, must lead your reader deeper and deeper into the details of what you're writing about. It is right here that you can trip over your own feet, so to speak, because the increasing depth of thought induced by the document's flow must tie in intimately with the completeness, or *depth of content,* of the document. In short, get the sequence wrong, and the completeness (to distinguish it from *completion*) can't take place because topics that belong together will be too scattered. On the other hand, if you haven't correctly or precisely calculated the depth of the document's content, you won't be able to decide how the flow should go. It's a juggling act, or perhaps a snake eating its own tail.

If document design sounds too complicated to deal with at this point, don't worry, because there is an easy way to get around this problem. That way is *recursive design,* which just means going over the design again and again. If you aren't certain of flow yet, put something in the outline anyway. Then, as you proceed to add greater and greater detail, be on the lookout for topics that suddenly seem to belong elsewhere.

When that happens, stop and begin to question the flow decisions you made. Very likely they don't fit the subject matter correctly. Start asking questions and cutting and pasting in the outline. When you have moved a topic to another location in the outline, be sure to ask yourself what that movement will do to the flow elsewhere in the document. Cut and paste, cut and try. Keep at it, and soon the fog will clear. Always try to look at it as if you're a reader, not the writer, and pretty soon this habit will make it easy for you to recognize when there is a flow and completeness problem, and also to recognize when you have it fixed.

Now, I fully realize that the previous discussion on designing a document is probably not like anything you're likely to find in texts on writing. That's because I have never seen one of those texts actually tell you what goes on in a writer's head while he or she is writing, which seems to me to be more valuable than a dry discussion of dangling participles. As a matter of fact, I made the same assumptions here that I did concerning the application design. I assumed that you're interested in writing, that you want to know what it is I do when writing, and why I do it that way.

Oh, and one last bit of advice about writing documentation for software: don't start designing the documentation until you have finished a prototype version of the software.

Of course, it's not enough to simply have a mental picture of what goes on in a writer's head while writing. Some mechanics are necessary as well. Specifically, you need some methods of organizing material, and you need to understand the mechanics of outlining.

First, look at the basic methods of organizing a document, paying particular attention to whether or not a method is suitable for software documentation. There are three broad organizing principles that you can apply to your document's design, as follows:

☐ *Teaching by example:* I think of this standard as the principle of illustration or analogy. The discussion is moving toward the full explanation of some particular point, but the content is illustrative. Specific instances of the subject, or even analogies to the subject, are used to bring out the point in a very concrete way. Concrete examples are the most useful kind, but metaphorical analogies can be used too—if you keep in mind that analogies have their limitations and dangers (that is, they may not be sufficiently exact). This organizing principle is perhaps most valuable in a how-to sequence, because it is the method that can most easily help the reader visualize a process or task. In addition to simple examples, this approach may make use of comparisons and contrasts, as well.

☐ *Analyzing the subject:* This organizing principle is well-adapted for the top-down approach to writing. Beginning with the most general considerations, the discussion moves into ever finer detail. Using this organizing principle is helpful to the reader also, because it begins with broad considerations that provide an easily discerned context that is readily remembered. It gives the reader a sense of place in the discussion that can help him think about the subject matter on his own, because he understands the relationships of all the parts of the discussion. You might want to use the analytical approach when guiding the reader through a discussion of why he or she might want to take this or that action.

☐ *Arguing the case:* The argumentative discussion is necessary when you want the reader to agree with you on some point that you recognize may be controversial. This is, perhaps, the least useful of the three organizing principles. I have most often found myself arguing a case when I am trying to convince the reader that some design decision is the right one—when I really don't like the result either. There *are* times when you'll need to do this, however. Computers aren't human in their flexibility, and it occasionally happens that a program must do things in a way different from a human approach. When using this approach to organize your document is necessary, be careful to always supply real evidence for your assertions. If you're not satisfied that an assertion will be intuitively and universally agreed upon, prove it.

Of the three organizing principles, the analytical approach is probably used most often in books like this one. If you go back and look at the table of contents, for example, you'll see that on each of the 14 days, I was attempting to move you more deeply into the construction details of the sample application. That movement in this book was accompanied by an increasing level of personal involvement on your part in the actual building of the software.

It is certainly true, however, that no one organizing principle is adequate for the design of a large document (anything, for example, more than the length of a school essay or paper). You may indeed section off the parts of the document that are suited to one approach or another.

As mentioned earlier, the way to express your document's organization on paper is to outline it. There are basically two outline styles you can choose from, as follows:

- [ ] *The sentence outline:* The sentence outline is an outline in which each entry (what I have been calling *bullets* and *heads*) is a complete sentence. With a sentence outline, you can understand very clearly what an entry will be about, because it is fully articulated.

- [ ] *The topic outline:* The topic outline is an outline in which each entry is only a phrase, or even a single word. With a topic outline, you must be careful to choose phrases for the entries that make clear what will be discussed in that section of the document. The phrases also must be indicative enough of the content that you can use them to judge the design's merits for coverage, flow, and completeness.

The sentence outline has very little use except for the shortest of documents. The reason, of course, is the resulting size of the outline after you flesh it out (develop it, as the texts say). One place you *can* use a sentence outline is in the so-called chapter outline. Needed only for a summary view of really long documents (such as a book), the chapter outline consists of the chapter number, chapter title, and as much as a short paragraph of descriptive material. You might want to use a chapter outline to review the large-scale flow of your document; but after that, you need to switch to a topic outline.

The topic outline is what I use to plan a book or a complete documentation manual. Because the content of a topic outline, however, just consists of phrases, you should already know the subject you'll write about. Otherwise, you may not be able to select entry phrases that are sufficiently descriptive to be of use to you or anyone else.

Once you have the major heads in your outline, develop the outline by adding more and more detailed entries, or subheads. Sometimes it really isn't necessary to outline very detailed levels. When the outline is sufficiently detailed, and you know you can write a

few pages for the most detailed entries, you're done. Notice that I didn't say, "two pages," or "five pages," or any other precise number of pages. That's one rule you would have to break right away.

Elements of Writing Style

So far, I've said quite a bit about what to say in your documentation. Now it's high time to think about how you should say it. It's time to talk about your writing style.

If you haven't done any writing before (or at least not much), you'll have exactly one writing style. You'll write exactly as you speak. Of course, failing that, you can do what I did when I began writing: you can try to get fancy and sound like a pompous jerk (some say I still do!). You probably realize that neither of these alternatives is really acceptable. So what should you do about writing style?

A compromise is probably in order. It is unnecessary to make a formal study of the art and craft of writing in order to be understood. All that's necessary is that you be able to read and speak in a relaxed tone on a serious subject.

Read what others have written with a critical eye, and ask whether or not you like the sound of their writing. If you do like another's style, try to determine what makes it sound good. If you don't like it, try to understand what it is that turns you off about the writing. Just this one exercise, or more properly, this one *habit*, will go far toward helping you adopt a writing style that's comfortable for you and for your readers.

The relaxed or comfortable style is always one that's easy to read, and it seems to convey the maximum amount of information with the minimum amount of effort. Being relaxed doesn't mean that you can't write a formal piece: it means you're at home with what you're doing as you write.

There are two reasons you might not be comfortable with your own writing (assuming that you have an adequate command of English grammar). The first reason—that *writing is new for you*—isn't very serious because it can be overcome with just a little experience. If you're uncomfortable with writing simply because it is a new thing for you, don't worry, just keep at it. The discomfort will soon disappear.

The second reason for being uncomfortable with your writing is a real showstopper, and is much more difficult to overcome. You might be uncomfortable about *what you're writing* because you think you have nothing to say and are instinctively (and correctly) aware that your readers will sense this.

Before you develop any phobias, let me say that this second kind of discomfort will haunt you for the rest of your writing career! If it is a permanent feature of your writing experience, perhaps you need to let someone else do the documentation. But if it is only an occasional thing, you can use it to help you with your writing.

What I mean is this: if you feel a discomfort that seems to say, "Hey, I don't know where I am headed with this piece," it's a signal that you should do one of two things. When documenting software, it might mean that your subconscious is telling you that the software itself hasn't been adequately developed in a particular area. Or it might mean that you need to go back and redesign the documentation and think about the magic three ingredients: coverage, flow, and completeness.

That's why I also said that the resolution of this second kind of discomfort with writing is very difficult. Redesigning some or all of the software (usually just some, thankfully) is, in itself, difficult; it means a rewrite of the documentation as well. On the other hand, redesigning the documentation also means a rewrite, and one that's potentially quite as difficult as a rewrite of the software.

In any event, as long as the feeling that something is wrong with the text doesn't arise from a true inability to write (an inability that almost no one has), listen to your subconscious on this issue, and do what it tells you. The great science fiction writer Damon Knight calls his subconscious "Fred" and places great stock in listening to it while he writes. I like to think of it as a kind of mental peripheral vision, an intellectual radar warning system. Just as you can practice using your real peripheral vision, you can practice using your mental warning radar. Before you know it, you can immediately feel when a piece is wrong— or when it is right.

As in the previous section, I have now delivered myself of some accumulated wisdom concerning the dark craft of writing. It is now time again to turn to a consideration of the nuts and bolts of the topic. Specifically, writing is the craft of building paragraphs from sentences, and sentences from words. What will you do with them?

The basic building block of writing is the *word*. Now, if you think that there is nothing to say about individual words in the craft of writing, you haven't developed your radar yet. Call Fred and see what he has to say about this. Did he mention the following things?

- [ ] Words can *denote* and they can *connote*. Clear discursive writing *denotes* meaning much more frequently than it connotes. Think of connotation as salt for your food (denotation). Too much salt, and the food will cloy and clog the taste buds, ruining the meal. It will also say amazingly little in the way of real information, while it may *sound* quite sophisticated. Connotation is one of the propagandist's favorite tools for misleading the unwary. I'm not being sarcastic, but look at your local newspaper, which is a good place to see how connotation can be used to twist meaning.

☐ The connotations of a word can be *emotionally loaded*. Words that denote and words that connote both have objective meanings fixed by common usage. But words that connote often go beyond this to include an emotional load, or a *poetic meaning,* one that perhaps appeals to the sensual side of human nature. Be especially sparing with these words in technical writing.

☐ Getting your message across successfully means using the *accurate word*. The accurate word is the word with the right denotation for your purpose. Novices in the art of communications often fail to choose the accurate word in one of three ways: by confusing similar forms, by confusing antonyms, and by failing to be clear about the point to be made.

Choosing and using the accurate word is extremely important: failure to do so will quickly cause the reader to conclude that the writer is ignorant, and thus the reader might dismiss the author's work.

☐ Words can be either *formal* or *informal*. Written English is usually formal in character, though this isn't always necessary. I have made considerable effort in this book, for example, to be informal in my language, in order to make learning a complex subject as much fun as possible. The problem in using informal language is that it is so easy to lapse into mere silliness (ask my editors about *this* one). When you want to be sure to get your point across accurately, it is better to err on the side of formality.

Moving from words to sentences, you need to understand what goes into the construction of an *effective sentence.* In short, an effective sentence is one that does the job with the least amount of fuss. Specifically, effective sentences have the following characteristics:

☐ Effective sentences have an *internal unity.* That is, they are constructed according to a single, clear purpose. One of my own most common errors in composition is to include parenthetical material that destroys the flow of thought expressed by the sentence. You can tell when I am doing this by noting the presence of parentheses or dashes setting off a part of the sentence—like this one (or this one.) The parenthetical aside isn't prohibited, but it is another one of those things that should be used sparingly. Unity of thought produces clarity of thought.

☐ Effective sentences exhibit an *economy of words*. Using more words than is necessary to express a thought distracts the reader from the intended point. Language that's too flowery is very distracting. Some people also have a tendency to be repetitive in an attempt to add force to their statements. It is most effective to just say it, and be done with it. Long sentences also can exceed the attention span of some of your readers. They will get lost easily when your sentences are too long. Come to think of it, I get lost when my sentences are too long! Brevity of speech leads to clear speech.

☐ Effective sentences are *active*. This doesn't mean you have to knock your readers down with language. It just means that you choose your words and the sentence's construction to express the point in the strongest way appropriate in the context. Both brevity and clarity are emphatic in nature. You also can be emphatic by using repetition (carefully!), active-voice verbs, or an emphatic word order. To use active-word order, you simply choose the subject of the sentence carefully. For example, "The sound barrier was first broken by Chuck Yeager" doesn't have the same impact as "Chuck Yeager broke the sound barrier first."

Finally, effective writing uses *effective paragraphs*. Knowing when to break paragraphs is important. If your writing has real continuity of flow in thought, this may be more difficult than you suspect. You should break paragraphs when the topic changes. Yet there should be a continuity between successive paragraphs.

One way to handle this problem of composition is to learn to think in paragraphs in the first place. Decide what the immediate point is and write a paragraph about it. The sentences and the paragraph breaks will take care of themselves.

Effective paragraphs also have the same or parallel characteristics as effective sentences. Paragraphs should have an internal unity, an economy of sentences, and a well-chosen emphasis. If you do it right, the reader won't be conscious of the design effort that went into the paragraph's construction. The reader *will* know that your writing is clear. That's the goal toward which we all strive.

Formatting the Documentation for Easy Reading

The visual appeal of a document has much to do with the reader's enjoyment of your work. With software documentation, as with any technical material, it is important that you make reading the document as enjoyable as possible.

Bookmaking and document production are, at the professional level, highly technical endeavors. Production and design are also art forms of which not everyone is capable. And poor production quality can absolutely destroy your document's effectiveness. This is a problem that I have thankfully never experienced as a writer, because I have always had some of the best professionals in the business producing my work (you can look at the front of this book to see who was involved in its production).

I fully realize that you might not have the editorial, design, and production resources that went into making this book. There are, however, some things you can do with the visual design of your document to enhance its appeal.

All the suggestions I am making concern what I call *visual breaks* (not a professional term, incidentally). The human eye sees boundaries more easily than a continuous collection of objects. Thus, visual differences, or breaks, between segments of your document relieve monotony, help highlight important material, and can make the document more visually appealing. The real trick is learning to select the right kind of visual breaks and not get too carried away with it. Documents that are either too plain, or are too busy are difficult to read.

At the simplest level, you can select fonts for different parts of your document. A *font* is the complete collection of all possible characters with the same typeface (*type style*). Bold, italic, and similar variations on the typeface are also referred to as type styles because they are usually spoken of as if they were different fonts.

Having selected a font, most word processors enable you to further control the type size to be used. Type sizes are ordinarily listed in *points*—a printer's point being approximately 1/72-inch. Thus, a 12-point typeface needs 1/6-inch to print one character. This is generally a good size for the ordinary text of your document.

When you consider what font to use for a particular part of the document, you should think in terms of *display type,* the type used for chapter and subheadings, and *text type,* the type used for the ordinary (prose) text of the document. The headings and text of your document should be set in different sizes of type, and possibly in different styles or fonts.

Display text for headings should be larger than the text type. You might pick 18-point type for chapter or major section headings. For example, reduce the size to 16-point and 14-point type for subordinate headings. In addition to using a larger type size for display text, you might consider using a different font or style. For example, a sans serif heading, possibly in italic or bold type, will set the heading off nicely from serif type text (such as Times Roman).

There are many things you can do within the body of the text. You also can use different typefaces to differentiate parts of the text. For example, in this book, `monospace type` is

used to set off the ObjectPAl listings, making them easier to see and read. Bold and italic text have their places too.

Another nifty way of introducing visual breaks into text while informing the reader is to insert pictures (screen shots work well in software documentation) and note boxes. Both of these objects break up the monotony of a page of nothing but text, as well as illustrate what the text is covering. (Ironically, this chapter is the one chapter in the book that's all text!)

When to use all these devices is another matter indeed. Only experience will teach you what works, and what doesn't work. There is one handy word of advice in this regard, however. If you're not a production professional (I'm certainly not), be conservative. Keep your designs simple and straightforward, and go for the clean look. Too much clutter is very confusing to the eye.

10

Desktop Publishing and Your Printer

Before I wrap up this chapter, I'll say something about desktop publishing and your PC's printer. If you're going to produce your own documents, you'll naturally need a printer; thus, the choice of printer becomes a real consideration.

There are three classes of printers from which you can choose: traditional dot-matrix printers, inkjet printers, and laser printers. My own experience with PC printers yields the following observations about them:

- ☐ Dot-matrix printers are unsatisfactory for the purpose of desktop publishing. Their output looks horrible (even the best dot-matrix printers have this problem), they are terribly noisy (I work late at night when the kids are asleep), and they are *slow*. There are fairly fast character-only printers on the market; but they are expensive, you can't control fonts, and you can't do graphics. Finally, adding insult to injury, a good dot-matrix printer costs about as much as any other printer.

- ☐ Inkjet printers produce much better output than do dot-matrix printers. There are still two problems with inkjet models. First, they are about as slow as an ordinary dot-matrix printer. Second, all that wet ink doesn't work well for graphic images that have a high pixel density: the paper soaks through with ink and can smear very easily, even after printing. Inkjet printers aren't really a viable alternative for desktop publishing.

☐ Laser printers are the remaining possibility, and these are the types of printers that I suggest you choose. You can get a really good six-page-per-minute laser printer for the same cost as a dot-matrix. A modern desktop laser printer is at least six times faster than a graphics-capable dot-matrix or inkjet printer. Laser printers are cleaner, dryer, and produce absolutely stunning output. In fact, if you get enough RAM in an ordinary laser printer, it is possible to produce truly camera-ready work. It doesn't seem to me that there is much choice in the matter. Go with a name-brand laser printer every time, and you won't lose. Oh, and the operational cost of laser printers works out to about the same as that for other printers too. You just have to shell out more money in a lump sum, for toner cartridges and the occasional photoconductor unit replacements. It works out in the long run, though.

The laser printer is really the only choice for serious desktop publishing, because they are capable of the finest graphic images—without which most documents come across as somewhat ho-hum.

Modification Notes

I bet that you're wondering just how I'm going to work "modification notes" into the subject of writing documentation. I admit that it gave me pause for thought, but the subject really does apply to documentation.

It is true that you can't plagiarize other documents outright. But you can borrow styles. There are writing styles, visual presentation styles, organization styles, heading styles, and all sorts of styles that you learn over time that will work well in one situation or another. That's why good word processors have a canned supply of style sheets that you can apply to your documents.

Therefore, you should constantly be on the lookout for styles that work well for the documents using them. Keep a critical eye on matters of style. Better than that, try out new styles to see how they work. And always remember that you're a unique individual for whom certain styles work better than others, just because you're you. Learn what those styles are by critically observing yourself at work. And then stick with the styles that work for you.

Debugging the Process

In a way, I have already covered the "debugging" process of writing. Debugging a document consists of constantly examining the success you're having (or aren't having, perhaps) with your document.

Never be afraid to go back and make corrections to the design's coverage, flow, and completeness. This should become habit, something you do even if you're already well into writing the text. Word processors make this much easier than it used to be, because you can cut and paste until everything is in the right place.

Also, never be afraid to go back and rebuild sentences and paragraphs. It is usually easy to tell when a sentence or paragraph isn't working. The trick is in figuring out what will work. The key to that mystery lies in having a clearly defined purpose for the document and for every part of it. A document with a clearly defined purpose will seem to write itself, whereas a document lacking purpose has to be forced out. The readers will see that immediately.

Writing the Application's Online Documentation

These are the days of fancy software packages. This can mean either that the software's components provide fancy functionality, or that the box and wrapper you first see are fancy. If you're like me, it is the first kind of fancy you're interested in.

When it comes to the utility of a software package, it also seems that *fancy* ought to mean *powerful,* with lots of easy-to-use features; fancy shouldn't mean *complicated.* If you stop to think about it, software documentation also can be complex and difficult; or it can be full-featured and powerful, with lots of information that is both helpful and easy to find.

By using the Windows help compiler and help engine, you can create online documentation for your applications that is indeed full-featured and powerful. Many of today's commercial Windows packages have made extensive use of Windows hypertext help features, giving the application a decided edge in usefulness.

In order to create Windows hypertext help documents, you will need at least the Windows help compiler (HC31.EXE), and for fancier effects, such as the ones you will see in this chapter, the Microsoft Hotspot Editor. You can get both of these tools from a variety of sources. I have them both, for example, in both the Windows SDK and the Borland C++ compiler packages. For those of you who do not have C compilers or SDKs, I'm also going to show you how to construct a hypertext help document using only Paradox for Windows forms. These can be just as nice, but they are a little more difficult to build—especially if they are very long.

Reviewing Hypertext Principles

The most general definition of a *hypertext document* is that it is a document controlled by a computer that provides easy, enhanced navigational facilities. That is, you can use the hypertext document to investigate and follow a train of thought, rather than having to simply read straight through it. Structured, assisted navigation is the feature that makes the hypertext format so suitable for online help.

Windows help databases qualify as hypertext documents by this definition. To build a Windows hypertext help document, there are several things you need to decide:

- ☐ What kind of document you input to the Windows help compiler, and how you structure this document
- ☐ How to define hotspots
- ☐ How to create hyperlinks (define jumps)
- ☐ How to include graphic images in the document
- ☐ How to embed intelligence in the document

☐ How to supply a help project file to the help compiler and run the compiler

For the rest of the day, you will see in detail how all these things are carried out. But before getting down into the nuts and bolts of the operation, take a summary preview look at each of these points:

☐ *What kind of document do you input to the Windows help compiler?* The Windows help compiler accepts only one kind of document as input: the Rich Text Format (RTF) document. An RTF document is stored with nothing but readable ASCII characters. All formatting is indicated by RTF commands or statements. Here is the beginning fragment of the VNOTES.RTF document:

```
{\rtf1\ansi \deff0\deflang1024{\fonttbl{\f0\froman Times New
Roman;}{\f1\froman Symbol;}{\f2\fswiss
Arial;}}{\colortbl;\red0\green0\blue0;\red0\green0\blue255;\red
0\green255\blue255;\red0\green255\blue0;\red255\green0\blue255;\red255\green0\blue0;
\red255\green255\blue0;\red255\green255\blue255;\red0\green0\blue127;
\red0\green127\blue127;\red0\green127\blue0;\red127\green0\blue127;
\red127\green0\blue0;\red127\green127\blue0;\red127\green127\blue127;
\red192\green192\blue192;}{\stylesheet{\s244 \fs16\up6\lang1033
\sbasedon0 \snext0 footnote reference;}{\s245 \fs20\lang1033
\sbasedon0\snext245footnote text;}{\fs20\lang1033 \snext0
Normal;}}{\info{\author Lee Atkinson}
```

Thankfully, you don't have to remember all these funny commands. You can use a word processor that handles RTF documents, such as Microsoft's Word for Windows, and it will handle all the command formatting for you.

☐ *How do you structure this document?* From your point of view, a Windows help document is structured as a series of *topics*. A topic is something that you can navigate to using a hyperlink, and read with no further navigation (except possibly paging up and down). The important thing to remember about topic structure is that you separate topics in the RTF document with hard page breaks. With Word for Windows, a hard page break is inserted into the document when you press Ctrl+Enter. Another way to look at topics is that a topic is what is named in each item of the document's table of contents. A table of contents should always be the first topic, too.

In the first paragraph of each topic you will need to insert at least three footnotes, using special footnote markers. These footnotes will define for the help compiler a *context string* identifying the topic, a *title* for the topic (used in the Windows help Search dialog window), and search *keywords* (also used in the Search dialog). Have no fear: I'm going to step you through all this one step at a time.

☐ *How do you define hotspots?* A *hotspot* is an area of the document page on which the reader can click the mouse to navigate directly to another part of the document. An item in the table of contents is a hotspot, for example. The document's readers can see the hotspot, but not the next item in the list.

☐ *How do you create hyperlinks (define jumps)?* A *hyperlink,* or jump definition, immediately follows the hotspot. The hyperlink is simply the *context string* associated with the new topic. Both hotspots and jump definitions are defined by applying special character formatting to them in the RTF document. You will also see plenty of this, very shortly.

☐ *How do you include graphic images in the document?* Really nice help documents include at least some graphic images. There are two ways to do this. One way is to use the help compiler's bitmap statements (RTF statements), and this is the way I have included graphic images in the VNOTES help document. Another way, when you're using a word processor like Word for Windows, is to insert the pictures directly in the document, right where you want them. I'll tell you why I didn't choose this option just a little later today.

☐ *How do you embed intelligence in the document? Embedding intelligence* is the hypertext way of saying *run a macro* or *run a program* when the user clicks a hotspot or enters a topic. This is an advanced hypertext feature, and fortunately you will get to see how this is done. I wanted to create a *talking* help document for the *Voice Notes!* application, so I had to "embed some intelligence" in it.

☐ *How do you supply a help project file to the help compiler and run the compiler?* The Windows help compiler has to pull many files together in order to create a finished Windows help (.HLP) file. All these files, and a few other things, too, are laid out in the help project (.HPJ) file.

Creating the Basic RTF Documents

The best way to learn is to do, so just jump right in there and create the VNOTES.RTF help source document. I won't make you look at every line of every page, but I'll show you a screen shot of the top of every topic in the help file, and explain what I did to it. It might be a good idea if you run the *Voice Notes!* application and click the HELP!!! button. Poke around in the VNotes help document, click the pictures and buttons, and see what happens. Getting familiar with the runtime help document might help you understand the following discussion better.

First things first, though. Before anything else happens, you have to create the initial RTF document. With Word for Windows, I generally use the **F**ile | **N**ew menu choice to create a new document, put just a little something in it, and **F**ile | Save **A**s an RTF file. Then open the RTF document normally. I create the file this way because Word for Windows sometimes tends to be a little tricky about files that aren't in its native .DOC format.

Now you are in the RTF document, and it's time to create the first topic, which is the table of contents. Figure 11.1 shows the first page of the document, with the footnotes window open.

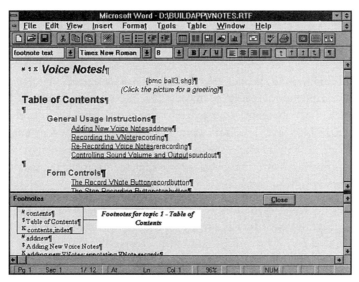

Figure 11.1. *The VNOTES.RTF file, showing the Table of Contents topic.*

The first thing you should notice about Figure 11.1 is the footnote text in the top-left corner. There are three of them: #, $, and κ. Now look down in the footnote window to see the corresponding footnotes. In the screen shot, I drew a box around the footnotes so you can find them easily; but there is no box in the real document. I also added the label out to the side of the footnotes, and you shouldn't try to type that in either.

The meaning of the three footnotes is as follows:

☐ The # footnote defines the *context string* for the topic. Think of this as the internal name of the topic. The help compiler uses the context string to determine where the jump should go when the reader clicks a hotspot.

☐ The $ footnote defines the topic's *title* that will be used, at runtime, in the Search dialog window. Obviously, a reader will not want to select search items based on the internal context string.

☐ The K footnote defines one or more *keywords* that the Windows help engine can use in a Search dialog. If there are more than one, separate the keywords with semicolons (;). You can use the same keyword in more than one topic, if it fits. The Search dialog will then be able to list several topic titles for the reader to select from.

At this point, I'll mention the {bmc ball3.shg} help command you see at the top center of the Table of Contents topic. This command includes a graphic image that has been processed with the Hotspot Editor. I think you will like the reason I did this, when you see it in just a bit.

In the Table of Contents proper in Figure 11.1, you see a series of hotspots defined. The first entry, Adding New Voice Notes, has double-underline formatting applied to it. This is what makes it a hotspot. Immediately following, you see the characters addnew formatted as hidden text. This is the context string that tells the help engine which topic to jump to when the user clicks the Adding New Voice Notes hotspot. If you look back down in the footnotes windows, you can see that addnew is the context string belonging to the very next topic.

There aren't any graphics in the next topic, Adding New Voice Notes. This topic is all text, as shown in Figure 11.2. Once again, notice the #$K footnote markers and the footnotes. The use is the same, although the content is necessarily different.

With all the super powers of hypertext composition at your fingertips, it's sometimes easy to forget the importance of simple text. Somewhere in there you have to tell the reader what he or she wants to know, and there is nothing more informative than plain English. Use pictures, sound, and even movies if you want to spice up the presentation and give it that finished quality. But remember that words are the most powerful information tool in the world; even with everything else available, there is no substitute for words.

Figures 11.3 and 11.4 continue in this same vein. These figures show the RTF topics concerning recording and re-recording a Voice. These topics are very straightforward— no pictures, no multimedia. (I know you're anxious—the multimedia part is coming!)

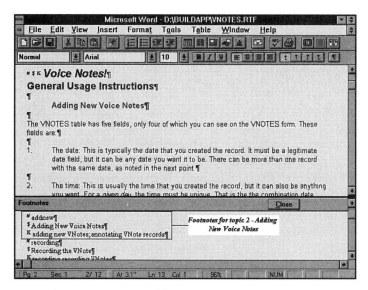

Figure 11.2. *The VNOTES.RTF file, showing the topic.*

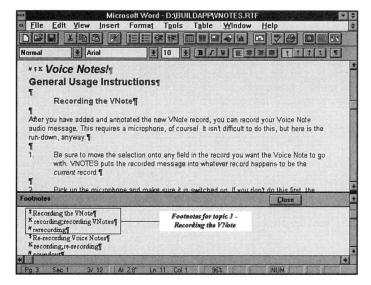

11

Figure 11.3. *The VNOTES.RTF file, showing the topic.*

Developer's Tip: One of the things to notice about the VNOTES help document is the way titles and captions are arranged. I call this style "quasi-standard" Windows help format. Although there is no enforced standard, you will find that many help documents do follow a similar formatting convention. At the top of the first page of each topic, you will generally find the name of the application or something similar in nature. This is a convenient place to stick a title, since the topic section's footnotes must appear at the beginning of the first paragraph in the topic. (The Windows help compiler requires this.) I like to do the application title in large, red letters. Just below that, you may see a section name. If I have sectioned off the table of contents, as I did in this document, I'll follow suit in the individual topics. I tend to make the section text a little smaller than the app name, and blue. Finally, I included the topic title itself. This is formatted a little smaller than the previous items, but still larger than the body of the topic text. I tend to make topic titles magenta. It just looks good to me; you're certainly free to style the text any way you like.

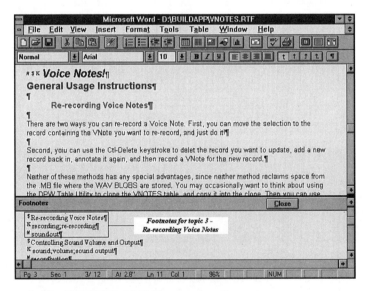

Figure 11.4. *The VNOTES.RTF file, showing the topic.*

Figure 11.5 shows the last of the pure-text topics, Controlling Sound Volume and Output. In this figure, you can see the hard page breaks surrounding the topic text. Sometimes I leave a blank line at the bottom of a topic, before the hard page break, and sometimes I don't. It doesn't matter to the help compiler, and it's only laziness on my part, I suppose.

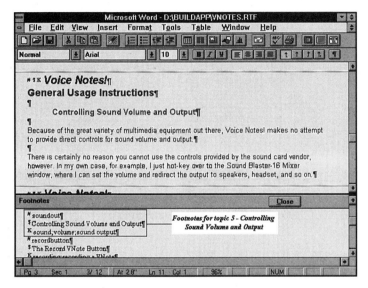

Figure 11.5. *The VNOTES.RTF file, showing the topic.*

In Figure 11.6, things get a bit more interesting. There are two features in this topic that go beyond simple text. Take a look at the figure now, and see if you can spot them. (Yes, I'm trying to make you look at the RTF document repeatedly and carefully.)

The first feature I want you to see in Figure 11.6 is the inclusion of the {bmc vnrecbtn.shg} help command. At runtime, this will appear as a copy of the Record VNote pushbutton, and can be clicked to hear a voice message from yours truly! This is a small thing, perhaps, but you don't see many multimedia Windows help files.

The other feature of interest in Figure 11.6 is in the last visible line of text. If you look carefully, you will see an embedded hyperlink in the text. There the reader is directed to jump to the Stop Recording Button topic. You can see how the context string is embedded in the text directly following the hotspot, just as it was in the table of contents.

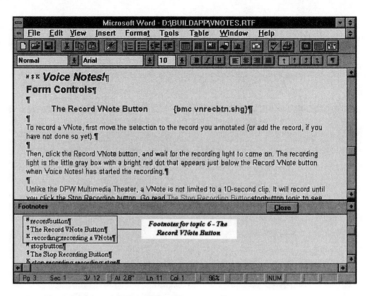

Figure 11.6. *The VNOTES.RTF file, showing the topic.*

The Stop Recording Button topic is similar in that it also has a talking pushbutton that is a copy of the control from the VNOTES form. It has no embedded hyperlinks, however. The Stop Recording Button topic structure also makes the hard page breaks visible, and is shown in Figure 11.7.

Topic 8, The Play VNote Button, and topic 9, The Extract WAV Button, are also similar in that they both include graphic images. Again, however, one of the main differences of this help document from others is that these graphic images (of pushbuttons) *talk*. Ordinary graphic images are .BMP files, not .SHG files. (I like to pronounce acronyms, so I call these last files *shag* files. It has a certain ring to it.) These topics are shown in Figures 11.8 and 11.9.

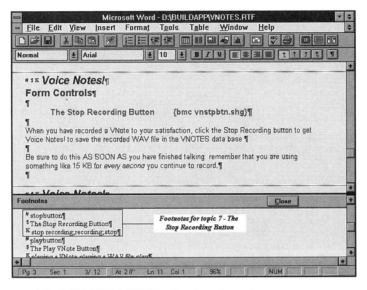

Figure 11.7. *The VNOTES.RTF file, showing the topic.*

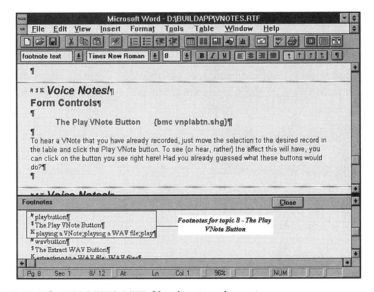

Figure 11.8. *The VNOTES.RTF file, showing the topic.*

Writing the Application's Online Documentation

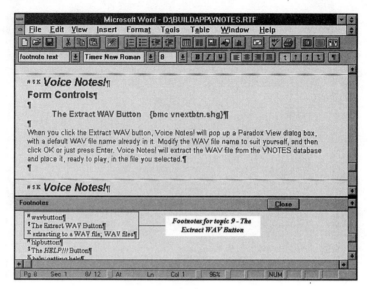

Figure 11.9. *The VNOTES.RTF file, showing the topic.*

The naming conventions for context strings are simple. A context string can consist of letters, numbers, and the underscore character. A context string must be unique within a document; otherwise, confusion of topics would result. I tend to use context strings that are all lowercase and look like C language variables. This helps me isolate them from other text surrounding them. These points are illustrated in topic 10, Figure 11.10, where the context string for the HELP!!! Button topic is simply hlpbutton.

The last of the figures for the RTF document is Figure 11.11, which depicts the Quit Button topic. Notice in this figure that the text typeface is Arial, a TrueType font. This is not required, but normal Windows help style uses a sans serif font like this. One last bit of information that may be of use to you is the fact the no single *topic* (not RTF document) may exceed 64K. If graphic images are pasted directly into the document, they do contribute to this size limit, since they are physically present. If, however, you use the {bmx *picture*.BMP} type command to include the graphic file, only the characters in the command contribute to this limit. Now you know why I use this type of command instead of pasting pictures directly into documents.

336

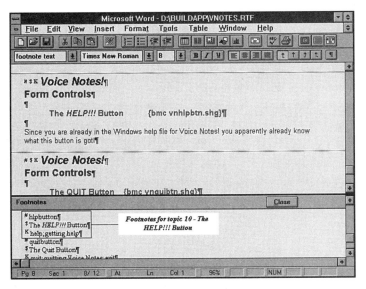

Figure 11.10. *The VNOTES.RTF file, showing the topic.*

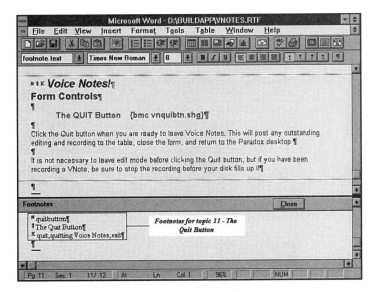

Figure 11.11. *The VNOTES.RTF file, showing the topic.*

> **Note:** There are three help commands for including graphic files in a help document, and all may name only Windows bitmap (BMP) or Hotspot Editor (SHG) files. The {bml ... } and {bmr ...} statements tell the help compiler to position the bitmap left- or right-justified, respectively, with the document margin. The {bmc ... } statement does not mean center the image however. It refers to character placement and indicates that the help compiler should place the image as if it were the next character in the text stream.
>
> In all cases, the help compiler will attempt to flow the text around the borders of the image, just as if it were a framed object in a word processor.

Finally, you get to see what the finished product looks like, in Figure 11.12. The {bmc ball.shg} statement isn't visible, but the ball3.shg image will be. Furthermore, if you click the ball3.shg image, I'll talk to you. Neat stuff! (You may prefer your own voice to mine, but I don't mind.)

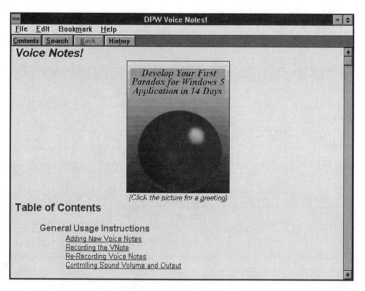

Figure 11.12. *The VNOTES help document at runtime, showing the topic.*

Figure 11.13 shows the first page of the Adding New Voice Notes topic at runtime. You can see how the footnote markers are also not visible. They did their work while the help document was being compiled, and are not needed now—although their effect is still certainly present in the .HLP file. All the text headers now line up properly.

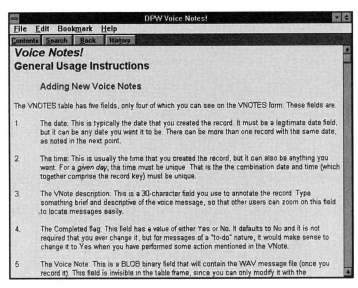

Figure 11.13. *The VNOTES help document at runtime, showing the topic (text only).*

In Figure 11.14, you can see the Record VNote Button topic with its talking pushbutton. You also can see how the embedded hotspot referring to another topic appears at runtime. Incidentally, all the WAV messages I used for this help document were recorded with VNOTES itself and extracted from its table. The table with those messages are on the CD-ROM that accompanies this book.

That wraps up the summary review of the RTF document's structure. Before I go on into further detail about how I added the multimedia features to the help document, however, I want to pause briefly and tell you how you can create hypertext help documents using only Paradox for Windows forms.

The basic approach to hypertext Paradox forms is simple: you use a multi-page form, with each page having a screen-sized text object placed on it. In a moment, you will add a couple of other objects to the form.

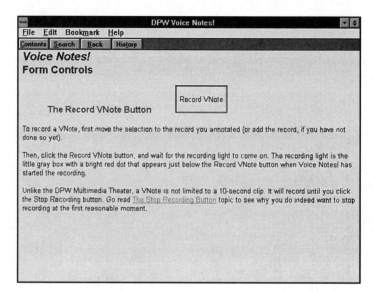

Figure 11.14. *The VNOTES help document at runtime, showing the topic (with a multimedia-connected pushbutton).*

To get the hypertext Paradox form going, create a new blank form and leave the background white, like a piece of paper. Drag a text object onto the page and size it to nearly fill up the window area. You can see how I started this in Figure 11.15, which is the first page of the TESTHYPR.FSL (or .FDL) document.

All the text in Figure 11.15, except for the hotspot text, is part of that one large text object. Now, since there is one large text object on the page, there are some limitations about where you can paste other objects, and about how you can access them separately from the main text object.

First, you can't just highlight some words in the one text object and attach methods to that fragment. The methods will apply to all of the text object, so that you would be limited to one page-sized hotspot. But as you can see in Figure 11.15, I wanted at least three hotspots on that page.

The solution is to paste other objects on top of the main text object. In this sample form, I pasted box objects wherever I wanted a hotspot, and inside the boxes I pasted yet other text objects (the hyperlink text). That is why the hotspot text appears to be a little out of line in Figure 11.16, the second page of the TESTHYPR form.

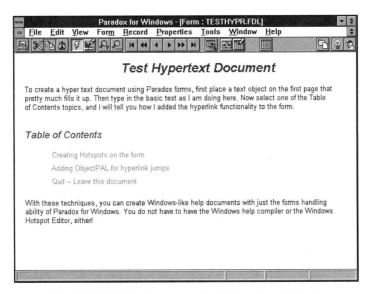

Figure 11.15. *The TESTHYPR form, page 1 of three hyperlinked pages.*

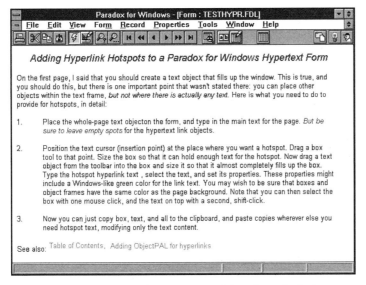

Figure 11.16. *The TESTHYPR form, page 2 of three hyperlinked pages.*

The next limitation you must deal with is the fact that you cannot paste other objects in the middle of the text of a text object. Paradox will move the new objects to a position where they do not interfere with the main text, no matter what you do. That leaves you with only one choice: the hotspot objects must be placed at the end of a line of text in the main text object. That is exactly what I have done on the first two pages, and on the third page of the form as well, which you can see in Figure 11.17.

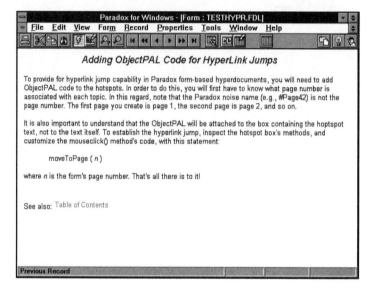

Figure 11.17. *The TESTHYPR form, page 3 of three hyperlinked pages.*

Once all the hotspot objects are in place, you can attach ObjectPAL code to them that performs the hyperlink jumps. I have attached the code to the `mouseclick()` methods of the boxes into which I then placed the hotspot text. The code is amazingly simple, and it is also shown in Figure 11.17: it is just a `moveToPage(n)` statement.

I suppose you could also have pasted other text objects directly on top of the main text object without using the boxes, made them line up a little better, and attached the ObjectPAL code directly to the new text objects. I haven't tried that, but it would make a good project for you to carry out. It's just another example of how old habits die hard. I did it that way as a novice when Paradox for Windows was new, and I just haven't stopped doing it. Oh, well!

Supplying Graphic Images in the Documents

Whether or not you supply multimedia features with a help document, pictures are always nice and add an extra dimension to the reader's pleasure in using the document. The question then immediately arises: "What kind of pictures should I use?"

Unless you're already into image scanning or video capture, there are only a couple of options. But they are fairly nice options and can add a lot to a help document.

First, you can use screen shots of the application itself. This requires a screen capture program but these aren't hard to come by. All the figures in this book, for example, were captured using a program named Collage Complete, which is a really nice Windows package. With Collage Complete, I could capture the screen image, convert it to gray scale (which the publisher required), and print it (which the publisher also required) with just a couple of keystrokes and a mouse click or two.

Because the sample help document you prepare in this chapter is for the *Voice Notes!* application, I thought it appropriate to illustrate this point with a screen shot of the *Voice Notes!* form. It appears in Figure 11.18, and would make a nice touch in the help document.

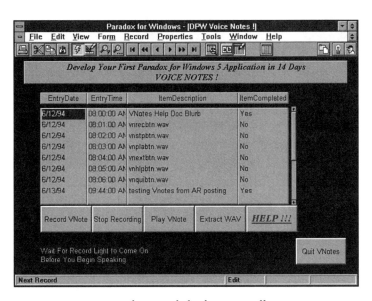

Figure 11.18. *Using a screen shot as a help document illustration.*

I admit, of course, that I did not use this shot in the actual help document, but I did use parts of it: I took the screen shot and then clipped out the control buttons, which all do appear in the document.

You also can roll your own images, using no more complex a program than Windows Paintbrush. Figure 11.19 illustrates a collection of text, graphic, and iconic effects that you can easily duplicate using Windows Paintbrush.

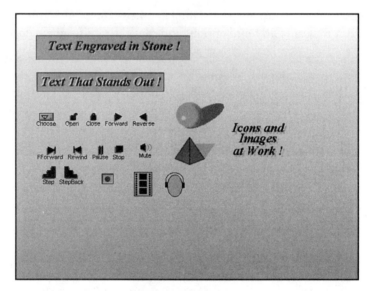

Figure 11.19. *Using text, images, and icons for dressing up a help document.*

The first thing I must confess about Figure 11.19 is that I went ahead and processed parts of the image with a product named Aldus Photostyler SE (Special Edition). With that tool, I enhanced the image by defocusing the text labels and the graphics depicting 3D effects. That is, I blurred them just slightly to give them a more realistic appearance.

Now, how did I produce the text effects in Figure 11.19? First, to achieve the Text Engraved in Stone! effect, I typed the text and copied it twice. I color-erased one copy to dark gray, and I color-erased the other copy to green (so I could color-erase it again in a minute without interfering with the grays).

Next I selected and dragged the dark gray copy of the text into its box. Then I selected and dragged the green copy into the box, placing it two pixels over and two pixels down from the original dark gray text's position. Next, I dragged the original black text on top of that, placing it just one pixel over and one pixel down from the dark gray position. That leaves the dark gray edge showing to the upper left of the text, and the green showing to the lower right of the black text. Last, I color-erased the green to white, and *voila!* Text engraved in stone!

To get the Text That Stands Out 3D effect requires only two copies of the text: a black original and another colored copy. Drag the colored copy into the box first and then drag the black copy on top of that, slightly offset. Then color-erase the colored copy to white, leaving the text appearing to be raised three-dimensionally above its surface. The Icons and Images at Work! shadowed text are done similarly, but you leave a little more separation between the two copies of the text, and no color-erasing is needed.

All the iconic and graphic images were created using the simple drawing tools of Paintbrush: lines, boxes, circles, and intersecting circles of slightly different shape (the head with the headset icon). Only the 3D ball and pyramid were processed by defocusing; you will probably want to leave icons sharp and clear.

Setting Up Speech and Video Support for the Documents

One of the things you have probably been bursting to know is how I made the ball logo and the pushbutton graphics talk in the help document. This is fun stuff, and it is really pretty easy, but it is somewhat detailed. A number of parts have to come together to make it happen.

Unfortunately, only C programmers have access to this sort of feature, as you will see in a moment. But you Paradox-only folks out there should not be disappointed. Remember that you can construct a hypertext Paradox form, and that earlier in this book you got a truckload of multimedia methods that can drive sound and video. In fact, you will see shortly that the C language DLL developed in this section is a conversion of the `playAnyMMClip()` method found in the PROJMGR form. You can do everything that is done here, you just can't use the Windows help compiler to do it.

Before you get deeply into it, here is a summary of the steps I took to add multimedia sound to the graphic images in the VNOTES.HLP document:

1. I used the Windows Hotspot Editor to define each entire graphic image as a hotspot, and to associate a macro call with it. The macro call is a custom call, and is just the function `playAnyMMClip()` that I later provide in the CMEDIA.DLL library.

2. I set up an INI file in the Windows directory that assists the CMEDIA.DLL in finding the WAV files it is supposed to play.

3. I wrote and compiled the CMEDIA.DLL itself. As I mentioned earlier, this is just a conversion of the `playAnyMMClip()` ObjectPAL method.

4. I declared the `playAnyMMClip()` function in the help project file using the `RegisterRoutine()` help macro.

Why all this had to happen is a bit involved, and will all be covered in this and the following sections.

Using the Hotspot Editor to process the original BMP files is the first order of business. This process is shown in Figure 11.20. The Hotspot Editor accepts a BMP file as input, and you Save **As** the file in a SHG (segmented hypergraphics) file. The SHG file is referred to as "segmented" since you can define several areas in the same graphic image as each being a separate hotspot.

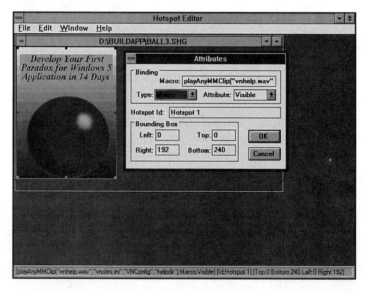

Figure 11.20. *Using the Hotspot Editor to attach a macro to a bitmap image.*

The BALL3.SHG file being processed in Figure 11.20 is not segmented. I dragged the cursor across the entire image to define a single hotspot. Then I right-clicked the selected area (sounds like Paradox inspection, doesn't it?) to pop up the Attributes dialog box. In that dialog box I selected the Macro attributes type and entered the macro call:

```
playAnyMMClip("vnhelp.wav","vnotes.ini","VNConfig","helpdir")
```

I used a similar procedure with each pushbutton image with which I wanted to record, varying only the name of the WAV file associated with the image.

An INI file is necessary because this help file will be invoked from a Paradox form. The problem with that is that the Paradox working directory (D:\BUILDAPP during development) is not the same as the Windows/DOS current directory. And it is only the Windows/DOS current directory that the CMEDIA C language routine knows anything about. Hence, you have to tell the routine where to find the media file it is supposed to play.

The VNOTES.INI file is located in the Windows (not the Paradox) directory. Its contents are as follows:

```
[VNConfig]
helpdir=d:\buildapp
```

There is only one section, and only one entry in that section, in this INI file. Notice that the call to playAnyMMClip() specifies the INI filename, the section name, and the entry name, so that the DLL will not be dependent on any particular INI file. That is, CMDEDIA.DLL can be used by *any* application, not just this one.

That brings us to the CMEDIA.DLL source itself. I won't go off into C programming details here, but look at the source code from the CMEDIA.C source file, and then I'll comment briefly on the features that interest us:

```c
#include <windows.h>
#include <mmsystem.h>
#include <string.h>
#include <stdlib.h>

#pragma argsused

int FAR PASCAL LibMain( HANDLE hInstance, WORD wDataSeg,
                        WORD wHeapSize, LPSTR lpszCmdLine )
{
  if ( wHeapSize > 0 ) UnlockData( 0 );
  return 1;
}

void FAR PASCAL playAnyMMClip( char *mmfilename,
                               char *inifile,
                               char *inisection,
                               char *inientry )
{
  char mciCmdStr[255];
  char fullMMName[255];
  char ReturnString[1025];
  DWORD ReturnCode, mmlength, mmpos;
```

```
/*
  The calling application must supply an INI file, with a section
  and an entry that specifies the PATH to use to access the MMfile.
  for Voice Notes! for example, the vnlotes.ini file looks like this:
    [VNConfig]
    helpdir=d:\buildapp
  or wherever the user installed the DPW apps.
*/
GetPrivateProfileString( inisection, inientry,
  "", fullMMName, sizeof(fullMMName), inifile );
strcat( fullMMName, "\\" );
strcat( fullMMName, mmfilename );
memset( ReturnString, ' ', 1024 );
strcpy( mciCmdStr, "open " );
strcat( mciCmdStr, fullMMName );
strcat( mciCmdStr, "  alias mmclip" );
ReturnCode = mciSendString(mciCmdStr, ReturnString, 1024, 0);
if ( ReturnCode ) {
  memset( ReturnString, ' ', 1024 );
  mciGetErrorString( ReturnCode, ReturnString, 1024 );
  strcat( ReturnString, "\n" );
  strcat( ReturnString, fullMMName );
  MessageBox( NULL, ReturnString, "CMedia Player", MB_OK );
  return;
}
memset( ReturnString, ' ', 1024 );
strcpy( mciCmdStr, "play mmclip" );
ReturnCode = mciSendString(mciCmdStr, ReturnString, 1024, 0);
if ( ReturnCode ) {
  memset( ReturnString, ' ', 1024 );
  mciGetErrorString( ReturnCode, ReturnString, 1024 );
  MessageBox( NULL, ReturnString, "CMedia Player", MB_OK );
  return;
}
memset( ReturnString, ' ', 1024 );
strcpy( mciCmdStr, "status mmclip length" );
ReturnCode = mciSendString(mciCmdStr, ReturnString, 1024, 0);
mmlength = atol( ReturnString );
memset( ReturnString, ' ', 1024 );
strcpy( mciCmdStr, "status mmclip position" );
ReturnCode = mciSendString(mciCmdStr, ReturnString, 1024, 0);
mmpos = atol( ReturnString );
while ( mmpos < mmlength ) {
  Yield();
  memset( ReturnString, ' ', 1024 );
  strcpy( mciCmdStr, "status mmclip position" );
  ReturnCode = mciSendString(mciCmdStr, ReturnString, 1024, 0);
  mmpos = atol( ReturnString );
}
memset( ReturnString, ' ', 1024 );
strcpy( mciCmdStr, "close mmclip" );
ReturnCode = mciSendString(mciCmdStr, ReturnString, 1024, 0);
if ( ReturnCode ) {
  memset( ReturnString, ' ', 1024 );
```

```
    mciGetErrorString( ReturnCode, ReturnString, 1024 );
    MessageBox( NULL, ReturnString, "CMedia Player", MB_OK );
    return;
  }
  return;
}
```

Most of CMEDIA.C is sufficiently close to the corresponding ObjectPAL method that it doesn't require extensive explanation, anyway. However, the call to `GetPrivateProfileString()` is very different. This is a call to a Windows service routine that will go and get the string value (the directory name, here) from the indicated INI file. The next few lines of code following concatenate the WAV filename to the directory name to form the full multimedia filename (the `fullMMName` variable).

Before compiling the CMEDIA . DLL (I used the Borland C++ compiler, of course), you have to supply a DEF file, as follows:

```
LIBRARY      CMEDIA
DESCRIPTION 'C MMedia Player'
EXETYPE      WINDOWS
CODE         PRELOAD MOVEABLE DISCARDABLE
DATA         PRELOAD MOVEABLE SINGLE
HEAPSIZE     4096
EXPORTS      playAnyMMClip
IMPORTS      MMSYSTEM.mciSendString
             MMSYSTEM.mciGetErrorString
```

The really important thing about the DEF file is that it declares what functions can be called by outside routines (the EXPORTS statement), and what outside routines it needs to call itself (the IMPORTS statement).

For you C programmers, all you have to do now is set the Application Type to DLL, MAKE the project, and this part is ready to go.

Creating the WinHelp Project Files

Before you can use the Windows help compiler to create the finished HLP file, you must supply it with a help project (HPJ) file. Naturally, there is one, named VNOTES.HPJ. (It is on the CD-ROM along with everything else.) The contents of VNOTES.HPJ are as follows:

```
[OPTIONS]
ROOT=D:\BUILDAPP
BMROOT=D:\BUILDAPP
TITLE=DPW Voice Notes!
WARNING=3

[CONFIG]
RegisterRoutine("CMEDIA", "playAnyMMClip", "SSSS" )
```

```
[FILES]
vnotes.rtf

[BITMAPS]
ball3.shg
vnrecbtn.shg
vnstpbtn.shg
vnplabtn.shg
vnextbtn.shg
vnhlpbtn.shg
vnquibtn.shg

[MAP]
contents 1
```

You probably noticed right away that the help project file is structured like a Windows INI file, with section names enclosed in square brackets and entries under the sections. This project file has a little more information than the bare minimum necessary, but not much more.

The [OPTIONS] section defines general characteristics for the help project that help identify the help document and tell the help compiler where to find things. The [OPTIONS] section is not optional! The ROOT entry tells the help compiler where all its input RTF and other files reside; BMROOT locates the graphics files, and can be different from the ROOT directories. The TITLE entry has a rather obvious use: it contains the Window title that the help engine will display in the help title bar at runtime. WARNING=3 tells the help compiler that I want to see all errors, critical or otherwise, at compile time.

[CONFIG] is an optional section, but you need it here to identify the CMEDIA.DLL and its functions. The RegisterRoutine() call is itself a help macro, and it defines the custom macro. The arguments to the call identify, in order, the DLL filename, the function within the DLL you will call, and the argument types expected by the DLL function. In this case, the "SSSS" indicates that the playAnyMMClip() expects to receive four far pointers to strings.

In the [FILES] section of the HPJ file you list all the RTF input documents that comprise the help file; there can be more than one file named here. The [BITMAPS] section serves a similar purpose: it lists all the image files here. If you were not using the SHG files defined as hotspots, you would simply name the BMP filenames. (PCX and other file types are not supported here.)

Finally, you can use the [MAP] section to assign identification *numbers* to context strings defined in the RTF file(s). This is not necessary for simple applications, but I have formed the habit of always mapping at the contents topic. It's really a useless habit because context ID mapping would be used to create browse sequences, when all the topics would need to be mapped. And you aren't doing that here.

Building the Windows Help Files

All the pieces are now in place. All that remains is to compile the help project using the Windows help compiler, and then take a quick look at how to invoke the Windows help engine for this document.

Oddly enough, the Windows help compiler is a DOS application. It can be run from a Windows DOS session, but you may run out of memory doing this. (I do run out of memory this way—too many resident drivers.) If this happens, just exit Windows and run the help compiler from a real DOS prompt.

Incidentally, I find it most convenient to copy the help compiler into the directory where all the help files are so that I don't have to type pathnames so often. You can always delete that copy of the help compiler later, but be sure you don't get rid of the original copy. Once all that is in place, run the help compiler using the following DOS command:

```
hc31 projectfilename.HPJ
```

In this case, the *projectfilename* is VNOTES. My advice is that if you receive any error messages at this time, go fix the problem and rerun the compiler until the project is entirely error-free.

Once back in Windows, you can run the Windows help engine in either of two ways. While I am still testing a new help document I use the Program Manager's **F**ile | **R**un menu selection and type in the following command:

```
winhelp projectfilename.HLP
```

where, again, the *projectfilename* is VNOTES for this project.

The other method is the one that is used to launch the help document from the VNOTES application itself. There I have attached ObjectPAL code to the HELP!!! button's `pushbutton()` method. It requires only one ObjectPAL statement to launch a help document, as follows:

```
helpShowTopic( "projectfilename.HLP", "contents" )
```

This call will invoke the `winhelp` engine, open the help document, and land in the Table of Contents topic. What could be easier, right?

Modification Notes

Developing Windows help documents is one time that boilerplating old documents is no help at all. If you copy another RTF file just to get the formatting, you will probably end up more confused than if you created the document fresh every time (because you will immediately have to go and delete *all* the text and *all* the footnotes before replacing them with the new document's contents). Just create a new RTF file and take it easy.

HPJ files may be another matter. Rather than having to remember all the section and entry names, or look them up every time, get an old copy of an HPJ file and modify it. You still have to remove all detailed information and supply new information, but that is not as large a process with the smaller HPJ file.

Debugging the Process

The kinds of errors that you will usually see from the help compiler will be errors involving topics that haven't yet been defined (I compile several times along the way, before everything is all there, to make sure everything is going according to plan), bitmap files that haven't been created yet, out-of-memory conditions, and other things like that.

These things aren't usually hard to resolve. Just think in terms of the connections involved. If you define a hotspot and jump, for example, make sure the target topic exists before you compile the project again. Common sense is really all you need to operate the help compiler.

Implementation

Part IV requires three days to complete. You're on the home stretch now. In Part IV, you learn about the following things:

☐ How to approach testing your application before releasing it to the users. You'll also develop some speed-test routines with ObjectPAL that demonstrate how to, and how not to, handle tables for best performance.

☐ How to package your application for distribution. You'll learn how to create your own installation apps along the way, too.

☐ How to support your users after you roll out the new application. In the final part of the book, you'll still be creating Paradox applications in the shape of user databases and problem logs. And you'll learn one final nifty technique: how to dynamically bind multiple tables to the same table frame (one at a time, of course), even while in edit mode.

12

Testing the
Application

Before you deploy your application to the end users, you should test it. Testing the application used to mean some really serious work because there were no debugging aids or automation tools for testing.

Today you'll see that with Paradox for Windows, not only isn't testing a pain, finding and correcting errors isn't all that bad either. You'll unit test the application's components, devise test data, perform integration testing on the whole package, learn how to use ObjectPAL's debugging tools, discover something about tuning Paradox applications for performance, and consider the three phases of testing software.

Unit Testing the Application's Components

You begin by unit testing the various components of the PDW AR/AP system. For that purpose, you should start and individually run each part of the application, apart from the whole. Run each form, for example, and do your best to break it.

That's right: break it. You may think this is silly, but I assure you it's not. Any stress you can scientifically devise for the application will be nothing compared to what the first nonthinking user will do to it.

That doesn't mean, of course, that the users will be either deliberately slow or malicious. What it does mean is that all users approach a new software package with many assumptions and prejudices—which are different from the ones you had while writing the software. This guarantees that users will do things to the software that you never dreamed of.

First, begin with the source version of the forms. Table 12.1 lists them all for you, for use as a checklist. Run each one and make sure that it compiles clean and runs properly. Do everything you can think of to each one, and observe how it withstands your efforts.

Table 12.1. Forms list for stand-alone testing.

Form name	When installed	Where installed	File size
appost.fsl	always	\BUILDAPP	24352
archart.fsl	always	\BUILDAPP	7584
arexport.fsl	always	\BUILDAPP	16864
arinq.fsl	always	\BUILDAPP	12688
armassc.fsl	always	\BUILDAPP	16080

Form name	When installed	Where installed	File size
arpost.fsl	always	\BUILDAPP	22080
arxtab.fsl	always	\BUILDAPP	9616
dbutil.fsl	always	\BUILDAPP	30496
dpwinstl.fsl	always	\BUILDAPP	171856
dpwmain.fsl	always	\BUILDAPP	53616
edmmfile.fsl	always	\BUILDAPP	6416
formlist.fsl	always	\BUILDAPP	6496
menus.fsl	always	\BUILDAPP	8528
mmstills.fsl	always	\BUILDAPP	7536
projmgr.fsl	always	\BUILDAPP	22384
pwmmplay.fsl	always	\BUILDAPP	268576
refdata.fsl	always	\BUILDAPP	15440
rptmgr.fsl	always	\BUILDAPP	19152
sysctl.fsl	always	\BUILDAPP	25872
tbutil.fsl	always	\BUILDAPP	47104
testhypr.fsl	always	\BUILDAPP	13872
testmmt.fsl	always	\BUILDAPP	10592
testole2.fsl	always	\BUILDAPP	86624
vnotes.fsl	always	\BUILDAPP	26528

When you test these forms, there are two that you will have to handle a little differently. These are the EDMMFILE and MENUS forms. The first of these is a support dialog for the Multimedia Theater, and really can't be tested apart from that form. The second of these, MENUS, comes up at runtime with the tool bar turned off. If you want to toggle to design mode, you'll have to use the **F**ile | **S**how Speedbar menu option (the Speedbar terminology was retained in this release for compatibility purposes; Paradox 5 for Windows now calls them toolbars).

The TESTOLE2 form may require some special handling, too. Because the form embeds the media clips as OLE objects, running the media clips requires that the media files be where they were when I created the form. That happened to be on my D: drive, which very likely isn't where you installed the sample software. You may have to go to design mode and insert the media objects again from the location you installed them.

12

I also ran into another interesting phenomenon when retesting TESTOLE2. It so happened that during the book project, I burned up my old computer (got the keyboard too hot, you know) and had to replace the whole computer. The problem turned out to be that both the sound equipment and the sound drivers were no longer supplied by Sound Blaster, my preferred vendor. This situation caused me to have to change the OLE verb number for the sound object, from 0 to 1, in order to get the clip to play. You may have to do something similar if you also are not running Sound Blaster equipment.

After testing each source version form, go back and run each delivered form. It may be that either you or I failed to deliver the form after the last change to the ObjectPAL. If that has happened, the delivered version may behave differently from the source version. That, of course, would be embarrassing when your users report an error that you thought you fixed some time ago. For your convenience, Table 12.2 lists all the delivered-form filenames in this part of the testing.

Table 12.2. Delivered forms list for stand-alone testing.

Form name	When installed	Where installed	File size
appost.fdl	always	\BUILDAPP	22912
archart.fdl	always	\BUILDAPP	7424
arexport.fdl	always	\BUILDAPP	13536
arinq.fdl	always	\BUILDAPP	11136
armassc.fdl	always	\BUILDAPP	14048
arpost.fdl	always	\BUILDAPP	21200
arxtab.fdl	always	\BUILDAPP	9424
dbutil.fdl	always	\BUILDAPP	24720
dpwinstl.fdl	always	\BUILDAPP	162752
dpwmain.fdl	always	\BUILDAPP	40608
edmmfile.fdl	always	\BUILDAPP	6800
formlist.fdl	always	\BUILDAPP	6704
menus.fdl	always	\BUILDAPP	6816
mmstills.fdl	always	\BUILDAPP	7408
projmgr.fdl	always	\BUILDAPP	19856

Form name	When installed	Where installed	File size
pwmmplay.fdl	always	\BUILDAPP	234208
refdata.fdl	always	\BUILDAPP	15088
rptmgr.fdl	always	\BUILDAPP	17104
sysctl.fdl	always	\BUILDAPP	20592
tbutil.fdl	always	\BUILDAPP	34896
testhypr.fdl	always	\BUILDAPP	13440
testmmt.fdl	always	\BUILDAPP	10240
vnotes.fdl	always	\BUILDAPP	20256

Reports, no less than forms, have behavior to check out. For example, do the headings line up where you want them to? Do page breaks occur at the right time? Do the labels all fit in the right places on the label page? Do the labels creep up or down the page? There are a host of things to look for when testing a report that you may not have thought of before. Use Table 12.3 as a checklist while testing the source version of the reports.

Table 12.3. Reports list for stand-alone testing.

Form name	When installed	Where installed	File size
arbill.rsl	always	\BUILDAPP	14336
arcust.rsl	always	\BUILDAPP	7504
armail.rsl	always	\BUILDAPP	5008
arrecv.rsl	always	\BUILDAPP	14240
custdetl.rsl	always	\BUILDAPP	10800

12

Delivered reports, like forms, may not be at the same level of readiness as the source version. It behooves you to test them as well. If there is an inconsistency, you may simply need to deliver the report again. Or you may really need to fix something. Table 12.4 lists all the delivered versions of the AR/AP reports.

Table 12.4. Delivered reports list for stand-alone testing.

Form name	When installed	Where installed	File size
arbill.rdl	always	\BUILDAPP	14336
arcust.rdl	always	\BUILDAPP	6864
armail.rdl	always	\BUILDAPP	5008
arrecv.rdl	always	\BUILDAPP	14240
custdetl.rdl	always	\BUILDAPP	10800

Table 12.5 lists all the queries, in both QBE and SQL versions, that are used by the application. You haven't seen some of them, such as the APPOPT query, because they first appear on Day 13. Don't worry about those yet. And anyway, those queries are for you to use when you package the AR/AP system for distribution, not for other users.

Table 12.5. Queries list for stand-alone testing.

Form name	When installed	Where installed	File size
appopt.qbe	always	\BUILDAPP	207
appopt.sql	always	\BUILDAPP	227
appreq.qbe	always	\BUILDAPP	203
appreq.sql	always	\BUILDAPP	225
custbal.qbe	always	\BUILDAPP	488
custbal.sql	always	\BUILDAPP	351

All the stand-alone Paradox scripts are listed in Table 12.6. As a matter of fact, you haven't seen any of these yet. But don't worry: you will! The speed*n*.sdl scripts are used later today in fact. The APPSIZE script comes into play on Day 13.

Table 12.6. Scripts list for stand-alone testing.

Form name	When installed	Where installed	File size
appsize.sdl	always	\BUILDAPP	5312
appsize.ssl	always	\BUILDAPP	6416
speed1.sdl	always	\BUILDAPP	5232
speed1.ssl	always	\BUILDAPP	5824

Form name	When installed	Where installed	File size
speed2.sdl	always	\BUILDAPP	5168
speed2.ssl	always	\BUILDAPP	5648
speed3.sdl	always	\BUILDAPP	5168
speed3.ssl	always	\BUILDAPP	5696

If you want to see or change the code, you'll have to open the script in design mode.

There isn't much you can do to test tables, but you can check to see that they are there, and that they have the correct structures. You also should check tables that are supposed to be linked by a referential integrity relationship. All the application's tables, including the main tables and some tables ordinary users won't see, are listed in Table 12.7.

Table 12.7. Tables list for stand-alone testing.

Form name	When installed	Where installed	File size
ahbk1.db	always	\BUILDAPP	4096
ahbk2.db	always	\BUILDAPP	4096
apay.db	always	\BUILDAPP	4096
apayhist.db	always	\BUILDAPP	4096
ar.db	always	\BUILDAPP	4096
arbk1.db	always	\BUILDAPP	4096
arbk2.db	always	\BUILDAPP	4096
arhist.db	always	\BUILDAPP	4096
class.db	always	\BUILDAPP	4096
constant.db	always	\BUILDAPP	532480
cubk1.db	always	\BUILDAPP	4096
cubk2.db	always	\BUILDAPP	4096
customer.db	always	\BUILDAPP	4096
dbanswer.db	always	\BUILDAPP	4096
ixanswer.db	optional	\BUILDAPP	2048
mainhelp.db	optional	\BUILDAPP	6144
method.db	always	\BUILDAPP	843776

continues

12

Table 12.7. continued

Form name	When installed	Where installed	File size
prjitem.db	always	\BUILDAPP	8192
prjmast.db	always	\BUILDAPP	4096
rianswer.db	optional	\BUILDAPP	4096
uiclass.db	always	\BUILDAPP	292864
vendor.db	always	\BUILDAPP	4096
vnotes.db	always	\BUILDAPP	4096

That's basically the score on unit testing. Just run every possible piece, and make sure that it at least runs properly when run by itself.

Tips for Supplying Test Data

There are at least two questions you should ask yourself when you design the test data you'll use to burn in your application. How many records are enough for real testing? What about boundary conditions for data values?

In the first instance, if you test with fewer than a sufficient number of test records in the tables, you'll almost certainly fail to uncover some trouble spot that real use will highlight immediately. This is something that I have seen time and time again.

On the other hand, some programmers are so worried about bugs in a new version of software that they will test with full-size files from the old version. Naturally, if this is the first version, that won't apply. You'll still have to devise some test data in that case.

My own experience seems to validate what mathematicians say. A minimum sample should consist of at least 30 items before any assurance can be had that things are going well. In such circumstances, each table should be populated with at least 30 records for testing purposes. These records can, of course, be removed before any users see the tables.

The second question deals with *boundary conditions,* as I call them. A boundary condition is nothing more or less than a data value that's set at the extreme limits of its valid range of values. Many interesting things happen to programs you thought were tightly written when they encounter boundary conditions.

You should therefore include some extra records (beyond the base number of 30) that contain values at the extreme possible ranges of their values. Further, if the data type being used to hold a field will permit greater or lesser values than you intend to handle, deliberately add some such records to the test suite. Seeing what the application does with those values is sometimes quite revealing.

Integration Testing the Entire Application

Integration testing ordinarily refers to testing that verifies the correct operation of parts of an application with respect to other parts of the application. If a Paradox form works well alone, it will almost certainly work well when called by another form.

Yet there is some integration testing that can be done. You can ask such question as: Do the posting routines permit the addition of data that cannot be archived later? Do I allow the user to enter all possible information that will be needed later, for writing checks, for example?

The longer you look at the application as a whole, the more likely you are to think of such questions. The reality, however, is that such questions will really be formulated by your users, because they use the application in their own world.

It may certainly be, however, that by this point in testing the application you'll have found something that doesn't work right—and for reasons you don't understand, either. Because that can definitely happen, I'll just take the time to walk you through the debugging tools that Paradox for Windows provides for you.

It is quite likely that you'll at least know what form the problem is in, and nearly as likely that you'll have some idea what method is involved in creating the problem. At any rate, you'll begin by investigating some method, so I will illustrate the process and debugging tools by debugging the pushbutton() method of the Do It button in the AREXPORT form. Pretend that for some unknown reason, the data isn't exported correctly. Now you have to find out why.

The first step is to open the form in design mode, inspect the button, and open its pushbutton() method. Because you don't know precisely where the problem is, just set a breakpoint on the first executable line of ObjectPAL code. A *breakpoint* is a place in the code that execution will stop—for the express purpose of enabling you to investigate the code there. Setting the breakpoint is shown in Figure 12.1.

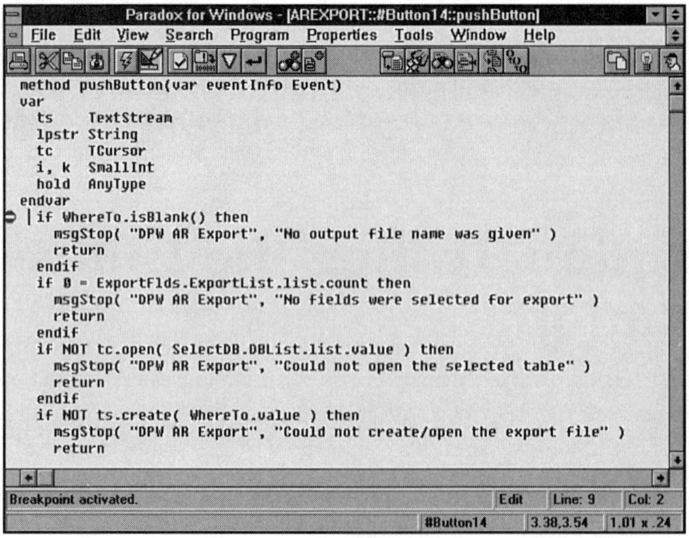

Figure 12.1. *Setting a breakpoint in the AREXPORT's Do It button method.*

You can set a breakpoint by using the **P**rogram | Toggle **B**reakpoint menu choice while inspecting the code for a method. Or you can postion the insertion point on the line of code where you want execution to stop, and click the Set breakpoint tool on the toolbar. You can turn a breakpoint off in exactly the same ways, using the controls as toggles for breakpoints.

Setting the breakpoint isn't all that's required to start the ObjectPAL debugger. After setting the breakpoint, you must start the program. Choose **P**rogram | **R**un from the desktop menu to do this. The form will begin execution and, in this case, just pop up waiting for inputs or button clicks, as shown in Figure 12.2.

When you make the required inputs and click the Do It! button, however, things begin to happen. This is shown in Figure 12.3, where the breakpoint has been reached and the Debugger window has opened automatically. Notice in that figure that when the Debugger window is open, whenever the mouse pointer is outside the Debugger window, it assumes the shape of a stop sign.

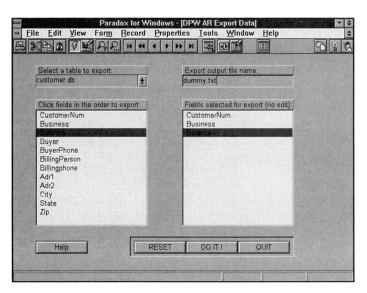

Figure 12.2. *After setting a breakpoint, choose* **Program** | **Run** *from the desktop menu and start the application.*

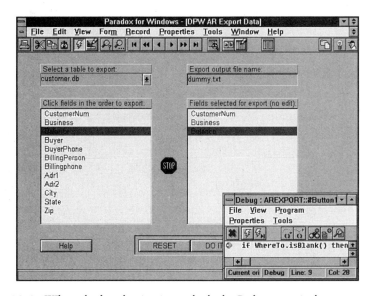

Figure 12.3. *When the breakpoint is reached, the Debugger window automatically opens.*

The Debugger window initially is as small as it can be and still conveys any information. The next step is to maximize the Debugger window so that you can see what is going on in the method's code. This is shown in Figure 12.4. It's a little difficult to see in this figure because the current position pointer and the breakpoint symbol are overlapping, but there is now a little current position marker in the shape of a right-pointing caret.

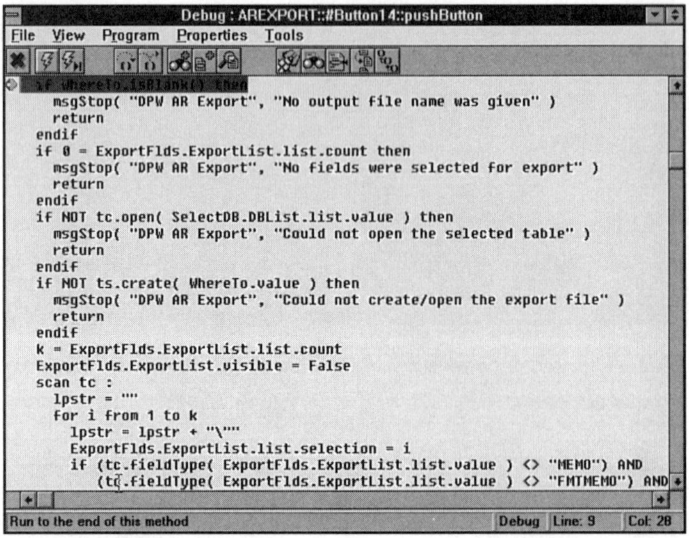

Figure 12.4. *Maximizing the Debugger window so you can follow what is going on.*

Now that the breakpoint has been reached and the Debugger window is open, the method's code is no longer executing automatically. Instead, the Debugger is waiting for you to do something. What you should do is step through the code, one line at a time, using the Step Over and Step Into toolbar buttons. These are the toolbar buttons with the bouncing arrow icons on them.

Stepping over means executing one line at a time in the current method; if another method is called, don't go down into it, but keep going in the current method. *Stepping into* also means executing the code one line at a time. When another method call is encountered, however, debugging execution "goes down into" the new method. Stepping over is what you'll do here. Figure 12.5 shows the current position pointer moving down through the code as you step over it.

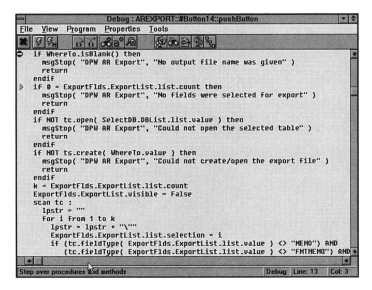

Figure 12.5. *Stepping through the code using the debugger.*

Stepping through the code (whether stepping over or stepping into it) is valuable because when you hit the line causing the problem, Paradox will show you the same error messages you get during normal execution. This time, you know exactly where the problem is.

There are also many other tools you can use while debugging. If you're debugging a complicated problem, for example, you may have set several breakpoints, not just one. You can review and manipulate them by opening the Breakpoints window. Open the Breakpoints window by using the toolbar button with the icon that looks like a position pointer caret pointing to a piece of paper. The Breakpoints window is shown in Figure 12.6

As you're stepping through the code, you may wonder what the value of some variable may be at that point. You can find out by opening the Inspect window. First click the Inspect toolbar button (the one with the magnifying glass). The Inspect dialog box will prompt you to enter the name of the variable to be inspected, as shown in Figure 12.7.

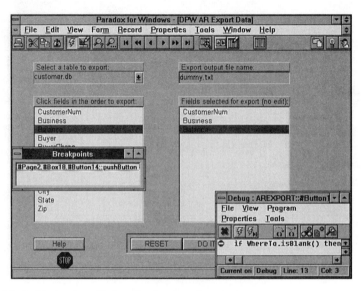

Figure 12.6. *Reviewing the breakpoints you have set.*

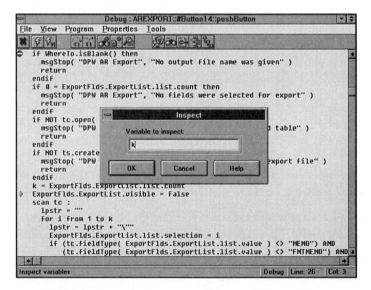

Figure 12.7. *Using the Inspect dialog box to check on a variable.*

Inspect will then display a small dialog box whose title is the type of the variable you selected, and whose contents contain the variable's value. For instance, I inspected the variable k, which is a SmallInt type, as shown in Figure 12.8.

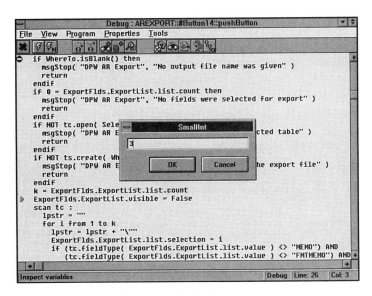

Figure 12.8. *Output from the Inspect dialog box.*

Furthermore, you can keep a running watch on the values of one or more variables all the time. This is called *setting a watch*. Clicking the Add Watch toolbar button will produce the prompting dialog box (shown in Figure 12.9), entitled Watches. (This toolbar button is the one with the binoculars and a plus sign on it.)

12

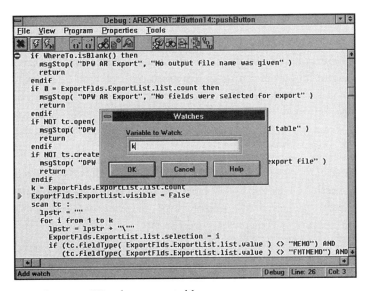

Figure 12.9. *Setting a Watch on a variable.*

Once you have added the variable to the Watch list, that dialog box goes away. However, you can still see the watched variables by opening the Watch window. Just click the Watch window toolbar button (the binoculars on top of a page symbol), and the Watch window pops up, as shown in Figure 12.10. Notice there that I have been watching the variable k, whose value is 3, and the string variable lpstr, which hasn't been used yet in the method. Therefore, its value is reported as Unassigned.

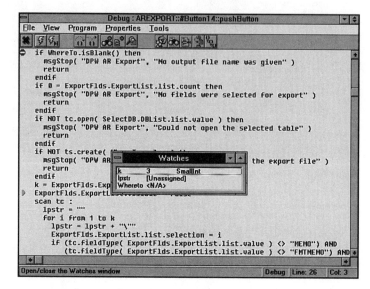

Figure 12.10. *Displaying all watched variables in the Watches window.*

Another tool may be needed if you need to know where ObjectPAL went before it got to the breakpoint. To determine this, you can use the Call Stack, which just lists the methods that have been called because execution began under the debugger. The Call Stack toolbar button has a picture of three large sets of parentheses (in a stack) connected by arrows. The Call Stack window displays a line for each object method that has been entered, as shown in Figure 12.11.

Finally, you can monitor events by using the Tracer window. By *events,* I mean each and every line of code executed—all of them. Open the Tracer window by clicking the toolbar button with three page symbols, two of which are connected by a curving arrow symbol. The Tracer window is shown in Figure 12.12.

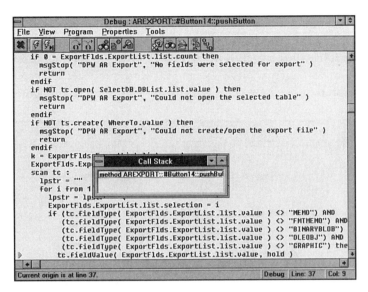

Figure 12.11. *Exploring program navigation using Call Stack.*

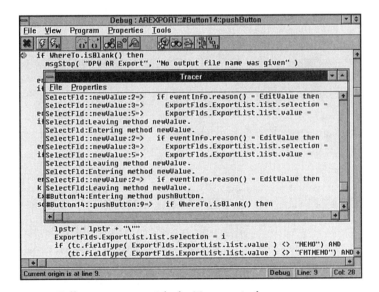

Figure 12.12. *Following events with the Tracer window.*

As you can see, tracing execution yields quite a lot of information. If this isn't enough for you, you can cause the tracer to descend into built-in methods' code, whether or not there is any ObjectPAL attached to that method. You do this by choosing **Properties** | **Builtins** from the Tracer window's menubar, which produces a dialog box just chock-full of checkboxes for all the built-in methods. This is shown in Figure 12.13.

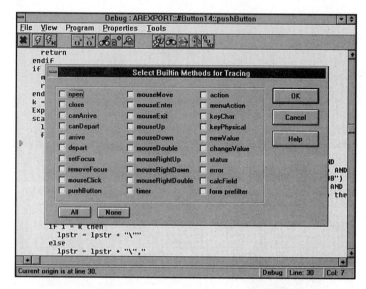

Figure 12.13. *Customizing the tracer to include the Paradox built-in methods.*

I think you'll agree that Paradox provides plenty of tools for debugging even the most stubborn application problems.

Performance Tuning—the Easy Way

Performance tuning with Paradox isn't too much of a problem, especially when you compare Paradox development to development with traditional tools, such as the C language. The reason for this ease of tuning is precisely Paradox's object-oriented nature, which tends to do so many things for you, that you must design and code with other tools.

Thus, the greatest tuning error that new users of Paradox usually make is to over-control the application by writing too much ObjectPAL code. As I've said several times, *Let the engine do the work* (wherever that's possible). Don't do too much, and ObjectPAL methods will usually do the job faster than your code.

To illustrate what I mean by these statements, I have written three ObjectPAL scripts (forms that never become visible, and have only one method: the run() method). These scripts are named SPEED1.SSL, SPEED2.SSL, and SPEED3.SSL. (For the actual benchmark runs, execute the delivered SDL scripts.)

Each one of these scripts runs through every record in the INFILES table (which you'll become familiar with tomorrow). In the first, I have very much over-controlled the code necessary to access each record in the table—and it runs the slowest of all three. The code isn't long, so take a look at it now:

```
method run(var eventInfo Event)
var
  tv TableView
  tc TCursor
  start, stop, elapsed, i, nrecs LongInt
endvar
  start = CPUClockTime()
  if tv.open( "infiles.db" ) then
    tc.attach( tv )
    nrecs = tv.nRecords
    for i from 1 to nrecs
      tc.moveToRecord( i )  ; in practice, this might be a locate function
      tv.moveToRecord( tc )
    endfor
  else
    msgStop( "Speed test 1:", "Oops!" )
    return
  endif
  tv.close()
  stop = CPUClockTime()
  elapsed = stop - start
  msgInfo( "Speed test 1:",
           "Elasped Time = " + strval(elapsed) )
endmethod
```

SPEED1 uses both a table view and a table cursor to access each record in the table. As the comment indicates, real code would probably be trying to use the table cursor to randomly locate a record, but this is just an example for comparing execution speeds.

Using a table cursor to locate each record and then synchronizing the table view with it turns out to be a slow process. Figure 12.14 shows the results of the first speed trial: it took over 30 seconds to read just over 240 records. Note that the speed trial times will vary greatly from one computer to the next, and possibly even from one trial to the next—depending on what you have going on in Windows. When I reran these tests on a 486/66 machine, things happened a *lot* quicker.

12

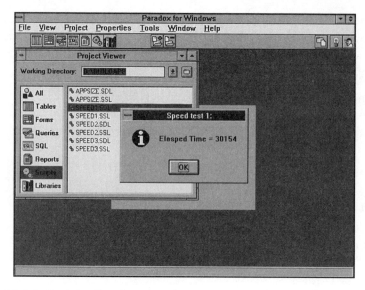

Figure 12.14. *Running Speed test number 1.*

Well, that was pretty slow. But you can tune it up by removing the table cursor altogether. That was a classic bit of overcontrol, because you can use just table view properties to get to each record. The corrected code looks like this:

```
method run(var eventInfo Event)
var
  tv TableView
  start, stop, elapsed, i, nrecs LongInt
endvar
  start = CPUClockTime()
  if tv.open( "infiles.db" ) then
    nrecs = tv.nRecords
    for i from 1 to nrecs
      tv.rowNo = i
    endfor
  else
    msgStop( "Speed test 2:", "Oops!" )
    return
  endif
  tv.close()
  stop = CPUClockTime()
  elapsed = stop - start
  msgInfo( "Speed test 2:",
           "Elapsed Time = " + strval(elapsed) )
endmethod
```

Now run SPEED2 and see what you get. The results are displayed in Figure 12.15. Things are a lot better now. The elapsed time is just under 12 seconds, better than twice as fast as the first speed run.

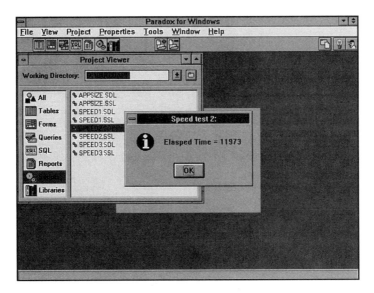

Figure 12.15. *Running Speed test number 2.*

However, there is a better way. Accessing all of a table's records is a true batch process, and one that no user looking at a screen can possibly assist (at least not fast enough). Therefore, ask yourself why there should be any visible user interface (UI) object associated with the process at all. Could that be the reason things are running so slow? It turns out that, yes, that is the reason. For the third speed trial, SPEED3, you go back to a table cursor without any table view. Here is the code for running the table this way:

```
method run(var eventInfo Event)
var
  tc TCursor
  start, stop, elapsed, i, nrecs LongInt
endvar
  start = CPUClockTime()
  if tc.open( "infiles.db" ) then
    nrecs = tc.nRecords()
    for i from 1 to nrecs
      tc.moveToRecord( i )   ; in practice, this might be a locate function
    endfor
  else
    msgStop( "Speed test 3:", "Oops!" )
    return
  endif
  tc.close()
  stop = CPUClockTime()
  elapsed = stop - start
  msgInfo( "Speed test 3:",
           "Elasped Time = " + strval(elapsed) )
endmethod
```

Now run SPEED3. What did you get? An elapsed time of just over two seconds? That's more than 5 times faster than the improved SPEED2 run, and 15 times faster than the first speed run.

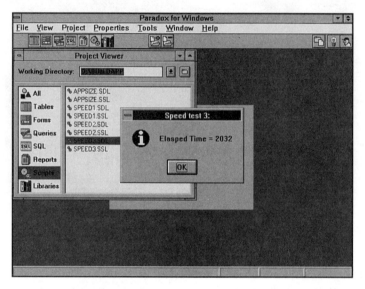

Figure 12.16. *Running Speed test number 3.*

The more code I used trying to make sure things went well, the worse the application ran. Of course, you have to have enough code to do the job. The moral of the story, however, is to look through the documentation to find the best code to do the job. That usually means picking the method with the least code.

Alpha, Beta, and Gamma Testing

There are three stages of software testing that the big software companies like to throw around. These are the alpha, beta, and gamma phases of testing. I say that they like to throw these terms around: it is getting so that there isn't much testing at all before a new product hits the retail shelves. Oh, well, that's the way it is!

However, you can use these concepts to test your code. Even if you don't have a formal testing protocol, you can still divide your testing into three rough phases that parallel the fancier names.

First of all, think about alpha testing. *Alpha testing* is the testing that you do before anybody else ever sees the product. This is the place to really wring things out—unless you enjoy being embarrassed.

Beta testing occurs when you let a limited number of others use the software, especially for the purpose of testing. That group of others are the famed *beta users,* of which *moi* is one for Borland's Paradox. Seriously, this is where things you never thought could happen tend to pop up. This is the time for really finding all the weird errors that can't happen, but do. This is the phase that bullet-proofs the code for public use.

It may be that you don't have a group of beta users. But you might find a friend or two who is willing to sit down at your machine for a while and play with the new toys. You should stress to this person that you want him or her to do things that don't look right, just to see what will happen. Be sure to take notes, now!

If your new software survives the beta-testing phase, it's time for gamma testing. In this phase of testing, all changes to basic design and functionality are frozen. All you are looking for are those final, tricky bugs you need to kill just before you let go of the product.

If your software gets past this phase of testing, you'll need to proceed immediately to Day 13, where I will show you how to package it up and get it out the door!

Modification Notes

Today there was one technique presented that you can use when benchmarking various techniques for best performance. That was the CPUClockTime() procedure call.

CPUClockTime() returns a LongInt number that's the number of milliseconds elapsed because the computer was turned on. That's why I interpreted 2032 as "a little over two seconds."

If you surround a few lines of code (as you just saw me do) and take the difference between the two values, you get a very accurate elapsed time for the process. So if you're trying to decide between two alternative methods of doing something, clock it, and make the decision based on the best time (presuming that both methods are safe).

Debugging the Process

How do you debug a day of debugging? You consider the possibility that I haven't told you those particular things that will be useful to you in your situation—that's how.

There isn't any possible way I can predict what will happen to your testing strategies; that's the very nature of testing. You don't know what is going to happen, but you want to find out. Therefore, take everything I just said with a grain of salt, and above all, do your own thinking and be fast on your mental feet.

Packaging the Application

When you buy a new piece of software, what's the first thing that you see? It's the packaging, isn't it? And when you get home, what's the next thing that you see? It's another kind of packaging: the installation procedure.

Odds are, if either of these two kinds of packaging aren't pretty slick, you won't trust the product from that time forward. If the vendor can't get the packaging right, then how in the world can anyone expect it to get the product right? There's usually some truth to that speculation, too.

Packaging the software is therefore at least as important as building quality software in the first place, at least as far as software that you want others to use is concerned. Today you'll see how I packaged the sample software for this book. It was a pretty big job and required attention to many of the considerations that would accompany packaging a commercial application. In most ways, it is a commercial application, because it all came with this book—which you bought on the open market.

Identifying the Application's Distribution Components

The foundation step of designing a package for a distributable application is being *sure* that you have every piece accounted for and in the package. I know I would feel pretty chagrined to find that you didn't get everything you need on the CD-ROM that comes with this book.

If there are a lot of pieces, as there were for me in putting this book together, some sort of automation for controlling the identification process is in order. It was doubly hard for me because I had to get all the pieces together that would go on the CD-ROM, and keep track of just those (several hundred) pieces that only I and the editors would see.

It seems like a Paradox for Windows table would do the trick, don't you think? Indeed it does, and indeed I built one. It is named INFILES.DB, and it contains the name, installation type (optional or required), target directory location, and size (in bytes) of everything that I planned to put on the CD-ROM. I used a cheater's trick to populate the table in the first place, but I will get to that a little later today.

Figure 13.1, then, shows the INFILES table with files and their information. If you look at that figure closely, you'll see that the records for the INFILE table itself don't contain file size notations. I will tell you the reason for that when I show you the automation tools I used to size the application's distribution.

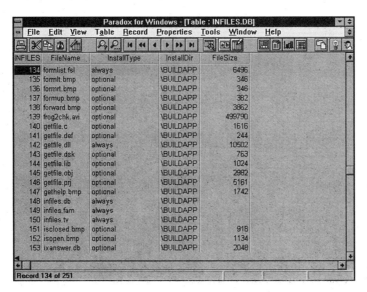

Figure 13.1. *Using the INFILES table to identify all the application's distribution components.*

Just as an example of the kind of table that's needed for recording distribution files, I took a screen shot of the table's structure information and included it here. It's shown in Figure 13.2.

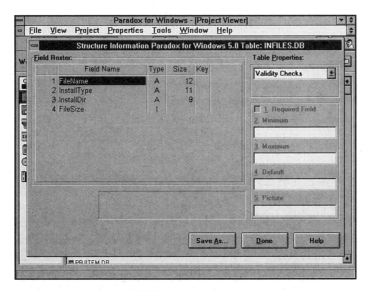

Figure 13.2. *Structuring the INFILES table.*

13

Now, the INFILES table by itself doesn't do anyone much good. For one thing, I needed to know how many bytes of free disk space are needed for each of the three possible types of installation (all files, required files only, or optional files only). That's in the next section, so hold that thought for a moment.

What the table by itself can do is provide some way of recording, which is what I did as I developed pieces of the application. That's the best time to make decisions such as whether or not the file is required or optional in the installation. It is also a handy way of keeping track of just how much disk resource you will be asking the user of the application to commit to when installing the application.

Sizing the Application's Distribution Components

With the INFILES table in place, I have almost everything I need to compute the total size of the distributable components of the application. I say almost, because it would be quite tedious, for example, to use the Windows File Manager to look up all the file sizes and manually enter them into the table.

You can guess my solution, no doubt. I wrote some ObjectPAL to do it for me. Because I didn't care about having a pretty form to look at for this app (I only wanted to get the work done as quickly as possible), I put that code in the run() method of a Paradox script—APPSIZE.SSL, appropriately enough. Because a picture is as quick a way as any to show that code to you, I opened the script in design mode and shot a picture of it. You can see it in Figure 13.3. (It's small enough that every bit of the code is visible).

You can see that our old friend, the table cursor, is hard at work again, and so is the scan loop. Of course, if the method can't open the INFILES table, it produces an error message and quits immediately. Otherwise, you go right on into the scan loop.

Within the loop, the FileSystem method findfirst() is used to get directory information for the file named in the current record. If it isn't found, a message (in the status bar) is produced, but the script continues operation. If the file is found in the directory, the file size information is extracted and the current record is updated with it.

The reason the records for INFILES itself had no size information is because I used search() to see if the table cursor was referring to itself, so to speak, and looped early if it was. This is necessary because you can't access size information for a table you have open and in edit mode; you get an error.

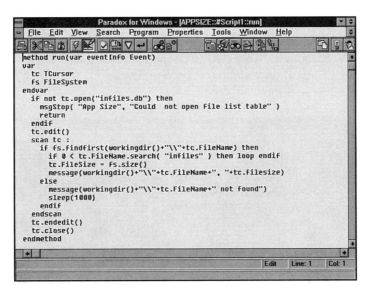

Figure 13.3. *The APPSIZE script acquires detailed sizing information and updates the INFILES table.*

If you remember the speed benchmarks from Day 6, you may think that displaying each filename and its size in the status bar, using the message() procedure, slows the script down too much. It does in fact slow it down some, but the real culprit in this ObjectPAL code is the findfirst() method. Reading the directory for each file is really expensive in time, much more so than the message() call. There isn't much way around that, however, so we'll let it go.

After running the APPSIZE script, the INFILES table now contains all the sizing information I need to code the installation procedure. There is only one small problem in the way: I now need some easy way of splitting out the required and optional aggregate file sizes. I will need to check the target hard drive during installation to see if there is enough room for a specific installation type, not just the All option. A user might just be able to install the required files, for example, but not all of them. One would not want to prevent that user from installing what he or she can.

All those file sizes are mingled together in the INFILES table, however. What shall I do? I'll write a Paradox query that will select just the required files and a query that will select just the optional files. Then I can summarize the file size column of the answer table, and *voila!*—there's my answer.

The first query is APPREQ, and as the name implies, it selects from INFILES just those files that are required for installation. APPREQ is easy to set up. Open a new query and pick the INFILES table. When the query view comes up, click the INFILES.DB box to check all the fields at once and type always in the InstallType field's condition box. The finished setup is shown in Figure 13.4.

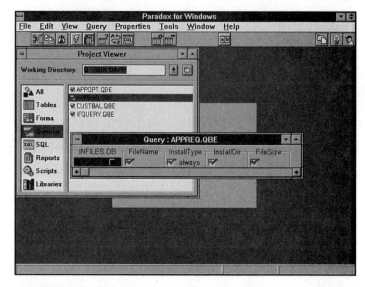

Figure 13.4. *The APPREQ query selects all the files that are required for proper installation of the product.*

When the query runs, you should get an answer table. The only thing unusual about this query is that I have overridden the default destination for the answer table. I named it DBANSWER.DB and directed it to my current working directory. This would not be a good move if I were sharing the app on a network. At any rate, the results of running the APPREQ query are shown in Figure 13.5.

Only one step remains in determining the aggregate size of the required installation files, and that's to sum the FileSize column of the just-obtained answer table. There is a handy tool available for this purpose, and it is the TBUTIL utility. Figure 13.6 shows the results of the column sum operation.

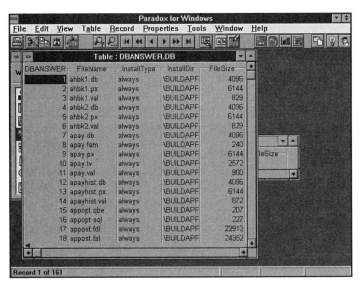

Figure 13.5. *Results of the APPREQ query in the DBANSWER table.*

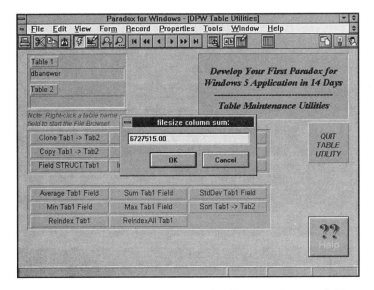

Figure 13.6. *Using TBUTIL to summarize the file sizes of required files.*

The APPOPT query is almost identical to the previous one. The main difference is that it selects records that have the value optional in the InstallType field. The design window for the APPOPT query is shown in Figure 13.7.

385

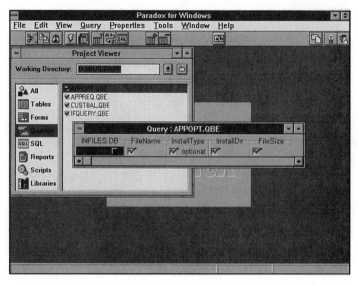

Figure 13.7. *The APPOPT query selects files that are optional in the application's installation.*

This query also yields an answer table, containing only the optional installation files. It is shown in Figure 13.8.

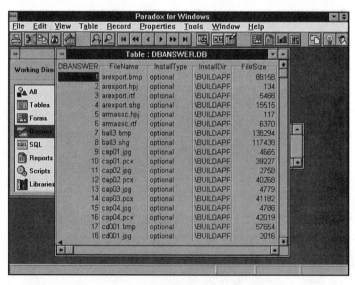

Figure 13.8. *Results of the APPOPT query in the DBANSWER table.*

Finally, you can get the aggregate size of the optional installation files by summing the `FileSize` column of the answer table again. Using TBUTIL again, you get the results shown in Figure 13.9.

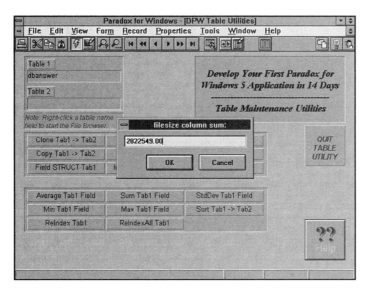

Figure 13.9. *Using TBUTIL to summarize the file sizes of optional files in the installation.*

Now that I have the required and optional file sizes, all I have to do is add them together to determine the total installation file size.

Of course, there is a better way to size the application. You can write another ObjectPAL application and form to do the job for you. You'll get to do just that when you get to the section titled "Modification Notes," later today. I just wanted you to see what the ingredients of the process are first, before you do it the easy way (no goofing off, now.)

Using Compression Tools to Keep Distribution Costs Down

If you're not packaging your application on a CD-ROM as I am, the disk space required for the distribution files may be a problem. In the first place, multiple disks can be expensive to package if you distribute many copies. They also can be time-consuming to create. Even a CD-ROM isn't a bottomless pit of storage space.

The obvious means of controlling the size of the distribution package disks is to compress the distribution files. There are a number of ways you can approach this, but one consideration must always be before any others. Do you have the rights to distribute the decompression part of the compression app? If not, or if it costs too much, a particular compression package may be useless for your purposes, no matter how well it works.

But let's survey the ordinarily available means of compressing and decompressing files by looking at their usefulness and relative costs. Then you can make your own choice in the matter.

The first compression package that comes to mind for distributing Windows applications is the Windows pair of programs, COMPRESS and EXPAND. The EXPAND utility comes with every retail Windows package, so you can be sure that all your users will have a copy of it. It works well, meaning it doesn't fail (at least that I have ever seen), and it yields pretty fair compression. On the other hand, neither the COMPRESS program nor the EXPAND program are particularly fast.

Because your users all have a copy of EXPAND anyway, there is no distribution packaging cost associated with these programs; you don't even have to put it on the distribution disks. You can just invoke the user's copy. There is a cost to you, however, as the developer because the COMPRESS utility doesn't come with retail Windows packages. It is part of the Windows SDK, which you have to buy. It's true that this is a one-time cost, but you have to factor it in.

One of the most popular compression programs out there today is PKZIP and its decompression pal, PKUNZIP. PKZIP is a technical winner. It's fast, it produces really amazing compression ratios, and it's everywhere. The only problem with PKZIP that I have is that it's not free, and I don't have the distribution rights for the PKUNZIP program—no pay, no rights. This doesn't mean that I'm down on PKZIP—I'm not. It's a fine program; I just can't afford to use it.

You might consider packages such as the old standby, ARC. This program works fine, too, but it also costs something to distribute. Furthermore, it has been completely surpassed, technically, by packages such as PKZIP and LHARC.

LHARC is my personal favorite. Although it's not *quite* as fast as PKZIP, it's close, and you can get really good compression ratios with it. The best feature of all is that you can distribute it free, as long as you acknowledge the owner's rights. Each recipient of this package is expected to individually register his or her own copy. It is a great notion for getting shareware out there, and it is a great all-round package. It gets my vote, anyway.

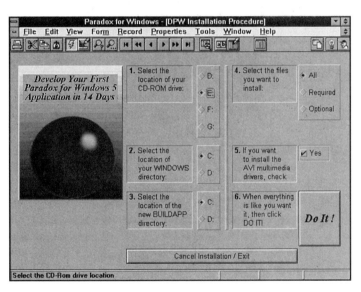

Writing Your Own Packaging and Distribution Applications

This is the section that I have been itching to get to today. Here, you'll roll your own distribution and installation application. It is packaged in the Paradox form DPWINSTL.FDL (.FSL for the source version). It's neat, if I do say so myself. I hope you like it too, especially since you had to use it to get the sample software installed on your hard drive.

The DPWINSTL form enables you to install all, just the required, or just the optional files from the sample CD-ROM drive. It also can update or install the latest Video for Windows and Indeo runtime drivers, as well. The DPWINSTL form is shown in Figure 13.10.

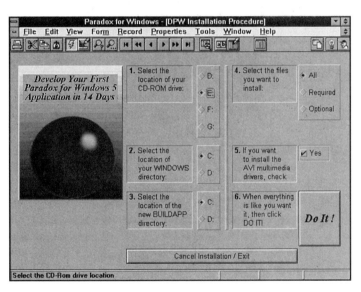

Figure 13.10. *The DPW Installation Procedure form, DPWINSTL.FDL.*

The form's open() method contains logic that you have seen before. In addition to normal default processing, the open() method sets up the radio buttons to their initial values, as follows:

```
;¦BeginMethod¦#FormData1¦open¦
method open(var eventInfo Event)
  if Not eventInfo.isPreFilter() then
    doDefault
```

```
    maximize()
    RomBtns.value = "E:"
    RomBtns.ePush.pushbutton()
    WinBtns.value = "C:"
    WinBtns.cPush.pushbutton()
    AppBtns.value = "C:"
    AppBtns.cPush.pushbutton()
    AVIBtn.value = "Yes"
    AVIBtn.aviCheck.pushbutton()
    FileBtns.value = "All"
    FileBtns.allPush.pushbutton()
  endif
endmethod
;¦EndMethod¦#FormData1¦open¦
```

The Cancel Installation/Exit button is easily covered, too, for you have seen it all before.
Here are the mouse and pushbutton methods for this control:

```
;¦BeginMethod¦#Page2.#Button40¦mouseEnter¦
method mouseEnter(var eventInfo MouseEvent)
  message( "Leave the installation utility..." )
endmethod
;¦EndMethod¦#Page2.#Button40¦mouseEnter¦

;¦BeginMethod¦#Page2.#Button40¦mouseExit¦
method mouseExit(var eventInfo MouseEvent)
  message( "" )
endmethod
;¦EndMethod¦#Page2.#Button40¦mouseExit¦

;¦BeginMethod¦#Page2.#Button40¦pushButton¦
method pushButton(var eventInfo Event)
  msgInfo( "DPW Installation Procedure", "Quitting Installation" )
  close(0)
endmethod
;¦EndMethod¦#Page2.#Button40¦pushButton¦
```

The `mouseEnter()` and `mouseExit()` methods for the `aviBtn` radio buttons are a nice
courtesy, letting the user know what would happen if the checkbox is on when
installation begins. You get the new Video for Windows and Indeo drivers. Here are
those mouse methods:

```
;¦BeginMethod¦#Page2.aviBtn¦mouseEnter¦
method mouseEnter(var eventInfo MouseEvent)
  message( "Choose whether or not to install the Video for Windows drivers..." )
endmethod
;¦EndMethod¦#Page2.aviBtn¦mouseEnter¦

;¦BeginMethod¦#Page2.aviBtn¦mouseExit¦
method mouseExit(var eventInfo MouseEvent)
  message( "" )
endmethod
;¦EndMethod¦#Page2.aviBtn¦mouseExit¦
```

Before getting deeply into the main logic of the application, you can just get the mouse methods out of the way for the Do It! button. They are coded as follows:

```
;¦BeginMethod¦#Page2.DoIt¦mouseEnter¦
method mouseEnter(var eventInfo MouseEvent)
  message( "Perform the selected installation process..." )
endmethod
;¦EndMethod¦#Page2.DoIt¦mouseEnter¦

;¦BeginMethod¦#Page2.DoIt¦mouseExit¦
method mouseExit(var eventInfo MouseEvent)
  message( "" )
endmethod
;¦EndMethod¦#Page2.DoIt¦mouseExit¦
```

The following pushbutton() method is for the Do It! button and contains all the real meat of the application. It is long enough that I will occasionally interrupt it with my comments. You start off with the local var block, declaring the variables you need for execution:

```
;¦BeginMethod¦#Page2.DoIt¦pushButton¦
method pushButton(var eventInfo Event)
var
  fs FileSystem
  freebytes, bytesloaded Longint
  romdir, appdir, windir, vfwdir String
  inpfile, outfile, pline String
  response String
  tc TCursor
  ts TextStream
endvar
```

Next, the variable bytesloaded is initialized to 0, and the code checks the user's target drive to be sure there is enough free space to perform the desired type of installation. A switch block sorts out the different kinds of installation and determines whether to proceed based on each kind. Notice that I have used size values just a little greater than those just determined with the sizing procedures (previously demonstrated).

```
  bytesloaded = 0
;------------------------------------------------------------
; Get the target drive size, to make sure it will fit
;------------------------------------------------------------
  message( "Checking free space" )
  freebytes = fs.freeDiskSpace( AppBtns.value )
  message( "Your ", AppBtns.value, " drive has ",
           StrVal(freebytes), " bytes free" )
  switch
    case FileBtns.value = "All" :
      if freebytes < 10000000 then
        msgStop( "DPW Installation",
                 "Installing with the ALL\noption requires about 10MB" )
        return
      endif
```

13

```
      case FileBtns.value = "Required" :
        if freebytes < 7000000 then
          msgStop( "DPW Installation",
                   "Installing with the REQUIRED\noption requires about 7MB" )
          return
        endif
      case FileBtns.value = "Optional" :
        if freebytes < 3500000 then
          msgStop( "DPW Installation",
                   "Installing with the OPTIONAL\noption requires about 3.5MB" )
          return
        endif
    endswitch
```

Once the code has determined that there is enough room to lay everything down on the user's drive, a check is made to verify that all the directories and drives the user selected are valid ones. This is done as follows:

```
;-------------------------------------------------------------
; Now validate the drives and directories named on form
;-------------------------------------------------------------
  message( "Verifying directories" )
  romdir = RomBtns.value + "\\BUILDAPP"
  appdir = AppBtns.value + "\\BUILDAPP"
  windir = WinBtns.value + "\\WINDOWS"
  vfwdir = RomBtns.value + "\\VFW"
  if not isDir( romdir ) then
    msgStop( "DPW Installation",
             "Installation source not found on\n" + romdir )
    return
  endif
  if not isDir( windir ) then
    msgStop( "DPW Installation",
             "Windows directory not found" )
    return
  endif
  if not isDir( vfwdir ) then
    msgStop( "DPW Installation",
             "Video for Windows directory not found" )
    return
  endif
```

Next, if the target directory exists, it is assumed that this run is a reinstall. Otherwise, the BUILDAPP directory is created for the first time, as follows:

```
  message( "Creating new application directory" )
  if not isDir( appdir ) then
    if not fs.makeDir( appdir ) then
      msgStop( "DPW Installation",
               "Couldn't create the new directory" )
      return
    endif
  else
    message( "DPW Installation", "Found app dir, reinstalling.." )
    sleep(1000)
  endif
```

Now begins the great, huge scan loop, which reads the INFILES table and determines what to do based on the user's selections on the form. The first order of business, of course, is to open a table cursor on the table:

```
;----------------------------------------------------------
; Open a TCursor on INFILES.DB (on ROM) and scan the table.
; For each file found that matches the install type (FilBtns.value),
; copy the file to appdir.
;----------------------------------------------------------
  message( "Copying files to new directory" )
  sleep(1000)
  if tc.open( romdir + "\\INFILES.DB" ) then
    scan tc :
```

There are three major case statements within the switch that follows. There is one for each of the three install types because files are selected for copying a little differently for each install type. Here we go, into the switch:

```
        switch
          case (FileBtns.value = "All") :
            if tc.filename.search("infiles")>0 then loop endif
            inpfile = romdir+"\\"+tc.FileName
            if tc.InstallDir = "\\WINDOWS" then
              outfile = windir+"\\"+tc.FileName
            else
              outfile = appdir+"\\"+tc.FileName
            endif
            message( "Copying " + inpfile + "..." )
            if not fs.copy( inpfile, outfile ) then
              response = msgYesNoCancel( "DPW Installation",
                        "File copy failed.\nGo ahead anyway?" )
              switch
                case response = "Yes" :
                  message( "Skipping file and continuing..." )
                case response = "No" :
                  message( "Quitting installation run..." )
                  tc.close()
                  close(0)
                case response = "Cancel" :
                  message( "Quitting installation run..." )
                  close(0)
              endswitch
            else
              bytesloaded = bytesloaded + tc.filesize
            endif
          case (FileBtns.value = "Optional") :
            if tc.InstallType = "optional" then
              inpfile = romdir+"\\"+tc.FileName
              if tc.InstallDir = "\\WINDOWS" then
                outfile = windir+"\\"+tc.FileName
              else
                outfile = appdir+"\\"+tc.FileName
              endif
```

13

393

```
            message( "Copying " + inpfile + "..." )
            if not fs.copy( inpfile, outfile ) then
              response = msgYesNoCancel( "DPW Installation",
                          "File copy failed.\nGo ahead anyway?" )
              switch
                case response = "Yes" :
                  message( "Skipping file and continuing..." )
                case response = "No" :
                  message( "Quitting installation run..." )
                  tc.close()
                  close(0)
                case response = "Cancel" :
                  message( "Quitting installation run..." )
                  close(0)
              endswitch
            else
              bytesloaded = bytesloaded + tc.filesize
            endif
          endif
        case (FileBtns.value = "Required") :
          if tc.filename.search("infiles")>0 then loop endif
          if tc.InstallType = "always" then
            inpfile = romdir+"\\"+tc.FileName
            if tc.InstallDir = "\\WINDOWS" then
              outfile = windir+"\\"+tc.FileName
            else
              outfile = appdir+"\\"+tc.FileName
            endif
            message( "Copying " + inpfile + "..." )
            if not fs.copy( inpfile, outfile ) then
              response = msgYesNoCancel( "DPW Installation",
                          "File copy failed.\nGo ahead anyway?" )
              switch
                case response = "Yes" :
                  message( "Skipping file and continuing..." )
                case response = "No" :
                  message( "Quitting installation run..." )
                  tc.close()
                  close(0)
                case response = "Cancel" :
                  message( "Quitting installation run..." )
                  close(0)
              endswitch
            else
              bytesloaded = bytesloaded + tc.filesize
            endif
          endif
      otherwise:
        message( "Install type not recognized" )
        sleep(500)
        message( "" )
    endswitch
  endscan
else
  msgStop( "DPW Installation",
```

```
                  "Can't open the installation file list" )
        return
   endif
   tc.close()
```

Regardless of the install type, if a file was copied to the user's drive, its size was tallied in the bytesloaded variable, which will be displayed at the end of the run.

Next, special consideration for the INFILES table itself is made. It wasn't copied during the table scan because it was open then; a sharing violation would have occurred if the code had tried to copy it (and its family of files). That task is therefore handled separately, as follows:

```
; -----------------------------------------------------------
; Copy the INFILES.DB separately, after the table cursor is closed
; -----------------------------------------------------------
   if FileBtns.value = "Required" or FileBtns.value = "all" then
      inpfile = romdir+"\\INFILES.DB"
      outfile = appdir+"\\INFILES.DB"
      message( "Copying " + inpfile + "..." )
      fs.copy( inpfile, outfile )
      inpfile = romdir+"\\INFILES.FAM"
      outfile = appdir+"\\INFILES.FAM"
      message( "Copying " + inpfile + "..." )
      fs.copy( inpfile, outfile )
      inpfile = romdir+"\\INFILES.TV"
      outfile = appdir+"\\INFILES.TV"
      message( "Copying " + inpfile + "..." )
      fs.copy( inpfile, outfile )
   endif
```

Now all but one of the files are copied over to the user's drive. The last one that wasn't copied was VNOTES.INI because it needs to be customized with the user's selected drive name, instead of just copied. A TextStream is used to perform that chore, as follows:

```
; -----------------------------------------------------------
; Customize the vnotes.ini file and write to Windows directory
; -----------------------------------------------------------
   outfile = windir+"\\VNOTES.INI"
   if not ts.open( outfile, "nw" ) then
      msgStop( "DPW Installation",
              "Can't create VNOTES.INI" )
      return
   else
      pline = "[VNConfig]"
      ts.writeline( pline )
      pline = "helpdir="+appdir
      ts.writeline( pline )
   endif
```

Last, but by no means least, you have to consider the Video for Windows installation process. Thank goodness Microsoft has its own installation procedure for that. All I have

13

to do here is invoke the VFW setup utility, if the user elected to install it at this time. Here is the code for that process:

```
;-----------------------------------------------------------
; Finally, go launch the Video for Windows installation
;-----------------------------------------------------------
  if aviBtn.value = "Yes" then
    message( "Launching Video for Windows setup..." )
    sleep( 1000 )
    message( "Executing "+romdir+"\\SETUP.EXE" )
    sleep( 2000 )
    execute( vfwdir+"\\SETUP.EXE", Yes, WinStyleDefault )
    bringtotop()
  endif
  message( "DPW installation is complete! " +
           StrVal(bytesloaded) + " bytes loaded." )
endmethod;¦EndMethod¦#Page2.DoIt¦pushButton¦
```

Returning to the more mundane level, there are also `mouseEnter()` and `mouseExit()` methods for the installation type radio buttons, the CD-ROM address radio buttons, the \WINDOWS directory drive location, and the application destination drive buttons. All the code for these mouse methods follows:

```
;¦BeginMethod¦#Page2.FileBtns¦mouseEnter¦
method mouseEnter(var eventInfo MouseEvent)
  message( "Select the files you want to install..." )
endmethod
;¦EndMethod¦#Page2.FileBtns¦mouseEnter¦

;¦BeginMethod¦#Page2.FileBtns¦mouseExit¦
method mouseExit(var eventInfo MouseEvent)
  message( "" )
endmethod
;¦EndMethod¦#Page2.FileBtns¦mouseExit¦


;¦BeginMethod¦#Page2.RomBtns¦mouseEnter¦
method mouseEnter(var eventInfo MouseEvent)
  message( "Select the CD-Rom drive location" )
endmethod
;¦EndMethod¦#Page2.RomBtns¦mouseEnter¦

;¦BeginMethod¦#Page2.RomBtns¦mouseExit¦
method mouseExit(var eventInfo MouseEvent)
  message( "" )
endmethod
;¦EndMethod¦#Page2.RomBtns¦mouseExit¦

;¦BeginMethod¦#Page2.AppBtns¦mouseEnter¦
method mouseEnter(var eventInfo MouseEvent)
  message( "Select the drive where the sample programs should go..." )
endmethod
;¦EndMethod¦#Page2.AppBtns¦mouseEnter¦

;¦BeginMethod¦#Page2.AppBtns¦mouseExit¦
```

```
method mouseExit(var eventInfo MouseEvent)
  message( "" )
endmethod
;¦EndMethod¦#Page2.AppBtns¦mouseExit¦

;¦BeginMethod¦#Page2.WinBtns¦mouseEnter¦
method mouseEnter(var eventInfo MouseEvent)
  message( "Select the drive where your \\WINDOWS directory is..." )
endmethod
;¦EndMethod¦#Page2.WinBtns¦mouseEnter¦

;¦BeginMethod¦#Page2.WinBtns¦mouseExit¦
method mouseExit(var eventInfo MouseEvent)
  message( "" )
endmethod
;¦EndMethod¦#Page2.WinBtns¦mouseExit¦
```

Just as a nicety, I have also provided mouseEnter() and mouseExit() method messages
even for the logo graphic on the form, like this:

```
;¦BeginMethod¦#Page2.#Bitmap3¦mouseEnter¦
method mouseEnter(var eventInfo MouseEvent)
  message( "Welcome to the DPW installation procedure..." )
endmethod
;¦EndMethod¦#Page2.#Bitmap3¦mouseEnter¦

;¦BeginMethod¦#Page2.#Bitmap3¦mouseExit¦
method mouseExit(var eventInfo MouseEvent)
  message( "" )
endmethod
;¦EndMethod¦#Page2.#Bitmap3¦mouseExit¦
```

Now that wasn't so bad, was it? The fact is, if you have done this sort of code before, it
isn't too bad. If you have never done this sort of thing before, however, it can be
intimidating. That's one of the big reasons I wrote the installation utility for the book's
sample code in ObjectPAL like this—just so you could see how I did it.

Using Commercial Packaging and Distribution Apps

13

For those of you who bought this book in *anticipation* of getting a copy of Paradox for
Windows, you had to use the alternative installation technique provided on the CD-
ROM. That installation utility is a stand-alone utility created by a commercial package
the Sams folks use to provide such services.

That raises the issue of using commercial packaging and distribution applications to
package your software for distribution. I won't go into much detail in this section. I just
want you to be aware that such things exist, and that you can buy them if you want.

One of the packages that I have at my disposal is the Microsoft Setup utility. It works and it creates standard Windows installation packages, but parts of it have to be run under DOS, not Windows—so I don't use it much. It does, however, provide a sample of what you'll encounter if you use such a utility.

In Figure 13.11, for example, you can see what a Setup utilities Windows-based disk layout program looks like. With that utility, you can indicate such things as which files are required and which are not, which files to compress for distribution (using COMPRESS, of course), and whether to version files or not.

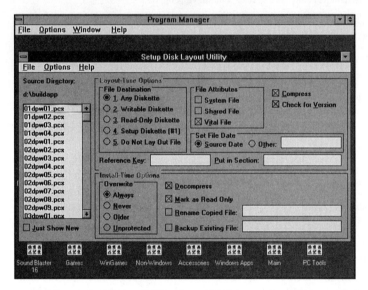

Figure 13.11. *Using the Microsoft Windows SDK Setup Disk Layout Utility to identify installation files.*

One of the main problems with the Setup utility is that it creates files that nothing but the setup utility can use, as shown in Figure 13.12.

They didn't count on my sneakiness, however. I did in fact use the layout utility's output to create the initial version of the INFILES table. I simply used the SYSCTL app's Import Variable ASCII file utility with the new INFILES table, and then cleaned it up. It sure beats finding all those files the hard way!

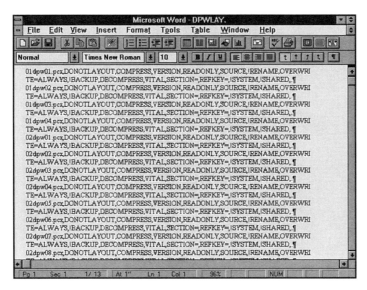

Figure 13.12. *Sample output from the Microsoft Disk Layout Utility.*

The moral is short. Whether you buy a third-party product or write it yourself, get some automation software for packaging apps if you'll be doing this sort of thing on a regular basis.

Modification Notes

Here is a nifty modification project for you. You already have several components for a complete application sizing package: the APPSIZE script, the APPREQ and APPOPT queries, an example of column-summing logic from TBUTIL, and of course the INFILES table itself.

You can take these elements and use them to build a form around INFILES, naming it, for example, AUTOSIZE. Put everything you need in this form to both maintain INFILES and to compute the sizes you need to know for the installation procedure. The form should look something like the one in Figure 13.13.

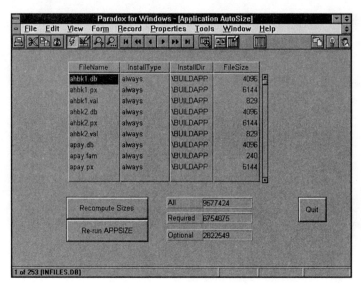

Figure 13.13. *Suggested layout for the AUTOSIZE form.*

By now, you need very little, if any, guidance through ObjectPAL procedures. Furthermore, because the source for the AutoSize application is (or should be) very short and simple, I will show you the code that I suggest you use (without saying anything at all about it). And here it is:

```
;¦BeginMethod¦#Page2.#Button11¦pushButton¦
method pushButton(var eventInfo Event)
  close(0)
endmethod
;¦EndMethod¦#Page2.#Button11¦pushButton¦


;¦BeginMethod¦#Page2.#Button7¦pushButton¦
method pushButton(var eventInfo Event)
var
  tc TCursor
endvar
  tc.attach( INFILES )
  if tc.isedit() then tc.endedit() endif
  play( "APPSIZE.SDL" )
endmethod
;¦EndMethod¦#Page2.#Button7¦pushButton¦


;¦BeginMethod¦#Page2.#Button14¦pushButton¦
method pushButton(var eventInfo Event)
var
```

```
 tc TCursor
 xall, xrequired, xoptional LongInt
endvar
  all = 0
  required = 0
  optional = 0
  xall = 0
  xrequired = 0
  xoptional = 0
  tc.attach( INFILES )
  tc.home()
  scan tc :
    xall = xall + tc.FileSize
    switch
      case tc.InstallType = "always" :
        xrequired = xrequired + tc.FileSize
      case tc.InstallType = "optional" :
        xoptional = xoptional  + tc.FileSize
    endswitch
  endscan
  all = xall
  required = xrequired
  optional = xoptional
  tc.home()
  tc.moveToRecord( 1 )
endmethod
;¦EndMethod¦#Page2.#Button14¦pushButton¦
```

Debugging the Process

Debugging the installation procedure is a must. There is only one way to do that: run it every possible way it can be run. If I ran DPWINSTL once, I ran it 50 times, trying out the features. (That was just today, incidentally.)

Even then, somebody out there will have a machine or software configuration with which the thing just won't work! Well, I tried. If it doesn't work on your machine, you can use an alternative installation procedure that does not depend on Paradox for Windows.

13

Rolling Out the
Application

It is now Day 14 of designing, building, and implementing the DPW AR/AP business application with multimedia features and many, many support utilities. The application itself, with all its varied parts, is complete, tested, and ready to go.

Now, in closing, it's time to turn to the subject of whether the developer is ready to go or not. Have you yet given any thought to the process of actually delivering the product to your end users?

If you're an individual just programming for yourself (and I hope a whole bunch of you bought this book), this chapter may not hold much interest for you at first glance. And if you're a professional developer who bought this book just to get a quickie introduction to Paradox for Windows, you may not need to further study product roll-out. It might seem, then, that today's text is just for the corporate developer who is going to deploy the product in a fairly localized manner.

But before you draw that conclusion, wait just a moment. In the first place, there may be some little glimmering here that you haven't thought of yet, particularly if you're an individual programmer. In the second place, even if you're an individual programmer, you'll still have to maintain your software for yourself, and I have some little goodies today that will help you do that.

So stick around, and see if there isn't one last bit of gold in the mine shaft. You'll at least get to check out one last neat application, and learn an ObjectPAL technique that you may not have seen before.

Documenting the Installation Process

If you and I have designed the installation utilities correctly, the average user will be able to merely look at the installation screen and immediately discern what needs to be done. The DPW Installation Procedure is, I feel, just that simple. It is so simple that I did not even put a Help button on the form.

Yet, even if the installation procedure is that simple, it is very likely that you should provide some written installation instructions with the application. There should be at least a one-page blurb that tells the new user in no uncertain terms what must be done to get the software on his or her computer.

What this documentation must contain, and how detailed it should be, must be determined in light of the intended audience for the product. A simple example, for instance, is the audience for this book—there is only a fine line between this book with its CD-ROM disk and a pure software package. You could say that you bought the

software, and the book is only the documentation for it. I often thought of it that way while I was writing the software and the book, although ordinary software packages don't expect the user to write part of the code.

So what do I know about my audience? Well, first I can be pretty sure that all of you have something more than just the average user's level of computer literacy. I know this from the fact that you bought a programming book—this one. And I know that many of you have actually done some programming before, at least to the extent of setting up basic applications with Paradox for Windows, or another tool like it.

Therefore, I can deduce that you folks won't need me to tell you which side of the CD-ROM goes up, nor what *current directory* or *current drive* mean. On the other hand, programmer types are always pointing out that *assume* can be broken up into three appropriate words, so don't assume anything about your prospective users.

What kinds of things, then, should you consider putting in the installation documentation? Here are a few handy ideas:

- [ ] *What kind of hardware and software must the user already have in order to support your application on his or her machine?* It is most embarrassing to find that you haven't told a new user all that he or she needs to know about this.

- [ ] *What kind of media is the software being distributed on?* The disk with this book, for example, is a standard CD-ROM, so there isn't much doubt about what kind of drive is needed to install it. But if you're distributing on disks, what kind do you provide? 5.25- or 3.5-inch disks? Low-density, double-density, or high-density disks? You need to say what is provided: not everybody can use every medium.

- [ ] *How much room is required to install the product?* The sample code from this book for example, requires about 10MB to install—about 7MB to install just the required files, and about 3MB to install the optional files.

- [ ] *What significant choices will have to be made?* For example, the DPWINSTL procedure can, but doesn't have to, launch the Video for Windows installation setup program. It is important to know this is coming, and what release of VFW is being supplied, because installing a back release of Video for Windows can foul up your whole multimedia system.

- [ ] *What setup parameters are absolutely required, and which can be flexibly modified?* The installation procedure for this book's sample code, for example, requires a target directory named \BUILDAPP to run. What if you already happen to have a directory by that name? You need to know that you can't install the product in a case like this. (Actually, DPWINSTL would install this stuff right in there along with whatever happened to be there first—which could be extremely troublesome.)

14

405

These are just a few of the things you might want to document for the install process. These things are in addition to a step-by-step, how-to instruction set, of course.

Getting the Application to the Users

This section is bound to be the shortest section in the book. If you're a commercial developer or an individual developing your own software, getting the software to the user isn't a problem. In the former case, you already have established distribution channels and methods. In the latter case, when you finish writing the app, it's already where it belongs.

That leaves the corporate developer, poor fellow. There is no pat solution for you, I'm afraid. Deploying applications is a matter that has been debated in the trade rags frequently. There are many problems associated with disk distribution, such as knowing whether users actually upgraded their software with the latest copy, or even really got the latest copy. There are also many problems associated with network deployment, all related to the humongous administrative efforts it takes to follow who has what, at what release level, and so on.

I'm afraid that there is just no one solution to this problem. Too much depends on what resources you have at hand, together with what resources the users have at their disposal. The only thing to say about it (cheap shot here) is that you should do whatever will most certainly see that the users get the software on their machines first, and after that, whatever costs the least effort. Sorry. The truth hurts sometimes.

Supporting Your Users After the Fact

After those last negative words, I'm glad that I can offer you some positive ones about how you can keep up with users and the problems they may have with the software. I also have one last chance to put a nifty little application before you that you just might be able to use.

You can probably tell that I have no intention of trying to teach you how to handle irate users calling you in the middle of the night. That part is strictly a human-relations skill. At any rate, what I can do is give you some automation tools for following users and what they do with your software. You can easily expand on these tools as well. And not least, I will show you a slick ObjectPAL trick you just may not have seen elsewhere.

What you are going to do here is to build two tables and a form. The tables will make up a user list, with memo fields for detailed notes on any user, and a problem log, also with memo fields for describing problems and bugs and their solutions. The form will be an integration tool for accessing the tables' information. It is the form that has the slick trick in it, naturally.

The first thing you need is the user list table. It will appropriately be named USERLIST.DB. The USERLIST table is shown in a table view in Figure 14.1.

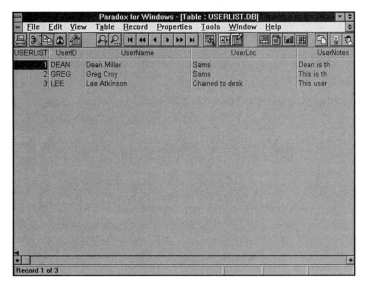

Figure 14.1. *The USERLIST table in a table view.*

In a simple table view, USERLIST doesn't look like much. It does, however, have sufficient structure for you to maintain basic information about each user of your software. The USERLIST record structure is shown in Figure 14.2.

14

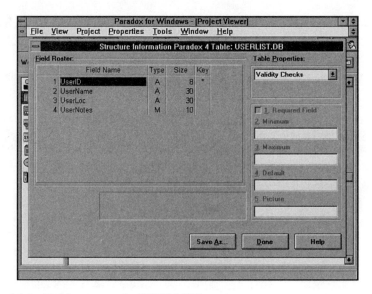

Figure 14.2. *Field structure for USERLIST.*

USERLIST uses the UserID field as the record key. This sort of assumes that the user is on a network, which may not actually be the case. If not, you'll still have to make up a user ID for a user. That isn't a bad idea, anyway, because even if there are several users who use just one machine (one at a time, of course), you'll want to keep track of them so you can assign passwords. (You did add password protection to the system, didn't you?)

Other information for each user is simple and straightforward. It includes the user's name, a location for the user, and the UserNotes Memo field. You can expand this structure, incidentally, any way you want to, without affecting the operation of the form you'll build in just a moment.

Now that you know who all the users are, you'll need some means of keeping track of problem reports, and what you did about them. A problem log is in order, so I built one for you. It is named PROBLOG.DB, and is shown in Figure 14.3.

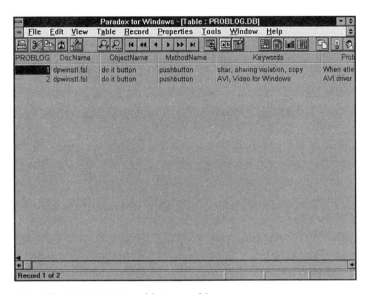

Figure 14.3. *The PROBLOG table in a table view.*

The PROBLOG table is nearly as simple as the USERLIST table, with one glaring difference. PROBLOG has no key. This is because, as you can see in Figure 14.3, it is possible that there may be more than one problem with a given document, object, and method. The structure of PROBLOG is displayed in Figure 14.4.

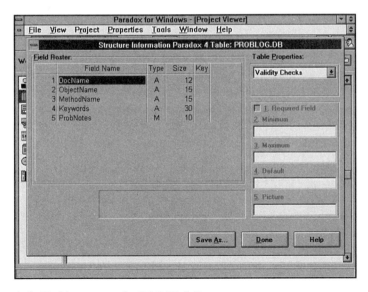

Figure 14.4. *Field structure for PROBLOG.*

14

Now it's time for the good part. Notice in Figure 14.5 that access to the two tables is integrated with the USERADM form. There are six control objects on the USERADM form, which are really three controls in pairs.

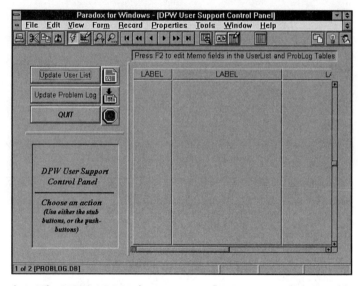

Figure 14.5. *The USERADM administration form running, but no table selected yet.*

For each pair of controls there is a pushbutton and a graphics object, either of which will access the function noted in the pushbutton's label. You can click the Update User List button, for example, or just click the graphics object (I call it a *stub*) to the right of the pushbutton. Notice that the graphics image looks like a page from a list. The mouseclick() method for each graphics object just calls its companion button's pushbutton() method. There is no reason for having pairs of objects like this except that I liked the notion, and wanted to experiment a little. I kind of like the effect. What do you think?

The other active control, of course, is the Update Problem Log button with its graphics stub. The basic idea is that you click one of these controls (or stubs) to activate the corresponding table—all in the same form, in the same table frame. That's where the trick comes in, but hold on a bit.

If you click the Update User List control, the USERLIST table is attached to the table frame, and displayed, as shown in Figure 14.6 (it's a list of good guys, naturally). Because this is a real table frame, it has real Paradox features behind it. You can edit the table, scroll and navigate through it, use the Zoom and More Zoom tools from the toolbar to find things quickly, and more.

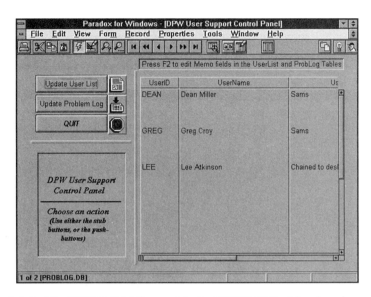

Figure 14.6. *The USERADM form with the USERLIST table selected.*

One of the primary things you can do, of course, is to move to the memo field and take up to 32KB of notes on any particular user. Using the memo field is illustrated in Figure 14.7.

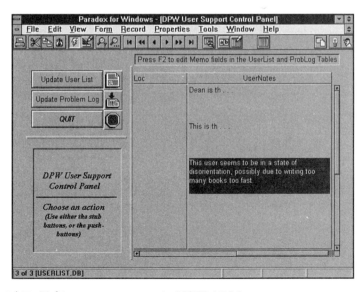

Figure 14.7. *Taking notes on a user in USERADM.*

The nice thing about USERADM is that you can work with one table, still be in edit mode, and instantly change to the other table simply by clicking the other control (or stub). Figure 14.8 shows USERADM now switched to the PROBLOG table.

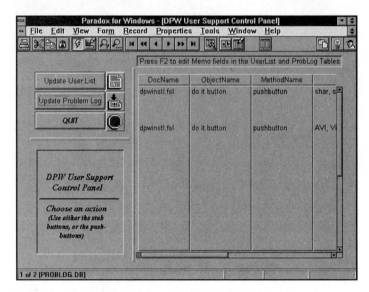

Figure 14.8. *The USERADM form with the PROBLOG table selected.*

Just as with the user list, the purpose of the problem log is to note the details about problems and bugs in the software. Documenting a bug for the DPWINSTL form using USERADM is demonstrated in Figure 14.9.

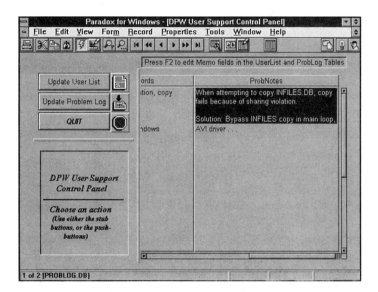

Figure 14.9. *Taking notes on a problem in USERADM.*

That's the last of the pictures. I am sure you're eager to see how I used the same form and table frame to access two different tables. (It could have been any tables; table format doesn't matter to USERADM.)

Well, then let's go right into the ObjectPAL code. First, you get the preliminaries out of the way. The form open() method has that startling sameness about it, as follows:

```
;¦BeginMethod¦#FormData1¦open¦
method open(var eventInfo Event)
  if NOT eventInfo.isPreFilter() then
    doDefault
    maximize()
  endif
endmethod
;¦EndMethod¦#FormData1¦open¦
```

You have seen how to use object frame styles to simulate pushbuttons (earlier in the book). That, plus a direct call to pushbutton() methods, is the main characteristic of the graphics object's mouseclick() methods, as follows:

```
;¦BeginMethod¦#Page2.#Bitmap11¦mouseClick¦
method mouseClick(var eventInfo MouseEvent)
  self.frame.style = Inside3DFrame
  quit.pushbutton()
  self.frame.style = Outside3DFrame
endmethod
```

14

413

```
;¦EndMethod¦#Page2.#Bitmap11¦mouseClick¦

;¦BeginMethod¦#Page2.#Bitmap10¦mouseClick¦
method mouseClick(var eventInfo MouseEvent)
  self.frame.style = Inside3DFrame
  problems.pushbutton()
  self.frame.style = Outside3DFrame
endmethod
;¦EndMethod¦#Page2.#Bitmap10¦mouseClick¦

;¦BeginMethod¦#Page2.#Bitmap9¦mouseClick¦
method mouseClick(var eventInfo MouseEvent)
  self.frame.style = Inside3DFrame
  users.pushbutton()
  self.frame.style = Outside3DFrame
endmethod
;¦EndMethod¦#Page2.#Bitmap9¦mouseClick¦
```

The form `close()` method is also an old friend by now. Here is its source:

```
;¦BeginMethod¦#Page2.quit¦pushButton¦
method pushButton(var eventInfo Event)
  close(0)
endmethod
;¦EndMethod¦#Page2.quit¦pushButton¦
```

Now you come to the secret of the app. Actually, it's so simple and easy to do that you may be disappointed that there isn't a mountain of ObjectPAL behind so seemingly complex a task as switching tables in a table frame. Once again, however, that's the beauty of ObjectPAL. It may take a while to locate what to do, but most often, how isn't going to be very complicated.

Here are the sources for both the active controls (pushbuttons). Look at them, and then I will tell you why they work:

```
;¦BeginMethod¦#Page2.problems¦pushButton¦
method pushButton(var eventInfo Event)
  message( "Changing table to ProbLog..." )
  self.moveto()
  sometable.visible = False
  sometable.TableName = "problog.db"
  sometable.visible = True
endmethod
;¦EndMethod¦#Page2.problems¦pushButton¦

;¦BeginMethod¦#Page2.users¦pushButton¦
method pushButton(var eventInfo Event)
  message( "Changing table to UserList..." )
  self.moveto()
  sometable.visible = False
  sometable.TableName = "userlist.db"
  sometable.visible = True
endmethod
;¦EndMethod¦#Page2.users¦pushButton¦
```

In the first prototype of this applet, I forgot to include the `self.moveto()` calls. All these calls do is move the focus onto the button that's doing the work. Does that seem trivial? It's not; it's the whole secret. If you don't do this, and if you have also clicked or edited a table field, attempting to change the table name associated with the table frame will yield a great big Paradox error dialog box. And it won't switch, either. It will just tell you over and over that you can't delete an object (the table frame) that's currently active (has the focus).

Bingo! Knowing and using that one little secret, you need only one line of code to assign a new value to the frame's `TableName` attribute. The `visible` attribute is also used to make it appear that the change is a sudden sharp one, no panting or crawling. Although, to be honest, I never tried it without first making the table frame invisible. I always assume that working with a visible UI object will slow things down. (Remember the speed tests?)

That's all there is to it. Really. Now you have a neat automation tool for keeping track of users and the problems they cause—excuse me, the problems they discover.

Starting All Over for the Next Release

There was a reason I wanted you to be able to track problems and their resolutions using USERADM. When the problem log gets to a certain critical mass, it's time to pull the next release together. The users will appreciate a clean release with all the bugs and bug patches gone. It will increase their use and enjoyment of the software, and their confidence in it. Who knows? It might just really work better, too.

The question then remains: *What is that critical mass of problems in the log?* No one can tell you that. It is strictly a judgment call. But one criterion you can use is this: if you change *too* many things in the next release, it may become incompatible with the previous release and cause your users some grief.

Don't let the problems pile up. Fix them as soon as they hit your door. Whenever it is economical to do so, roll out a new release of the software. They will love you for it.

Modification Notes

There is nothing more to modify until you begin your next project. That project you'll have to undertake without me, but I will be there in spirit.

I won't mind a bit, either, if some of my code, or something derived from it, is there too. In fact, I would be proud to know that you think it is good enough to seed future ideas and future ObjectPAL methods. So feel free to use the code you got from this book in any way you see fit. If it helps you to roll out a nice-looking, full-featured, well-behaved application, so much the better.

There are two ways you use the sample code from this book as a boilerplate for other applications. The first way is to use the FORMLIST utility to get the ObjectPAL to a text file. Then you can roll your own forms, and copy and paste code from a text editor into the new form's methods.

The second way is to use Paradox to copy the form or report to a new name, and modify the result right in place. Having been through this book with me, you're experienced enough to use this second method. Just don't forget to sweat the small stuff—it will come to get you when you aren't looking.

There are several things you got from this book that won't go directly into other applications, but that you can use to build new applications. Here is a list of those things.

- [ ] You have the application sizing tools, especially the AUTOSIZE app you got unexpectedly at the end of the previous chapter. This is a handy tool for keeping up with what you have developed so far. You can copy INFILES.DB, the AUTOSIZE form, and the APPSIZE script into a new working directory; then empty the table and start adding new entries as you move through the development stages.

- [ ] Speaking of emptying tables, you also can use the TBUTIL and SYSCTL utilities while developing just about any application. I only used them several million times while I wrote this book.

- [ ] If you really want to get into heavy help files for your Windows apps, you also can transport the C language module CMEDIA.DLL right over. You'll probably have to modify it slightly so that it doesn't depend on just the VNOTES.INI file; but if you're this serious, it won't be much of a problem.

- [ ] For apps that support multimedia features, you have a truckload of sources from this book that will help you implement those features. Those sources include a lot of ObjectPAL, and even some C language modules. (Remember the GETFILE.DLL for that pure-Windows look at open file selection time?)

- [ ] You also can port the *Voice Notes!* application into your new development with almost no modification. All you need to do here is get rid of the DPW annotations in the form and the Windows help file.

□ The DPW Multimedia Theater is a nice touch for added value, too. Port it on over. Of course if you're going to use this app or the *Voice Notes!* as is, I would appreciate it if you left something in them that identifies them as having come from this book (for example, the DPW logos and annotations). That's not a requirement, however. The code is yours to do with what you want, as long as you don't copy it, write a book, and claim that you originated it. Sams would probably come get you in the middle of the night for that.

□ The Report/Print Manager is another piece that you can use almost directly as a support utility in another application. You can impress your users by demonstrating duplexed laser printing.

□ Last but not least, you can use the User Administration app to support your users after roll out, just like you learned today.

There are many other fragmentary pieces that you can pick up and adapt to other applications, as well. I have tried to supply a smorgasbord of techniques and code examples, so dig in!

Debugging the Process

Alas, there is now nothing to debug in the new application. Until, that is, the very first user touches the keyboard. That's when you get your first irate phone call. And it is there that I will leave you to your fate.

14

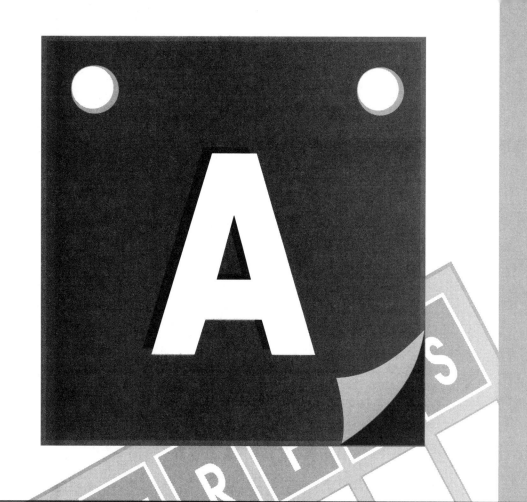

Glossary of Terms

alias   A shorthand name you assign to a drive and directory path combination. The alias :work: is your current working directory (not the same as the DOS current directory).

answer table   The table ordinarily located in your private directory that received query output. I have often overridden this default table with DBANSWER.DB in the current working directory in this book.

AVI   Audio Video Interleaved. The file format used by Microsoft's Video for Windows to store full-motion video plus sound multimedia clips. This is also the file extension for Video for Windows files.

axis   The horizontal (*x*) or vertical (*y*) directions on a chart or graph.

band   An area on a report design. Default areas include the report, page, and record bands. Define a group band if you want to take control of breaks or force a page break at certain points.

binary field   Also known as a BLOB field. Used by Paradox to store data as a simple stream of bits (data that Paradox cannot interpret). This doesn't mean that the data is useless. This book uses binary fields, for example, to store WAV files in the *Voice Notes!* application.

bind   Used to associate a table with a design object. In the USERADM application in Day 14, different tables are *dynamically* bound to a table frame.

blank   A field that does not contain any value. In Paradox, this is not the same as a field that contains a zero or even null value: those fields are not considered blank.

BLOB   A binary object.

cascade delete   One of the two possible delete options you can specify in a referential integrity relationship (prohibit delete is the other). If you have defined cascading deletes, deleting a record in the master table will cause all linked records in all detail tables to be deleted also. This option is *not* used for the AR/AP system.

child table   The dependent table in a referential integrity relationship. This is also called a detail table, although that terminology is somewhat loose. (Detail tables aren't necessarily permanently linked to master tables.)

click   To press and release the left mouse button.

column   The vertical stack that one field makes in a table.

composite index   A secondary index composed of two or more contiguous fields of a table.

composite key   A primary key composed of two or more contiguous fields that occur at the beginning of the record of a table.

compound index   Same as a composite index.

compound key   Same as a composite key.

container   A UI object that completely encloses objects within it. Deleting or moving a container object also affects the contained objects. Contained objects are moved with the container object.

crosstab   A UI object that resembles both a table frame and a spreadsheet grid and is used to summarize (tabulate) data.

data integrity   The assurance that data will not be corrupted. You can assure data integrity by using validity checks, table lookup, and referential integrity relationships.

data type   A kind of data with certain characteristics, such as currency, date, numeric, and integer.

default   An action or value that Paradox will use if you don't tell it to do something different. This book often uses the `doDefault` statement to indicate that Paradox should go ahead with default processing of forms and other objects. Once or twice, this book even used the `disableDefault` statement to expressly prohibit this from happening. (See the sections on programming the AR/AP engine.)

design object   The same as a UIObject. These are fields, boxes, pictures, and so on that you place on your forms and reports.

Desktop   The main window in Paradox.

detail table   A dependent table in a form's data model. This is also loosely called a child table, even though this table doesn't necessarily participate in a referential integrity relationship.

dialog box   A small window used to present messages or to solicit input from the user. Frequently, the `msgInfo()` and `msgStop()` procedures are used to display informational dialog boxes in the AR/AP application and its utilities.

DLL   See *dynamic link library*.

double-click   To quickly press and release the left mouse button twice. This is a standard Windows action that is consistently used in the Paradox user interfaces.

drop-down listbox   A text box with a button at the right end that you can click to drop down a list of items. Clicking one of those items chooses it to be the new value of the field (the drop-down listbox).

dynamic link library   A library of compiled routines used in Windows to package function groups. This book uses two DLLs: The GETFILE.DLL for file selection services (which behave a little differently from the Paradox File Browser) and the CMEDIA.DLL for driving multimedia services right out of a Windows help file.

field view   An editing mode that enables you to move through a field one character at a time for editing (using the standard Windows editing keystrokes). In a regular field, press F2 to enter field view. Pressing Ctrl+F2 enters persistent field view, which enables you to move through multiple records in a table without leaving field view mode. In a memo field, Shift+F2 enters memo view, which is analogous to field view.

focus   A Windows term meaning the place the input will come from next. If a field on a form *has the focus,* any typing you do will go into that field. Whether an object has the focus or not can determine whether it is active or not. In the USERADM form, for example, you have to move the focus off the table frame before you can bind a different table to it.

form   The main design document type in Paradox. You mostly draw forms in the from design window to create the user interfaces for your applications. ObjectPAL programming is done by inspecting the properties of design objects on the form and attaching methods to those objects, or customizing their built-in methods. This is the object-oriented concept that makes Paradox for Windows such a great prototyping tool; you can create applications with great speed and accuracy using Paradox forms design.

graphic   A picture, usually in the form of a Windows BMP file. Graphic objects can be pasted directly into forms and reports. In forms, you also can attach ObjectPAL code to a graphic object's methods. You could, for example, modify a graphic object's mouseClick() method to make the picture behave like a pushbutton. (This book does some of that.)

grid   The network of horizontal and vertical lines separating fields in table frames and crosstab objects. You can customize the color and style of grids in your forms and reports.

group   To identify a set of records having a common value or characteristic. Thus, you can define group bands in a report when you want to take a control break or a page break on, say, the customer number (as this book does in some of the AR reports so that different customers in the report appear on separate pages of the report).

index   A file containing indexes for Paradox keyed tables. There is one file for the primary index and for each of the secondary indexes (if there are any). Note that the primary index is established by the key of a table (which may be more than one field).

inspect   To view or modify an object's properties. Inspect an object by right-clicking it to see its properties menu. This is how you access a design object's methods. You inspect it and choose **M**ethods from its properties menu. Then you choose the method to customize from the Methods menu. (You also can choose to add a new custom method of your own devising.)

key   One or more fields at the beginning of a table's records that are used to uniquely identify each record. When a table has a key, only one record with that key can exist in the table. Establishing a key is required before you can define a referential integrity relationship. Sometimes, secondary indexes are also referred to as keys or as secondary keys, but this terminology is loose.

link   A relationship between two or more tables. You can establish a permanent link between two Paradox for Windows tables by defining a referential integrity relationship on the child table and linking it to the parent (master) table. This option was not available in earlier DOS versions of Paradox. You also can establish a temporary relationship between two tables by linking them in the data model of a form. This was the only way to link tables in DOS paradox.

listbox   A box object containing a list of selectable entries. This book uses listboxes in the AREXPORT form to enable the flexible structuring of exported data, as well as to illustrate how to write ObjectPAL code to handle listboxes.

lock   A software protocol that permits the *serialization of a resource.* This fancy term just means that you can control who gets control of an object, and when. You can use locks to ensure that a table or even a record is edited by only one user on a network at a time.

master table   The independent table in a linked table relationship. Sometimes, this is also used to refer to the parent table of a referential integrity relationship, but only when the context makes it clear what is going on (some Paradox messages do this, for instance).

MCI   Media Control Interface, which is the set of programming interfaces Microsoft has provided as a standardized means of controlling media devices. The MCI includes the string command interface used extensively in this book.

memo field   A text field that the manuals say can be of "virtually any length." They can be up to 32MB, which is a considerable improvement over the old

days when databases supported up to 32KB memos, if at all. Memo fields are stored in the table's MB file, the same place that graphics and BLOBs are stored. A *formatted* memo field will also enable you to apply text styling to all or portions of the text, very much like a full-fledged word processor.

message   Informational text displayed in a form window's status bar, at the bottom. This book's applications often used the `message()` procedure to inform the user what was going on.

method   The ObjectPAL code attached to an object that determines the object's behavior. Pushbuttons, for example, do nothing by default until you customize the `pushButton()` method. You also can define custom methods that do anything you want them to do for any object.

MMSYSTEM   The MCI command interface DLL uses in this book to provide multimedia features for our applications.

MPC   A Multimedia PC. This has various meanings, but a multimedia PC is generally understood to be at least a 386DX, 33MHz machine, with at least 4MB RAM, an 80MB hard drive, an 8-bit sound card, and a double-spin CD-ROM drive. Anything less than this is not worth having, and you can get considerably more for not too much more money. If you want to know more about this topic and a host of other things related to multimedia, read Ron Wodaski's books (from Sams Publishing, naturally).

multimedia   The combination of multiple media—text, graphics, sound (*real* sound, not just beeps), and full-motion video—to present information. In this book, you learn how to write multimedia Paradox for Windows applications.

multi-record object   A design object on forms and reports that displays several records from a table at one time. This book uses a multi-record object, for example, to lay out the labels in the AR Mailing Labels report. You can control how many records are displayed, and in what order they are displayed (left to right, and then down, for instance).

object   A form, report, table, query, or script. This book didn't use many scripts, but the one it did use, APPSIZE, was quite important. That is typical of scripts: you don't use many, but when you do, they really count.

parent table   The independent table in a referential integrity relationship. This is also referred to as a master table, but this is not the precisely correct language. (See *master table*).

primary index   The file containing the index on a table's primary key. Remember that the primary key can be either simple (one field) or composite (several contiguous fields).

Project Viewer   The browse window that lets you launch forms, reports, queries, scripts, or view tables directly from the browse list. You can double-click an item to launch it immediately, or right-click it to inspect its properties menu.

properties   The attributes possessed by an object. The properties of a design object, for instance, include its size, color, and position on the form or report.

prototype   To design an application by a process of repetitive redefinition, using provisional versions of the software to inform the next round of design. Often thought of as design by trial and error (it is not), this is a powerful and rapid way to bring a new application to production. It is almost impossible to do using traditional third-generation compilers to create the software.

query   An inquiry you make to Paradox for information in one or more tables. Queries are normally defined in a query window, where you check the fields you want to be included in the answer table (which is a separate table from the input table) and where you define the conditions for including a record in the query's results. Paradox implements queries with QBE (query By Example) tools. Paradox 5 for Windows now also supports local SQL queries.

record   A group of related fields that comprise one row of a table. This is similar to a row in a spreadsheet or in a printed tabulation.

referential integrity   A relationship between a parent and child table that you define, which permanently links the two tables. The relationship is defined on the child (detail) table so that each of its records must have a counterpart in the parent table. Each AR transaction record, for example, has a customer number field that must match the key of the customer table. The parent (master) table keeps a record of all of its dependent tables in its VAL file.

restructure   To change the record layout of a table. Restructuring can involve changing the indexes of a table, field attributes, adding or deleting fields, and other things. There are some restrictions on restructuring a table that has referential integrity defined on it.

right-click   To click and release the right mouse button. In Paradox, a right-click indicates that you want to inspect an object's properties. One interesting use in Paradox 5 for Windows is right-clicking a field in a table view. You can do this to set filter values for that field so that only those records whose field has the values you specify are displayed in the table view or table frame.

script   A stand-alone ObjectPAL program. Scripts are actually forms that are always invisible and have only one method—the run() method. It is the run() method that you customize to write a script. Scripts are mostly useful for

launching other functions that have visible forms. This book used one, however, that was launched by a form when we needed some processing done that didn't require another, independent form (the APPSIZE script).

secondary index   A file containing one of a table's secondary indexes, or just the secondary index itself. The context of the statement using the term usually makes clear which meaning is indicated.

sidebar   The vertical bar at the extreme left side of the report design window, used to set page breaks. This book used this feature in a couple of the AR/AP reports.

table   A collection of data records maintained by Paradox for Windows, with your information in them. Actually, a Paradox table consists of several files; the .DB file is the one with the main body of your data records. Other files in the table's *family* include index files (such as the .PX primary index file), memo/ BLOB files (.MB files), field validation files (.VAL files), and others.

table frame   A design object placed on a form for displaying a table's records. Note that a table frame is not the same as the table. The table frame is said to be *over* the table. When you edit fields and records in a table frame, changes must be posted to the underlying table. In the User Administration utility, you saw how to dynamically bind a table to a table frame while running a form (as opposed to defining the table frame's table in design mode).

toolbar   The ribbon of iconic buttons at the top of the desktop window for selecting frequently used tools and actions. The text tool, for example, enables you to drop a text field onto a form in its design window. Other tools include pushbutton, graphic, field, chart, and crosstab.

UIObject   A User Interface Object. These are the objects you drop onto forms and reports and can customize for the behavior you want. A pushbutton, for example, is a UIObject.

validity check   A limitation on what a user can put into a field, defined by you while creating or restructuring the table. This is one very important means of ensuring the integrity of the table's data.

B

Contents of the
Companion
CD-ROM

A list of all the files contained on the sample CD-ROM is contained in this appendix, plus the installation instructions. Each file is listed with the installation requirement appended to the filename, in parentheses. There are two classes of installation files: always installed, and optional.

To install all the sample material from the CD-ROM to your hard drive, you will need about 10MB of free space on your hard drive. If you choose to install just the required files, you will need about 7MB. Even if you install all the files, the sample video clips remain on the CD-ROM; they are too large to install on the hard drive.

To use all the features of the DPW sample applications, you will need a Sound Blaster or compatible sound card on your system, as well as the CD-ROM drive for installation. The basic functions of the sample code, however, can function without sound support.

To install the sample applications and files on your hard drive where you can use them, perform the following steps:

1. Place the CD-ROM disk in the CD-ROM drive. Let's assume this drive is E:, for illustrating the install process.

2. Start Paradox for Windows and change the current working directory to E:\BUILDAPP (using your real CD-ROM drive's address).

3. Open the DPWINSTL.FDL form. You can do this by using the Project Viewer, listing the forms, and double-clicking on DPWINSTL.FDL. Alternatively, you can choose **File | Open | Form** from the Desktop menu, and either select the form from the browse window or type it in.

4. Click the radio buttons on the installation form until they reflect your computer's configuration. You will need to indicate the CD-ROM drive, the drive location of the \WINDOWS directory, and the drive where you want to install the sample material.

5. Click the checkbox for Video for Windows installation on or off. If you don't have these drivers at all, or just want to update them to the latest releases, check this option on. Video for Windows installation will follow DPW installation.

6. When you have all the buttons and checkboxes set up to your satisfaction, click the DO IT pushbutton. DPW, and optionally Video for Windows, will install themselves.

You also can install the DPW software without running Paradox 5 for Windows. Follow these steps to install the files to your hard drive:

1. From Windows File Manager or Program Manager, choose **File | Run** from the menu.

2. Type *x*:INSTALL and press Enter. Substitute your CD-ROM drive letter for *x*. For example, if the disc is in drive G, type G:INSTALL.

3. Choose **F**ull Install to install all the software; choose **C**ustom Install to install only the some of the software. When the installation is complete, the Video for Windows setup program will start automatically.

Once you have installed the sample material, you can start the main user interface to the DPW applications by opening the DPWMAIN.FDL form. There are other forms from the book that are not launched by the main selection panel, but you can refer to the chapters in which these forms are designed and built.

The complete list of sample files is as follows:

ahbk1.db	*(always)* Sample backup table of the AR history table, created by the backup feature of DPWMAIN main selection panel.
ahbk1.px	*(always)* Primary index file for the ahbk1 table.
ahbk1.val	*(always)* Validation file for the ahbk1 table.
ahbk2.db	*(always)* Sample backup table of the AR history table. Created by the backup feature of DPWMAIN main selection panel.
ahbk2.px	*(always)* Primary index file for the ahbk2 table.
ahbk2.val	*(always)* Validation file for the ahbk2 table.
apay.db	*(always)* The AP (Accounts Payable) transaction table. This table is permanently linked to the master table VENDOR by a referential integrity relationship.
apay.fam	*(always)* The AP transaction table's FAM file (related file list).
apay.px	*(always)* The AP transaction table's primary index file.
apay.tv	*(always)* The AP transaction table's table view file.
apay.val	*(always)* The AP transaction table's validation file.
apayhist.db	*(always)* The AP (Accounts Payable) history transaction table. This table is permanently linked to the master table VENDOR by a referential integrity relationship.
apayhist.px	*(always)* The AP transaction table's primary index file.
apayhist.val	*(always)* The AP transaction table's validation file.
appopt.qbe	*(always)* The QBE version of the APPOPT (application optional files) inquiry.
appopt.sql	*(always)* The SQL version of the APPOPT (application optional files) inquiry.
appost.fdl	*(always)* The delivered AP posting form.

B

appost.fsl	*(always)* The source AP posting form.
appreq.qbe	*(always)* The QBE version of the APPREQ (application required files) inquiry.
appreq.sql	*(always)* The SQL version of the APPREQ (application required files) inquiry.
appsize.sdl	*(always)* The delivered version of the APPSIZE application sizing automation ObjectPAL script.
appsize.ssl	*(always)* The source version of the APPSIZE application sizing automation ObjectPAL script.
ar.db	*(always)* The AR (Accounts Receivable) transaction table. This table is permanently linked to the master table CUSTOMER by a referential integrity relationship.
ar.px	*(always)* The AR transaction table's primary index file.
ar.val	*(always)* The AR transaction table's validation file.
ararc.ini	*(always)* The Windows INI file for the AR/AP backup restore system. This INI file stores the current backup version number. The version number will be accessed and then incremented to get ready for the next backup run. The version number is just accessed to determine the current version number, for a restore run.
arbill.rdl	*(always)* The AR billing report, delivered version.
arbill.rsl	*(always)* The AR billing report, source version.
arbk1.db	*(always)* Sample backup table of the AR transaction table; created by the backup feature of DPWMAIN main selection panel.
arbk1.px	*(always)* The primary index files for the arbk1 table.
arbk1.val	*(always)* The validation files for the arbk1 table.
arbk2.db	*(always)* Sample backup table of the AR transaction table; created by the backup feature of DPWMAIN main selection panel.
arbk2.px	*(always)* The primary index files for the arbk2 table.
arbk2.val	*(always)* The validation files for the arbk2 table.
archart.fdl	*(always)* The AR chart by date form, delivered version.
archart.fsl	*(always)* The AR chart by date form, source version.
arcust.rdl	*(always)* The AR customer summary report, delivered.

`arcust.rsl`	*(always)* The AR customer summary report, source.
`arexport.bmp`	*(optional)* An optional Windows bitmap file of the AREXPORT window that you can use to modify the AREXPORT Windows help document, using the Hotspot editor (if that is available to you).
`arexport.fdl`	*(always)* The AR export data form, delivered version.
`arexport.fsl`	*(always)* The AR export data form, source version.
`arexport.hlp`	*(always)* The "live" Windows help file for the AR export data application.
`arexport.hpj`	*(optional)* The AR export project file for the Windows help compiler.
`arexport.rtf`	*(optional)* The Rich Text Format document file for the AR export data help system
`arexport.shg`	*(optional)* The segmented graphics file that was created by the hotspot editor for the AR export data help document. Multiple areas of the bitmap have been defined as hotspots for the help engine, so that it will know what topic to jump to when a user clicks on part of the image.
`arhist.db`	*(always)* The AR history transaction table. This file is permanently linked to the CUSTOMER table with a referential integrity relationship.
`arhist.px`	*(always)* The primary index file for the AR history table.
`arhist.val`	*(always)* The validation file for the AR history table.
`arinq.fdl`	*(always)* The AR inquiry form, delivered version. The six canned inquiries for the AR system are launched from here, depending on user choices made in the form.
`arinq.fsl`	*(always)* The AR inquiry form, source version.
`armail.rdl`	*(always)* The AR Mailing Labels report, delivered version.
`armail.rsl`	*(always)* The AR Mailing Labels report, source version.
`armassc.fdl`	*(always)* The AR Mass Charge posting form, delivered version.
`armassc.fsl`	*(always)* The AR Mass Charge posting form, source version.
`armassc.hlp`	*(always)* The AR Mass Charge Windows help document.
`armassc.hpj`	*(optional)* The AR Mass Charge project file for the Windows help compiler.

B

`armassc.rtf`	*(optional)* The Rich Text Format document for the AR Mass Charge help system.
`arpost.fdl`	*(always)* The AR Posting form, delivered version. This is where all AR transactions and payments against transactions are posted.
`arpost.fsl`	*(always)* The AR Posting form, source version.
`arrecv.rdl`	*(always)* The AR Receivables Detail report, delivered version.
`arrecv.rsl`	*(always)* The AR Receivables Detail report, source version.
`arxtab.fdl`	*(always)* The AR Crosstab form, showing a crosstab of receivables by customer and date, delivered version.
`arxtab.fsl`	*(always)* The AR Crosstab form, showing a crosstab of receivables by customer and date, source version.
`autosize.fdl`	*(always)* The application sizing automation tool, used when designing the delivery package for a finished application, delivered version.
`autosize.fsl`	*(always)* The application sizing automation tool, used when designing the delivery package for a finished application, source version.
`ball3.bmp`	*(optional)* The 3D ball logo for the book, Windows bitmap format.
`ball3.shg`	*(optional)* The 3D ball logo for the book, Windows segmented hypergraphics format.
`cap01.jpg`	*(optional)* The JPEG format image for the first frame of the El Capitan AVI clip that was used briefly to illustrate the PW Multimedia Theater.
`cap01.pcx`	*(optional)* The Paintbrush format image for the first frame of the El Capitan AVI clip that was used briefly to illustrate the PW Multimedia Theater.
`cap02.jpg`	*(optional)* The JPEG format image for the second frame of the El Capitan AVI clip that was used briefly to illustrate the PW Multimedia Theater.
`cap02.pcx`	*(optional)* The Paintbrush format image for the second frame of the El Capitan AVI clip that was used briefly to illustrate the PW Multimedia Theater.

cap03.jpg	*(optional)* The JPEG format image for the third frame of the El Capitan AVI clip that was used briefly to illustrate the PW Multimedia Theater.
cap03.pcx	*(optional)* The Paintbrush format image for the third frame of the El Capitan AVI clip that was used briefly to illustrate the PW Multimedia Theater.
cap04.jpg	*(optional)* The JPEG format image for the fourth frame of the El Capitan AVI clip that was used briefly to illustrate the PW Multimedia Theater.
cap04.pcx	*(optional)* The Paintbrush format image for the fourth frame of the El Capitan AVI clip that was used briefly to illustrate the PW Multimedia Theater.
cd001.bmp	*(optional)* The Windows bitmap format image of the first frame of the CDLOAD, and fifth frame of the CDUNLOAD sample AVI clips.
cd001.jpg	*(optional)* The JPEG format image of the first frame of the CDLOAD, and fifth frame of the CDUNLOAD sample AVI clips.
cd002.bmp	*(optional)* The Windows bitmap format image of the second frame of the CDLOAD, and fourth frame of the CDUNLOAD sample AVI clips.
cd002.jpg	*(optional)* The JPEG format image of the second frame of the CDLOAD, and fourth frame of the CDUNLOAD sample AVI clips.
cd003.bmp	*(optional)* The Windows bitmap format image of the third frame of the CDLOAD, and third frame of the CDUNLOAD sample AVI clips.
cd003.jpg	*(optional)* The JPEG format image of the third frame of the CDLOAD, and third frame of the CDUNLOAD sample AVI clips.
cd004.bmp	*(optional)* The Windows bitmap format image of the fourth frame of the CDLOAD, and second frame of the CDUNLOAD sample AVI clips.
cd004.jpg	*(optional)* The JPEG format image of the fourth frame of the CDLOAD, and second frame of the CDUNLOAD sample AVI clips.

cd005.bmp	*(optional)* The Windows bitmap format image of the fifth frame of the CDLOAD, and first frame of the CDUNLOAD sample AVI clips.
cd005.jpg	*(optional)* The JPEG format image of the fifth frame of the CDLOAD, and first frame of the CDUNLOAD sample AVI clips.
choose.bmp	*(optional)* A Windows bitmap image used to label a pushbutton in the PW Multimedia Theater application.
class.db	*(always)* A Tabular enumeration of ObjectPAL classes, created by the REFDATA application.
class.px	*(always)* The primary index file for the class table.
close.bmp	*(optional)* A Windows bitmap image used to label a pushbutton in the PW Multimedia Theater application.
cmedia.c	*(optional)* The C-language source code for the Windows help system multimedia interface (DLL) constructed while building components of the AR/AP system.
cmedia.def	*(optional)* The Windows DEF file for the CMEDIA C-language DLL project. Used by the C compiler while building the DLL executable file.
cmedia.dll	*(always)* The executable Windows help system multimedia interface used by some of the AR/AP system's Windows help documents.
cmedia.dsk	*(optional)* A desktop file used by the Borland C compiler, for building the CMEDIA project. If you are one of the brave ones and want to tinker with the little bit of C code that comes with this book, you will need this and several other files as well.
cmedia.obj	*(optional)* The unlinked machine code output from the compiler for the CMEDIA.C source compilation.
cmedia.prj	*(optional)* The Borland C/C++ project file for building the CMEDIA DLL multimedia interface.
commdlg.dll	*(always)* A redistributable common dialog DLL from the Windows SDK. This DLL is used by the GETFILE.DLL you integrated into the AR/AP systems.
constant.db	*(always)* A Tabular enumeration of ObjectPAL constants, created by the REFDATA application.

constant.px	*(always)* The primary index file for the constant table.
cubk1.db	*(always)* Sample backup table of the AR customer table; created by the backup feature of DPWMAIN main selection panel.
cubk1.fam	*(always)* The cubk1 table's FAM file (related file list).
cubk1.px	*(always)* The cubk1 table's primary index file.
cubk1.tv	*(always)* The cubk1 table's table view settings file.
cubk1.val	*(always)* The cubk1 table's validation file.
cubk2.db	*(always)* Sample backup table of the AR customer table; created by the backup feature of DPWMAIN main selection panel.
cubk2.fam	*(always)* The cubk2 table's FAM file (related file list).
cubk2.px	*(always)* The cubk2 table's primary index file.
cubk2.tv	*(always)* The cubk2 table's table view settings file.
cubk2.val	*(always)* The cubk1 table's validation file.
custbal.qbe	*(always)* The customer balance query, QBE format.
custbal.sql	*(always)* The customer balance query, SQL format.
custdetl.rdl	*(always)* The customer detail report, delivered format.
custdetl.rsl	*(always)* The customer detail report, source format.
customer.db	*(always)* The AR customer table. This is the master table for the AR side of the application; the transaction and transaction history files are linked to this table permanently with a referential integrity relationship.
customer.fam	*(always)* The customer table's FAM file.
customer.px	*(always)* The customer table's primary index.
customer.tv	*(always)* The customer table's table view file.
customer.val	*(always)* The customer table's validation file.
dbanswer.db	*(always)* The overridden answer table for queries and some of the utilities.
dbutil.fdl	*(always)* The database and query manager utility, delivered version.
dbutil.fsl	*(always)* The database and query manager utility, source version.

dpwinstl.fdl	*(always)* The DPW installation procedure form, delivered version.
dpwinstl.fsl	*(always)* The DPW installation procedure form, source version.
dpwmain.fdl	*(always)* The DPW Main Selection Panel form, delivered version. This is the main entry point into the AR/AP system.
dpwmain.fsl	*(always)* The DPW Main Selection Panel form, source version. This is the main entry point into the AR/AP system.
dpwmain.hlp	*(always)* The Windows help file for the Main Selection Panel.
dpwmain.hpj	*(optional)* The DPWMAIN project file for the Windows help compiler.
dpwmain.rtf	*(optional)* The Rich Text Format file input to the Windows help compiler for the DPWMAIN help system.
editfile.exe	*(always)* The DPW NotePad stand-alone scratch pad utility. Since this is a C language program and is included "just for fun," there is no source for this program.
edmmfile.fdl	*(always)* A Support form for the Multimedia Theater, for prompting the user for a filename for storing a WAV file that was just recorded. Delivered version.
edmmfile.fsl	*(always)* A Support form for the Multimedia Theater, for prompting the user for a filename for storing a WAV file that was just recorded. Source version.
elcap.avi	*(optional)* The El Capitan full-motion video clip. This was put together using VistaPro to generate the discrete scenes (the key frames) and PhotoMorph to create the AVI file from the scenes.
fforward.bmp	*(optional)* A Windows bitmap image used to label a pushbutton in the PW Multimedia Theater application.
film.bmp	*(optional)* A Windows bitmap image that can be used to label a pushbutton.
formdn.bmp	*(optional)* A Windows bitmap image used to label pushbuttons in some of the AR/AP application forms.
formlist.fdl	*(always)* A Windows bitmap image used to label pushbuttons in some of the AR/AP application forms.
formlist.fsl	*(always)* A Windows bitmap image used to label pushbuttons in some of the AR/AP application forms.

B

`formlt.bmp`	*(optional)* A Windows bitmap image used to label pushbuttons in some of the AR/AP application forms.
`formrt.bmp`	*(optional)* A Windows bitmap image used to label pushbuttons in some of the AR/AP application forms.
`formup.bmp`	*(optional)* A Windows bitmap image used to label pushbuttons in some of the AR/AP application forms.
`forward.bmp`	*(optional)* A Windows bitmap image used to label pushbuttons in some of the AR/AP application forms.
`frog2chk.avi`	*(optional)* A sample AVI file, generated from the PhotoMorph samples.
`getfile.c`	*(optional)* The C-language source for the GETFILE DLL module, used to select input files, Windows-style.
`getfile.def`	*(optional)* The compiler DEF file for the GETFILE DLL module.
`getfile.dll`	*(always)* The GETFILE executable DLL module.
`getfile.dsk`	*(optional)* The compiler's desktop file for the GETFILE project.
`getfile.lib`	*(optional)* Compiler output from the GETFILE project.
`getfile.obj`	*(optional)* Compiler output from the GETFILE project.
`getfile.prj`	*(optional)* The compiler project file for GETFILE.
`gethelp.bmp`	*(optional)* A Windows bitmap image used to label pushbuttons in some of the AR/AP application forms.
`infiles.db`	*(always)* The master distribution file list for the DPW installation utility.
`infiles.fam`	*(always)* The `infiles` table's FAM file.
`infiles.tv`	*(always)* The `infiles` table's table view file.
`isclosed.bmp`	*(optional)* A Windows bitmap image used to label pushbuttons in some of the AR/AP application forms.
`isopen.bmp`	*(optional)* A Windows bitmap image used to label pushbuttons in some of the AR/AP application forms.
`ixanswer.db`	*(optional)* An output file from the Table Utilities form, used to hold index structures while a table is being cloned.
`lister.bmp`	*(optional)* A Windows bitmap image used to label pushbuttons in some of the AR/AP application forms.
`loadcd.avi`	*(optional)* The load CD video example.

mainhelp.db	*(optional)* The `mainhelp` table. This table was used to collate and collect the topics and topic numbers for the DPWMAIN help system. For a help file of any size or complexity, it is a good idea to organize the help topics this way.
mainhelp.px	*(optional)* The primary index file for the `mainhelp` table.
menus.fdl	*(always)* The `menus` form, delivered version. This form was supplied to illustrate how to create Windows-style menus using ObjectPAL, but was not used to build the main application.
menus.fsl	*(always)* The `menus` form, source version.
method.db	*(always)* The ObjectPAL methods reference table, created by the REFDATA application. This is one of the handiest tables I have ever discovered.
method.px	*(always)* The primary index file for the `method` table.
mmcntrl.bmp	*(optional)* The original Paintbrush file in which all the graphic controls for the Multimedia Theater are developed.
mmstills.fdl	*(always)* The Multimedia Stills form, delivered version. This form is launched by the Multimedia Theater (MMT) whenever the user selects a graphic image format file rather than a video or audio file.
mmstills.fsl	*(always)* The Multimedia Stills form, source version.
mute.bmp	*(optional)* A Windows bitmap image used to label a pushbutton in the PW Multimedia Theater application.
open.bmp	*(optional)* A Windows bitmap image used to label a pushbutton in the PW Multimedia Theater application.
pagedn.bmp	*(optional)* A Windows bitmap image used to label pushbuttons in some of the AR/AP application forms.
pagelt.bmp	*(optional)* A Windows bitmap image used to label pushbuttons in some of the AR/AP application forms.
pagert.bmp	*(optional)* A Windows bitmap image used to label pushbuttons in some of the AR/AP application forms.
pageup.bmp	*(optional)* A Windows bitmap image used to label pushbuttons in some of the AR/AP application forms.
pause.bmp	*(optional)* A Windows bitmap image used to label a pushbutton in the PW Multimedia Theater application.

B

pdmhello.wav	*(always)* A "Hello" audio file for the DPW Project Development Manager.
pencil.bmp	*(optional)* A Windows bitmap image used to label pushbuttons in some of the AR/AP application forms.
pencil.ico	*(optional)* An icon image from which the pencil.bmp file was taken.
prjitem.db	*(always)* The items table for the Project Development Manager.
prjitem.px	*(always)* The primary index file for the prjitem table.
prjitem.val	*(always)* The validation file for the prjitem table.
prjmast.db	*(always)* The master table for the Project Development Manager application. One row in this table represents a day's work, whereas a row in the items table shows a discrete task performed on that day.
prjmast.fam	*(always)* The FAM file for the prjmast table.
prjmast.px	*(always)* The primary index file for the prjmast table.
prjmast.tv	*(always)* The table view file for the prjmast table.
prjmast.val	*(always)* The validation file for the prjmast table.
problog.db	*(always)* The problem log table for the USERADM (User Administration) application.
problog.mb	*(always)* The memo/BLOB file for the problog table.
probs.bmp	*(optional)* A Windows bitmap image used to label pushbuttons in some of the AR/AP application forms.
projmgr.fdl	*(always)* The Project Development Manager form, delivered version.
projmgr.fsl	*(always)* The Project Development Manager form, source version.
pwmmplay.fdl	*(always)* The DPW Multimedia Theater form, delivered version.
pwmmplay.fsl	*(always)* The DPW Multimedia Theater form, source version.
record.bmp	*(optional)* A Windows bitmap image used to label a pushbutton in the PW Multimedia Theater application.
refdata.fdl	*(always)* The ObjectPAL Reference Data form, delivered version.

`refdata.fsl`	*(always)* The ObjectPAL Reference Data form, source version.
`reverse.bmp`	*(optional)* A Windows bitmap image used to label a pushbutton in the PW Multimedia Theater application.
`rewind.bmp`	*(optional)* A Windows bitmap image used to label a pushbutton in the PW Multimedia Theater application.
`rianswer.db`	*(optional)* A table used to hold referential integrity structure by the TBUTIL form while cloning a table.
`rptmgr.fdl`	*(always)* The DPW Report/Print Manager, delivered version.
`rptmgr.fsl`	*(always)* The DPW Report/Print Manager, source version.
`speakers.bmp`	*(optional)* A Windows bitmap image used to label a pushbutton in the PW Multimedia Theater application.
`speed1.sdl`	*(always)* The Speed-1 test form, delivered version.
`speed1.ssl`	*(always)* The Speed-1 test form, source version.
`speed2.sdl`	*(always)* The Speed-2 test form, delivered version.
`speed2.ssl`	*(always)* The Speed-2 test form, source version.
`speed3.sdl`	*(always)* The Speed-3 test form, delivered version.
`speed3.ssl`	*(always)* The Speed-3 test form, source version.
`step.bmp`	*(optional)* A Windows bitmap image used to label a pushbutton in the PW Multimedia Theater application.
`stepback.bmp`	*(optional)* A Windows bitmap image used to label a pushbutton in the PW Multimedia Theater application.
`stop.bmp`	*(optional)* A Windows bitmap image used to label a pushbutton in the PW Multimedia Theater application.
`stopsign.bmp`	*(optional)* A Windows bitmap image used to label pushbuttons in some of the AR/AP application forms.
`sysctl.fdl`	*(always)* The DPW System Control Panel, delivered version.
`sysctl.fsl`	*(always)* The DPW System Control Panel, source version.
`tbutil.fdl`	*(always)* The DPW Table Utilities form, delivered version.
`tbutil.fsl`	*(always)* The DPW Table Utilities form, source version.
`testhypr.fdl`	*(always)* The test hyperdocument form, delivered version.
`testhypr.fsl`	*(always)* The test hyperdocument form, source version.
`testmmt.fdl`	*(always)* The Test MMT form, delivered version. The Test MMT form demonstrates launching the Multimedia Theater form remotely.

`testmmt.fsl`	*(always)* The Test MMT form, source version.
`testole2.fsl`	*(always)* The test OLE2 form, source version only. This form tests pasting OLE2 objects directly onto forms.
`uiclass.db`	*(always)* The UIObject class reference table, created by the REFDATA application.
`uiclass.px`	*(always)* The primary index file for the `uiclass` table.
`unloadcd.avi`	*(optional)* The unload CD video clip.
`useradm.fdl`	*(always)* The User Administration form, delivered version.
`useradm.fsl`	*(always)* The User Administration form, source version.
`userlist.db`	*(always)* The user list table for the USERADM application.
`userlist.mb`	*(always)* The memo/BLOB file for the `userlist` table.
`userlist.px`	*(always)* The primary index file for the `userlist` table.
`vendor.db`	*(always)* The AP vendor master table. The APAY and APAYHIST tables are permanently linked to this table using referential integrity relationships.
`vendor.fam`	*(always)* The FAM file for the `vendor` table.
`vendor.px`	*(always)* The primary index file for the `vendor` table.
`vendor.tv`	*(always)* The table view file for the `vendor` table.
`vendor.val`	*(always)* The validation file for the `vendor` table.
`vnextbtn.bmp`	*(optional)* A Windows bitmap graphic image for the *Voice Notes!* application.
`vnextbtn.shg`	*(optional)* A Windows segmented graphic image (hotspot) for the *Voice Notes!* application.
`vnextbtn.wav`	*(always)* A WAV file used by the *Voice Notes!* application.
`vnhelp.wav`	*(always)* A WAV file used by the *Voice Notes!* application.
`vnhlpbtn.bmp`	*(optional)* A Windows bitmap graphic image for the *Voice Notes!* application.
`vnhlpbtn.shg`	*(optional)* A Windows segmented graphic image (hotspot) for the *Voice Notes!* application.
`vnhlpbtn.wav`	*(always)* A WAV file used by the *Voice Notes!* application.
`vnotes.db`	*(always)* The *Voice Notes!* audio notepad's master table.
`vnotes.fdl`	*(always)* The *Voice Notes!* application form, delivered version.
`vnotes.fsl`	*(always)* The *Voice Notes!* application form, source version.

`vnotes.hlp`	*(always)* The Windows help file for the *Voice Notes!* application.
`vnotes.hpj`	*(optional)* The Windows help project file for *Voice Notes!*
`vnotes.ini`	*(always)* The *Voice Notes!* Windows INI file. This file will be customized and copied to the Windows directory when you run the installation utility.
`vnotes.mb`	*(always)* The *Voice Notes!* table's memo/BLOB file.
`vnotes.px`	*(always)* The *Voice Notes!* table's primary index file.
`vnotes.rtf`	*(optional)* The Rich Text Format source document for the *Voice Notes!* help system.
`vnotes.val`	*(always)* The *Voice Notes!* table's validation file.
`vnotes.wav`	*(always)* A WAV file used by the *Voice Notes!* application.
`vnplabtn.bmp`	*(optional)* A Windows bitmap graphic image for the *Voice Notes!* application.
`vnplabtn.shg`	*(optional)* A Windows segmented graphic image (hostspot) for the *Voice Notes!* application.
`vnplabtn.wav`	*(always)* A WAV file used by the *Voice Notes!* application.
`vnquibtn.bmp`	*(optional)* A Windows bitmap graphic image for the *Voice Notes!* application.
`vnquibtn.shg`	*(optional)* A Windows segmented graphic image (hostspot) for the *Voice Notes!* application.
`vnquibtn.wav`	*(always)* A WAV file used by the *Voice Notes!* application.
`vnrecbtn.bmp`	*(optional)* A Windows bitmap graphic image for the *Voice Notes!* application.
`vnrecbtn.shg`	*(optional)* A Windows segmented graphic image (hostspot) for the *Voice Notes!* application.
`vnrecbtn.wav`	*(always)* A WAV file used by the *Voice Notes!* application.
`vnstpbtn.bmp`	*(optional)* A Windows bitmap graphic image for the *Voice Notes!* application.
`vnstpbtn.shg`	*(optional)* A Windows segmented graphic image (hostspot) for the *Voice Notes!* application.
`vnstpbtn.wav`	*(always)* A WAV file used by the *Voice Notes!* application.
`welcome.wav`	*(always)* A sample WAV file you can play with the Multimedia Theater.

JASMINE1.AVI, AIRJET.AVI, RAFTING.AVI are copyrights of Jasmine Multimedia Publishing.

Building WinHelp
Databases

To create a Windows help file, you need three things: the Windows 3.1 help compiler (HC31.EXE), a help project file for the particular help file you are building, and a Rich Text Format (RTF) document as the primary input to the help compiler.

You can get the Windows help compiler from either the Windows SDK, or from a professional version of a major compiler, such as the Borland C/C++ Professional compiler package. You will have to compose the other components of the help project. This appendix contains reference material you can use for creating the project files and RTF files you need for building Windows help.

Help project files are divided into sections, much like INI files are. Each section is introduced by the section name in square brackets. The help project files you see in this book, for example, all begin with the [OPTIONS] section.

You can place comments in a Windows help project file. Use a semicolon (;) to introduce a comment. The help compiler will ignore all the text from the semicolon to the end of the line. Blank lines are also permitted in a project file. All help project file statements begin in column 1.

All the possible sections in a help file, with all their possible statements, are as follows:

[OPTIONS]:	Specifies options that control the help compiler's operation. This section is optional, but if used, it should be the first section to appear in the help project file.
BMROOT	Designates the directory in which the compiler can find the bitmap files used in bmc, bml, and bmr references in the Help topic files. You can specify multiple paths in this statement, as follows: BMROOT=*pathname[,pathname...]*
BUILD	Determines which topics to include or exclude in the build. Use the BUILD statement only if you define build tags in the RTF document(s) and in the [BUILDTAGS] section. The BUILD option uses the following syntax: BUILD=*expression* where *expression* is composed of build tag names in a logical expression with the following operators: ( ) Parentheses & AND operator ¦ OR operator ~ NOT operator tag Build tag

COMPRESS	Specifies what type of compression to use during the build. There are several forms of compression you can apply to the help file:
	The following forms of the option specify no compression:

```
COMPRESS = NO
COMPRESS = FALSE
COMPRESS = 0
```

	The following form of the option specifies medium compression:

```
COMPRESS = MEDIUM
```

	The following forms of the option specify high compression (block and key-phrase):

```
COMPRESS = YES
COMPRESS = TRUE
COMPRESS = 1
COMPRESS = HIGH
```

CONTENTS	Specifies the context string of the contents topic for a Help file. This optional statement enables you to predefine the context string for the main contents topic, as follows:
	`CONTENTS=context-string`
COPYRIGHT	Adds a unique copyright message for the Help file to the About dialog box. This statement specifies a text string of your choosing:
	`COPYRIGHT=copyright-notice`
ERRORLOG	Puts compilation errors in a file during the build. This statement simply names the text file in which the error log should be recorded:
	`ERRORLOG=textfile.ext`
FORCEFONT	Forces all authored fonts in the RTF files to appear in a different font when displayed in the Help file. Specify this optional statement as
	`FORCEFONT=fontname`
	where font name can be any font that appears in the Fonts dialog box of the Windows Control Panel. Font names cannot exceed 20 characters.

Building WinHelp Databases

ICON	Specifies the icon file to be displayed when the Help file is minimized: `ICON=iconfile.ICO`
LANGUAGE	Specifies a different sort ordering for Help files authored in a Scandinavian language. There is only one possible value for this option: `LANGUAGE=scandinavian`
MAPFONTSIZE	Maps a font size in the RTF file to a different font size in the compiled Help file. The syntax is as follows: `MAPFONTSIZE=m[-n]:p` meaning to change font size m [optionally through range n] to font size p in the output help document.
MULTIKEY	Specifies an alternate keyword table to use for mapping topics. You specify a case-sensitive character to use for the topic's footnote, as follows: `MULTIKEY=footnotechar`
OLDKEYPHRASE	Designates whether the compiler should use the existing key-phrase table or create a new one during the build.

OPTCDROM	Optimizes the Help file for CD-ROM use. Any of the following statements will turn this option on:
	
	`OPTCDROM = YES`
	`OPTCDROM = TRUE`
	`OPTCDROM = 1`
	`OPTCDROM = ON`

REPORT	Controls the display of messages during the build process. To get more detailed messages about the build process, specify `REPORT=ON`
ROOT	Designates the directories used to locate topic and data files listed in the project file. There can be more than one root path. If there are, all paths specified will be searched by the Windows help compiler, looking for a topic file. The syntax is `ROOT=path[,path...]`

<table>
<tr><td>TITLE</td><td>Specifies the text that is displayed in the title bar of the Help window when the file is open. You can specify a title of up to 50 characters, as follows:

TITLE=titlestring</td></tr>
<tr><td>WARNING</td><td>Indicates the level of error message reporting the compiler displays during the build. The warning levels are as follows:

WARNING=1 ; Reports only several errors
WARNING=2 ; Reports intermediate-level errors
WARNING=3 ; Reports all errors; use this at first</td></tr>
<tr><td>[FILES]</td><td>Specifies the topic files to be included in the help build. This section is always required. You can simply list the individual filenames, which can include drive and path specifications; or you can list them in another file and use the #include directive, as follows:

#include <<em>filename</em>></td></tr>
<tr><td>[BUILDTAGS]</td><td>Specifies build tags for the build. This section is optional. Use this section only if you include build tags in the topic (RTF) files and you specify which topics to include in the build with the BUILD statement in the [OPTIONS] statement.</td></tr>
<tr><td>[CONFIG]</td><td>Specifies user-defined menus, buttons, and built-in macros used in the help file, and registers DLLs and DLL functions used as macros within the Help file. This section is required if the Help file uses any of these features. This section was used, you may recall, to set up the CMEDIA DLL for the VNOTES help project. The RegisterRoutine() was used to define CMEDIA.DLL and its call arguments. The general syntax of the RegisterRoutine() statement is as follows:

RegisterRoutine("DLL-name", "function-name", "format-spec")

The RegisterRoutine() macro registers a function within a DLL with WinHelp. Registered functions can be used in macro footnotes within topic files, or in the [CONFIG] section of the project file—the same as standard Help macros. The parameters used by RegisterRoutine() are as follows:</td></tr>
</table>

DLL-name	The filename of the DLL being called. The filename must appear in quotation marks. If WinHelp cannot find the DLL, it displays an error message and does not perform the call.
function-name	The function executed in the designated DLL.
format-spec	Contains a string specifying the formats of parameters passed to the function. The format string must appear in quotation marks. Characters in the string represent C parameter types, as follows:

u   unsigned short (WORD)
U   unsigned long (DWORD)
i   short int
I   int
s   near char * (PSTR)
S   far char * (LPSTR)
v   void

Look at the VNOTES help project to see the RegisterRoutine() used in a real setting.

[BITMAPS]	Specifies bitmap files to be included in the build. If segmented graphic files containing hotspots are used by the help document, they are also included here (using the .SHG file extension). This section is *not* required if the project file lists a path for bitmap files using the BMROOT or ROOT option. I usually include this section to document what I have done in the help project.
[MAP]	Associates context strings with context numbers. This section is optional. For use with Paradox for Windows, I always code at least a contents=1 map entry, where contents is the actual context string of the contents topic.
[ALIAS]	Assigns one or more context strings to the same topic. This section is optional.
[WINDOWS]	Defines the characteristics of the primary help window and secondary windows used in the Help file. This section is required if the Help file uses secondary windows.
[BAGGAGE]	Lists files that are to be placed within the help file's .HLP file, which contains its own file system. This section is optional.

The RTF document that is the primary input to the help compiler must have a specific format. In discussing that format, I will assume that you are using the Word for Windows word processor, since that is the only one I have ever found that has all the combinations of features you need to create your RTF help document.

The RTF document must have the following characteristics:

☐ The RTF document is composed of a series of topics, which are separated by hard page breaks (use the Ctrl+Enter keys to create a hard page break).

☐ The contents topic should be the first topic in the RTF document.

☐ At the beginning of the first paragraph of every topic, you must specify one or more special footnotes that tell the help compiler things about the topic, such as its context string (required), the topic title string, and search keywords for the topic (optional but highly recommended).

☐ Bitmaps can be inserted directly into the document. There are WinHelp macros for this, which are illustrated in Day 11, "Writing the Application's Online Documentation." The easiest way, however, is to just insert them directly.

The footnotes used in a WinHelp RTF document must use certain special, predefined footnote characters. To see footnote characters in use, consult Day 11. The following list tells you what all the available footnote characters are

*	Build tag for the current topic.
#	Context string of the current topic.
$	Title string of the current topic.
+	Browse sequence number of the current topic.
K	Keywords for the current topic.
n	Alternative keywords for the current topic. The placeholder n represents a letter other than K, which is reserved for regular keywords.
!	Execution macros of the current topic.

WinHelp macros can be specified either in the [CONFIG] section of the project file, or in a topic's ! footnote. If a macro is embedded in a topic, it is executed as soon as the topic is entered. The following list contains all possible WinHelp macros:

About	Displays the About dialog box
AddAccelerator	Assigns a macro to an accelerator key

Annotate	Displays the Annotation dialog box
AppendItem	Appends a menu item
Back	Displays the previous topic in the history list
BookmarkDefine	Displays the Define dialog box
BookmarkMore	Displays the More dialog box
BrowseButtons	Adds browse buttons
ChangeButtonBinding	Assigns a macro to a button
ChangeItemBinding	Assigns a macro to a menu item
CheckItem	Checks a menu item
CloseWindow	Closes a window
Contents	Displays the contents topic
CopyDialog	Displays the Copy dialog box
CopyTopic	Copies current topic to the clipboard
CreateButton	Adds a new button to the button bar
DeleteItem	Removes a menu item
DeleteMark	Deletes a text marker
DestroyButton	Removes a button from the button bar
DisableButton	Disables a button
DisableItem	Disables a menu item
EnableButton	Enables a button
EnableItem	Enables a menu item
ExecProgram	Executes a program
Exit	Exits WinHelp
FileOpen	Displays the Open dialog box
FocusWindow	Changes the focus window
GotoMark	Jumps to a marker
HelpOn	Displays the Help on Using topic
HelpOnTop	Toggles on-top state of help
History	Displays the history list
IfThen	Executes macro if the marker exists
IfThenElse	Executes one of two macros if the marker exists
InsertItem	Inserts a menu item

InsertMenu	Inserts a new menu
IsMark	Tests if a marker is set
JumpContents	Jumps to the contents topic
JumpContext	Jumps to the specified context
JumpHelpOn	Jumps to Using Help file
JumpId	Jumps to the specified topic
JumpKeyword	Jumps to the topic containing the keyword
Next	Displays the next topic in the browse sequence
Not	Reverses the IsMark macro
PopupContext	Displays a topic in a popup window, using a context string
PopupId	Displays a topic in a popup window, using a context ID number
PositionWindow	Sets the size and position of a window
Prev	Displays the previous topic in browse sequence
Print	Prints the current topic
PrinterSetup	Displays the Printer Setup dialog box
RegisterRoutine	Registers a DLL function
SaveMark	Saves a marker
Search	Displays the Search dialog box
SetContents	Sets the Contents topic
SetHelpOnFile	Sets the Using Help help file
UncheckItem	Unchecks a menu item

Running the help compiler is quite easy, though it must be done either from DOS or from a DOS window, if running Windows. (You may not have sufficient memory for this option, though; I frequently don't.) To invoke the help compiler, first make sure that HC31.EXE is either in your current directory or available through the DOS PATH statement, and type in the following command:

```
HC31 projectfile.HPJ
```

where *projectfile* is the name of your help project file. If you get error messages, correct the problems and rerun the help compiler until you get no error messages.

The VNOTES help project was dissected in detail in Day 11. You can refer to that chapter for information on how to put a help project file and RTF document together,

and even on how to create segmented hypergraphic images as hotspots for your help document. Since other help projects were not documented there, they are included in this appendix for reference. The RTF documents that go with them are included on the CD-ROM; so you can look at them directly with your word processor. Note that only the HLP files are always-install files: you may have to go back and install the optional files from the CD-ROM to see the other documents.

The AREXPORT.HPJ project file has the following contents (change the drive name in path specifications to wherever you installed the sample software):

```
[OPTIONS]
ROOT=D:\BUILDAPP
TITLE=DPW AR Export
WARNING=3

[BITMAPS]
arexport.shg

[FILES]
arexport.rtf

[MAP]
contents 1
```

The ARMASSC.HPJ project file has the following contents:

```
[OPTIONS]
ROOT=D:\BUILDAPP
TITLE=DPW AR Post Mass Charges
WARNING=3

[FILES]
armassc.rtf

[MAP]
contents 1
```

The DPWMAIN.HPJ project file has the following contents:

```
[OPTIONS]
ROOT=D:\BUILDAPP
TITLE=DPW Main Selection Panel
WARNING=3

[FILES]
dpwmain.rtf

[MAP]
contents    1
postar      2
exportar    3
archivear   4
```

```
bill          5
masscharge    6
armailview    7
arinq         8
arback        9
arrestore    10
arviewhist   11
billprint    12
armailprint  13
postap       14
exportap     15
archiveap    16
pay          17
apmailview   18
apinq        19
apback       20
aprestore    21
apviewhist   22
payprint     23
apmailprint  24
mmt          25
tabutil      26
dbutil       27
sysctl       28
playcd       29
stopcd       30
vnotes       31
rptmgr       32
quit         33
```

As you can see, only the DPWMAIN.HPJ project file has a complete map of all the topics so that the individual topics may be invoked directly from different applications.

Multimedia
Reference
Summary

In this appendix, you will find summaries of Windows Multimedia specifications. This is not a multimedia tutorial: you can consult several of Ron Wodaski's books from Sams on this subject. The material presented here is only meant to round out the practical examples of multimedia programming presented in this book. After all, the best way to learn a subject is to do it, and nowhere is that more fun than with multimedia.

First, the following list presents all the standard Windows multimedia device types:

animation	Animation device
cdaudio	CD audio player
dat	Digital audio tape player
digitalvideo	Digital video in a window (not GDI-based)
other	Undefined MCI device
overlay	Overlay device (analog video in a window)
scanner	Image scanner
sequencer	MIDI sequencer
vcr	Videocassette recorder or player
videodisc	Videodisc player
waveaudio	Audio device that plays digitized waveform files

You probably recognize the types of multimedia devices that you wrote ObjectPAL (and a little bit of C) for. The *animation* device was used to play the AVI clips, and the *waveaudio* device was used to play my voice notes to you. The *cdaudio* device type was used to play your favorite music (by the CDAudio feature of the DPW Main Selection Panel).

Note that Windows comes out of the box with only the *sequencer* and *waveaudio* drivers. For video clips, you have to have the Video for Windows drivers (which you get with this book) or other third-party drivers.

The next list summarizes the *animation* device-type commands, many of which are used in this book:

capability	Obtains the capabilities of a device
close	Closes the device
info	Obtains textual information from a device
open	Initializes the device

pause	Pauses the device
play	Starts playing an animation sequence
put	Defines the source, destination, and frame windows
realize	Tells the device to select and realize its palette into a display context of the displayed window
set	Sets the operating state of the device
status	Obtains status information from the device
step	Steps the play one or more frames forward or reverse
stop	Stops playing
update	Repaints the current frame into the display context
where	Obtains the rectangle specifying the source or destination area
window	Tells the device to use a given window for display instead of the default window

The following list summarizes the commands for the *waveaudio* device. This book used many of these commands, too:

capability	Obtains the capabilities of a device
close	Closes the device
cue	Prepares for playing or recording
delete	Deletes a data segment from the MCI element
info	Obtains textual information from a device
open	Initializes the device
pause	Pauses playing or recording
play	Starts transmitting output data
record	Starts recording input data
resume	Resumes playing or recording on a paused device
save	Saves data to a disk file
seek	Seeks forward or backward
set	Sets the operating state of the device
status	Obtains status information from the device
stop	Stops playing or recording

The CDAudio commands were some of the simplest commands used in this book, but they yielded some of the most pleasing results. The *cdaudio* device commands supported are as follows:

capability	Obtains the capabilities of a device
close	Closes the device
info	Obtains textual information from a device
open	Initializes the device
pause	Pauses playing
play	Starts playing the device
resume	Resumes playing or recording on a paused device
seek	Seeks forward or backward
set	Sets the operating state of the device
status	Obtains status information from the device
stop	Stops playing

There is a required set of commands that every multimedia device must support. These required commands include the following:

capability	Obtains the capabilities of a device
close	Closes the device
info	Obtains textual information from a device
open	Initializes the device
status	Obtains status information from the device

There is also a handful of system commands that can be used to control the multimedia system. These commands are as follows:

break	Sets a break key for an MCI device
sound	Plays sounds from the [sounds] section of the WIN.INI file
sysinfo	Returns information about MCI devices

You saw throughout the book how command strings were passed to the MCI system (MMSYSTEM.DLL). Every Paradox form that uses the MCI string command services must have a USES block attached to the form, as follows:

```
Uses MMSYSTEM
  mciSendString( lpstrCommand CPTR, lpstrReturn CPTR,
                 wReturnLng CWORD, hCallBack CWORD ) CLONG
  mciGetErrorString( dwError CLONG, lpstrReturn CPTR,
                     wLength CWORD ) CWORD
endUses
```

The mciSendString() is used to pass the command to MCI. In addition to passing the initial command, mciSendString() is used to issue the status MCI command to get key information for controlling the playing of a media clip. The mciGetErrorString() is used to retrieve error text if errors occur.

Argument types for the mciSendString command include strings, signed long integers, and rectangles (which are specified as an ordered list of long integers). You may recall all these features were used in the PWMMPLAY form (the Multimedia Theater). The following ObjectPAL code, for example, defined the window (the rectangle) for playing a Video for Windows AVI clip:

```
mciCmdStr = "put movie destination at " +
            strVal(pxMBTopX+3) + " " +
            strVal(pxMBTopY+3) + " " +
            strVal(pxMBWide-8) + " " +
            strVal(pxMBHigh-8)
...
ReturnCode = mciSendString(mciCmdStr, ReturnString, 1024, 0)
```

String arguments were also used extensively. For example, to determine the length of a MIDI file, the following code fragment was used:

```
    mciCmdStr = "status midis length"
    ReturnCode = mciSendString(mciCmdStr, ReturnString, 1024, 0)
```

A full discussion of multimedia programming is, of course, beyond the scope of this appendix. Other resources you can consult on the subject include Ron Wodaski's Sams books on the subject, as well as Paul Perry's *Multimedia Developer's Guide,* also from Sams.

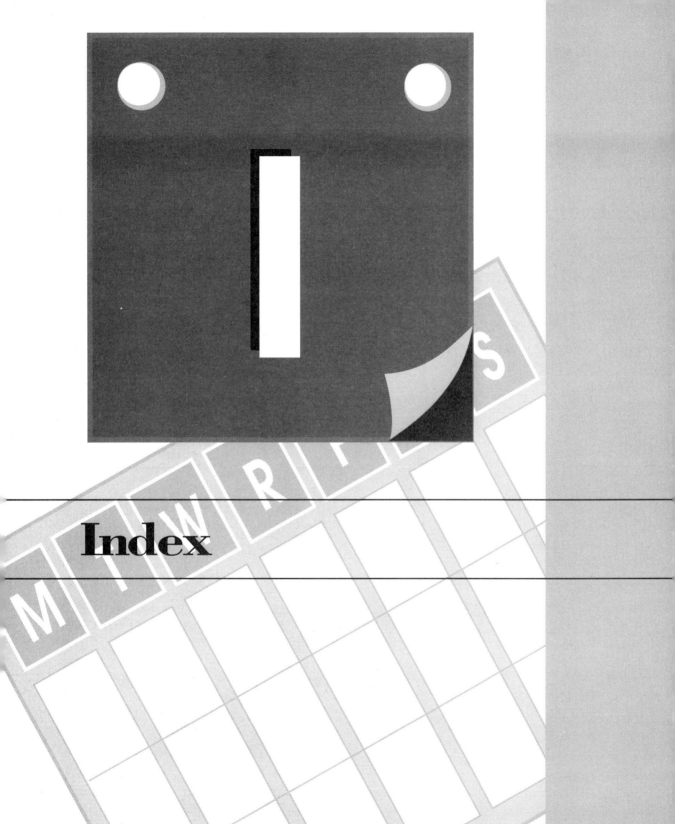

Index

DPW AR/AP system

methods

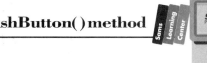

tables

Add to Your Sams Library Today with the Best Books for Programming, Operating Systems, and New Technologies

The easiest way to order is to pick up the phone and call

1-800-428-5331

between 9:00 a.m. and 5:00 p.m. EST.

For faster service please have your credit card available.

ISBN	Quantity	Description of Item	Unit Cost	Total Cost
0-672-30533-X		What Every Paradox 5 for Windows Programmer Should Know (Book/Disk)	$45.00	
0-672-30322-1		PC Video Madness! (Book/CD-ROM)	$39.95	
0-672-30391-4		Virtual Reality Madness! (Book/CD-ROM)	$39.95	
0-672-30160-1		Multimedia Developer's Guide	$49.95	
0-672-30496-1		Paradox 5 Developer's Guide (Book/Disk)	$45.00	
0-672-30320-5		Morphing Magic (Book/Disk)	$29.95	
0-672-30362-0		Navigating the Internet	$24.95	
0-672-30315-9		The Magic of Image Processing (Book/Disk)	$39.95	
0-672-30308-6		Tricks of the Graphics Gurus (Book/Disk)	$49.95	
0-672-30456-2		The Magic of Interactive Entertainment (Book/CD-ROM)	$39.95	
0-672-30376-0		Imaging and Animation for Windows (Book/Disk)	$34.95	
0-672-30270-5		Garage Virtual Reality (Book/Disk)	$29.95	
0-672-30413-9		Multimedia Madness!, Deluxe Edition (Book/CD-ROMs)	$55.00	
0-672-30352-3		Blaster Mastery (Book/CD-ROM)	$34.95	
		Shipping and Handling: See information below.		
		TOTAL		

❏ 3 ½" Disk

❏ 5 ¼" Disk

Shipping and Handling: $4.00 for the first book, and $1.75 for each additional book. Floppy disk: add $1.75 for shipping and handling. If you need to have it NOW, we can ship product to you in 24 hours for an additional charge of approximately $18.00, and you will receive your item overnight or in two days. Overseas shipping and handling adds $2.00 per book and $8.00 for up to three disks. Prices subject to change. Call for availability and pricing information on latest editions.

201 W. 103rd Street, Indianapolis, Indiana 46290

1-800-428-5331 — Orders   1-800-835-3202 — FAX   1-800-858-7674 — Customer Service

Book ISBN 0-672-30597-6

The Companion CD-ROM

The CD-ROM included with this book contains complete source code and database files for all the applications created in the book, including a financial transaction system with voice mail hooks, a multimedia theater, and various database utilities.

Installing the Software

Insert the CD-ROM in your drive and follow these steps to install the software. You'll need 10 megabytes of free space on your hard drive to install all the files, or 7 megabytes to install just the essential files. (Several video clips are not installed, to conserve hard drive space.)

1. Start Paradox 5 for Windows.

2. Choose **F**ile | **O**pen | **F**orm from the Paradox 5 menu.

3. Select the file *x*:\BUILDAPP\DPWINST.FSL. Substitute your CD-ROM drive letter for *x* in this filename.

4. Follow the instructions in this form to install the software.

You also can install the software without running Paradox 5 for Windows. Follow these steps to install the files to your hard drive:

1. From Windows File Manager or Program Manager, choose **F**ile | **R**un from the menu.

2. Type *X*:\INSTALL and press Enter. Substitute your CD-ROM drive letter for *X*. For example, if the disc is in drive G, type G:\INSTALL.

3. Choose **F**ull Install to install all the software; choose **C**ustom Install to install only some of the software.

The files will be installed to a directory named C:\BUILDAPP unless you change the drive letter during the install program. When the installation is complete, the setup program for Microsoft Video for Windows will start automatically. See Appendix B for more information on these files.